THE CAMBRIDGE COMPANION TO

ADORNO

Each volume in this series of companions to major philosophers contains specially commissioned essays by an international team of scholars, together with a substantial bibliography, and will serve as a reference work for students and nonspecialists. One aim of the series is to dispel the intimidation such readers often feel when faced with the work of a difficult and challenging thinker.

The German philosopher and aesthetic theorist Theodor Wiesengrund Adorno (1903–69) was one of the main philosophers of the first generation of the Frankfurt School of Critical Theory. An accomplished musician, Adorno first focused on the theory of culture and art. Later he turned to the problem of the dialectic of modern reason and freedom. In this collection of essays, imbued with the most up-to-date research, a distinguished roster of Adorno specialists explore the full range of his contributions to philosophy, history, music theory, aesthetics, and sociology.

New readers will find this the most convenient and accessible guide to Adorno currently available. Advanced students and specialists will find a conspectus of recent developments in the interpretation of Adorno.

Tom Huhn teaches aesthetics and philosophy at the School of Visual Arts in New York.

D1570975

The Cambridge Companion to
ADORNO

Edited by
Tom Huhn

CAMBRIDGE
UNIVERSITY PRESS

CAMBRIDGE UNIVERSITY PRESS
Cambridge, New York, Melbourne, Madrid, Cape Town, Singapore,
São Paulo, Delhi, Dubai, Tokyo, Mexico City

Cambridge University Press
32 Avenue of the Americas, New York, NY 10013-2473, USA

www.cambridge.org
Information on this title: www.cambridge.org/9780521775007

© Cambridge University Press 2004

First published 2004

A catalog record for this publication is available from the British Library

Library of Congress Cataloging in Publication data
The Cambridge companion to Adorno / edited by Tom Huhn.
    p. cm. – (Cambridge companions to philosophy)
   Includes bibliographical references and index.
   ISBN 0-521-77289-3 – ISBN 0-521-77500-0 (pbk.)
    1. Adorno, Theodor W., 1903–1969. I. Huhn, Tom. II. Series.
  B3199.A34C36   2004
  193 – dc22
                                    2003055910

ISBN 978-0-521-77289-1 Hardback
ISBN 978-0-521-77500-7 Paperback

For my parents,
John and Naomi Huhn

CONTENTS

ix

x Contents

CONTRIBUTORS

J. M. BERNSTEIN is University Distinguished Professor of Philosophy at the New School for Social Research. His publications include *Adorno: Disenchantment and Ethics* (Cambridge University Press, 2001) and the forthcoming *Against Voluptuous Bodies: Adorno's Late Modernism and the Idea of Painting.*

ANDREW BOWIE is Professor of German at Royal Holloway, University of London. His books include *From Romanticism to Critical Theory* (Routledge, 1997), *Aesthetics and Subjectivity: From Kant to Nietzsche* (Manchester University Press, 2003), and *Introduction to German Philosophy from Kant to Habermas* (Polity Press, 2003). He is writing a book, *Music, Philosophy, and Modernity.*

SAMIR GANDESHA is Assistant Professor of Modern European Thought and Culture in the Department of Humanities at Simon Fraser University in Vancouver, Canada. In 2001–2, he was an Alexander von Humboldt Research Fellow at the Institut für Philosophie, Universität Potsdam. He has published numerous articles and book chapters on Critical Theory, including "Schreiben und Urteilen: Adorno, Arendt und der Chiasmus der Naturgeschichte" in *Arendt und Adorno*, edited by Dirk Auer, Lars Rensmann, and Julia Schulze Wessel (Suhrkamp, 2003). He is currently writing a book addressing Adorno's critique of Heidegger.

LYDIA GOEHR is Professor of Philosophy at Columbia University. She is the author of *The Imaginary Museum of Musical Works, An Essay in the Philosophy of Music* (Oxford University Press, 1992), and *The Quest for Voice: On Music, Politics and the Limits of Philosophy*

(Oxford University Press, 1998). She is currently working on a book on the relationship between philosophy and music in the work of Adorno.

TOM HUHN teaches aesthetics and philosophy at the School of Visual Arts in New York and has taught philosophy and aesthetics at New York University, Sarah Lawrence College, and Wesleyan University. His recent book is *Imitation and Society: The Persistence of Mimesis in the Aesthetics of Burke, Hogarth, and Kant* (Penn State Press, in press).

ROBERT HULLOT-KENTOR is a professor of literature and philosophy at Southampton College. He has recently completed a reconstruction of Adorno's *Current of Music: Elements of a Radio Theory* for the Adorno Archive, which will be published as volume 3 of Adorno's *Nachgelassene Schriften*, and is preparing new translations of Adorno's *Philosophy of New Music* and *Negative Dialectics*.

SIMON JARVIS is Gorley Putt Lecturer in English Literary History at the University of Cambridge. He is the author of *Adorno: A Critical Introduction* (Polity Press, 1998) and is currently editing a four-volume collection of articles on Adorno for Routledge.

MARTIN JAY is Sidney Hellman Ehrman Professor of History at the University of California, Berkeley. Among his most recent publications are *Cultural Semantics* (University of Massachusetts Press, 1998) and *Refractions of Violence* (Routledge, 2003). He is finishing a book on the discourse of experience in modern European and American thought.

ROBERT KAUFMAN is Assistant Professor of English and Affiliated Assistant Professor of German Studies at Stanford University. His essays on poetry and the other arts in relation to aesthetic and critical theory have appeared in various journals, including *Critical Inquiry, October, American Poetry Review, Das Brecht-Jahrbuch (The Brecht Yearbook), Modern Language Quarterly*, and *Studies in Romanticism*. He is presently completing two related studies, *Negative Romanticism, Almost Modernity: Keats, Shelley, and Adornian*

Critical Aesthetics and *Experiments in Construction: Frankfurt School Aesthetics and Contemporary Poetry.*

CHRISTOPH MENKE is Professor of Philosophy at the University of Potsdam and Fellow at the Max Weber-Kolleg in Erfurt. His publications include *The Sovereignty of Art: Aesthetic Negativity in Adorno and Derrida* (MIT Press, 1998) and *Reflections of Equality* (Stanford University Press, forthcoming).

STEFAN MÜLLER-DOOHM is Professor of Sociology at the University of Oldenburg. He is the author of *Adorno: Eine Biographie* (Suhrkamp, 2003) and *Die Soziologie Theodor W. Adornos* (Campus, 2001) and editor of *Das Interesse der Vernunft: Rückblick auf das Werk von Jürgen Habermas* (Suhrkamp, 2000).

MAX PADDISON is Professor of Music at the University of Durham. He is the author of *Adorno's Aesthetics of Music* (Cambridge University Press, 1993) and *Adorno, Modernism and Mass Culture* (Kahn and Averill, 1996; second edition 2003). He has published widely on the aesthetics and sociology of nineteenth- and twentieth-century music, the avant-garde, and rock music and is coeditor (with Irène Deliège) of the book *Musique contemporaine: Perspectives théoriques et philosophiques* (Mardaga, 2001), to which he has also contributed chapters on Adorno and issues in contemporary music and postmodernism.

JAMES SCHMIDT is Professor of History and Political Science at Boston University. He is the editor of *What is Enlightenment? Eighteenth-Century Answers and Twentieth-Century Questions* (University of California Press, 1996) and the author of articles on Kant, Hegel, Horkheimer, Adorno, Foucault, and Habermas. His current work involves German responses to the Enlightenment.

GERHARD SCHWEPPENHÄUSER is Professor of Aesthetics at the Free University of Bolzano. His publications include *Ethik nach Auschwitz: Adornos negative Moralphilosophie* (Argument Verlag, 1993), *Grundbegriffe der Ethik* (Junius Verlag, 2003), and *Adorno zur Einführung* (Junius Verlag, 2003). Together with Wolfgang Bock, he edits the journal *Zeitschrift für kritische Theorie*.

ROLF TIEDEMANN was Adorno's assistant from 1959 to 1965 and is the founder and former director of the Adorno Archive in Frankfurt. He is editor of Adorno's *Gesammelte Schriften* and the ongoing *Nachgelassene Schriften* and is coeditor of Walter Benjamin's *Gesammelte Schriften*. His books include *Dialektik im Stillstand* (Suhrkamp, 1983), *Studien zur Philosophie Walter Benjamins* (Suhrkamp, 1973), and *Mystik und Aufklärung* (edition text + kritik, 2002).

JOEL WHITEBOOK is a practicing psychoanalyst in New York City and is on the faculty of the Columbia University Center for Psychoanalytic Training and Research. He is also the author of *Perversion and Utopia: A Study in Psychoanalysis and Critical Theory* (MIT Press, 1995).

Introduction
Thoughts beside Themselves

Theodor Wiesengrund Adorno was a philosopher, composer, essayist, and social theorist. He was born in 1903 in Frankfurt, Germany, where his father, Oskar Wiesengrund, was a prominent wine merchant and assimilated Jew who had converted to Protestantism. His mother, Maria Cavelli-Adorno della Piana, was a Catholic and had enjoyed a successful career as a singer until the time of her marriage to Adorno's father. (In 1938 Adorno had his name changed from Wiesengrund to Adorno.) Adorno was an only child in a quite well off household that he described as presided over by two mothers. His other "mother" was his mother's sister, Agathe Calvelli-Adorno. She too had had a successful musical career, as a pianist.

At the age of fifteen, Adorno began weekly study meetings with Siegfried Kracauer, a man fourteen years his senior and then editor of the liberal newspaper *Frankfurter Zeitung*. The weekly meetings continued for many years and had Kant's *Critique of Pure Reason* as their first object of study. Adorno later reported that he owed far more of his intellectual development to these meetings than to his academic teachers. Adorno began his university studies in Frankfurt in 1921, studying philosophy, sociology, music, and psychology. It was during the time of his studies that Adorno met and befriended Max Horkheimer and Walter Benjamin; the latter would become especially influential for Adorno's philosophical work. In 1924 Adorno completed a doctorate in philosophy. In 1925 he went to Vienna, where he stayed on and off for months at a time through 1927, with the idea of continuing his musical training and possibly pursuing a career as a composer and concert pianist. In Vienna Alban Berg taught him composition and Eduard Steurmann piano; both were members of the Schoenberg circle. Adorno also continued writing the music criticism he had begun publishing in 1921. As Richard Leppert notes in his introduction to the recent collection of Adorno's writings on music, "Between 1921, while still a teenager, and 1931 he published dozens of opera and concert reviews, reviews of published new music, as well as essays on aesthetics, and heavily favoring new music."[1]

Back in Frankfurt in 1927 Adorno began to associate with Horkheimer and other members of the Institute for Social Research, which later would be referred to as the "Frankfurt School."[2] The Institut für Sozialforschung opened in Frankfurt in 1924 and had as its mission the combining of philosophy and social science into a critical theory of social existence. Adorno's publications for the Institute began in 1932 in the first issue of its journal. As the Institute's commitment to a version of Marxist insight was never concealed, the police closed its offices six weeks after Hitler assumed the power of the German state on January 30, 1933. A few months later the Nazis took from Adorno his official right to teach. After the Second World War the Institute was officially reopened in Frankfurt in 1951. The members of the Institute spent the Nazi period in exile, many of them in the United States, where they established ties with Columbia and Princeton Universities. Adorno arrived in New York in 1938 and remained there until 1941, when he moved to Los Angeles, where he would spend almost eight years and adopt United States citizenship. In a 1957 letter, Adorno wrote of his eleven-year exile in America: "I believe 90 percent of all that I've published in Germany was written in America."[3] Adorno returned to Germany in 1949; in 1953 he was appointed to a tenured faculty position in Frankfurt. He became the director of the Institute after Horkheimer's retirement in 1958, and he remained director until his death from a heart attack, on holiday in Switzerland, in 1969.

Though Adorno is perhaps best known in the English-speaking world for two major philosophical publications, *Negative Dialectics*, published in German in 1966, and *Aesthetic Theory*, not quite finished at the time of his death, we would do well to heed two recent observations regarding Adorno's work. The first is Richard Leppert's reminder of the large place that music occupied in Adorno's life. Indeed, Adorno continued composing throughout his adult life, and, as Leppert calculates, nearly a third of Adorno's 23 volumes of published writings (the posthumous writings are estimated to appear in roughly the same quantity) are concerned with music.[4] The second is

Henry Pickford's acknowledgment of the very wide public life that Adorno led in West Germany from 1950 to 1969. Pickford writes, "His engagement in the mass media was a logical consequence of his eminently practical intentions to effect change."[5] Adorno participated in more than 150 radio programs and published often in the leading newspapers and journals.

As a thinker Adorno shunned systematic philosophy and doubted whether true thinking could ever achieve transparency: "True thoughts are those alone which do not understand themselves."[6] His complaint against systematic philosophy was of a piece with his sweeping objection to *methodological* thinking: Both suffer an avoidance of the purported object of inquiry by the very constraints that allow them to have a goal or isolate a phenomenon in the first place. Systematic philosophy and methodological thinking share a predilection for reaching conclusions that too often cannot help but confirm whatever presuppositions are embedded in their premises. In this way, thinking becomes not only opaque to itself but also rigid, like a thing, before it has the opportunity to allow things to encounter it or for it to become something else. Adorno's involvement with music, art, and literature, but so too especially his interest in philosophy, is then best considered as a means of overcoming, or rather at least eluding, the rigidification of experience by thought. And yet Adorno was no anti-thinker, no Luddite of the mind, but rather one of the most probing and accomplished *thinkers* of the twentieth century.

The most extensive effects of the pervasiveness of the stiffening character of thought can be found in the forms of subjective life. The human subject, bound up by its hard edges, comes to be like – even especially to itself – an object. But just as Adorno is not against thought *in toto*, so is he also not against subjectivity. In *Dialectic of Enlightenment*, Adorno and coauthor Horkheimer famously read Odysseus as the prototype of rigid, albeit successful, subjectivity. It is the cunning calculation of Odysseus, as well as his readiness to sacrifice his men and himself, which makes him the prototype of subjectivity. We might say that the clever strategies of Odysseus are the precursors of systematic thought. This aspect of subjective life is best characterized according to the ascendancy of reflexiveness in it. That is, what makes Odysseus so successful is not just his heroic mastery over and domination of the men, matter, and monsters that he encounters but also his having raised mastery and domination to the guiding principle of all his actions. And the success of this principle is to be attributed, according to Horkheimer and Adorno, to its peculiar reflexive character.

At first glance, this reflexivity seems rather curious in the case of mastery and domination, for how could reflexivity be appropriate when the whole point of mastery and domination – their concept, we might say – is that they submit to no other force. And yet, consistent with their concept, mastery and domination require subjectivity to submit itself to them. In short, whatever mastery Odysseus achieves requires a previous submission and mastery of the self. It is thus by means of its ability to submit that subjectivity becomes masterful. This is no small accomplishment; great and terrible things have followed hard upon it. The victorious thumping of the chest is the most vivid illustration of this reflexivity; the victor thereby demonstrates his willingness to subdue and master himself as the very sign – and the price – of his victory over others.

Now one might imagine that Adorno's response to this critique of the structure and provenance of subjectivity would be to recommend its transcendence, a kind of Nietzschean overcoming of all the previous forms of mastered (and submitted) subjectivity. But such an imagined response forgets Adorno's commitment to avoiding the sweeping obfuscations and dead ends of systematic philosophizing. To respect that commitment means then that Adorno's critique implies that subjectivity needs, at most, reform rather than revolution. Yet this realization does not diminish the scope and penetration of Adorno's critique of subjectivity. It means instead that Adorno understands the development of subjectivity as a dialectical, historical process. Therefore, what is required, according to him, is not a return to an earlier form of subjectivity but rather some forward movement from within what subjectivity has already become. And it's just here that the centrality of aesthetics, and especially the dynamic of mimesis, is to be understood in his thought. One might arrive at this central insight of his by following Adorno's critique of the limitations of subjective thought.

If the historical task for thinking is like that for subjectivity, then the forward path is not through some overcoming but rather by way of a certain reflexiveness in, and reflection upon, thought. In this regard, one might hazard that Adorno could not be more traditionally philosophical, if traditional philosophy is taken to have its ground in self-examination. But what here sets him apart from so much of western philosophy is the place where and the manner in which reflection occurs. If thinking cannot turn upon itself to reflect without bringing along its rigidifying tendencies and objectifying impulses, it would thereby doom whatever reflection it might achieve to become but another reified version of what it has already been. And yet the dialectical advantage of objectifying thought – like that of reifying subjectivity – is that it leaves in its wake a great many deadened things. The aim is not to revivify these ossified objects, as if we might unlock some life trapped in them, but instead to allow subjectivity to become, reflectively, something else in response to them, perhaps by allowing them to become something other than what systematic, strategic thinking would have us continue to make of them.

Thoughts and other dead things might be taken to be object lessons for life because they exhibit the stasis wherein life, for whatever reason, neglected to continue, except in a damaged and damaging fashion. And this means that life might be something more than whatever it is that blossomed and withered in the coming to be of objects, including especially that premier object, the subject. The thoroughness of Adorno's dialectical thinking is apparent in *Negative Dialectics*, one of his most important works. There he reconsiders the supposed inevitably forward trajectory of the dialectic and examines whether what Hegel called "determinate negation," the antithetical moment of the dialectic, has always been followed by a recuperative, integrative synthesis. Adorno famously contends that historically it has not and that the best evidence of this failure lies in the fact that even philosophy missed its own opportunity to realize itself as a form of life.

Thinking tied too tightly to concepts – philosophy's tragic flaw – is to be countered by objects that elude, and thoughts that turn away from, the objectifications of thinking. How might we think here about experience without reducing it to the contours of thought or conversely valorizing it as some transcendent category? Adorno's attempt seems to have been to try to follow, intellectually and experientially, the shape of certain objects, namely those that themselves seemed irreducible to thoughts alone. This intellectual mimetic tracing of the object might be called experience, if by that term we intend an encounter with an object that itself is something not wholly objective. Artworks – and especially the experiences they spark – are just such objects for Adorno. But rather than characterize artworks as resisting thought or objecthood, thereby enjoining just the kind of agonistic struggle that helped Odysseus make himself into an opposition to that which he imagined resisted him, we might instead pragmatically describe artworks as objects which, in their incompleteness, invite a like-minded subjectivity. Artworks are incomplete in at least two senses. One is that they unavoidably address subjects whose experience or interpretation of them they presuppose. The other constitutive incompleteness of artworks can be mined from Hegel's insight that each artwork is a symbol – or sole inhabitant – of a world that is nonetheless implied by the very achieved singularity of its existence. This incompleteness is then a kind of dislocation, for the artwork is the displaced and lonely sole example of a world that cannot otherwise bring itself more completely into existence. The incompleteness of the object becomes for thoughtful experience a symptom of an incompleteness elsewhere. Put differently, what we might call the robustness, or the very existence, of the admittedly singular object is evidence of an incompletely realized world. Why don't other objects imply incompletely realized worlds? Perhaps they might, if only we did not encounter so much difficulty imagining them.

Marx's analysis of the commodity also proceeded by taking an object's identity to be premised upon a constitutive absence. In the case of the commodity, its appearance depended on the disappearance of the social relations that allowed its coming into being. We might imagine the artwork for Adorno as a kind of reverse image of the commodity: The artwork, rather than efface a world for the sake of its coming into being, instead projects a possible world. But it seems this projection must avoid both the sweep of conceptual thought as well as its impulse toward completion. For Adorno the most striking possibility of a world is not glimpsed by thought alone. Rather, possibilities reside in the particular ways in which experience has been thwarted. Adorno's dialectical appreciation of experience – aided by Freud's psychoanalytic theory – entails the observation that experience is constituted also, or even especially, by the specific ways in which it has been thwarted.

But how does experience come to be thwarted if it comes to be possible only by the very limitations that constitute it? Space and time, as Kant observed, are not encroachments upon experience but are instead the boundaries within and according to which experience is made possible in the first place. So too might we observe for Adorno that dialectically the object, and subject, are not mere impediments to some imagined experience. They are instead the very stuff of, in, and out of which experience is made. Hegel understood the artwork as the object *par excellence* for subjective experience precisely insofar as it could not – despite its overwhelmingly subjective character – escape the constraint that it remain objective, which is to say an object rather than a thought. That is, for Hegel, just as beauty must always be a human artifact, so too can the artwork never entirely escape its materiality, which seemed to guarantee its remaining objective. For Hegel then, the artwork's inescapable objecthood – which signals the inability of subjectivity to ever fully consume the art object without remainder – makes the artwork the most fruitful object in the path of subjective becoming. The artwork object is thus a goad rather than impediment to experience. And this characterization of the productive thwarting of experience by art is not so far afield from a psychoanalytic conception of experience, which posits the ego as the rigidification and armature within which experience comes to be. And just as the force of the ego is fundamentally negative, as that which throws itself up against whatever is imagined as opposed to it, so too is the artwork a mimetic projection of where subjectivity might most productively founder. Perhaps the artwork is a kind of cunning mimetic device that subjectivity somewhat unwittingly puts up in front of itself as a trap. The artwork is a mimetic reenactment of subjective foundering.

Artworks and the aesthetic judgments that follow them are mimetic reproductions of thoughts and objects which themselves are deadened bits of subjectivity. They thereby provide cues for what subjectivity once might have been – or failed to become. Could there not then be a form of life, a form of subjectivity, which takes up these mimetic residues as objects for reflection? Thus we might understand reflection as the further unfolding of subjective possibility. Here mimesis in Adorno becomes the name for the projection and reprojection of subjectivity, of an unfolding of aspects. Mimesis is not then the copying or imitation of what has been but the continuity from reflection to reflection, of the multiple aspects and movements of subjective possibility.

The artwork is central to the project of reflection and the possibility of further subjective unfolding because, for Adorno (following Hegel), the artwork is the most thoroughly subjective of objects. The subjectivity of the artwork is due to the peculiar character of its objectivity: The artwork is an unfinished, incomplete object, and by dint of this it invites reflection. We might observe that all objects are incomplete insofar as they are but truncated aspects of subjectivity. But the artwork, unlike all other objects, is also mimetic and reflexive insofar as it is an image of the ongoing incompleteness of subjective activity. The task of subjectivity is not of course to become complete, for that would signal but another version of static rigidification. The task is rather for subjectivity to go on with itself, to become more of what it already is. But to become more of what it already is is problematic because, not only is it difficult to distinguish what is living from what is dead in the form of the subject, it is also unclear how to distinguish between those dead objects that might repay subjective regard and those that might not.

The artwork – and in this Adorno follows the Kantian tradition regarding the efficacy of aesthetic judgment – is an occasion for subjective dissolution and reconstitution. It is precisely the artwork's unfinishedness that holds the greatest promise for the subject. The artwork is not the occasion for the subject to complete itself; instead, what Adorno calls its truth content is the open-endedness of an object at rest within its lack of completion. Its content is not something, especially not some truth, to be deciphered by the subject. The artwork is instead an occasion for the subject to liken itself to a state of unfinishedness. The subject is thereby afforded a mimetic model of the pitfalls of subjective becoming, of how to forestall becoming fixed and fixated, rigid and further bound up.

The larger issue here is the relation of objects to subjective becoming. I want to suggest that, for Adorno, mimesis was the key term according to which he came to understand the dialectical relations between subjectivity and objects, and, more importantly, between subjective and objective becoming. Were Adorno not so adverse to metaphysics, not to mention sweeping philosophical formulations, we might even claim that all things come to be mimetically. But what might this mean? And why do art and aesthetic theory come to be the primary modes for Adorno of encountering crucial aspects of mimetic production and reproduction?

To begin to answer these questions requires that we heed Adorno's oft-repeated critique of "first philosophy," that is, of philosophy having any first principles from which everything subsequently is to be deduced. This means that to continue here is to give up the hope of finding some origin of mimesis. Instead, Adorno in effect posits mimesis as having always been there, or here. He characterizes it as "archaic," indeed as an "impulse," suggesting even in one passage of his *Aesthetic Theory* that to trace back its history might well deposit us in the realm of biology.[7] And in response to the more or less common art historical supposition that cave drawings are the first instances of mimesis, Adorno responds that "the first images must have been *preceded* by a mimetic comportment" and adds – in what I take to be the most direct, though nondialectical, specification of mimesis in his *Aesthetic Theory* – that this mimetic comportment is "the assimilation of the self to its other" (AT, 329).

There is much to be gleaned from this single passage: Mimesis precedes image making, by extension all thing making (production), and is thereby initially a praxis rather than a poiesis, a doing rather than a making. If we then ask, "A doing of what?" the answer appears: the assimilating of self to other. There is a still more pressing opposition, which we might approach by asking what activity in particular mimesis, as a dynamic act of assimilation, stands in contrast to. Adorno's answer might be harvested from the following: "Mimesis is an archaic comportment that as an immediate practice . . . is not knowledge" (AT, 111). Knowledge, we might say, stands at the farthest remove from the archaic mimetic comportment. Of course, this constellation changes drastically when art comes to be the vehicle of mimesis. We can understand this turn of events by appreciating another consequence of mimesis being subject to the critique of first philosophy. That is, for Adorno, the inability to say how or when mimesis originates entails the dialectical consequence that the contrary of mimesis is posited simultaneously with it. In other words, the dialectical complement to the mimetic impulse is what Adorno designates the mimetic taboo. And though we likewise cannot identify the origin of this taboo on mimesis, we nonetheless are given some inkling of what undergirds it when Adorno remarks that "immediately back of the mimetic taboo stands a sexual one: Nothing should be moist" (AT, 116).

This provocative formulation calls forth two brief digressions. The first is perhaps out of place in a discussion of Adorno, as it begins with a film reference (Adorno noted that, despite his vigilance, film viewing always made him stupid). In David Lean's film about T. E. Lawrence, titled *Lawrence of Arabia*, Peter O'Toole, playing Lawrence, says, "I love the desert, it's so clean." The desert is of course not so much clean as it is *not* moist, hence the best instantiation of the sexual taboo. This leads to a second digression, by way of Freud's *Civilization and Its Discontents*, whose original German title relates directly to Adorno's definition of mimesis as assimilation, since *Das Unbehagen in der Kultur* might better be translated as *The Inassimilable in Civilization*. Recall Freud's remark in that book that the history of civilization might be written according to a chart documenting the increase in the use of soap. I take the thrust of that remark to be not simply that we are now cleaner than we have ever been but that what appears to us inassimilable – dirt by definition is the inassimilable *par excellence* – looms larger than ever, leading to the call for ever more soap to flush out whatever nooks and crannies still serve as refuge for dirt. Soap is anti-mimetic; it is the means by which the fear of an object's deliquescence – its assimilating return to nature – is thwarted. In this light, soap appears as the primary instrument of Nietzsche's *principium individuationis* – the principle of individuation – a recurring motif in the *Aesthetic Theory*. Soap not only polices but also helps erect the boundary between self and other.

Though we cannot fix the origin of the mimetic taboo, we nevertheless can perceive its contours by understanding this taboo's relation to art making and artworks, as follows: "Mimetic comportment...is seized in art – the organ of mimesis since the mimetic taboo – ...[and] becomes its bearer" (AT, 110). Not only does mimetic comportment migrate to art – perhaps it might be appropriate to say it now hibernates there – it also thereby becomes a dialectically entwined impulse and taboo. But why does art become the "refuge" and organ for mimetic comportment? This seems easy to answer, but I'm not sure how satisfying the answer is, for it appears to be founded on a preexisting *likeness* between mimesis and art. Adorno characterizes both as a "comportment" [*Verhalten*].

For example, he states that "art in its innermost essence is a comportment" (AT, 42), that the "mimetic element...is indispensable to art" (AT, 41), and, still more strongly, that art is "the indigenous domain of mimesis" (AT, 92). Yet, "comportment" on the face of it seems too general and vague a notion to support an essential and indigenous affinity between art and mimesis, unless we transpose comportment back into the opposition between praxis and poiesis. In that pair of terms, comportment readily aligns itself with praxis and thereby stands in contrast to poiesis, that is, in contrast to art making. So what art and mimesis initially share is a way of doing rather than making. But how then does what we might call art doing (praxis) become art making (poiesis) and artworks?

I believe the answer to this is to be found by way of the taboo on mimesis, especially its pervasiveness, and the effect of that pervasiveness on art doing transformed by the mimetic taboo. I take the extensiveness of the taboo on mimesis to be, if you will, the mimetic counterpart to what Adorno calls the spell of reality: "Because the spell of external reality over its subjects...has become absolute, the artwork can only oppose this spell by assimilating itself to it" (AT, 31). That is, art's a priori mimetic substance is the counterweight to the sway of the absolute character of what we might call the spell of the mimetic taboo. To put it still otherwise, "Mimesis was displaced by objectifying imitation" (AT, 162). A difficulty here will be to avoid understanding art's objectification of imitation, of a transformation of mimesis from doing into making, in solely negative terms and instead like the dialectical, ambivalent character of objects. That is, whatever one's judgment regarding the fate of mimesis, the fate of art coupled inextricably with mimesis is not necessarily the same. Mimesis transformed by art, perhaps even into a version of its opposite, might nonetheless constitute what Adorno calls the "fulfillment of objectivity" (AT, 15).

We might here offer a preliminary surmise: Art succeeds when mimesis fails; alternatively, mimesis succeeds by way of art. Before bequeathing any laurels on either art or mimesis, we might consider the path success follows regardless of its origin. And proceeding along this path, the path on which mimesis unfolds, quickly brings us to the difficulty of understanding what Adorno means by "expression." Though it is readily apparent that expression is thoroughly mimetic – a point Adorno makes in saying that "expression is a priori imitation" (AT, 117) – it is less easy to discern the content of expression. Consider, for example, the latter half of this formulation: "Artistic expression comports itself mimetically, just as the expression of living creatures is that of pain" (AT, 110). This claim poses its own obstacle to mimesis, to assimilation, since it seems to entail the presupposition that living creatures express only pain. I do not want to suggest that this cannot be the case, yet I do not want to give fuel to those who would dismiss Adorno out of hand as pessimistic and cynical, which I take to be the real charge lying just below the surface of the common dismissal of him as an elitist. Instead, I would have us recall that Adorno's characterization of expression needs to be understood in the context of what he often took his philosophical enemy's position to be: vitalism. Indeed, he thought even Nietzsche suffered from an aspect of vitalism in his opposition of form to life. Incidentally, Adorno does at one point write that the mimetic impulse is "the antithesis of form" (AT, 144), but he does not, contra Nietzsche, collapse together life and mimesis.

If form is not to stand opposed to life, just as objects are more than impediments to subjectivity, then artistic expression must be formulated as continuous with life rather than some break with it. Expression therefore needs to be already embedded in life, as the following passage indicates: "The mimetic impulses that motivate the artwork, that integrate themselves in it and once again disintegrate it, are fragile, speechless expression. They only become language through their objectivation as art. Art, the rescue of nature, revolts against nature's transitoriness" (AT, 184). This is true even though, as he adds a few pages later, "art is in sympathy with diffuseness" (AT, 188). Adorno's characterization of expression is reminiscent of the early Marx's depiction of religion: hardly a mere affirmation of the status quo, as it encompasses an embedded critique of things as they are as well as a demand for a better life. So too Adorno's notion of expression, which he takes to be a mimetic continuation of life offering some cipher or token that might nonetheless preserve or put itself forward as something more than a fragile, speechless moment. For expression to expand into language, the artwork becomes more than a mere organ of mimesis, it becomes its very fulfillment: "Through expression art closes itself off...and becomes eloquent in itself: This is art's mimetic consummation. Its expression is the antithesis of expressing something" (AT, 112).

But what is the nature of expression opposite the expression of something? I fear that the only way to pursue this question is with Adorno's own somewhat metaphorical formulations regarding the alternation of movement and stasis. These terms come most often into play in his remarks on objectivation. For example, he writes, "Art objectivates the mimetic impulse, holding it fast at the same time that it disposes of its immediacy and negates it" (AT, 285). Art, in other words, by holding fast the mimetic impulse, embodies it. The artwork is thus an objectivated mimetic impulse. The artwork is an *image* of the mimetic impulse, transformed by the taboo that disallows mimetic immediacy. In this regard, art fully respects the taboo on mimesis.

Consider the following: "The tension between objectivating technique and the mimetic essence of artworks is fought out in the effort to save the fleeting, the ephemeral, the transitory in a form that is immune to reification and yet akin to it in being permanent" (AT, 219). I want to suggest that there is nothing a priori of value in whatever is fleeting, ephemeral, and transitory. Rather, the momentary comes to have value only in the context of the absolute spell of external reality; that is, only in the realm of a thralldom to things does the momentary *appear* valuable. The task of the artwork – or, perhaps we might now just as readily say, the task for mimesis – is to objectivate the momentary in such a way that it stands in contrast to reification. Yet the very technique of art, what might also be called its inseparability from form, is in tension with its mimetic essence. The trick for art – and since art is the refuge for mimesis, the task for mimesis – is to somehow objectivate without reification, to express without expressing something, and to think without being too well thought. In the register of motion, it would mean being held fast without becoming rigid, pausing without withering.

The impulse of art, which Adorno claims runs through its entire history, is to "objectivate the fleeting, not the permanent" (AT, 219). And yet "the greatest justice that was done to the mimetic impulse becomes the greatest injustice, because permanence, objectivation, ultimately negates that mimetic impulse" (AT, 219). It is, however, difficult to reconcile this claim, that objectivation negates the mimetic impulse, with Adorno's claim elsewhere that "[M]imesis itself conforms to objectivation, vainly hoping to close the rupture between objectivated consciousness and the object" (AT, 285), as if mimesis were the attempt to reconnect the thinking subject with its alienated thought object. We must either admit that these are in contradiction with one another or complicate our understanding of mimesis, perhaps achieving something akin to just that complication of the nature of objects that we find in Adorno. I propose to do the latter, and to do so by framing a further elaboration of mimesis within a consideration of some of Adorno's remarks on the relation of art to society.

Let us continue by way of the most oft cited passage from *Aesthetic Theory*: "[A]rt becomes social by its opposition to society, and it occupies this position only as autonomous art" (AT, 225). Or as he puts it elsewhere, "What is social in art is its immanent movement against society" (AT, 227). Society's immanence to the artwork, coupled with the latter's mimetic essence, reveals the artwork as the locus of the emphatic intimacy between the social and the mimetic. The issue, if you will, of this intimacy is the autonomy of the artwork.

Art is then something that achieves autonomy rather than having its freedom bestowed upon it by something else, for example, by a supposedly free context in which it is made. And this achieved freedom, by dint of which the artwork becomes social, is complicated by the inherently social character of the artwork in the first place: As artifact, the artwork begins as a product of social labor. How is it that the artwork both begins as a social fact and yet also only *becomes* social if it achieves autonomy? Are there two *societies* at work here, one that corresponds to, indeed consists of, empirical reality (and its spell) and another somehow autonomous one? The short answer is yes, and what I want to sketch is how these two societies are mimetically related – or more strongly, how one society proceeds mimetically out of the other.

First, these two societies correspond to what Adorno calls the double character of art: Art is at once both autonomous and a *fait social* (AT, 5). As he puts it, the artwork's autonomy consists of resembling – but without imitating – the society of empirical reality: "It is by virtue of this relation to the empirical that artworks recuperate, neutralized, what once was literally and directly experienced in life and what was expelled by spirit" (AT, 5). There is then a

respiritualization of society by art, and this respiritualization reproduces what was once deadened by spirit's initial evisceration of experience by means of concepts and alienated thoughts. What qual-
ifies this respiritualization as mimesis rather than mere mimicry
or parody is the participation of spirit in the original expulsion of
direct, unmediated experience. To formulate this in regard to autonomy would be to understand the artwork's initial autonomous
stirrings – that is, mimetic impulses – as directed entirely against
society, and yet the work's mature, achieved autonomy is one fully
at home within society. Hence the need for two kinds, or at least
two understandings, of society. These two societies, however, might
just as readily be conceived as two aspects of autonomy or, finally,
as two versions of mimesis. The first autonomy is then a movement against itself, an autonomy of mere choice, of only choosing
among the proffered alternatives, just as the first kind of mimesis,
objectivating imitation, is a movement against the immediacy of
experience and toward formal differentiation, which is to say, in accord with the principle of individuation. Adorno wants neither to
valorize nor to denigrate this first pass at assimilation, the mimesis
that proceeds by moving against itself. He is therefore at pains to
indicate that autonomy and mimesis are incomplete if they remain
at this stage. Since the dialectic of assimilation, that is, mimesis, is
ultimately aimed at producing self-identity, it is as if such an identificatory procedure must begin by shunning whatever aspects of
self appear as false casing. And since the most pervasive false casing is the whole empirical reality of stunted society, it is this in its
entirety against which mimesis – and the art that is its vehicle –
turns.

Insofar as all artworks attempt to conjure a world in which each
work would be the exemplary member, each work thereby mimetically opposes not so much external reality per se but more the pervasiveness of its spell upon us. It is specifically the entirety of external
reality's spell that the artwork mimetically opposes – this logic is
directed in particular against the *spell* of that reality rather than its
material constituents. The artwork's mimetic charge is against the
legacy of magic within the artwork itself. This is what allows Adorno
to claim that art is an enlightening force – it moves against the spell
that artifacts are complicit in weaving over us. Thus the artwork's

unshakeable dependence on the artifactual. Put otherwise, mimesis requires the artifact in the same way that contemporary reality requires the commodity. The artwork mimetically produces itself by reproducing the nature of the requirement. I take this to be the meaning of what Adorno calls the "inner-aesthetic development" of the artwork. Art's "contribution to society is not communication with it but rather something extremely mediated: It is resistance in which, by virtue of inner-aesthetic development, social development is reproduced without being imitated" (AT, 226). Now, since that requirement – society's requirement of the commodity and art's requirement of the artifact – is itself illusory, the mimetic artwork is structurally endowed to reveal just this illusoriness. The artwork thus comes to be as appearance, albeit the appearance of autonomy: "In the context of total semblance, art's semblance of being-in-itself is the mask of truth" (AT, 227).

Another way to describe the artwork's masking of truth is to say that, instead of having or containing truth, the artwork *reflects* truth, so long as reflection is here understood as a mode of mimesis. So too is art's semblance of being-in-itself – its appearance as autonomous – a reflection, or at least an indication of real autonomy. Though this seems to imply that the work of art remains unfinished, unable to do more than indicate or point, I want nonetheless to suggest – in light of Adorno's remark that fully mimetic art would constitute a fulfillment of objectivation – that art and mimesis are complete. Further, the only context in which this suggestion might have some purchase is that of history. Consider the following: "Society is not only the negativity that the aesthetic law of form condemns but also, even in its most objectionable shape, the quintessence of self-producing and self-reproducing human life" (AT, 226). Adorno continues the passage by asserting that society revealed itself, at a certain moment in its history, as a process of "self-annihilation." It will not do to assume that the reference here is solely to the midcentury Holocaust; instead, the term is meant to encompass the destruction of subjectivity. It is by means of the latter, as the most advanced form of the principle of individuation, that the whole – society – is produced and reproduced. It is in this light that we might best understand Adorno's remark to the effect that history occurs in art, if nowhere else. Art's history, in contrast to the ahistory of external reality, is the unfolding of subjectivity according to the twists and turns of mimesis. Put differently, the dialectic of mimesis, borne by the artwork, represents – but only as semblance – what subjectivity might otherwise have become.

For Adorno, what maintains a spell as a spell is its nonconceptual, or at least preconceptual, character. To be under the spell of something is to sanction some power over the self by dint of that power's failure to be subdued by a concept. A spell is curiously like a concept or thought. Both are capable of engaging and holding thinking. And yet, still more curiously, in one regard the spell is a more enlightened engagement of thought than the concept. That is, whereas the spell is a kind of embrace and acknowledgment of a thralldom to thought, the concept suffers from the illusion that it is not a product or consequence of such thralldom. The concept, in short, is constituted by a kind of mythic denial that the *power* of thought is irrational. In other words, the concept comports itself as if it were autonomous. The spell, by contrast, is enlightened to the extent that it does not conceal what it takes to be the sheer heterogeneity of thought. The spell, we might even say, is a kind of mimetic approximation of thought's heterogeneity to itself. Likewise the artwork. That is, the artwork, as well as the aesthetic theory that mimetically attempts to continue it, is an approximation of life's nonidentity to itself. The artwork is a model of a thought beside itself. And Adorno's thinking might be described as the attempt to hold thoughts without mastering or being subsumed by them.

NOTES

1. Theodor W. Adorno, *Essays on Music*, ed. Richard Leppert (Berkeley: University of California Press, 2002), 5.
2. A detailed history of the Institute can be found in Rolf Wiggershaus, *The Frankfurt School: Its History, Theories, and Political Significance*, trans. Michael Robertson (Cambridge, Mass.: MIT Press, 1994), and in Martin Jay, *The Dialectical Imagination: A History of the Frankfurt School and the Institute of Social Research, 1923–1950* (Boston: Little, Brown, 1973).
3. Quoted in Martin Jay, "The Frankfurt School in Exile," in *Permanent Exiles: Essays on the Intellectual Migration from Germany to America* (New York: Columbia University Press, 1985), 41.

4. Introduction to Adorno, *Essays on Music*, 13–15. Leppert also notes here Adorno's participation throughout the 1950s and 60s in the Darmstadt International Vacation Courses on New Music.

5. Preface to Theodor W. Adorno, *Critical Models: Interventions and Catchwords*, trans. Henry W. Pickford (New York: Columbia University Press, 1998), ix.

6. Theodor W. Adorno, *Minima Moralia: Reflections from Damaged Life*, trans. E. F. N. Jephcott (London: New Left Books, 1974), 192.

7. Theodor W. Adorno, *Aesthetic Theory*, trans. Robert Hullot-Kentor (Minneapolis: University of Minnesota Press, 1997), 329. Hereafter cited as AT.

1 Negative Dialectic as Fate
Adorno and Hegel

[T]he unity of the system derives from unreconcilable violence. Satanically, the world as grasped by the Hegelian system has only now, a hundred and fifty years later, proved itself to be a system in the literal sense, namely that of a radically societalized society.

Adorno

That Adorno entitled his major work of theoretical philosophy *Negative Dialectics* is enough, all by itself, to indicate the pervasive nature of the presence of Hegel in his thought.[1] While Hegel is occasionally the object of Adorno's thought, most notably in "World Spirit and Natural History: An Excursion to Hegel," a chapter of *Negative Dialectics*, and in *Hegel: Three Studies*, he is more routinely and emphatically present as its orientation, its method, approach, style, or *conatus*. An extreme way of stating this claim would be to say, flatly, that Adorno was a Hegelian, that however he departs from Hegel, he accepts the rudiments of Hegelian idealism. Adorno might be said to be an objective idealist to the extent to which he denies there is a philosophical "first,"[2] a fundamental ground, origin, or telos, be it mind or nature, subject or object: There can be no mediation without "something" which is mediated, and no presentation of pure immediacy without its mediations. And those mediations will be social and historical.[3] Even more significantly, Adorno's project could be said to aim at "speculative identities" that are the product of dialectically working through experiences of radical separation, diremption: Two apparently opposing items are shown to be internally related to one another, to somehow belong together. In Hegel the governing speculative identity is that of subject and substance:

Everything that is subject must be shown to be just as much (historical) substance, and what is regarded as substance must be shown to
be also subject.[4] In Adorno the governing speculative proposition, his
version of the identification of subject and substance, is that history
and nature are one, whose fullest expression is the claim that philosophy, as the domain of the presumptively autonomous concept,
and art, as the practice that preserves the materiality of the sign,
are one.[5]

Yet if Adorno is a Hegelian, he cannot be an orthodox Hegelian.
But then maybe the thought of anyone being an orthodox Hegelian is
contradictory. If for Hegel philosophy is one's own time and the history producing one's own time expressed in thought, then historical
change transforms the possibilities of philosophical expression. To
be writing philosophy after the French Revolution is significantly
different from writing philosophy "after Auschwitz" (ND, 361–5).
Hegel conceived of the French Revolution, including "the Terror,"
as formative for our education toward freedom and its embodiment
in the modern liberal state; Adorno thought Auschwitz revealed the
intransigent moment of violence in the modern conception of reason, the idea and ideals of reason as given by Kant and, however
differently, by Hegel. The reason that promised reconciliation was,
despite itself, a form of domination and violence because, in truth,
the "Hegelian subject-object is subject."[6] So perhaps I can state my
hyperbolic claim this way: Adorno's philosophy is the articulation
of what it is to be a Hegelian *after* Hegel, after Marx, after Nietzsche,
and above all after two centuries of brutal history in which the moment to realize philosophy, the hope of left Hegelians like Marx,
was missed (ND, 3). This is a quixotic position because whether one
thinks of Hegelianism in terms of Hegel's idea of an end of philosophy in "absolute knowing" or in terms of its political, left Hegelian
equivalent, an ideal transparent society in which philosophy is no
longer necessary because it has been realized, the result is the same:
Hegelian philosophy after Hegel is philosophy after philosophy was
supposed to have ended. So philosophy continues, "lives on" (ND, 3),
through critical engagement with the conceptions of reason that
were to enable us to stop philosophizing and live a human life. We
have philosophy because such a life is not available, which is also
an Hegelian idea, namely, that philosophy speaks to the *need* of culture which that culture cannot satisfy. And, again, just to take us

full circle, the categorial expression of need in a culture consists of unreconciled dualities, say, between history and nature.

To do any kind of justice to my hyperbolic thesis, that Adorno is a Hegelian doing philosophy after Hegel, requires showing what Hegelian ideas, conceptual figures, look like when pursued after Hegel. And accomplishing this end is best achieved, at least initially, by showing how Hegelian conceptual figures, transformed in response to their new historical setting, concretely shape Adorno's thought. I shall pursue this demonstration in three stages. First, I will argue that the dialectic of enlightenment is, finally, a transformed embodiment of Hegel's causality of fate doctrine. Next, I will examine the idea of negative dialectics as a response to the historical dialectic at a standstill. Finally, turning to the *Three Studies*, I will explore dialectic as the exposition (or tracking) of a repressed material meaning in concepts.

I. DIALECTIC OF ENLIGHTENMENT AS A CAUSALITY OF FATE

Dialectic of Enlightenment is the attempt to provide a conceptual analysis of how it was possible that the rational process of enlightenment which was intended to secure freedom from fear and human sovereignty could turn into forms of political, social, and cultural domination in which humans are deprived of their individuality and society is generally emptied of human meaning. Horkheimer and Adorno's goal is thus to elaborate an account of the conceptual underpinnings of the process of societal rationalization (as originally delineated by Max Weber), a process of which capital class domination and reification (as theorized by Marx) constitute the disastrous apotheosis. While *Dialectic of Enlightenment* has other aims, above all the sheer revealing of enlightened reason as violent and dominating, I take the "how possible?" question to be the heart of the matter. Horkheimer and Adorno's official answer is that instrumental or subjective reasoning, in which items are understood and explained by being subsumed under general theories, is only a part of reason, that part whose job is to enable our coping with and mastering of threatening nature. When this part of reason is taken to be the whole of reason, theoretically *and* practically, then we end up in the apparently ever-moving but, in reality, static iron cage of modernity.

While uncovering the substitution of a part of reason for the whole is a plausible beginning for a conceptual analysis, it does not, as stated, take us very far.

Although rarely noted, Horkheimer and Adorno explicitly conceived *Dialectic of Enlightenment* to be a generalization and radicalization of "The Enlightenment" chapter of the *Phenomenology of Spirit*.[7] The antagonists of the Enlightenment are pure insight and religious faith. The speculative proposition orienting the dialectic is that pure insight and faith are one; that is, enlightened rationality and faith turn out to be necessarily dependent on one another, and when that mutual dependency is repudiated, they become equally and analogously empty forms of the self. The two-part structure of Hegel's chapter involves, as the first step, "The Struggle of the Enlightenment with Superstition," in which enlightenment thought construes religious belief, faith, as nothing but an anthropomorphic illusion, the projection of human meaning onto material nature, and, oppositely, conceives itself as the permanent critique of all illusion, pure negativity. In step two, "The Truth of Enlightenment," it is shown that enlightenment rationality, pure insight as permanent critique, *because* it has no content of its own, because its goodness or worth comes solely from the dissolving of illusion, can be, finally, nothing but the empty thinking of the self thinking itself. Enlightenment reason, shorn of its critical object, becomes subject without substance. Hence, what enlightenment seeks to repudiate as blind faith in the absolute other is nothing but substance, the object of thought and what would give thought in general real content.

In broad terms, this *is* the dialectic of enlightenment. Horkheimer and Adorno simply extend the basic structure so as to enable it to form the underpinning for societal rationalization generally rather than being the logic of only a certain moment in history. Thus the first part of Hegel's chapter provides the model for the idea that enlightenment is the critique of myth, where myth is understood as anthropomorphism, the projection of the human onto nature.[8] Even more significantly, the first part of Hegel's chapter forms the model for the idea that the essence of enlightenment thought, pure insight, *becomes* the pure, transcendental self: By making itself the critique of all positive content, the self transforms itself into the transcendental center of experience, which as such is necessarily empty (DA, 29). Enlightenment reason is subjective reason. The second part of

Hegel's chapter forms the model for the idea that enlightenment is systematically dependent on what its seeks to repudiate, religion and its mythic avatar being in fact irrational forms of object dependence, but forms of object dependence nonetheless. There is, finally, a third borrowing. Hegel contends that because pure faith refused to think anything concretely, it is, despite itself, nothing but an empty yearning of the self for substance, and because enlightenment has nothing to think, the enlightened self collapses back into dumb thinghood. I take this dialectic to be the origin of the claim that becomes "enlightenment reverts to mythology" (DA, xvi).[9] Negatively, enlightenment partakes of the emptiness it creates in its object.

This is rushed and deserves detailing. Its guiding thought, however, is not implausible, namely, that the Enlightenment critique of religion models generally the critique of illusion and that the critique of illusion models the crucial moments in the process of societal rationalization.[10] One might nonetheless query the appropriateness of such an immediate overlap between Hegel's regional dialectic and one aimed at a wider historical process. The appropriation pans out so neatly because, for Hegel and for Horkheimer and Adorno, the dialectic of enlightenment is equivalent to or a dialectical version of the conflict between reason and faith as seen through the lens of Kant's account of concept and intuition: Reason is to faith as concept is to intuition. So, enlightened or subjective reason is a version of concepts without intuitions (which are of course empty), and faith a version of intuitions without concepts (which are of course blind); where Kant's dictum is itself just *the* epistemic version of the dialectic between subject and substance, history and nature. Hence, the critique of religion *can* model the overcoming of illusion generally because that process is, finally, the transfiguration of nature into an object of pure insight. I take the following as pivotal: "In the relation of intuition (i.e., direct perception) and concept, philosophy already discerned the gulf which opened with that separation [the separation of the pure sign, and so science, from particular images which become the substance of art], and again tries in vain to close it: philosophy, indeed, is defined by this very attempt" (DA, 18). So reason is to faith as concept is to intuition, which becomes the relation of science to art. I shall return to this.

Now even if it is conceded that Hegel's dialectic of faith and pure insight does form the model for the dialectic of enlightenment (the battle between enlightenment and myth), it is still not obvious why, even conceding the concept-intuition thesis, this should form a *general* model for the process of societal rationalization – the overcoming of illusion seems too intellectualist to be the conceptual key to a historical dynamic, and, further, it is not obvious why the dialectic should become *self-stultifying* when appropriated by Horkheimer and Adorno. The answer to each question will require the introduction and deployment of a further Hegelian conceptual figure. Hegel did not conceive of the dialectic of faith and pure insight (or concept and intuition) as unique or autonomous; on the contrary, he understood the moments of faith and pure insight to point back to a more fundamental antagonism. One can conceive of faith and pure insight as highly refined epistemic crystallizations of more fundamental anthropological moods: Faith expresses unconditional *trust* in the other or, at least, the yearning or need for unconditional trust. Hence the figure of God is just the figure of an object of unconditional trust. So Hegel states that faith

puts its trust in it [the object], i.e. it finds itself as *this particular* consciousness, or as self-consciousness, precisely *in the object*. Whomsoever I trust, his *certainty of himself* [what is projected onto God] is for me the *certainty of myself*; I recognize in him my own being-for-self, know that he acknowledges it and that it is for him purpose and essence.[11]

Faith thus expresses an absolute trust in the other, which is a recognition of my absolute dependence on the other, which, if deserved, gives me back my independent self. If the figure of faith is a rationalized, and so ruined, version of trust,[12] and trust the recognition of self in otherness, then pure insight as permanent critique is a figure of the mood of *suspicion*; suspicion sees in trust only the threat of self-loss. Hence, if trust involves my perfect confidence in the other through which I can attain perfect confidence in myself, then the mood of suspicion is one of not seeing myself in the other at all but of seeking or conceiving of myself as possessing perfect independence from the other.

For Horkheimer and Adorno, enlightenment is the general epistemic expression of distrust, suspicion, and the desire for independence, while myth is the epistemic expression of the need for trust, the acknowledgement of our epistemic dependence on the objects of cognition. Horkheimer and Adorno could reasonably hope that the dialectic of enlightenment had historical generality because they could reasonably construe it as an epistemic expression of the anthropologically basic moods of suspicion (fear and anxiety, misrecognition and nonacknowledgment, critique and skepticism) and trust (acknowledgment, recognition), which, in Hegel, originally take shape in the dialectic of independence and dependence – nothing less than the famous dialectic of master and slave. To be sure, for Hegel the one thing that is not present in the dialectic of independence and dependence is trust – that is the point. Rather the master, who enters the battle for pure recognition in order to demonstrate his independence from nature, in winning the battle comes to conceive of himself as independent from nature, not needing to trust it or others because he has successfully made himself transcendentally independent of nature within and without through violently dominating the human other. What the master does not see is that he is fully dependent on the slave twice over: Only the slave offers him recognition *as* master, and the slave mediates the master's relation to nature so that nature can be seen by him as nothing other than what spontaneously and immediately satisfies his desire (compare DA, 13). While the slave knows full well that he is dependent on the master, that fact is intolerable to him, so he seeks to become independent, transforming nature, through science and labor, in his own image. In both cases, dependence is conceived of as negative.[13]

Adorno and Horkheimer's fundamental strategy is to appropriate Hegel's analysis of the dialectic of master and slave, independence and dependence, both directly *and* by turning it back into the logic of reason and object. Reason (the master concept) depends on object (the slave intuition). The initial anti-idealist premise of this transposition is that so-called intersubjective practices are forms of interacting between beings who are, also and ineliminably, "body or blood" (DA, 29), *objects* of a certain kind. Recognition is always, at least, the recognition of another bodily being. Whatever else is involved in recognizing another, the minimum of recognizing is *perceptual* and *sensible*. If the concepts employed in giving recognition necessarily pass over this perceptual and judgmental beginning, or acknowledge it only in terms of the application of what is already conceived of as logical or rational in itself, then what is recognized will be misrecognized at the same time. Rationalized reason, that formation of reason that emerges through seeking to detach itself from reliance on nature by mastering it, is systematic misrecognition because it eschews reason's dependence on objects. Horkheimer and Adorno could make this transposition because they, correctly, understood the dialectic of pure insight (subjective reason) and faith as an epistemic version of the dialectic of master and slave: "Enlightenment dissolves the injustice of the old inequality – unmediated lordship and master – but at the same time perpetuates it in universal mediation," in, that is, equalizing what was different through the concept (DA, 12).[14] In seeing the dialectical connection between pure insight and faith, on the one hand, and master (independence) and slave (dependence), on the other, folding the former into the latter so that it is present from the outset, both sides of the logic contributing to the forming of the other side, Horkheimer and Adorno give Marxist history (the battle of classes) a Weberian, rationalizing, twist. Once we recognize the connection between the dialectic of enlightenment and the dialectic of master and slave in Hegel, then the linking of the critique of instrumental reason to Odysseus commanding his rowers as he binds himself to the mast in order to hear the song of the sirens turns out to be logically austere in Hegelian terms.

So my claim is now that we understand the dialectic of enlightenment, as taken over from Hegel, as one fundamental expression of the dialectic of desired independence from nature and disavowed dependence: Reason or enlightenment seeks through knowing and labor to master nature and become independent of it without acknowledging its pervasive dependence. The critique of myth is fundamental in this process, as mythic thought represents, however inadequately, the moment in cognition in which dependence on nature is acknowledged. But this can be generalized, because if what makes myth unacceptable is its projecting of the human on to nature, then the lesson of the critique of myth is that all cognitions of nature which depend on it for their content are illusory. Reason can thus be rational only if independent from nature, only if, then, its content is pure, that is, a priori. Logic, mathematics, mathematical physics, and the methods of permanent critique thus become the ideals of reason, and its eventual taking those on as its proper identity is how it rationalizes itself.

For Horkheimer and Adorno, unlike Hegel, the drive to independence derives not from the desire for recognition but from the fear of nature, the fear of self-loss. By construing history from the standpoint of the master, so to speak, Horkheimer and Adorno make plausible the idea that the process should have a static result. In Hegel the position of the master is a dead-end because in receiving recognition from the slave he no longer has to act in relation to the natural world: He can immediately enjoy it.[15] In this respect, the master has become absented from history and returns to a natural existence, just a bit of nature – which is just how Horkheimer and Adorno envision us.

I think it is both helpful and accurate to see the conceptual figures of pure insight and faith, suspicion and trust, desired independence and disavowed dependence, mastery and slavery as structuring the dialectic of enlightenment. But there is still a problem. In Hegel's story, the standpoint of the master is, finally, static whilst the slave makes history. In Horkheimer and Adorno's story, the struggle is between humans and nature, which is why the language of independence (of reason and the concept) and dependence is more appropriate. But though it is clear how the master's nonrecognition of the slave leads to the master's stasis, it is unclear why our nonacknowledgment of our dependence on nature should be not only self-stultifying but dominating, a form of violence.

At the strictly epistemic level, the answer is fairly direct. Adorno and Horkheimer contend that the vehicle of enlightenment misrecognition is abstraction: "Abstraction, the tool of enlightenment, treats its objects as did fate...: it liquidates them... [T]he leveling domination of abstraction... makes everything in nature repeatable" (DA, 13). Nothing is wrong in abstraction itself; it is a necessary feature of any conceptual practice. However, when the results of abstraction are *systematically* detached from what they have been abstracted from and are thereby, what is the same thing, reified as independent, then the forms of knowing and reasoning that result are themselves a mastering of the object, approaching the object as nothing other than what reason *determines* it to be, hence as *merely* a token or case or example or specimen of what is already known. Hence, if reason or the concept is conceived of as wholly independent from nature – Platonically expressed in the separation of the intelligible from the sensible, the eternity of reason from the time of life, Kantianly expressed by reason being the lawgiver to nature – then either reason will be empty, a pure thinking of itself, always conceiving of the world as nothing but an image of the self, or reason will collapse into skepticism, for if reason is permanent critique, which is what the mood of suspicion becomes, then eventually it will have to critique its own most fundamental ideas, truth and rationality. Hence, the best explanation for our highest values devaluing themselves is that those values express an overwhelming drive for independence from nature. But this skeptical denouement is weaker than Horkheimer and Adorno's contention that enlightened reason is violent and destructive in its nonacknowledgment of dependence.

Although I am not aware of Horkheimer or Adorno anywhere drawing attention to the doctrine of the causality of fate, this seems to me the version of the dialectic of independence and dependence that comes closest to their own.[16] What separates the lament over abstraction from the nominalist critique of universals with which it is in league is that both the activity of abstraction and what is abstracted from must, indeterminately, be rooted in or parts of anthropomorphic nature, the nature implicit in our animal embodiment and its objects: what is seeable by the human eye, touchable by the human hand, whose size and heft are measured in relation to the human body, what appears desirable or useful in relation to our natural needs, and so on. Saying anything very compelling or clear about anthropomorphic nature is immensely difficult because it is this nature which has been liquidated by enlightenment, to be replaced by the mechanical nature of Newtonian science and the autonomous culture of capital – the system of exchange value making every object a commodity.

With this thought, Horkheimer and Adorno return the dynamic of independence and dependence to Hegel's early formulation of it as a logic of "life." Here is how Hegel originally formulated his doctrine of independence and dependence:

In the hostile power of fate, universal is not severed from particular in the way in which the law, as universal, is opposed to man or his inclinations as the particular. Fate is just the enemy, and man stands over against it as a power fighting against it. Only through a departure from that united life which is neither regulated by law nor at variance with law, only through the killing of life, is something alien produced. Destruction of life is not the nullification of life but its diremption, and the destruction consists in its transformation into an enemy.[17]

In this confused account, Hegel opposes the subsumptive logic of universal (law) and particular, against which he is bringing the same accusation as Adorno will, to a part-whole logic of life where, roughly, the notion of life is being used to figure human communities as organic communities, literally and metaphorically, of a certain kind. Hence, in acting against the other (suppressing her) I act against myself, removing myself from the organic totality of which I am a part and which gives me my life. Hence what I as criminal suffer is nothing other than "the reactive force of a life that has been suppressed and separated off."[18]

There is no need to oppose a logic of conceptuality to a logic of life, once life is interpreted as anthropomorphic nature, and the issue of universal and particular concerns not them as such but a particular regime of concept and object, namely, one in which reason is taken to be and to operate in accordance with the notion that it is, ideally, independent and self-determining. Once these substitutions are made, the logic of life and the logic of independence and dependence can be thought together: Instrumental reasoning, as the rational expression of and means for securing the desire for self-preservation, misrecognizes itself when it reifies the process of abstraction through which it proceeds, when it comes, finally, to think of itself as reason as such. In so doing, it separates itself from anthropomorphic nature, conceiving itself as independent and separate, and nature as its alien other – an other whose shape, as a system of objects governed by mechanical laws, shares nothing with it. In denying the anthropomorphic life of its other, it liquidates its own life; reification is literal and not metaphorical. Finally, what it suffers in terms of fate, now the debilitating consequences of rationalized modernity, our iron cage, is still the "reactive force of a life that has been suppressed and separated off." Broadly speaking, this is Horkheimer and Adorno's narrative.

In order to underline this claim, let me put together Hegel's causality of fate doctrine with Horkheimer and Adorno's epistemic version of it. In the following passage I have placed in square brackets what Adorno and Horkheimer add to Hegel in order to transform the causality of fate doctrine into the dialectic of enlightenment:

The trespasser [humans as seeking their self-preservation through the rational domination of nature] intended to have to [rationally and epistemically] do [away] with another's [nature's anthropomorphically conceived] life [through rational mastery], but he has only destroyed his own [anthropomorphic nature], for [anthropomorphic] life is not different from [anthropomorphic] life. . . . When the trespasser feels the disruption in his own [now repressed, voided anthropomorphic] life... or knows himself [in his bad conscience [in his guilt]] as disrupted [reified], then the working of his fate commences, and this feeling of a [anthropomorphic] life disrupted must become a longing for what has been lost [become an immanent critique of enlightened knowing].[19]

This yearning figure appears in *Dialectic of Enlightenment* as Odysseus bound to the mast maddened in desire for the world of nature no longer available to him. By the time we reach Sade's Juliette, which is to say, ourselves, even that yearning is unknown to itself.

2. NEGATIVE DIALECTICS AS DIALECTIC AT A STANDSTILL

Adorno interprets Samuel Beckett's *Endgame* as a degenerated logic of master (Hamm) and slave (Clov). Hamm depends on Clov to do what is necessary in order to keep them both alive; but in a situation in which all they possess is their dependence on one another, without meaning or purpose, this is of dubious value. Given the emptiness of their situation, something worse than death is palpable: "the fear that they will be unable to die." To be able to die would be something; so the possibility of death stands for possibility, that something might happen, that things might change. The nonmovement of the play, its plot as the curtailment of plot, tells against this: "The servant is no longer capable of taking charge and doing away with domination. The mutilated Clov would scarcely be capable of it, and in any case, according to the historico-philosophical sundial of the play it is too late for spontaneous action." The best, perhaps only move left to Clov is simply to leave, which is what he prepares to do toward the end of the play. Yet, the play ends not with his exit (finale, death, whatever), but with him standing motionless at the door, his eyes fixed on Hamm. Adorno interprets this as an "allegory whose intention has fizzled out," that is, even the allegorical significance of exiting limply collapses. Worse, apart from differences that may or may not be important, this ending is identical with the beginning of the play: "No spectator, and no philosopher, would be capable of saying for sure whether or not the play is starting all over again. The pendulum of the dialectic has come to a standstill."[20]

That parenthetical "and no philosopher" is telling. The authority of Beckett's presentation, Adorno is claiming, is to make the master-slave dialectic unavailable as an interpretive scheme through which philosophers might interpret the world. Foremost among those "philosophers," the irony is painful, would be Marx, who interpreted all history as the history of class conflict and the dynamic of capital as the conflictual dialectic of proletariat and bourgeoisie. That dialectic is unavailable for interpretive purposes because it has withered, come to a standstill. So the "historico-philosophical sundial" of the play is just the historico-philosophical sundial of the present. Adorno did not have to await Beckett to have this thought; the original project of the Frankfurt School in the 1930s was to diagnose a situation in which the revolutionary dynamics of the European left had "fizzled out."

Beckett's "endgame," the dialectic of master and slave at a standstill, converges all too well with the immobilization with which the dialectic of enlightenment expires. Indeed, the point of *Dialectic of Enlightenment* was to explain why the dialectic of class had come to a standstill. If it is "too late for spontaneous action," then Adorno's new question is, how possibly can the immobile present be set into motion? Two features of the argument of *Dialectic of Enlightenment* make responding to this question appear to be all but impossible. First, though it may well be the case that what is repressed by instrumental reason is anthropomorphic nature, that nature has disappeared from view and thus become unavailable for critical purposes. How can lost nature be critically mobilized when there is none about? Second, if reason has fairly successfully *become* autonomous, then what *rational* resources could there be for demonstrating its actual reliance on its other; I assume that the "in-principle" dependence of reason on its other was shown in *Dialectic of Enlightenment*. The demonstration that in principle reason is dependent on its other – and self-defeating, irrational, and skeptical when that dependence is systematically and reflectively repressed – however diagnostically and genealogically significant, is idle for the purpose of explaining how we might respond to this situation. In the Beckett essay, Adorno repeats the central emancipatory logic of the earlier work but does not explain how it is to be carried it out: "*Ratio*, which has become completely instrumental, devoid of self-reflection and reflection on what it has disqualified, must inquire after the meaning that it itself has expunged."[21]

How can reason inquire after the meaning that it itself has expunged? *Negative Dialectics* is intended as a response to this dilemma. The beginning to an answer to this question is to recognize that *reason* as such cannot undertake this inquiry, not on its own or in its own now stifled voice. What is required is a shift in levels, away from the discourse of reason and rationality and to that of the concept: "Insight into the *constitutive character of the nonconceptual in the concept* would end the compulsive identification which the concept brings unless halted by such reflection. Reflection on its own meaning is the way out of the concept's seeming being-in-itself as a unity of meaning" (ND, 12, emphasis added). I anticipated this move earlier when I argued that part of what made the dialectic of pure insight and faith generalizable is that it was an articulation or version of the dialectic of concept and intuition. For Adorno, consonant with the German idealist tradition, not only is the concept the vehicle or medium of reasoning, in so being it is the medium of cognition generally. At the micrological level, the dialectic of assumed independence and disavowed dependence takes the form of the concept, which, although general in its very nature, becomes ever more general by subsuming low-level conceptual graspings, say, the kind of conceptual graspings that track objects in their sensuous appearance, under ever higher and more general conceptualities, ever more embracing unities. Hence, the movement of abstraction occurs by means of conceptual ascent to higher and more unifying modes of subsumption and explanation.[22] Logic and modern science are the quintessential expression of conceptual unification theoretically, while practically it is the relegation of use value to exchange value that performs the task. Abstraction through conceptual ascent will do for the explanation of the liquidation of anthropomorphic nature.

In accordance with what has come to be called the semantic thesis of idealism, "the structure and unity of the *concept* is the same as the structure and unity of the *self*."[23] For Adorno, this double unity is the product of the dialectic of enlightenment, the process of conceptual ascent to ever more embracing unities. This is why, for Adorno, conceptual ascent, when cut free from other forms of reflection and rational comprehension, is taken to be a triumph of subjective reason: the world as mirror of the unity the self achieved in the self abstracting itself from anthropomorphic nature. Thus, the dialectic of enlightenment just is the coming-to-be of the semantic thesis of idealism: The activity of the self unifying and individuating itself through the repression of nature within – "man's domination over himself...grounds his selfhood" (DA, 54) – occurs simultaneously with and is the same action as its unification of the world through the concept. Each unification of the world through conceptual ascent produces an increment in the self's abstraction from its inner nature, and each repression of inner needs and impulses enables a further dominating (via unification) of nature without. The semantic thesis of idealism is thus the stakes in the claim that "the history of civilization is the history of the introversion of sacrifice" (DA, 55). *The semantic thesis of idealism represents the deepest structure of occidental rationality; and it is for that reason that the critique of enlightened modernity transpires as the critique of idealism.*

The achievement of unity, as in the doctrine that the "I think" must be capable of accompanying all my representations, which is the same as the achievement of independence, occurs at the philosophical level when the schema for all possible conceptual unifications is legislated a priori. The consequences of this achievement, philosophically, are the contrasts of concepts with intuitions,

first as *form* to *matter*, which they structure or organize. Second, they contrast with intuitions as *general* to *particular*. Finally, they contrast with intuitions as products of *spontaneity* or intellectual activity, as opposed to products of receptivity.

In the first, the conceptual is distinguished from the *material*, that which provides *content*, as opposed the form (more specifically the *normative* form or rulishness), which is the contribution of concepts. In the second, the conceptual is distinguished from the particular, as what *classifies* to what is *classified*. In the third, the conceptual is distinguished from what is imposed on us from without, as what *we do* as opposed to what is *done to* or imposed on us.[24]

Again, these contrasts or dualities are for Adorno products of the dialectic of enlightenment. If one interprets Adorno's notion of mimetic response, not as a self-sufficient conception of cognition, which is the standard view, but rather as a primitive or developmentally early conception of the moment of sensuous receptivity, then

Kantian intuition, as the blind slave of the master concept, is the remnant form of mimetic response that occurs once the concept becomes ideally independent. Within this schema, anthropomorphic nature or sensuous particularity is captured as what the dominating concept suppresses. As a consequence, in *Negative Dialectics* anthropomorphic nature is represented logically rather substantially; it is called the nonidentical.

So the austere philosophical expression of dialectics at a standstill is the series of contrasts that make up the duality between concept and intuition. In typical Hegelian fashion, dialectical critique involves showing that these are indeed dualities and that as such the structure is self-defeating. One good reason for thinking that these are dualities is that the intuitive moment is so deprived of content that it becomes imponderable how it could play the functional role – of guiding and constraining conceptualization – assigned to it; all the cognitive action, so to speak, occurs in the forming, classifying, imposing, with what is formed, classified, and imposed upon appearing solely and only in the light of its presumptive uptake. Because nothing can be said about what is taken up other than the result, the concept appears to commune only with itself, the self with itself, and the world becomes only a shadow cast by the light of reason.

Optimistically, the relation between the contrasting items can be set in motion if it can be shown that the items relegated to blind intuition have a content of their own. First, intuitions cannot be reductively the dumb matter or content of concepts but must have a form or rulishness of their own (the suppressed rulishness of anthropomorphic nature; call it the language of nature). Second, then, particulars must be capable of possessing a content or identity on their own and not merely through that which accrues to them as member of a class of like items. Third, the link connecting spontaneity (freedom) with the self-determining movement of reason must be broken so that what is suffered or undergone, our power of receptivity, can itself be a source of meaning. To perform each of these reversals is to reinflate, to expand and thicken, the intuitive moment of conceptuality. In accordance with the logic of independence and dependence, this involves showing how the presumptive independent moment of the concept, call it the logical moment, is dependent on its material moment, which would entail showing how the material moment possesses some independence from the logical moment, for an item cannot be dependent on a second item unless the second possesses some independence of its own. But this of course is the normative message of the master-slave dialectic.

Taking up again Hegel's critique of Kant's formalism, for that is what is at issue here, is more difficult than my account thus far has made it appear, since the fundamental move which enabled Hegel to do the job is unavailable to Adorno. Hegel reconfigured the relation between concept and intuition into, first, the relation of one subject to another, intersubjectivity as such, and then into social practices more generally. For Hegel, recognitive logics replace subject-object logics. But a generalized logic of intersubjectivity is useless for Adorno's purposes because it eschews the moment of materiality that he diagnoses as the suppressed moment of the concept; the slave can only be recognized if recognized as a fully embodied (natural) subject. Adorno accomplishes the task, to the degree he does, in two stages: the *preparatory* stage of negative dialectic and a second, more robust stage in which dialectic is seen to be a way of tracking or establishing material inferential relations among concepts.

Negative dialectics begins, or better the experience of negative dialectics begins, *precisely* at the place where we left off from the causality of fate several paragraphs back. Recall, as a consequence of the trespass, which is now the domination of anthropomorphic nature by instrumental reason, the trespassers, us, feel our own life disrupted or reified; in our bad conscience, which is to say, in our feeling of guilt about what we have done, the working of fate commences, and the feeling of guilt and disruption becomes a longing for what has been lost. Adorno reformulates this in terms of the experience of contradiction. As things stand, the world appears as a closed logical order; this order is that which has been imposed upon the world by instrumental reason. Because the totality is structured to accord with the demands of logic, above all the law of excluded middle (everything *must* be either true or false, belong or not belong; no indeterminacy or heterogeneity is to be tolerated), then

whatever differs in quality, comes to be designated as a contradiction. Contradiction is nonidentity under the aspect of identity; the dialectical primacy of the principle of contradiction makes the thought of unity the measure of heterogeneity. As it collides with its limit it exceeds itself. Dialectics is the consequent consciousness of nonidentity. It does not begin by taking a standpoint. My thought is driven to it by its own insufficiency, by my guilt of what I am thinking. . . . What we differentiate will appear divergent, dissonant, negative for just as long as the structure of our consciousness obliges it to strive for unity. (ND, 5)

I do not know how convincing this is, but it is a stunningly delicate transformation of Hegel's romantic thought into a historico-logical register. Dialectics cannot begin by taking a standpoint because to do so would presume the subject was in possession of a method through which she could reverse the damage; however, method so conceived is the assumption of the independence of reason, which is the cause of the problem (DA, 4).

Dialectics can commence only by understanding the dominant logical mechanism of reason from a reverse angle. Under standard conditions, contradictions are signs that reason has failed and hence a spur to seek a better, more consistent, and more unifying account. But if the unity and so consistency of the phenomena facing us is the problem, a sign that we have imposed an order on it, then the emergence of a contradiction signifies differently; it means that something has slipped through the unifying net, which is to say that contradictions testify to antagonisms in reality (between what is demanded of things and the things). What slips past the unifying net is nonidentical with the concept that was supposed to grasp it. Hence, the experience of contradiction becomes the experience of an object claiming against its unifying concept; my experience of that claim is, first, my experience that the now indigent, dissonant item is so as a consequence of my reasoning, and, second, my experience, my dawning recognition, that I could not have rationally dominated the item in the first place without *its* claiming – a claiming, again, which only appears as reason fails. So my experience of guilt is a two-sided acknowledgment of my dependence on the object: I am responsible for or to the object for what has been done to it, and I am responsible to the object for the possibility of thinking it at all.

Adorno presses the guilt, responsibility, yearning logic of the negative experience thus: "While doing violence to the object of its syntheses, our thinking heeds a potential that waits in the object, and it unconsciously obeys the idea of making amends to the fragments for what it has done; in philosophy this unconscious tendency becomes conscious" (ND, 19). Philosophical reflection is the conscious form of the unconscious experience of guilt and debt; thus, philosophical reflection, in experiencing contradiction, experiences it as the token of a past violence that as such requires, as Melanie Klein would have it, reparation.[25] This is why Adorno can claim that pain and negativity are "the moving forces of dialectical thinking" (ND, 202) and hence that the "need to lend a voice to suffering is a condition of all truth" (ND, 18).[26] Although reductive, it would not be wrong to say that *Negative Dialectics* is structurally the experience of contradiction, the recognition of guilt and the need for reparation, and the reflective activity of reparation – call it critique of the rationalized concept of the concept.

Negative dialectics, austerely thought, is nothing other than the reflective version of the experience of contradiction; it is that experience raised to the level of the concept. What makes this dialectic negative is that it nowhere claims or even attempts to state the truth of an indigent item; rather it is riveted to the moment in which the object appears as "more" than what its covering concept has claimed it is. The nonidentical would be, thus, "the thing's own identity against its identifications" (ND, 161); but that identity appears now only as the claim of the necessary insufficiency of the covering concept, and hence not in itself. But the very idea of an item having an identity in excess of what its identitarian form demands is equivalent to claiming that a thing *must* be capable of having an identity other than that which has accrued to it through being the member of a class, and therefore it *must* have a cognitive content other than that which is provided for it by its conceptual formation. What follows the two "musts" is what logically emerges from, is the conceptual upshot of, the experience of contradiction; what follows the two "musts" thus constitutes the meaning of nonidentity. Nonidentity is the form of identification that would be satisfied if the two "musts" were satisfied. Conversely, once it is acknowledged that the intuitive moment contributes to conceptual content in this way, it follows that the logical element of the concept must be overreaching itself in its claimed independence and autonomy. And, indeed, it is this moment, the moment of examining and criticizing the claim to hegemony of the logical element of the concept, hence the idealist concept of a concept in general ("Concepts and Categories"), as well as, in the light of that critique, criticizing a few specimen rationalized concepts (freedom, world history, and metaphysics), that is the primary task of *Negative Dialectics*.

Rationalized reason substitutes part for whole, Horkheimer and Adorno's original claim, *through* illegitimately abstracting the logical element of the concept from its material moment. The critique of concept-intuition dualism thus fulfils the promise of the dialectics of pure insight and faith, enlightened reason and myth, independence and dependence, because it forms the micrological infrastructure of those logics. The reflective comprehension of the experience of contradiction is insight into the essential irrationality of that concept of the concept which is specified by the three contrasts between concept and intuition.

Adorno states that "dialectics is the ontology of the wrong state of things" and that the right state of things "would be free of it: neither a system nor a contradiction" (ND, 11). Dialectics is the reflective comprehension of the experience of contradiction; contradiction now occurs because there is an antagonism between the social system, rationalized society as formed through the demands of capital, and the particular subjects and objects formed. Contradiction, when it occurs, points to the claim of the particular, the nonidentical, against its social identifications. Since contradiction is the moving force of negative dialectics, negative dialectics will continue only so long as domination continues. Thus contradiction, understood not as what empties a thought of content but as what shows the inadequacy in the form of thought seeking consistency (which is the precise difference between logical and dialectical contradiction), is bound to unreconciled experience.[27] If there were no closed system, then there would not be dialectical contradiction. So, not only is negative dialectic not totalizing, an attempt to arrive at absolute knowing or the absolute idea, and not only is dialectic negative because it is moved by the negative experiences of pain and suffering, and not only is dialectic negative because it lives through a continual awareness of contradiction, but dialectic is negative because its condition of possibility is the negative or wrong state of things.

What negative dialectic *offers*, in contrast, is the conceptual possibility of there being actual possibility. If there is "more" to an item than what its covering concept determines, then there must be more possibilities for the object to be than what system dictates.

Contradiction does not reveal what those possibilities are, only that if what specifies the object's possibilities is precisely what deprives the object of possibility, then the contradiction betwixt concept and object entails an indeterminate possibility in the object. The very thing that Hamm and Clov hoped, that something might happen (which is the very thing that the form of Beckett's play deprived them of), is ignited by the procedure of negative dialectics. So perhaps we might imagine Clov suddenly able to stop staring at Hamm and turn his eyes to the door. Clov, finally, is truly preparing to leave; something might happen. That would not be much, but pointing to a possible exit when one thought there was none is something.

3. DIALECTIC AS CONSTELLATIONS OF MATERIAL INFERENCE

Hegel's texts are antitexts.

It is at this juncture that critics of Adorno routinely balk. If giving the Copernican turn an axial turn toward the object (ND, xx), of over and over again turning Clov around to face the door, and just this movement of turning *exhausts* the capacities for rational critique, then it is too little, no different *in fact* from a negative theology, even if its historical ambitions are logically incommensurable with negative theology. And if Adorno's philosophy was stuck at the moment of turning, a purely logical conversion, then Adorno's critics would have a point. But precisely what distinguishes negative dialectic conceptually from negative theology entails that logically this cannot be all. What is more than the reflective appropriation of the experience of contradiction is equally a question of dialectics, of what makes dialectical contradiction more than logical contradiction. Contradiction can be dynamic only if the content of the concepts concerned is synthetic. Hence, if a contradiction – say, humans are free and determined – carries synthetic content, then it cannot be fixed by arbitrarily changing definitions.[28] Again, contradiction can reflect an antagonism in the object.

I read "Skoteinos, or How to Read Hegel," the final essay in *Three Studies*, which is equally a reprise of the whole, as explicating "How to Read Adorno." "Skoteinos" means darkness or obscurity; the essay is thus a critique of the ideal of Cartesian clarity and distinctness and a defense of whatever is necessary in order that the content of concepts demonstratively reveals their extraconceptual, nonlogical, nonanalytic content.[29] Adorno's defense of Hegel turns on the idea that Hegelian dialectic, despite the fact that it is a subjective subject-object dialectic (it expresses the semantic thesis of idealism), despite the fact that it disowns the significance of language, despite the fact that it aimed at conceptual closure, and despite the fact that the closure aimed at transpired as the closed system of late capital, nonetheless, in its very attempt to conceptually exhaust the world, to make concept and world be at one, to utterly bind thought and being, transcends itself: "Hegelian dialectic finds its ultimate truth, that of its own impossibility, in its unresolved and vulnerable quality, even if, as the theodicy of self-consciousness, it has no awareness of this" (H, 13).[30] The very ambitiousness of Hegelian dialectic, a conceptual system that would saturate empirical-historical existence, is what makes it turn into its opposite. Reality cannot be shown to be conceptually saturated, rational, unless conceptuality, the very movement of what Hegel calls "Spirit," can be shown to be empirically saturated. The latter, which is intrinsic to Hegelian dialectic, ruins its rationalism and takes it beyond itself. Hegelian dialectic was always a negative one – conceptualities undoing themselves through or in virtue of their claim to sufficiency – but without the claim to sufficiency, the undoing, the stress of reality in the concept, would not have occurred.

Adorno thinks that there are two key premises to Hegel's dialectic. First, it operates as a critique of Kantian formalism: "In Kant, critique remains critique of reason; in Hegel, who criticizes the Kantian separation of reason from reality, the critique of reason is simultaneously a critique of the real. The inadequacy of isolated particular definitions is always also the inadequacy of the particular reality that is grasped in those definitions" (H, 77). Because thought-forms are socially and historically formed, come to be, they bear within themselves the social reality forming them. It is this that makes Hegel's *Phenomenology* at least in part a genealogy of reason. For example, consider how Hegel explicates the possibility of skepticism in relation to simpler forms of consciousness and the world surrounding it and how the contradictions of skepticism tell against the world that calls it into being. My account of the placement of the semantic thesis of idealism is intended to bear analogous dual weight.

Dialectic is thus "reason's critical consciousness of itself and the critical experience of its objects" (H, 10). Second, what permits the critique of the separation of form from matter is the recognition that transcendental form, the "mystery" behind the synthetic unity of apperception (the articulation of and vehicle for the semantic thesis of idealism), is "none other than social labor" (H, 18; see 18–27). If this means that Kant is only able to claim the transcendental unity of apperception in the light of the achieved mastery over nature which social labor had achieved, then it is a reasonable half-truth. If the stronger thesis is meant, namely, that labor is the archetype or origin of synthetic thought, then it is false. Labor could not labor without conceiving of the object as matter to be formed; but then so conceiving of things is the work of abstraction achieved through conceptual activity. This latter, however, is sufficient for Adorno's purposes, since it perceives conceptualization and laboring as intrinsically connected if distinct activities of which it makes no sense to see one or the other as primary: They both signify the coping of an animal lacking a natural niche who must reproduce itself in the absence of reliable instinctual mechanisms. In putting the matter this way, I am claiming that the coming-to-be of the semantic thesis of idealism is a consequence of both the dialectic of enlightenment and the master-slave dialectic; the labor of the concept is both the concept's own as well as anticipations or memories of forms of social labor.[31] It is the connection between the two dialectics, their dialectical relation to one another, that entails the illicitness of the distinction between form and matter.

Once it is conceded that concepts are not masters of their own contents, that they are historically conditioned repositories of events of successful and unsuccessful conceptualization and hence transmit contents they do not originate, then in opposition to logical system one would anticipate that the characterizing features of dialectic would be expressions of the excess of empirical content, in its particularity, over conceptual form. Each of Adorno's characterizations of dialectic is or is intended as an element in the undoing of concept-intuition dualism, or as an expression of the insufficiency of that dualism, and by extension an elaboration of the notion of material inference or implication. Broadly speaking, the idea of material inference claims that what connects two or more concepts is their specific content rather than a topic-neutral logical connective – the laws of logic. In learning a concept, what we learn are its logical powers, that is, what inferences it licenses. To know that Nashville is *south* of Chicago, one must grasp that Chicago is *north* of Nashville; that is what it is to grasp *south* and *north*. Equally, to appropriately comprehend the concept *lightning*, one needs to know that if there is lightning, then soon there will be *thunder*. To have the concept *tomato* is to know that tomatoes are for eating, that you pick them when red and not green (unless you intend to fry them).[32] The logical powers of concepts bespeak their contentful connection to other concepts, how the relations of concepts relate to, reflect and express, relations between objects or events (lightning and thunder), how features of objects are connected to human practices (the color of tomatoes with respect to their picking and ways of being prepared for eating), and so on. Because the logical powers of some concepts are so immediate, as with *north* and *south*, it can appear that what is at issue is an analytic truth whose validity is thus dependent on a law of logic, but the way color, ripeness, readiness for eating, and modes of preparation are connected in our appreciation of tomatoes, and thus in our having the concept *tomato*, reveals the illusion in that belief. Dialectic is the attempt to reveal how concept-concept relations express or are tethered to concept-world relations. But those two sets of relations are the connection of the concept-intuition relation *in* each concept.

In order to expose how concept-concept relations relate to concept-world relations, Adorno, arguing both for and against Hegel, reveals how language is necessary for the presentation of dialectic. Dialectic transpires, in part, through the constitution of language. Language contains two axes, an expressive axis oriented toward the object (language is to express the thing itself, *name* it) and a communicative axis. The two axes are construed as linguistic analogues of the intuitive and logical moments of the concept respectively. Hence, neither axis is reducible to the other; classical rationalism is the attempt to reduce expression to communication (H, 105). Everything that ruins conceptual transparency, every element of conceptuality that appears in language as vagueness, indeterminacy, rhetorical or material excess, is the expression of the excess of the object in relation to its logical concept. The tension between the axes is what keeps the dialectic open. Because the axes are functionally differentiated, that openness is permanent. So this tomato's greenness does not strictly entail unripeness if ripeness means ready to eat and here; in Tennessee, we do eat green tomatoes. There is no context-independent way of comprehending tomatoes if such comprehending involves knowing how to recognize them (e.g., through their color) and what their color means. The desire for transparency and determinacy may lead to the idea that to see something as red strictly involves only seeing it as a color that is not orange or yellow or green, and so forth, while only metaphorically or symbolically is what is red ripe or healthy or flushed or hot. But those connections are not obviously metaphorical at all: In context they can express a causal fact or the connection between such a causal fact and a human practice. What are considered as the metaphorical or symbolic or rhetorical dimensions of language, what gives on to the idea that the expressive axis of language expresses the subject and not the object, are often, in fact, the most object-dependent features of a concept, its concrete material meaning (the way its meaning is bound to the object in a practical context), and hence what bears most on a judgment's objectivity.

If the conceptual powers of concepts imbricate experiences with practices and their history, then the exposition of a concept cannot be presented deductively without falsifying how those powers actually accrue to a concept. Dialectic refers to another mode for exposing the logical powers of a concept, one that makes perspicuous its "materiality" – its experience, object, practice, and history dependence. If the structures of conceptual inference demanded in dialectic, the "configuration of moments" Adorno calls "constellation" (H, 109), are conceived as displacing the logical component of the concept by its material component, then dialectical movement takes on a "mimetic" character, a "kind of gestural or curvilinear writing," possessing a "musical quality" (H, 122). Following or tracking a set of material inferences is more like tracking or following a piece of music than like following a logical argument. Adorno interprets this moment of dialectic as the attempt to rescue, in the medium of the concept, "the mimesis the concept represses." Hegel achieves this by disempowering "individual concepts, using them as though they were imageless images of what they mean" (H, 123). "Imageless image" is meant, again, to try to capture how connections between or among concepts are more than logical; if a concept is like an image, thick with empirical (experiential and historical) content, then it is that content itself that must connect it to adjoining concepts. To interpret concepts as imageless images is to interpret the logical aspect of the concept as a vehicle for expressing its intuitive content. In so doing, Adorno is reading back in conceptuality as such Hegel's claim at the conclusion of the *Phenomenology* that the slow-moving succession of forms of consciousness is "a gallery of images."[33]

Perceiving inferential relations among concepts as imbricating process in their objects is what explains and vindicates Hegel's "phenomenological" procedure of "simply looking on," surrendering passively to the thing itself (H, 6), adopting a stance of "spontaneous receptivity" (H, 7; see also 81, 94). If the goal of expressing an object is not to place it in a deductive, explanatory system but to track its connection with contiguous objects (events, practices, etc.), then what is wanted is a mode of writing that is experience sensitive, sensitive to how experience itself unfolds, develops, swerves, halts, collapses, is transformed almost beyond recognition. Such experience sensitivity requires adopting a different cognitive stance toward the object, one in which there is an experiential following – as we do in listening to music or following narratives or watching films or as occurs in Hegelian phenomenology. This moment of adopting a receptive, experience-sensitive stance is the one that overcomes the duality between the alignment of meaning with spontaneity, freedom, and self-determination and of passivity with suffering, nonmeaning, irrationality, which was the third element of concept-intuition dualism. Spontaneous receptivity can be a form of rational response if particulars on their own can be rulish and so meaningful. (It is the way artworks and our experience of them entwine the three revisions to concept-intuitional dualism that makes them paradigmatic for a reformed conceptuality for Adorno.)

My favorite summary of all this is the claim that traditional philosophy, in reifying the object under its covering concept, freezes the object in just the way that a photograph freezes an object, making it forever "like that" (H, 100). Dialectic, on the other hand, in recognizing process as constitutive of the object, wants to convey substance as process (including the process of its conceptualization and rationalization). In order to carry this out, dialectic attempts to overcome its textual character and approach the ideal of film (H, 121). It follows that, in reading Hegel, one must for the most part go along with the flow, only occasionally halting as one notes that a certain moment is being relayed in slow motion rather than at speed (H, 123). Film, about which Adorno was notoriously ambivalent, in its natural evanescence, "the fact that its events exist only in motion, in passing,"[34] becomes the ideal analogue for the perception of relations of material inference.

Now these characterizations of dialectic, which all deserve and would benefit from extended elaboration, are a bit of a rogues' gallery. Part of their roguishness, the defense of obscurity, is that Adorno wants to put as much space as possible between dialectical and logical forms of inference. Equally, he thinks that under existing conditions the possibility of forming compelling constellations of concepts, constellations that would release objects from existing conceptual domination, is not good. Thus, only the extremes of the difference between logical and material inference can display either – as if relations of material inference were really, say, contiguous images rather than matters of "if-then," "because," and the like. Nonetheless, what Adorno is about in all this is neither obscure nor philosophically untoward. The contention is that if concepts are dependent on their objects, and if conceptual rationalization therefore can only occur through repressing the material moment *in* the concept through and in which that dependency is transmitted and acknowledged, so the logical "snapshot" of the object in fact depends upon a filmic movement which its, the snapshot's, form repudiates or disavows, then even rationalized concepts will have an excess of material meaning beyond their logical meaning. If even red, when it is the red of a tomato, records process (biological and social), then substance is process, a process whose hypertrophy, like the hypertrophy of the master-slave dialectic, is repeated when logical inference, as in a deductive system, displaces material inference. Dialectic is the causality of fate, the return of the repressed, in the concept, minimally the process stored in it, hence its possibilities, future or past, realized and/or ruined. Hence, dialectic is that form of conceptual awareness that acknowledges the repressed material moment of the concept. It does so by revealing relations of material inference among concepts. In this essay, in Sections 2 and 3, I attempted to conjure a constellation of material inferential relations among the micrologics of pure insight and faith, suspicion and trust, concept and intuition, independence and dependence, master and slave, together with the semantic thesis of idealism. The object illumined by that constellation was, I hope, the dialectic of enlightenment. Thus, if I have managed to nondeductively explicate the nature of enlightenment reason, at least in part, then I have shown how dialectical reason is possible.

Of course, detailing the conception of conceptuality necessary for a viable conception of material inference and showing how that conception of inference is, indeed, the very one at stake in Hegel's development of dialectic would require a great deal more exposition and argument. Nonetheless, if I am right that Adorno needs a conception of material inference to explain the difference between logical and dialectical contradiction, then there is necessarily more cognitive substance to Adorno's thought than its "negative" self-characterization invites. Taking heed of that excess is what it means to be an Hegelian after Hegel, after Marx, after Nietzsche, and after two centuries of brutal history in which the hope of realizing philosophy was, for good reason, missed.

NOTES

1. Although the idea of negative dialectics has an austere meaning, as a book title one should hear it ironically, on analogy with the way *Minima Moralia* ironically relates to Aristotle's *Magna Moralia*.
2. Theodor W. Adorno, *Negative Dialectics*, trans. E. B. Ashton (New York: Seabury Press, 1973), 138–40. Hereafter cited as ND.
3. Hence every object conceived of is mediated by the object itself, its presentation (image), its concept, the linguistic mediation of that concept, the social location of the relevant linguistic mediation, and the historical formation of social practice and linguistic medium. As we shall see, the cornerstone of mediation for Adorno is conceptual mediation.
4. G. W. F. Hegel, *Phenomenology of Spirit*, trans. A. V. Miller (Oxford: Clarendon Press, 1977), 9–10; see also 37–40 for speculative propositions.
5. This way of stating the Adorno-Hegel connection follows the lead of Simon Jarvis, "The 'Unhappy Consciousness' and Conscious Unhappiness: On Adorno's Critique of Hegel and the Idea of an Hegelian Critique of Adorno," in *Hegel's Phenomenology of Spirit: A Reappraisal*, ed. Gary Browning (London: Kluwer Academic, 1997), 57–72. I have benefited immensely in writing this essay from Jarvis's example. My argument here develops a line of thought I essayed in "Being Hegelian: Reply to Simon Jarvis," in the same volume, pp. 73–7. Another go, in English,

at the Adorno-Hegel connection is to be found in Michael Rosen, *Hegel's Dialectic and Its Criticism* (Cambridge: Cambridge University Press, 1982), chap. 7.

6. Theodor W. Adorno, *Hegel: Three Studies*, trans. Shierry Weber Nicholsen (Cambridge, Mass.: MIT Press, 1993), 13. Hereafter cited as H.

7. Hegel, *Phenomenology of Spirit*, 328–55.

8. Max Horkheimer and Theodor W. Adorno, *Dialectic of Enlightenment*, trans. John Cumming (New York: Seabury Press, 1972), 3, 6. Hereafter cited as DA.

9. When Horkheimer and Adorno state that myth is already enlightenment, they mean, more precisely than the vague idea that the self of myth is finally the same as the empty self of enlightenment, that mythic thought in part intends to explain and comprehend the world (the enlightenment project) as well as to narrate it. Here the difference between Hegelian faith as religious belief under secular conditions (Pascalian faith as religious belief after the arrival of modern science) and mythic thought as thought before the arrival of subjective reason is significant.

10. It is worth recalling here that Marx modeled the critique of ideology on the critique of religion and that Weber conceived societal rationalization as the rationalization of religious belief. Analogous ideas appear in Nietzsche and Durkheim. For reasons we shall come to, Adorno and Horkheimer regard the Hegelian model as the most general account of something close to the classical sociological theory of the development of Western rationality.

11. Hegel, *Phenomenology of Spirit*, 334.

12. Faith is trust which has been isolated from reason.

13. Willhem van Reijen, in his *Adorno: An Introduction*, trans. Dieter Engelbrecht (Philadelphia: Pennbridge Books, 1992), notes the structuring role of the master-slave dialectic in *Dialectic of Enlightenment* (pp. 36–40). If I am right, this is too direct. What structures the analysis is the dialectic of faith and pure insight, but this structure is, and was doubtless construed by Horkheimer and Adorno as, an expression of the dialectic of independence and dependence. As always with Hegel, "later" structures embed earlier ones, which means that any given historical moment in fact reenacts phenomenologically more primitive structures. Horkheimer and Adorno compress the work of embedding so that the different "logics" or forms of consciousness are interconnected almost from the outset.

14. Of course, the insight is originally Marx's, contained in his analysis of the shift from feudalism to capitalism. Because Horkheimer and Adorno

see capital as itself an expression of the domination of the universal over the particular, they can push back and generalize Marx's thought.

15. Hegel, *Phenomenology of Spirit*, 116.
16. The doctrine of the causality of fate was formulated by Hegel in "The Spirit of Christianity and Its Fate" (1798–9), in *On Christianity: Early Theological Writings*, trans. T. M. Knox (New York: Harper and Row, 1961), 224–39. Once Hegel came to recognize that the conception of organic community which this doctrine assumes is incommensurable with modern society as portrayed by Adam Smith and company, the doctrine had to be recast. The dialectic of independence and dependence is that recasting. My contention here is that, in order to bring nature into their account, Horkheimer and Adorno are implicitly reforming the causality of fate doctrine itself as a logic of independence and dependence.
17. Hegel, "Spirit of Christianity and Its Fate," 229.
18. Jürgen Habermas, *The Philosophical Discourse of Modernity*, trans. Frederick Lawrence (Cambridge: Polity Press, 1987), 28. For my critique of Habermas's handling of Hegel's causality of fate doctrine, see my *Recovering Ethical Life; Jürgen Habermas and the Future of Critical Theory* (London and New York: Routledge, 1995), esp. 82–7, 176–91.
19. Hegel, "Spirit of Christianity and its Fate," 229–30.
20. Theodor W. Adorno, "Trying to Understand Endgame," in *Notes to Literature*, vol. 1, trans. Shierry Weber Nicholsen (New York: Columbia University Press, 1991), 269.
21. Adorno, "Trying to Understand Endgame," 273.
22. Conceiving of conceptual ascent as a mechanism of abstraction explains how abstraction is logically involved in concept formation, sidestepping thereby the perfectly correct standard criticisms of the empiricist analysis of concept formation through abstraction.
23. Robert B. Brandom, "Some Pragmatist Themes in Hegel's Idealism: Negotiation and Administration in Hegel's Account of the Structure and Content of Conceptual Norms," *European Journal of Philosophy* 7, no. 2 (1999): 164. Brandom is intent on defending the semantic thesis of idealism; Adorno construes it as *the* source of the disaster.
24. Robert B. Brandom, *Making It Explicit: Reasoning, Representing, and Discursive Commitment* (Cambridge, Mass.: Harvard University Press, 1994), 616.
25. See, for example, Melanie Klein, "Love, Guilt and Reparation," in Melanie Klein and Joan Riviere, *Love, Hate and Reparation* (New York: Norton, 1964), 57–119.
26. Adorno continues this thought: "For suffering is objectivity that weighs upon the subject; its most subjective experience, its expression, is

objectively conveyed" (ND, 18). If I have understood the second clause correctly, the suffering is my suffering at the violence done to the object, so lending a voice to suffering is making explicit the demands of the object as they are experienced subjectively. This hones the logic of reparation closely to the Hegelian romantic paradigm. I am grateful to Ståle Finke for correcting my original reading of this sentence.

27. In Hegel and Adorno, dialectical contradiction feeds off the aspiration to completeness, satisfaction, stability, or, what is the same, the antagonism produced by that aspiration as a social fact.

28. The Kantian antinomy of freedom and determinism is the pivot of the "Freedom" chapter of *Negative Dialectics*. To say that the concepts are synthetic is to say that they express their social and historical formation and hence carry empirical content. It is this Adorno demonstrates for freedom and determinism, thus showing why the phenomena-noumena distinction or "two views of one reality" thesis reflect rather than dissolve the contradiction. The unresolved character of the Kantian antinomies has led Hauke Brunkhorst, in his *Adorno and Critical Theory* (Cardiff: University of Wales Press, 1999), to cite them as the origin of the idea of negative dialectics (p. 21).

29. Throughout his writings, Adorno is ambiguous about the extra-conceptual; the ambiguity should not be dissolved. He does mean both: conceptual content that is irreducible to conceptuality as such, that bears within itself essential reference to experience, and what is so referred to in such experience. The former without the latter would be idealism; the latter without the former skeptical realism. That both limbs on their own are suspect and that there is no easy or direct synthesis of them is precisely the knot which dialectics unties for Adorno. The argumentation of the "Skoteinos" chapter replicates some of the introduction to *Negative Dialectics* and also "Essay as Form."

30. The introduction to the English translation by Shierry Weber Nicholsen and Jeremy J. Shapiro does a fine job of tracing how Adorno appropriates Hegel at his points of greatest vulnerability.

31. There are too many features of conceptuality – reflective, inferential, expressive – for which any direct analogy with laboring seems ruinous. This is to deny, not that the separation of mental from manual labor may not be an important moment in the genealogy of occidental rationality (its egregious and dominating separation of the intelligible from the sensible and how rational culture arises only through forgetfulness of nature and embodiment), only that the use of the tag "labor" will not itself re-form the connection. Hence, the doctrine of the illegitimate separation of mental and manual labor is useful for the genealogy of rationalized culture, but apart from the reminder that thinking is always

also in a practice in relation to other practices and depends on its objects (materials) for its content and shape, it is false as a contribution to the historico-anthropology of the concept.

32. Brandom, *Making It Explicit*, 98–101. For an account of Adorno's version of material inference, see my *Adorno: Disenchantment and Ethics* (New York: Cambridge University Press, 2001), chap. 6.

33. Hegel, *Phenomenology of Spirit*, 492.

34. Stanley Cavell, "The Thought of Movies," in *Themes out of School: Effects and Causes* (Chicago: University of Chicago Press, 1984), 11–12.

2   Weighty Objects

On Adorno's Kant-Freud Interpretation

I

Adorno was vehemently anti-Hegelian. He was also one of the most thoroughly Hegelian thinkers of the century. He was anti-Hegelian insofar as he opposed final closure – reconciliation or *Aufhebung* – in philosophical inquiry. His opposition was based on combined theoretical and anthropological considerations concerning what might be called the anthropogenesis of the concept. Adorno believed that conceptual thinking arose out of the need for adaptation – for mastering inner and outer nature – and because of that always carried the seeds of domination within it. As Western rationality developed from its inception in pre-Socratic philosophy through the creation of modern science and technology, that potential in fact became realized on a global scale. With Hegel's system, Adorno argued domination in the material sphere was reflected by domination in the conceptual sphere. The totalitarianism of the system – where the whole swallows up the parts – was the counterpart of the overt totalitarianism of fascism and the velvet-gloved totalitarianism of the culture industry. For this reason, Adorno rejected the Hegelian system – and systematizing thought in general – as well as any impulse toward a final synthesis, and he asserted the right of the nonidentical against them.

At the same time, and for the same reason, Adorno relentlessly adhered to the movement of the Hegelian dialectic detached from the system. He never rested content with given conceptual synthesis but always found the negative within it, so that the dialectical movement would recommence immediately. This was dialectics without end. Adorno often had more solutions available to him than he was willing to make use of, but his commitment to the untruth of the whole and the priority of the negative compelled him to end his arguments with aporias rather than with less conflicted conclusions. This is the case in *Negative Dialectics*, where Adorno brings Kant and Freud into confrontation with one another. There, Adorno brilliantly (and repetitiously) elucidates the same aporia from innumerable angles but never gets beyond it. My claim is that the concept of sublimation would have allowed him to get beyond this situation. And although he implicitly makes use of the concept he cannot embrace it; sublimation apparently lacks the requisite negativity and comes too close to a Hegelian notion of reconciliation – which, in contemporary society, for Adorno, always means false reconciliation.

Adorno is not the only one who is suspicious of the concept of sublimation. Among psychoanalytic theorists and philosophers who write about psychoanalysis, it has generally fallen into disfavor. Though this decline has taken place for a number of reasons, one is central. Sublimation has always smacked of a certain sentimentalization or spiritualistic mystification that backtracks from Freud's courageous materialism. Its critics charge that it represents a flight from his tough-minded critique of the hypocrisy of bourgeois morality and of philosophical and aesthetic idealism into a more reassuring and uplifting view of human nature. It threatens, so they charge, to defuse his explosive claim that we are not masters in our own psychical households but are largely motivated by powerful forces that work behind our backs. The concern about the spiritualizing dangers of a theory of sublimation is well taken. But it ignores another, if less publicized, Freudian insight; namely, that the products of Spirit are most successful precisely when they remain closely connected with the subterranean layers of the human mind.

Yet whatever the difficulties psychoanalysis cannot do without a theory of sublimation. Indeed, as I have argued elsewhere,[1] only such a theory – or an alternative theory that performs the same conceptual work – can safeguard psychoanalysis from conceptual and practical self-cannibalization. Psychoanalysis offers an account of cultural achievements, including the achievements of psychoanalytic theory and practice itself, in terms of the genetic conditions out of which they emerge. By itself, however, a genetic approach cannot avoid the genetic fallacy, that is, avoid reducing a cultural object to the conditions of its becoming. To avoid this reductionism, it must be supplemented by another approach, which, moving in the opposite direction, explains the process by which genetic material undergoes a change of function and achieves a degree of freedom that transforms it into something else. "There is," as Loewald has observed, "a vast difference between, on the one hand deriving something from its origins and antecedents, thus reconstructing its structure and functioning, and, on the other hand, reducing some now extant structure to its original rudiments, as though no development had taken place."[2]

Thus, regarding psychoanalysis itself, without a concept of the analyst's sublimation,[3] one cannot explain how, given its origins in unconscious instinctual life, his or her analyzing activity surpasses the products of the analyst's drives and unconscious to any significant degree. If it did not, the activity of analyzing would, in principle, be indistinguishable from – and therefore be swallowed up by – its object domain. We would be confronted with a form of biological monism or monistic materialism in which the ego of the analyst was simply one natural object among many.[4] For example, psychoanalytic theories about theories of infantile sexuality would be on the same epistemological level as those infantile theories themselves, which is to say, they would be drive-related fantasies. And analytic interpretations of transference would be on the same conceptual level as the patients' associations. They would, in other words, be solely the products of the analysts' transference to the patient.[5] If this were so, psychoanalytic theory and practice would be deprived of all claims to legitimacy.

Let me be clear: I am not maintaining that psychoanalysis requires a full-blown separation of the transcendental from the empirical – which by now we know is unattainable. I am only arguing that, for the concept of legitimacy to have any legitimacy, there must be a "good enough" distinction between the level of theoretical reflection and the theory itself.[6]

Because of its genetic approach and the profound dilemmas this raises, psychoanalysis has been particularly attractive to many of the historicizing theorists of postmodernism. Indeed, by introducing the concepts of transference and the unconscious, it has provided new ammunition for what is often understood as Nietzschean geneticism.[7] As we have seen, when psychoanalysis is stripped of a theory of sublimation, the genetic point of view becomes totalized. With such a totalization thus eradicating the distinction between the realm of objects and the realm of reflection – between questions of fact, *quid facti*, and questions of legitimacy or validity, *quid juris* – without a trace. And this is precisely what the more radical postmodernists are after.

Indeed, in the wake of Kuhn, Feyerabend, and Foucault, a broad genealogical turn has taken place in which the philosophy of science is often replaced by the anthropology, sociology, economics or politics, including the gender politics, of science. As the theoretical heirs of Marxism – a fact which is generally denied – these strategies aim to reduce theories to the various pretheoretical interests that produced them. However, like psychoanalytic reductionism, it is structurally impossible for this sort of interest-positivism to elucidate the validity of its own claims. To be sure, pre-Kuhnian analytic philosophy of science was basically Kantian and tended to repress the question of genesis altogether.[8] Questions of genesis were typically relegated to the inconsequential "realm of discovery," as opposed to "realm of validity," and the question of how the two realms might be related was rarely addressed. The post-Kuhnian theorists of science, on the other hand, often with stubborn disregard for the problem of self-reference, tend to elevate genesis into the whole story, thus losing sight of the question of validity. Both approaches are equally one-sided. The real task is *to elucidate the relation between genesis and validity*.[9] That would require investigating how genetic material – whether it be economic, psychosexual, sociological, political, or what have you – with all its historical contingency and particularity, gets transformed into cultural objects that can claim the type of value appropriate to their particular domain. Again, though it is radically undeveloped, the concept of sublimation is a marker for that elucidation.

The task is especially pressing, for today we are all, in one way or another, post-Nietzscheans. That is, in some sense, we accept the contingent origins of our epistemological, normative, and aesthetic structures. We have learned that no cultural object – a theory, a sonata, a mathematical proof, a piece of legislation, a socialized ego – is immaculately conceived. They all emerge out of "the slime of history," as Sartre put it. Furthermore, one would be hard pressed today to find a contemporary philosopher defending a strong version of foundationalism that provides an unshakable ground for our thinking. (Apel is a notable exception.) Indeed, to continue to polemicize against foundationalism or transcendentalism in the current context strikes me as a wasted effort. As I see it, however, without something like a theory of sublimation, which accounts for the relation between genesis and validity, our post-Nietzschean situation cannot avoid a slide into unacceptable forms of relativism and nihilism.

II

Against this backdrop, then, I want to turn to Adorno. For on these questions, as on so many others, he anticipated the postmodern and poststructuralist positions by several decades.[10] One source of Adorno's postmodernism *avant la lettre* is his appreciation of Nietzsche, whom he placed on a par with the other two titans of German philosophy, Kant and Hegel. Indeed, Adorno believed that, far from abandoning the Enlightenment, as is often assumed, Nietzsche had radicalized it and therefore counted as "one of the most advanced enlighteners of all."[11] (The difference between Habermas, who tends to see Nietzsche only as an irrationalist, and Adorno is due in no small part to this fact.)[12] Yet, although Nietzschean intuitions and insights form an essential part of Adorno's philosophical makeup, this is not the end of the story. For as a result of the influence of Hegel, his thinking is also dialectical – albeit in his own particular way! Dialectic for Adorno refers to the fact "that objects do not go into their concepts without leaving a remainder."[13] The movement of the dialectic is animated by the perpetual pursuit of the "remainder," that is, the excess that is left over after the *necessary* failure of each attempt to grasp the nonidentical conceptually. This continuous movement drives negative dialectics to take up the deficiencies, as well as the truth content, of each one-sided moment and thus constantly to move from one position to its antithesis, attempting to extract the truth content of each. Unlike the Hegelian dialectic, however, negative dialectics is interminable and does not end with an ultimate reconciliation, or *Aufhebung*.

I believe it would be possible to demonstrate that most of the major theses of the radical historicogenetic position are taken up in the movement of Adorno's negative dialectics. And this in fact gives some credence to poststructuralist and postmodernist claims that Adorno is one of theirs.[14] But in contrast to central tendencies in postmodernism, Adorno is not content to rest with the aporia of the Nietzschean-geneticist position. Instead he is continually compelled to move back to the truth content of what might be called the Kantian-idealist position to correct its deficiencies. While Adorno's strongest impulse may be to defend the nonidentical against the philosophy of identity, he also wants to do justice to the legitimate demands of identitarian thinking.

The "Metacritique of Practical Reason" – the first section of the third part of *Negative Dialectics* – seems to end with a standoff between the Nietzschean and Kantian positions regarding the question of genesis and validity. My thesis is, however, that he actually provides us with the elements of a mediation between them. This mediation, in fact, amounts to the outline of a theory of sublimation. If there is anything that approaches a positive desideratum in the *Dialectic of Enlightenment* – something that could unlock the self-vitiating unfolding of instrumental reason – it is the "remembrance of nature in the subject."[15] I am claiming, then, that a more nuanced theory of sublimation could flesh out the concept while simultaneously avoiding the simplifications of the utopian move.

In "The Metacritique of Practical Reason," Adorno brings Kant and Freud into a confrontation with each other. With the aim of empiricizing Kant's transcendental philosophy, Adorno reads it through Freudian eyes, and he attempts to elucidate the philosophical dynamics of Freudian theory by viewing it through a Kantian lens. However, if the "Metacritique" were to end in a standoff, as it appears to, the Kantian moment would have triumphed over the Freudian. Insofar as Kant's theory is more dualistic and antinomic than Freud's, a standoff, which is to say, an antinomy, would represent a confirmation of his position. Granted, there is a familiar reading of Freud – prominent among certain ego psychologists – that sees him as Kantian dualist. On this reading, the pleasure principle is opposed to the reality principle, the id to the ego, the primary process to the secondary, and so on, and the goal of psychoanalysis is to subordinate the second term in each dichotomy to the first. But there is less schematic and more productive interpretation of Freud, which understands him as a *frontier thinker*. On this reading, his most fertile ideas – namely, the drives, the ego, and, most especially, sublimation[16] – are seen as concepts "on the frontier between"[17] two psychological, if not quasi-ontological, realms: soma and psyche, the inner world and the outer world, nature and culture. As a frontier concept, a term that

Adorno uses but does not thematize, sublimation can also provide a mediation between the Nietzschean and Kantian positions.

In his "theoretical writings," particularly, *Negative Dialectics*, Adorno employs a skeletal theory of sublimation but does not name it as such. But in his culture critique and aesthetic theory his attitude toward the subject is uniformly hostile. Adorno adds a specific sociohistorical twist to the general theoretical suspicion of sublimation, discussed above. He argues that sublimation constitutes a flight into a false reconciliation that denies the antagonistic character of contemporary social reality. In today's totally administered world, he argues, "every 'image of man' must be ideological except the negative one" and every anticipation of "a more human existence" must be damaged rather than harmonious. Under these conditions, the synthesis of the diffuse elements of inner nature into an apparently well integrated self can be accomplished through violence. He maintains, moreover, that the pursuit of the well-integrated ego – often thought to be the goal of sublimation – is not only a politically and culturally dubious enterprise. On the basis of the economics of intrapsychic life, he argues, it is systematically unattainable as well. With the retreat from sociopolitical reality into the private realm, the irreconcilable conflicts of the world are simply displaced onto the psyche, which in no way possesses the resources to resolve them: "In an irrational society ... the ego is necessarily burdened with psychic tasks that are irreconcilable with the psychoanalytic conception of the ego."[18]

The polemical context in which Adorno made these assertions was the ego psychology of the Hartmann era, whose main theoretical contribution was the addition of the adaptive standpoint to Freudian metapsychology.[19] And it cannot be denied that – as the Frankfurt School and the Lacanians have argued – adaptation can easily slip into mere adjustment to the status quo. It has often been claimed that the insecurities of the émigré analysts played a major role in their apoliticism and conformism, and that is undoubtedly true. Not only had they fled the realities of a Europe torn by war and fascism, they were also confronted with American xenophobia and McCarthyism. In choosing to follow the perhaps prudent but unfortunate course of accommodating themselves to the conservative American culture of the 1950s, they withdrew from political reality altogether.[20] Theoretically, the concept of society gave way to an empty placeholder, namely, the "average expectable environment."[21] And it is not going

too far to argue that many of the difficulties of present-day psychoanalysis can be traced to this retreat.

Adorno expresses his contempt for the notion of aesthetic sublimation in the provocative assertion that "artists do not sublimate."[22]
Again, however, the polemical context in which this statement
was made restricted his thinking on the subject. In this case, it
is his disdain for the "vacuous sublimity of bourgeois consciousness"(ND, 205) into which self-satisfied *Bildungsburgers* try to escape the horrors of sociopolitical reality. Artists, he argued, "oppose
idiosyncrasies...to anything sublimated. They are implacable toward aesthetes, indifferent to a carefully-tended environment, and
in tastefully-conducted lives they recognize diminished reactions
against pressures to diminution." Just as today "every 'image of
man' " must be fractured, so "legitimate works of art" must "without exception" be "socially undesired."[23] Adorno is, in fact, tacitly
equating sublimation with the creation of works of beautiful illusion for an affirmative culture. His hostility toward the notion of
sublimation follows from this equation.

But aren't the legitimate works of art he champions – while scandalous, fragmented, and perhaps even ugly – infinitely more socially
desirable, in some emphatic sense, than the fetishistically repeated
classics of high culture or the pulp produced by the culture industry
precisely to mask the realities of social life? And Adorno de facto
says as much when he does not see Beckett's *Endgame* – which is,
for him, an exemplary work of advanced art – as an apolitical piece
of existentialist or absurdist theater. Instead, he sees it as negating,
but not *denying*, sociohistorical reality – that is, he sees it as a work
of critique. The bleak and fragmented world presented in *Endgame*
not only unmasks the reality that is denied by beautiful illusions and
the culture industry but does this by referring to an idea of true reconciliation, albeit in a highly oblique manner. Just as "consonance
survives in atonal harmony,"[24] a reconciled self and world are at least
dimly pointed to in atonal theater as a referent for illuminating the
falseness of the contemporary world.

Adorno is only willing to soften his self-imposed prohibition on
utopian speculation with respect to the truly advanced work of art.
In his aesthetic theory, he considers the way that "consonance survives" – and is anticipated – in the avant-garde work of art after the
violent synthesis of the well-integrated work of bourgeois art breaks

down. The type of logic that is manifest in the truly advanced work of art is opposed to the logic of identifying thought. Identity thinking subordinates the particular to the universal and constitutes the unity of the object through the forced synthesis of the manifold. In contrast, aesthetic rationality, as Wellmer has put it, "does not do violence to the particular, the suppressed, the nonidentical"[25] but synthesizes its material – the diffuse, the nonidentical, and the split-off – into a "nonviolent togetherness of the manifold."[26] Consequently, it provides "a glimmer of messianic light glimpsed in the here and now, an anticipation of reconciliation in the real world."[27] Although Adorno recognized that these new forms of aesthetic expression were connected with alternative forms of subjectivity, he never allowed himself to examine new possibilities for psychic synthesis – for integration of the self – after the dissolution of the classical bourgeois subject. For example, Adorno did not pursue the ramifications for postconventional identity contained in the following tantalizing passage: "The core of individuality would be comparable to those utterly individuated works of art which spurn all schemata and whose analysis will rediscover universal moments in their extreme individuation – a participation in a typicality that is hidden from the participants themselves" (ND, 162). For him, the end of the bourgeois individual meant the end of the individual as such, and he refused to countenance any images of postbourgeois individuality.

Because he had polemically deprived himself of the idea of sublimation, and because the concept of integration was too closely associated with the conformist ego psychology of his day, Adorno did not possess the theoretical resources to consider alternative forms of psychic synthesis that would constitute new forms of postconventional selfhood. Given the facts of infantile omnipotence and the ubiquity of aggression in the psychic life of human beings, it is undoubtedly going too far to speak of the "nonviolent togetherness" of the self.[28] We can, nevertheless, entertain new less violent, increasingly flexible, and more spontaneous forms of postconventional psychic integration. Such forms of selfhood would, as Castoriadis puts it, involve

another relation between the conscious and the unconscious, between lucidity and the function of the imaginary, in *another attitude* of the subject with respect to himself or herself, in a profound modification of the activity-passivity mix, of the sign under which this takes place, of the respective place of the two elements that compose it.[29]

If the well-integrated ego of the ego psychologists is rejected as an instance of false reconciliation, and if no alternative is put in its place, then postmodern hostility toward the ego as such and the call for its dissolution is the only remaining alternative. Although Adorno objected to the manic celebration of nonidentify – which, for him, was in no way superior to the violent synthesis of harmonious identity – he provided nothing to offer in its place.

III

Let me now try to make good my claim that Adorno uses a concept of sublimation in his theoretical writings without naming it. Significantly, he begins his metacritique of practical reason with the assertion that the antinimous outcome of the Kantian construction – in both the *Critique of Pure Reason* and the *Critique of Practical Reason* – results from the original separation of (transcendental) philosophy from (empirical) psychology. According to the standard philosophical reading, Kant insisted on this strict separation to guarantee the autonomy of the moral subject and the purity of the moral law. Following the analysis of the Juliette chapter of the *Dialectic of Enlightenment* – where the Sadean orgy, with its instrumentalized pursuit of pleasure and pain, and not the categorical imperative, is proclaimed the real moral content of the bourgeois world – Adorno gives a more intraworldly explanation of the source of this separation of the transcendental and the empirical. He argues that Kant was fulfilling "an unexpressed mandate," which the bourgeoisie had bequeathed to philosophy "ever since the seventeenth century," namely, "to find transparent grounds for freedom." The bourgeoisie was confronted with a dilemma. On the one hand, because of the marriage of the commodity form and instrumental reason in the market, it was "in league with" the "progressive [scientization]" of the world that threatened to engulf all realms of existence. On the other hand, it had to "fear scientific progress as soon as that progress [interfered] with the belief that its freedom...is existent." The solution was to transfer freedom from the empirical world into the noumenal realm, and that produced a convenient twofold result: Freedom was insulated from the steady march of instrumental reason, and morality was excused from intervening in the affairs of the so-called real world. "This," Adorno writes, "is the real background of the doctrine of the antinomies" (ND, 214).

In addition to the internal antinomies of Kant's own position, this separation of the transcendental and the empirical led to the mutual impoverishment of both philosophy and the human sciences:

The idea of freedom comes to be contrasted with the research of the individual sciences, of psychology in particular. Kant banishes the object of this research to the realm of unfreedom; positive science is assigned its place beneath speculation – in Kant's case, beneath the doctrine of the noumena. (ND, 214)

The "narrow-mindedness" of the empirical social sciences results from dismissing all questions that could make a difference as unscientific. And in the other direction, as "more of its substance is confiscated by the individual sciences," philosophy pays the price with its "noncommittal vacuity" – it tends towards "jejune edification" in Hegel's sense (ND, 214–5). In a claim that is revealing for my argument, Adorno notes one topic that could provide philosophy with substance and conviction: "The genesis of character" – and, I would add, the question of genesis in general – which was "commandeered" by psychology, a field poorly equipped to handle it properly. Deprived of a theory of the genesis of character, Adorno argued, "the philosophemes on freedom of the will deteriorate into declamations" (ND, 214). An adequate theory – which would lie somewhere "between philosophy and science"[30] – must integrate what the modern theoretical division of labor has separated and account for the psychobiological unity of the person. In other words, it has to account for both the moment of autonomy and the moment of determinism – the moment of freedom and the moment of nature – in individual and social existence.

Adorno's statements on genesis are corollaries of his doctrine of the "preponderance of the object," which is an attempt to reinterpret the "materialism" of Marx and Freud. When Adorno asserts that "identitarian thinking is subjectivistic even when it denies being so," he means the following: It is obvious that idealist philosophy imposes its subjective forms on the object. But scientific objectivism is no less subjectivist when it imposes its mathematical grid on nature, its realist self-interpretation notwithstanding. Adorno's alternative to identitarian thinking in both its modes is not to seek some equitable "balance" between subject and object. "Mediation," he argues, is inherently inequitable and does not involve splitting the difference. "The preponderance of the object" means, rather, that "the subject enters into the object altogether differently from the way the object enters into the subject." Although an object is always conceived by a subject, it is also something in its own right, independent of the subject; "we can," therefore, "conceive of an object that is not a subject." This is not the case, however, with the subject, which "by its very nature is from the outset an object as well" (ND, 183) and cannot be conceived independently of its embodiment. Indeed, even Kant "refused to be talked out of the moment of object preponderance" (ND, 184) and posited the thing-in-itself at the outermost perimeter of his thinking in order to at least mark the ultimate independence of the object from subjectivity.

The Frankfurt School's turn to the "underground history" of Europe – that is, to the "fate of the human instincts and passions which are displaced and distorted by civilization" (DA, 231) – marked a radical innovation in social theory. Adding an entire new dimension to Marxism, it pitted the claims of the *material* body against the (ideological) illusions of theoretical and moral idealism. The widespread focus on the body in social theory over the past several decades appears to be a continuation of that tradition. But a curious reversal has taken place, in which the materialism of the Marxian and the Freudian traditions has been supplanted by a Foucauldian-inspired constructivism.[31] Almost unnoticed, *the constructed body has been slipped in to replace the material body*. This substitution is motivated by an understandable desire to replace Freud's perceived biologism, which would condemn us to an immutable essentialism in sexual matters, with constructivism. Stressing the symbolic malleability of the body would make the historical transformation of gender relations possible. But this attempt to avoid biologism moves us to an equally unacceptable theoretical position – in fact, a hypostatization in the opposite direction. It results in a linguistic idealism where the Symbolic's ability to shape the body is extended almost without limit – to an "imperialism of the signifier."[32] To put it in Adorno's terms, it is a shift to the "preponderance of language.[33]

We must immediately correct two possible misunderstandings of Adorno's position. To begin with, the assertion of the preponderance of the object does not entail undoing the "critique of naive realism" (ND, 184). Immediate access to the object does not follow from the fact that the object possesses a priority *in res* vis-à-vis the subject. This is especially important with respect to the interpretation of psychoanalysis. The Freudian insistence on the preponderance of the object – that is, to insist on the centrality of the body – does not mean that one has unmediated access to the soma itself. Freud's alleged biologism notwithstanding, we must constantly remind ourselves that the drive is a concept on the frontier between soma and psyche and, similarly, that we never have direct access to the unconscious but only through its derivatives.

That there is no first nature to be gotten back to – in this realm or any other – does not, however, validate the transcendental position. This is the point where Adorno's approach becomes truly original and radical. The fact that we are always *in media res* – in the middle of consciousness, language, history, tradition, and so on – and therefore can only approach the object in the *"intentio obliqua"* (ND, 181) is the point where transcendental phenomenologists, hermeneuticists, deconstructionists, and contextualists of various stripes prematurely terminate their reflections. As a result, they elevate the moment of reflecting consciousness or language into an absolute. But Adorno, in his attempt to defend the truth content of a materialist tradition, is unwilling to stop here.[34] Instead, he takes the next step beyond this hypostatization: "Nor does an ontological supremacy of consciousness [or language] follow from the counter-argument, that without a knowing [or speaking] subject nothing can be known about the object." An insistence on too much transcendental sophistication in fact results in a piece of philosophical obtuseness. From the standpoint of transcendental reflection, consciousness or language, as the means of access to the object, is obviously prior to the object. But transcendental rigorism disallows a proposition which would be absurd to deny: namely, that consciousness or language, which (transcendentally) constitutes the object, is itself (empirically) constituted by the object and cannot exist independently of it.[35] To be sure, to subjectivist philosophy this proposition "will always sound like a transcendental dogma."[36] Nevertheless, it convicts the *"prius"* of subjectivist philosophy "of aposteriority" (ND, 181). As Adorno puts it, "Every statement to the effect that subjectivity [or language] 'is,' no matter what or how, includes an objectivity which the subject [or language], by means of its absolute being, claims to have established." Ultimately, "consciousness [and language] is a function of the living subject, and no exorcism" – for example, a transcendental deduction, an ideal language or a Husserlian *epoché* [37] – "will expel this from the concept's meaning" (ND, 185).

Against transcendental philosophy's charge of dogmatism, Adorno responds that identity thinking can only live up to its requirements of reflective rigor by eliminating the object through its absorption into the subject. Identitarian thought, that is, solves the problem of the immanent circle of consciousness or language by dragging the object into that circle – by forcibly imposing the a priori laws of thought on it "even where the object does not heed the rules of thinking." In contrast, dialectical thinking tries to expand the circle to meet the object. In this sense, "dialectical logic is more positivistic than the positivism that outlaws it. As thinking, dialectical logic respects that which is to be thought – the object – even where the object does not heed the rules of thinking. The analysis of the object is tangential to the rules of thinking" (ND, 141). Like magic – and unlike the conceptual thinking that replaced it – dialectical thinking "really [concerns] the object" and tries mimetically to mold itself to it (DA, 231). Unlike magic, however, dialectical thinking pursues this approach with the help of the concept: "To represent the mimesis it supplanted, the concept has no other way than to adopt something mimetic in its own conduct, without abandoning itself " (ND, 14). Adorno notes, moreover, that the distinction in everyday usage between "identifying an object" and "identifying with people and things" provides a key to the "the Greek argument whether like is known by like or by unlike." He argues that, in general, an awareness exists of an "indelible mimetic element in all cognition and human practice," thus validating the thesis that like is only known by like. In identifying thought, however, "this awareness grows untrue when the affinity [between knower and known]...is posited as positive." That is, in identifying thought, the affinity collapses into a complete identification and is effaced when the "false conclusion" is drawn "that the object is the subject. Identity thinking believes that it knows the unlike by likening it to itself, while in so doing it really knows itself only" (ND, 150). The affinity between subject and object is not pursued, but their likeness is presumed from the start.

Dialectics also answers that like is known by like, but it pursues this likeness as a task to be pursued rather than a preexisting condition. If identity thinking seeks to assimilate the object to itself by identifying the object within its conceptual grid, dialectics attempts to identify *with* the object mimetically and conceptually. In dialectics, the subject does not remain the static "subject of knowledge" but is transformed in the process of knowing. This process does not result, however, in the mere mirror reflection of the object by the subject but, as Rabinbach has put it, in "a form of mimicry or semblance that appropriates rather than replicates its object in a nonidentical similitude."[38] To examine the way Adorno pursues this mimetic appropriation of the object, which, by its very nature, cannot be methodologically "expounded" (ND, 33), would require a separate essay – at least. Suffice it to say, such an examination would involve a consideration of his notion of constellation and his connected views on language – with their insistence on an "idiosyncratic precision in the choice of words, as if they were to designate things" (ND, 52) – as well as an incursion into his *Aesthetic Theory*.

Adorno recognizes that any frontal assertion of the preponderance of the object will be futile and be simply dismissed by idealism as dogmatic objectivism. He assures us, however, that "there is no need for analysis to abdicate" in the face of this fact, for it is possible to undertake an immanent critique of idealism in terms of the concept of spontaneity. His thesis is that "spontaneity breaks through an idealism whose inmost core was christened 'spontaneity' " (ND, 181–2). Because it represents a moment of outsideness with the inside, nonidentity within identity, and nature within the subject, spontaneity provides a foothold for the immanent critique of idealism. Furthermore, because the most archaic impulses and the highest principle of reason dialectically converge in it, the notion also points to a bridge between subjectivity and objectivity, theory and practice, instincts and rationality.

IV

The doctrine of the will is supposed to resolve a central dilemma at the heart of Kant's philosophy: How can reason, once it has been purified of all empirical content in order to guarantee its autonomy and universality, be practically effective in a sensible world governed by natural causality? Kant conceives the will so formally or rationalistically as to make it too dissimilar to the sensible world – and especially to the faculty of desire, which is itself part of the sensible world – to serve its mediating function. "As the pure [*logos*], the will becomes a no-man's-land between subject and object, antinomical in a manner not envisioned in the critique of reason" (ND, 228). Indeed, as long as there is "no *movens* of practice but reason" (ND, 229) thus conceived, there can be no practice. The only way to solve the problem – this is Adorno's main anti-Kantian claim – is to reintroduce the moment of nature that was "eliminated in this abstraction [from empirical reality]." He calls this moment "the addendum" (ND, 229). And he turns to psychoanalysis, with its genetic approach, to help accomplish this task and make up for the radical deficiency that necessarily results from the "layout of [Kant's] system" (ND, 289): "What became Kant's fearfully majestic a priori is what psychoanalysts trace back to psychological conditions" (ND, 232).

Adorno identifies the addendum with "the archaic impulse, not yet steered by any solid I" (ND, 221), and the introduction of the impulse sets the dialectic of spontaneity, mentioned above, in motion. His thesis is that "in spontaneity, the philosophical concept that does most to exalt freedom as a mode of conduct above empirical existence, there resounds the echo of that by whose control and ultimate destruction the I of idealistic philosophy means to prove its freedom" (ND, 222), that is to say, an echo of the drives. Originally, the ego forms itself in opposition to the immediate spontaneity of the impulse. The identity and autonomy of the solid, orderly, and unified I is established and maintained by expelling the impulse "to the zone of unfree bondage to nature" (ND, 22). In so doing, it establishes a boundary between itself and internal nature as its "inner foreign territory."[39] Furthermore, with the extrojection of the impulse, the notion of spontaneity undergoes an apparent split. On the one hand, (1) the mode of immediate spontaneity that characterizes the archaic impulse now assumes the meaning of an unconscious, involuntary, and reflexive phenomenon, that is, of nature and unfreedom – at least from the perspective of the unified ego. And on the other, (2) with respect to the ego that has differentiated itself from nature, spontaneity is now defined in purely intramental terms and is seen as the highest moment of freedom, namely, the I's ability to initiate thinking without itself being determined by prior conditions. It is spontaneity in this second sense that is celebrated in idealism.

Adorno, however, detects traces of the first, natural mode of spontaneity in this second, transcendental form, which not only gives the lie to the purism of Kant's position but also points to a solution for the mediation of freedom and nature and theory and practice. Thus, the return of the repressed addendum breaks through "in the two-fold exegesis of " (ND, 230) this second, supposedly purified mode of spontaneity.

(2a) Intramental spontaneity denotes transcendental subjectivity's "unconscious and involuntary" (ND, 230) unification of our experience, which itself cannot become an object of experience. As long as the physiological substratum of our mind is intact, this form of spontaneity functions as involuntarily as our autonomic nervous system; it is as impossible to be transcendentally stupid as it is to make one's heart stop beating simply by willing it. Although it supposedly represents the highest stratum of mental functioning, transcendental spontaneity still has something naturelike (*naturwüchsig*) about it insofar as it operates involuntarily and without consciousness. This naturelike functioning indicates, moreover, that while the transcendental unity of the subject contains an aspect, that can be seen as transcending nature, it is also part of nature insofar as it has evolved out of the exigencies of self-preservation. The capacity to unify and organize experience – to discover lawful regularities in it – enables the human subject to master itself and external nature in the struggle for existence. The unconscious synthetic activity of the subject is therefore one of the most crucial adaptive endowments the human species has acquired in the course of evolution. The transcendental unity of the subject is outside nature in a formal sense, namely, insofar as it is its organizer. But, more importantly for Adorno's argument at this point, it is inside nature as an organ of adaptation and cannot prescribe ends that transcend self-preservation.

(2b) Intramental spontaneity also refers to the capacity of empirical, thinking consciousness to freely initiate chains of thought. Adorno argues, however, that "contemplative conduct" and logic,[40] which is the "correlate" of theoretical consciousness, are not original phenomena but the results of real acts of abstraction or "bracketing" that require the "negation of the will": "Contemplative conduct... is the conduct that wills nothing," and "logic is a practice insulated against itself." Kant, however, skips over this genetic moment in his account of supposedly pure thought and logic thus suppressing the fact that "pure consciousness – 'logic' – itself has come to be; it is a validity that has submerged its genesis." Moreover, "without the kind of will that is manifested in the arbitrary nature of every thought act – the kind that furnishes our only reason to distinguish such an act from the subject's passive, 'receptive' moments – there would be no thinking in the proper sense of the word" (ND, 230). Without the active willful direction of our thoughts, only the passive mirrorlike registration of reality would remain. This is exactly the opposite of the active and spontaneous side, which, as Marx famously observed, was stressed by German idealism.

The unassailable core of Kant's moral theory is his insistence that, if we did not transcend nature (to some degree) by organizing the diffuse impulses of our inner nature into the unity of a personal identity (of some sort), the idea of freedom would be meaningless. Thus, "subjects are free, after the Kantian model," Adorno observes, "in so far as they are aware of and identical with themselves" (ND, 299). (The corollary is that they are also "unfree as diffuse, nonidentical nature.") However, Kant's intentional disregard for the genesis of that transcendence and unity – or what Adorno explicitly calls the "sublimation" of the "individual impulses" into the unity and permanence of the self (ND, 238) – has an unfortunate consequence. Without the addendum, not only is the mediation of theory and practice impossible, but the unity of the self must necessarily be *coercive*. Kant, as we have noted, believed he had circumvented the problem of genesis and thereby avoided the heteronomy of the will by defining it in purely formal terms. The presumption – which is not as self-evident as Kantians often assume – is that formalization on its own can lift us out of the realm of temporality and becoming. But qua formal, the unity of the self must be "compulsive," for it is achieved by dragooning all the diffuse and conflicting forces of inner nature into its service and regimenting them according to the external demands of "the ego principle" (ND, 26). Thus, qua formal, subjects are also unfree "in so far as they are subjected to, and will perpetuate, [the ego's] compulsion" (ND, 229).

Like Freud, Adorno believes that pathological states – where things appear under a higher degree of magnification, so to speak – often help to illuminate the less apparent nature of normal conditions. He thus contends that the coercive, which is to say, the unfree character of the Kantian (and everyday) conception of the ego, is manifest in the obsessions and compulsions of the neurotic. And from the other side, as against this compulsive formal identity, subjects are free qua diffuse, nonidentical nature. They are free in this case "because their overpowering impulse – the subject's non identity with itself is nothing else – will also rid them of identity's coercive character" (ND, 299). For example, the *jouissance* of the orgasm, religious rapture, or Isolde's *Liebestod* can all dissolve the compulsive unification of the self and free us from the coercive demands of identity.[41] But these releases from compulsive identity are transient; they cannot provide a lasting solution. For in states like schizophrenia, where dedifferentiation exists as an ongoing state, the subject has not surpassed determinacy but is in fact "less than determined" and is therefore incorporated "so much more in the spell of nature" (ND, 241)[42] – Deleuze and Guattari notwithstanding.

However, if Adorno criticized idealism for prematurely terminating its theorizing with the notion of our oblique access to the object, this is the point where his own thinking comes to a halt too quickly. Characteristically, Adorno has elucidated the aporia of freedom and nature, unity and dispersion, in what borders on obsessional detail, but he never moves beyond it. Although the elements of the next step are implicit in his analysis his assumption that the unity of the self must necessarily be coercive prevents him from appropriating his own insights. He maintains that, viewed synchronically, the addendum appears irrational, for "it denies the Cartesian dualism of *res extensia* and *res cogitans*." Viewed genetically, however, this same fact has a different meaning: It points to a developmental "phase in which the dualism of extramental and intramental was not thoroughly consolidated,"[43] when it was "neither [volitionally] bridgeable nor an ontological ultimate." This means that the addendum is not only a remnant of "something long past, something grown all but unrecognizable," but also a prefiguration of something which "some day might come to be" (ND, 228–9). By pointing to a phase in which the "archaic impulse [was] not yet steered by any solid I" (ND, 221), psychoanalysis also awakens "the phantasm of reconciling nature and mind." The best that Adorno can say about the relation between the archaic past and a possible future, however, is that the addendum is "a flash of light" between them. Had he not been so leery about the concept of sublimation he could have unpacked that metaphor and provided more conceptual illumination about possibly achieving "a state that would no more be blind nature than it would be oppressed nature" (ND, 229).

Adorno was unwilling to do for the modern subject what he did for the modern work of art, although he had a similar analysis of both. He claimed that the unity characterizing the bourgeois subject and the traditional work of art was forced and therefore false or artificial. In both cases, the integration of the whole – and the appearance of harmony – was achieved by "suppressing and excluding that which is disparate or cannot be integrated, that which remains unarticulated and repressed."[44] The logic that governed the synthesis of the aesthetic and psychic entity was instrumental or identifying in that it subordinated the particular to the demands of the whole. As I pointed out above, the sole place where Adorno detected the workings of an alternative logic of synthesis in a totally reified world – which therefore represented an alternative to the forced integration of the whole – was in avant-garde art. Only the advanced work of art gathered its constituent elements together in such a way as to achieve the "the non-violent togetherness of the manifold."[45] To be sure, there is no direct translation from art into life. Nevertheless, Adorno did provide at least a glimpse of the sort of *logic* that might govern the integration of a nonreified society in the future, where whole and part, universal and particular, would be held together in a different way. This was as close as he came to utopian speculation.

The work of Hans Loewald – who, not accidentally, had studied philosophy with Heidegger before becoming a psychoanalyst – can help us take the next step beyond Adorno's elegant aporias. For Adorno's understanding of the sociohistorical situation was not the only thing that prevented him from trying to extrapolate an alternative notion of psychological integration from the nonreifying synthesis manifest in the advanced work of art. There was a theoretical factor at work as well: Adorno did not simply believe that obsessive-compulsive pathology *revealed something* important about the nature of ego. Like many psychoanalytic theorists in the fifties, including Lacan,[46] he unwittingly took "over much of the obsessive neurotic's experience and conception of reality"[47] *and identified the obsessional ego with the ego as such.* Because the ego was seen as reified by its very nature, it could not be reformed but had to be rejected in its entirety. The acceptance of this equation, tacit or otherwise, prevented Adorno from considering less coercive forms of ego integration that could become the basis for possible forms of postconventional identity. Instead, he was forced to posit "the end of the individual."

It is, however, precisely this equation between the obsessional ego and the ego as such that Loewald challenges. To accomplish this he introduces the distinction between psychic "processes that dam up, countercathect instinctual life and processes that channel and organize it."[48] Defense, especially repression, is the primary example of the former, and internalization and sublimation are the chief representatives of the latter. Where defense seeks to maintain the existing unity of the ego by *excluding* alien unconscious-instinctual forces, that is, the addendum, from its domain defense (cf. identitarian thinking), internalization and sublimation aim to expand and enrich the ego's identity by *including* those same forces into its structure. "The weakness of the 'strong ego'," that is, the ego "strong in its defenses,"[49] results in an undifferentiated unity that is narrow, brittle, and rigid. The strength of the inclusive ego results in a more differentiated and structured whole that is broader and more flexible.

The fact that Loewald sees internalization and sublimation, as they are understood in Freud's later structural theory, as forms of reconciliation suggests an important point of possible convergence with Adorno. In 1918, Freud first understood the process of internalization as a *specific* mechanism involved in the *pathogenesis* of melancholia. His thesis that melancholia resulted from the identification with an ambivalently loved object was encapsulated in this memorable line: "The shadow of the object falls across the ego."[50] The strong mimetic character of internalization and mourning – where the subject meets Adorno's requirement and becomes like the object – can be dramatically observed in the common phenomenon in which the bereaved person actually assumes certain characteristics and mannerisms of the deceased. Then, in 1923, Freud expanded his theory of internalization and came to see it not as a specific pathogenic process but as a *universal path of ego formation.* The thesis of this new position was captured in another equally memorable phrase: "The ego is the precipitate of abandoned object-cathexes."[51] This means that the ego, the subject, is formed through the internalization of objects that are then transformed into psychic structures. This internalization of the object – through which the subject becomes like the object – is identification in the strict psychoanalytic sense. At the same time, moreover, this process is also a transformation of object-libido into narcissistic-libido – a transformation of desire that, Freud believes, constitutes "a kind of sublimation." Indeed, he raises the question "whether this is not the universal road to sublimation, whether all sublimation does not take place through the mediation of the ego, which begins by changing sexual object-libido into narcissistic libido and then gives it another aim."[52]

The growth of an expanded and more differentiated ego takes place through the internalization of the object, which, at the same time, is a sublimation of desire. Taking these observations as his point of departure, Loewald argues that the ego, which has been transformed by this process, is *now mimetically closer to the object and stands in a new relation to it.* The act of sublimation-identification thus results in a new object relation – a new "constellation" between subject and object, to use Adorno's language. Indeed, going further, Loewald maintains that this new object relation also represents a form of reconciliation between subject and object. Expanding on Freud, he argues thus: "Equally, the shadow of the altered ego falls on objects and object relations. Sublimation is a kind of reconciliation of the subject-object dichotomy ... and a narrowing of the gulf between object libido and narcissistic libido, between object world and self."[53] We should stress that Loewald says a "narrowing," not an "elimination," of the "gulf" between subject and object. For he was every bit as opposed to any act of final *Aufhebung* as Adorno. Indeed, for him any ultimate reconciliation would be tantamount to psychic death.

Adorno was caught in a particular historical situation that prevented him from appreciating these aspects of Freud's theory. His antipathy to a totally administered world and what he saw as the philistinism of bourgeois culture made it impossible for him to seriously entertain the concept of sublimation, despite the fact that his theory calls for it. Had he been able to do so, he would not have been left with the unsavory choice between the rigidly integrated ego of conventional identity and the Dionysian dissolution of the self, which is to say, the choice that postmodernism seems to offer us. But this need not prevent a later generation of Critical Theorists from taking up the essential yet discredited notion of sublimation and exploring its theoretical meaning in detail.

NOTES

1. See Joel Whitebook, *Perversion and Utopia: A Study in Psychoanalysis and Critical Theory*, (Cambridge, Mass.: MIT Press, 1995), chap. 5. This essay returns to the investigation I began there in the hope of clarifying and elaborating my original position.

2. Hans Loewald, "Instinct Theory, Object Relations, and Psychic Structure Formation," in *Papers on Psychoanalysis* (New Haven, Conn.: Yale University Press, 1980), 210. See also Paul Ricoeur, *Freud and Philosophy: An Essay on Interpretation*, trans. Dennis Savage (New Haven, Conn.: Yale University Press, 1970), 490.

3. See Cornelius Castoriadis, "Psychoanalysis: Project and Elucidation," *Crossroads in the Labyrinth*, trans. Kate Soper and Martin H. Ryle (Cambridge, Mass.: MIT Press, 1984), 112, n. 47.

4. This is what is at stake in the controversy concerning the narcissistic origins of the ego.

5. See Castoriadis, "Psychoanalysis," 90.

6. See Cornelius Castoriadis, "Logic, Imagination, Reflection," in *World in Fragments*, ed. and trans. David Ames Curtis (Stanford: Stanford University Press, 1997), 246–72.

7. Nietzsche's own position was perhaps more subtle. See, for example, Raymond Geuss, "Nietzsche and Genealogy," *European Journal of Philosophy*, 2, no. 2 (1994): 274–92.

8. The French School of Bachelard and Canguilhem, in which Foucault was trained, was much more historical in its approach. See Gary Gutting, *Michel Foucault's Archaeology of Scientific Reason* (Cambridge: Cambridge University Press, 1989), 9–54.

9. A biographical note may be in order here. I was first trained as a philosopher, more or less in the Kantian mode. In transcendental bootcamp, which is to say, graduate school, one was drilled in the distinction between *quid juris* and *quid facti* and trained to seek out and destroy any trace of the reductionist fallacy. Then, after completing my philosophical studies, I trained as a psychoanalyst at a Freudian institute. There of course the analysts were supremely skilled at genetic interpretations but they evinced little awareness of, much less concern with, the problem of validity. As a result of these experiences, I began to think that the strict separation of the question of genesis and validity represented

a form of theoretical "splitting" and that the real goal was to bring them together.

10. See Peter Dews, "Adorno, Poststructuralism and the Critique of Identity," *The Limits of Disenchantment: Essays on Contemporary European Philosophy* (New York: Verso, 1995), 19–38.

11. Quoted by Anson Rabinbach, "The Cunning of Unreason: Mimesis and the Construction of Anti-Semitism in Horkheimer and Adorno's *Dialectic of Enlightenment*," in *In the Shadow of Catastrophe: German Intellectuals between Apocalypse and Enlightenment* (Berkeley: University of California Press, 1997), 191.

12. See Jürgen Habermas, "The Entwinement of Myth and Enlightenment: Max Horkheimer and Theodor Adorno," in *The Philosophical Discourse of Modernity: Twelve Lectures*, trans. Frederick G. Lawrence (Cambridge, Mass.: MIT Press, 1987), 106–30.

13. Theodor W. Adorno, *Negative Dialectics*, trans. E. B. Ashton (London: Routledge and Keagan Paul, 1974), 5. Hereafter cited as ND.

14. See Dews, "Adorno, Poststructuralism and the Critique of Identity," 20, 36 n. 5.

15. Max Horkheimer and Theodor W. Adorno, *Dialectic of Enlightenment*, trans. John Cumming (New York: Herder and Herder, 1972), 40. Hereafter cited as DA. Because of the self-imposed prohibition on utopian speculation, however, Adorno never elaborated this suggestive idea. But Marcuse – who was less subtle philosophically and more active politically – did: He tried to break out of the dialectic of enlightenment by translating the notion of "the mindfulness of inner nature" into the directly utopian idea of the emancipation of inner nature. See Jürgen Habermas, "Psychic Thermidor and the Rebirth of Rebellious Subjectivity," in *Habermas and Modernity*, ed. Richard J. Bernstein (Cambridge, Mass.: MIT Press, 1985), passim.

16. Winnicott's theory of the transitional phenomena – which are neither wholly created nor wholly found, that is, neither subjective hallucinations nor external objects – represents an attempt to explore the realm of "thirdness" to overcome the dualistic tendencies in Freud's thinking. See D. W. Winnicott, "Transitional Objects and Transitional Experience," in *Through Pediatrics to Psycho-Analysis*, intro. M. Masud R. Khan (New York: Basic Books, 1975).

It would be interesting to explore the difference between the fetish, as a form of thirdness that attempts to overcome dichotomy through a defensive denial, and the transitional object, which attempts to "sublate" it through creative symbolization. See Phyllis Greenacre, "The Fetish and the Transitional Object" and "The Transitional Object and the Fetish: With Special Reference to the Role of Illusion," in *Emotional*

Growth: Psychoanalytic Studies of the Gifted and a Great Variety of Other Individuals (New York: International Universities Press, 1971).

In a more philosophical mode, I might also mention that Kant's third *Critique* – which attempts to overcome the opposition between the first and second *Critique*s and provides the point of entrée for Hegel's dialectic – can be viewed as an attempt at frontier thinking. According to this interpretation, reflective judgment, which is neither constitutive nor arbitrary, neither purely objective nor subjective, can be seen as his frontier concept.

17. Sigmund Freud, "Instincts and Their Vicissitudes," in *The Standard Edition of the Complete Psychological works of Sigmund Freud* (hereafter cited as SE), vol. 19 (London: Hogarth Press, 1975), 121–2. In this canonical formulation, Freud is referring to the concept of the drive, but I would argue it can be applied to other concepts as well.

18. Theodor W. Adorno, "Sociology and Psychology," *New Left Review* 46-47 (1968), p. 87.

19. See especially Heinz Hartmann, *Ego Psychology and the Problem of Adaptation*, trans. David Rappaport (New York: International Universities Press, 1958).

20. In this they invite comparison with the members of the Institute for Social Research during their sojourn in the United States.

21. See Hartmann, *Ego Psychology and the Problem of Adaptation*, 46.

22. Theodor W. Adorno, *Minima Moralia: Reflections from Damaged Life*, trans. E. F. N. Jephcott (London: New Left Books, 1974), 213.

23. Adorno, *Minima Moralia*, 213.

24. Theodor W. Adorno, "Trying to Understand *Endgame*," in *Notes to Literature*, vol. 1, trans. Shierry Weber Nicholsen (New York: Columbia University Press, 1991), 248.

25. Albrecht Wellmer, "Reason, Utopia and the *Dialectic of Enlightenment*," in *Habermas and Modernity*, ed. Richard J. Bernstein (Cambridge, Mass.: MIT Press, 1985), 48. See also Whitebook, *Perversion and Utopia*, 152 ff.

26. Albrecht Wellmer, "Truth, Semblance and Reconciliation," in *The Persistence of Modernity: Essays on Aesthetics, Ethics and Postmodernism*, trans. David Midgley (Cambridge, Mass.: MIT Press, 1991), 14.

27. Albrecht Wellmer, "The Dialectic of Modernism and Postmodernism," in *The Persistence of Modernity*, 63.

28. Upon reflection, I have weakened my position since the publication of *Perversion and Utopia*.

29. Cornelius Castoriadis, *The Imaginary Institution of Society*, trans. Kathleen Blamey (Cambridge, Mass.: MIT Press, 1987), 104.

30. See Jürgen Habermas, "Between Philosophy and Science: Marxism as Critique," in *Theory and Practice*, trans. John Viertel (Boston: Beacon Press, 1973), 195–252.
31. See Joel Whitebook, "Freud, Foucault and The Dialogue with Unreason," *Philosophy and Social Criticism* 25 (1999): 29–66.
32. Peter Dews, *The Logics of Disintegration: Post-Structuralism and the Claims of Critical Theory* (London: Verso, 1987), 110.
33. Interestingly, Leo Bersani, who is certainly no advocate of biological determinism, sees this dematerialization of the body as a deradicalization of social theory. Although he doesn't want to deny that "the ideological exploitations" of the human body and its "fantasmatic potential have a long and inglorious history," he is willing to take the risk of defending the radical potentiality of the *material* body against the intellectualized pseudo-subversive flight into the Symbolic. As an example of this intellectualization, he notes that "among intellectuals, the penis has been sanitized and sublimated into the phallus as the originary signifier; the body is to be read as a language." Leo Bersani, "Is the Rectum a Grave?" *October* 43 (Winter 1987): 217, 220.
34. Thus, concerning poststructuralism's attempt to appropriate Adorno as one of their own, Dews writes the following: "The assumption has been that a more consistent pursuit of anti-metaphysical themes – and, by implication, a more politically radical approach – can be found in the work of the French Heideggerian [Derrida] than that of the Frankfurt Marxist.... First, although there are undoubtedly elements in Adorno's thought which anticipate Derridean themes; he has in many ways equally strong affinities with the mode of recent French thought that is usually known as the 'philosophy of desire.' It is only the exaggeration of the constitutive role of language in poststructuralism, it could be argued, and a corresponding antipathy – even on the intellectual left – to the materialist emphases of Marxism, which have led to this aspect of Adorno's work being overlooked or underplayed. Second, from an Adornian perspective, it is precisely this lack of a materialist counter-weight in Derrida's thought, the absence of any account of the interrelation of consciousness and nature, particularly 'inner nature,' which can be seen to have brought forth the equally one-sided philosophy of desire" (Dews, "Adorno, Poststructuralism and the Critique of Identity," 20). It would also be fruitful to ask how and to what extent the materialist dimension has survived in Habermas's linguistification of Critical Theory.
35. "That the *constituens* is to be the transcendental subject and the *constitutum* the empirical one does not remove the contradiction, for there is no transcendental subject other than one individualized as a unit of

consciousness – in other words, as a moment of the empirical subject"
(ND, 241).

36. The Habermasian claim that the aporia of Adorno's position results from
his entrapment in the philosophy of consciousness – which pictures the
opposition of an object to a knowing consciousness – and can be overcome by moving to an intersubjective philosophy of language does not
work. From Adorno's perspective, the intersubjective position is every
bit as much subjectivist philosophy as the philosophy of consciousness.
To be sure, the move to the philosophy of language may help to solve
some difficulties with respect to the knowledge of other speaking subjects. But the problem of reaching the nonhuman, that is, the nonlinguistic, object – *including the nonlinguistic inner nature within us* – is just
as difficult for the philosophy of language as it was for the philosophy of
consciousness. Where the latter faced the problem of breaking out of the
circle of subjective interiority in order to reach the object, now the former is confronted with breaking out of the circle of the intersubjective
interiority of language. While the circle may be larger, it is no easier to
transcend. This is manifested in the fact that the question of reference –
of how the intersubjective web of language hooks up with the world –
is as daunting in the philosophy of language as the question of access
to the object in the philosophy of consciousness. See Jürgen Habermas, *The Theory of Communicative Action*, vol. 1, *Reason and the
Rationalization of Society*, trans. Thomas McCarthy (Boston: Beacon
Press, 1984), 390 ff., and "Entwinement of Myth and Enlightenment,"
chap. 11.

37. The case of Habermas's ideal speech situation is more complex than
these other two examples. For the ideal speech situation does not, in
fact, claim to escape the material conditions of embodied thought and
speech in the manner of transcendental philosophy in the strict sense;
this is the way Habermas's opponents regularly construe it. Rather, it
claims to provide a theoretical device for elucidating the counterfactual
idealizations that must exist for empirical speech to be possible. The
relation between counterfactual idealizations and empirical reality then
becomes the important question.

38. Rabinbach, "Cunning of Unreason," 176.

39. Sigmund Freud, "New Introductory Lectures on Psycho-Analysis," SE,
vol. 22, 57.

40. By which he means "general" rather than "transcendental" in Kant's
sense.

41. Adorno's observation that "a common adjective for a libertine is 'disso-
lute,' dissolved" (ND, 238) helps to illuminate an internal link in the
poststructuralist position. For it highlights the systematic connection

between advocating the dispersion of the self and elevating the alpha libertine, de Sade, to the rank of a cultural hero.

42. Hegel also considered madness "a reversion to nature." See G. W. F. Hegel, *Philosophy of Mind: Being Part Three of the Encyclopaedia of The Philosophical Sciences*, trans. William Wallace (Oxford: Clarendon Press, 1973), sec. 408 and *Zusatz*, and Daniel Berthold-Bond, *Hegel's Theory of Madness* (Albany: SUNY Press, 1995), 25 ff.

43. This description cannot help but call to mind three important psycho-analytic theories of early development, namely, Winnicott's concept of "transitional phenomena," Mahler's idea of "dual unity," and Loewald's notion of an "undifferentiated psychic matrix."

44. Albrecht Wellmer, "Truth, Semblance and Reconciliation: Adorno's Aesthetic Redemption of Modernity," in *Persistence of Modernity*, 19.

45. Wellmer, "Truth, Semblance and Reconciliation," 14.

46. See Whitebook, *Perversion and Utopia*, 121 ff.

47. Hans Loewald, "Ego and Reality," in *Papers on Psychoanalysis*, 30.

48. Hans Loewald, *Sublimation: An Inquiry into Theoretical Psychoanal-ysis* (New Haven, Conn.: Yale University Press, 1988), 5.

49. Hans Loewald, "On the Therapeutic Action of Psychoanalysis," in *Papers on Psychoanalysis*, 231.

50. Sigmund Freud, "Mourning and Melancholia," SE, vol. 14, 249.

51. Sigmund Freud, *The Ego and the Id*, SE, vol. 19, 29.

52. Freud, " The Ego and the Id," 30.

53. Loewald, *Sublimation*, 20.

3   Adorno, Marx, Materialism

We have become used to thinking of "materialism" as a name for demystification. Materialism is understood as that kind of thinking which relieves us of deluded beliefs in immaterial entities or of "ideological" conceptions of society. It has also, sometimes, been thought of as the easiest of all philosophical or social-scientific creeds to grasp. Only matter, and material needs, are real, it seems to say; any claims to know anything beyond them are "metaphysical," or "idealist," or "ideological." Materialism's job is imagined as a relatively straightforward one: to break those idols and to leave us undeluded.

In practice this task of getting rid of illusions has proved much more difficult than the above remarks suggest. Materialism has found it hard to stand outside the illusions which it wants to dispel. It is easier to call oneself a materialist than it is to be one, because self-declared materialism has an unfortunate tendency to turn into its opposite. Something like this difficulty can be seen right at the origins of the tradition which came to be called "materialism." For the early Greek philosopher Democritus, matter was the absolutely real. Amongst his chief principles was that "[n]othing will come of nothing and nothing which is can be annihilated." The idea has had an impact well beyond Greek thought, right through to Newtonian physics and the modern common sense determined by it. Yet such an axiom already indicates how hard it is to separate the tradition of materialism from kinds of thinking with which one might expect it to have little in common. Here, for example, the Eleatic and very unmaterialist notion of substance as that which is eternal and can suffer no decay migrates into Democritus' conception of matter: "Nothing which is can be annihilated."

This kind of connection is no accident. Far from being in any straightforward way opposed to metaphysics, any thinking which starts out from the principle that "only matter is real" is itself dependent on a metaphysical claim. It makes, that is, a claim about the nature of the world in advance of an assessment of the means by which knowledge of the world is to be secured. Nor is this kind of problem confined to philosophical materialism. Suppose, for example, we were to decide that materialism should be regarded not as a metaphysical theory of what is real but instead as a "method." What makes a method a method is that the same procedures are followed to investigate different kinds of material. If the method remains the same whatever it is used to investigate, it can hardly be materialist at all, because it will remain an unchanging invariant, unaffected by any changes in the objects which it is to consider. Materialism, apparently the most straightforward and commonsensical of creeds, in practice keeps turning into its opposite, into just what it was supposed not to be.

For Adorno himself, wanting to be a materialist means starting from, not a set of fixed metaphysical or methodological commitments, but something which could more accurately be named an impulse: the utopian wish for undeluded happiness, including bodily pleasure, the wish for an end to suffering. This wish may be simple, even naïve; but it requires all the cunning of philosophical artifice if it is not to be deformed, turned into a parody of itself, from the outset. Adorno starts out, that is, from an acute awareness of how difficult it is to be a materialist. The more rapidly and brutally thought cuts itself free from illusion, the more it is entangled.

The fact that materialists have so often ended up saying such idealist things means that it must be much harder to stop saying them than we have thought. In particular, it means that materialist thinking has a peculiarly vexed relationship to the demand for systematic philosophical consistency. It cannot simply ignore that demand. If materialism thinks it has said farewell to philosophy, it has only said hello to some much cruder set of involuntary philosophical commitments. Yet a seamlessly noncontradictory system could never be "materialist," because what makes such a system a system is the reduction of the different and the variable to unchanging identity. Materialism thus has an unavoidably contradictory relation to system. It cannot live with it and cannot live without it.

Nowhere is this better illustrated than in the reception of Marx's thought. Its systematic elements have been petrified in different ways by different kinds of systematizers until it has come to resemble a *Summa Economica*, a body of unshakeably dogmatic doctrine, a special science demanding esoteric kinds of wisdom and armoured in its own untranslatable terminology. This has been done above all by taking far too literally Marx's own farewell to philosophy. What this farewell has come to mean in the history of Marxism is less a proper caution about the need for empirical evidence and research than a licence to make all sorts of philosophical claims whilst placing them dogmatically beyond the reach of philosophical scrutiny. The dogmatic worldview in the "dialectics of nature" developed by Soviet Marxism-Leninism is only the most striking instance of this kind of treatment; the same kind of maneuvre is in place wherever "historical" or "cultural materialism" regards its own procedures as operating in a special zone beyond the reach of philosophical questioning. Adorno's reading of Marx, instead, emerges from attempts in the early years of the twentieth century to remobilize Marx's thought by reconnecting it with the classical German philosophy in which Marx himself was trained – a body of work which, for all Marx's own rejection of Hegel and Hegelianisms, left a deep impact on the vocabularies and contours of his thought. Adorno focuses on those aspects of Marx's work which are hard to coerce into systematic consistency. These, for Adorno, are just those aspects from which the materialist truth content of Marx's authorship can best be understood. Above all, no special privilege is given to Marx's thought, which is read, not as speaking a peculiarly insulated and "Marxist" language, but as engaging with difficulties faced both by classical German philosophy and by the whole materialist tradition. From this engagement emerges Adorno's own attempt at formulating a nondogmatic materialism, an attempt which considers that much, but not everything, is to be learned from Marx's example.

For Adorno, the critical importance of Marx lies in his having brought together two very different and in many ways opposed strands of materialist thinking. Materialism is by no means guaranteed to be an emancipatory kind of thinking or one critical of existing political orders. We need only think of the work of Hobbes, where one of the most thoroughgoing materialisms which had thus far existed was put in the service of a powerful defence of the absolute authority of the state, as personified in the monarch. Adorno makes a distinction between some ancient materialisms such as that of Epicurus, concerned less with a cosmology or a metaphysics than with the revaluation of bodily pleasure as the highest good, and a materialism such as Hobbes's, in which political life and social life are interpreted in ways heavily influenced by the success of mathematics and the natural sciences. Marx brings these currents together in an especially fateful way. In his thought, "the attempt is made to bring together the utopian moment, found in early materialist efforts, with this anti-utopian moment, which sets out the impotence, sheer weakness and contingency of the nature of individual human beings."[1] As a result, *materialism* in and of itself is no kind of goal: "[T]he telos, the Idea of Marxian materialism is to do away with materialism, that is to say, to bring about a situation in which the blind compulsion of material conditions over human beings is broken, and in which alone the question as to freedom could first become truly meaningful" (PT, vol. 2, p. 198).

This essay is divided into four parts. First I discuss the main ways in which Adorno's conception of materialism, and his relationship to Marx, developed during the course of his life. I then turn to an account of Adorno's reading of Marx, following which I examine its significance for some central features of Adorno's own analyses of culture and society. Finally I offer an account of the nature of Adorno's broader materialism as evidenced in his mature thought.

THE DEVELOPMENT OF ADORNO'S MATERIALISM

Adorno's official early education was not conspicuously materialist. The dominant figure in his philosophical training was Kant, whether the straightforwardly epistemological Kant offered by his academic supervisor, Hans Cornelius, or the rather more complicated Kant presented by his intellectual mentor, Siegfried Kracauer. In any case, Adorno's early readings of Kant with Kracauer were important. Kracauer taught Adorno to regard the contradictions of major philosophical authorships less as an occasion for easy triumph than as symptoms of real antagonisms in historical experience. He thus opened the way to a decoding of the historical experience sedimented within the concepts and organization of philosophical texts, a decoding which was to become Adorno's characteristic mode of philosophical interpretation.

Three intellectual developments of the 1920s can be selected from many as having been of particular importance for the shape which Adorno's materialism eventually took. The first was the rethinking of Marxism undertaken by several philosophically informed Marxists in that decade, above all Georg Lukács. In his *History and Class Consciousness*, Lukács was able to show that central aspects of Marx's thought were being treated simplistically in current communist debate. Lukács showed how, despite Marx's apparent farewell to philosophy, certain critical issues in his thinking, such as the relation between theory and practice, could hardly be understood without some understanding of the way in which they had emerged from classical German philosophy, especially the thought of Hegel. For Lukács, neglect of this dimension of Marx's thought had led to some serious errors. Lukács argued that the effects of the transformation of all aspects of life, including intellectual life, brought about by capitalism, in particular by the fetishism of commodities, were so far-reaching as to influence the thought of critics of capitalism themselves. The division between subject and object, which Lukács took to characterize all modern thought, could not therefore be superseded without the supersession of the capitalist mode of production itself. Lukács thus came to understand the revolutionary proletariat as a kind of "collective subject" of history. Only from the standpoint of this collective subject would the problems of modern epistemology be susceptible of a solution. Not all parts of this Lukácsian programme (which was for Lukács himself only an intermediate stage between his own early romanticism and a later much more orthodox Marxism-Leninism) appealed to Adorno. Adorno never forgot the lesson taught by Lukács about the need to understand Marx through his philosophical background as well as through his break with that background. He was also impressed by Lukács's understanding of the pervasive importance of commodity fetishism for all aspects of cultural and intellectual life. He found himself sceptical from an early stage, however, about the notion that the revolutionary proletariat could be thought of as a collective subject of history.

In this regard, two other leading left-wing thinkers of the 1920s were of paramount importance to Adorno. From Walter Benjamin in particular, Adorno learned something which was to become one of the most salient characteristics of his materialism, the idea that the material specificity of the minute particulars uncovered by historical and philological enquiry rather than the highest, most general, and hence emptiest concepts should be the starting points for philosophical interpretation. The attentiveness with which Adorno, in *Minima Moralia*, dwells on a fleeting facial expression or a posture in order to allow them to begin to speak of the historical experience which is sedimented in them could hardly be imagined without Benjamin's similar attentiveness to the texts of Baroque drama in his *Origin of the German Play of Lamentation*. Benjamin's influence on every aspect of Adorno's thought can in most ways hardly be overestimated, but so far as the specifically *materialist* aspects of that thought were concerned, the influence of Max Horkheimer was perhaps still more important. It was Horkheimer, a long-standing admirer of Schopenhauer as well as of Marx, who relentlessly forced Adorno back over and over again to the relationship between philosophy and bodily human suffering. It was Horkheimer who insisted that materialism had to be defined not primarily as a body of metaphysical doctrine, nor as an invariant method which could be applied to any subject matter whatever, but rather as a practice of thinking orientated toward the utopian goal of the end of suffering.

It was in developing this necessarily initially rather imprecise idea that Adorno and Horkheimer were engaged for much of the 1930s. Records of the lengthy discussions between them in America toward the end of that decade show how fierce were the arguments from which Adorno's later materialism emerged. Horkheimer continually worried that Adorno would lose sight of what was to him the crucial point, the connection of materialist thinking with particular suffering-desiring-thinking human lives. Adorno, conversely, worried that Horkheimer's suspicion of epistemological abstraction would push him into a philosophically indefensible set of dogmatic assertions. Over the course of a decade, a remarkable intellectual collaboration emerged. Adorno was profoundly influenced by Horkheimer's idea that bodily affectivity is not merely inseparable from human knowledge but a necessary condition of it. As Horkheimer put the matter, "[A] god is incapable of knowing anything because it has no needs."[2] Yet at the same time Adorno convinced Horkheimer that philosophical abstraction was not something which any materialism could rapidly get rid of, because such abstraction was itself part and parcel of our – material – experience. The abstractions would, instead, have to be unpacked, interpreted, listened to until they disclosed the living experience buried in them.

There is a critical, and rather comical, moment in the records of the discussions among the American members of the Institute for Social Research which reveals Adorno and Horkheimer's unanimity on this point:

LÖWENTHAL: Sein ist Sein.
ADORNO und HORKHEIMER: Nein.[3]

Löwenthal's remark accurately gives the flavour of the distrust felt by several members of the circle around the Institute for Social Research: an impatience with Adorno's and, increasingly, Horkheimer's engagement with the subtleties of Hegelian logic and a worry that such an engagement would lead to a neglect of the really urgent tasks of political economy and the sociology of culture. At the same time, the remark exemplifies the danger around which Adorno's remarks to Horkheimer repeatedly circle: the danger that materialism might lead to a "dogmatic" truncation of philosophical reflection. Against Löwenthal's confidence that "Being" is the emptiest and therefore most useless of concepts, only susceptible of being addressed by this empty tautology, Adorno offers, not a "fundamental ontology" in which the "meaning of Being" could somehow be addressed without thinking about particular or "merely ontic" beings, but an awareness of the aporetic status of certain fundamental philosophical concepts: "aporetic" in the precise sense that they are repeatedly shown to lead to contradictions which are not simply the result of weak argumentation and cannot currently be got rid of.

These discussions had important implications both for Adorno and Horkheimer's social theory and for their conception of philosophical writing. It became impossible to think of the tasks of a materialist social theory as being likely to be fulfilled simply by assembling results from individual empirical social enquiries and subjecting them to theoretical assessment. Instead Adorno increasingly tended to develop still further the idea of materialism as a kind of *interpretation*. No analysis which simply subordinated philosophical questions to a prior set of dogmatically assumed sociological or historical theses could carry philosophical conviction. Instead of being subjected to an external set of standards, philosophical texts were to

be made to speak, as it were, from the inside out. The key concepts
of philosophical texts, even, and indeed especially, the most apparently abstract concepts, carried historical experience sedimented inside them. The contradictions, fractures, or slips in those texts could
be used to make those texts themselves speak of the suppressed historical experience which had made them possible.

It was out of these discussions on the nature and possibility of
a "materialist logic" that Adorno and Horkheimer's collaborative
Philosophical Fragments, later given the title *Dialectic of Enlightenment*, emerged. Although the topic of "materialism" does not receive
much explicit treatment there, the problem which it sets out is in
fact decisive for the whole character of Adorno's later materialism.
The book is preoccupied above all with how it is that apparently
demystificatory practices of thinking have become in their turn a
kind of mystification. The ways in which materialism, once converted into a method or a worldview, turns into its opposite afford a
striking instance of just what Adorno and Horkheimer mean by the
"dialectic of enlightenment." In the wake of that work, it became
clearer than ever to Adorno that attempts to confer on materialism
a seamlessly noncontradictory character would destroy it. Instead
Adorno began developing an "aporetic" materialism, that is to say,
a materialism which would exhibit and interpret, rather than efface,
those contradictions which could not be eliminated in the course of
its enquiry. This materialism was given its final shape in Adorno's
late and most important philosophical work, *Negative Dialectics*.

REREADING MARX

In contrast to his treatment of, say, Kant or Hegel, Adorno devoted
no single book or complete course of lectures to Marx. Yet Marx's
significance for Adorno is unmissable, not only because of the important articles centrally concerned with the contemporary consequences of Marx's work – articles such as "Late Capitalism or Industrial Society?" "Reflections on the Theory of Class," or "Theses on
Need" – or the lengthy passages from lecture courses such as
Philosophische Terminologie dealing with Marx's thought, but,
above all, because of the Marxian idiom in which so much of
Adorno's philosophical criticism, as well as his social and cultural
theory, is couched. Even in works in which Marx's name never

appears, such as the eventual text of *Dialectic of Enlightenment*, his presence can be felt throughout.

Reading Marxist accounts of Marx is often like watching the construction of a large but rather unstable toy. Marx's writings are converted into a terminological kit in which each piece is to have a fixed and peculiar meaning, as though they were written in an idiolect in which individual words will eternally retain the single special significance conferred on them by the author. For Adorno, this is the opposite of what reading Marx should be like. His Marx has the rare and timely advantage of being a human being: not the humorless system builder and sponsor of the imaginary pseudoscience of "Marxism" but a flexible, ironic, and alert intelligence, the contradictions in whose work are not to be loudly demonstrated away because of the difficulties they might cause to the faithful but rather to be attended to for what they tell us about its historical truth content as well as its limitations.

Although the subtitle of *Capital* directly calls the work a "critique" of political economy, it has more often been read as though it were an encyclopaedia. Of course, this is not to deny its systematic character. For Adorno, Marx's authorship, better than any other, exemplifies his view that materialism has a necessarily contradictory relationship to system. Yet its systematic character comes from the claim to systematic unity and coherence which capitalist society itself sets up. Marx seeks to understand the systematic character of capitalist society without giving in to its claim to be a natural or inalterable state of affairs: "Marx's system, in so far as one can speak of his 'system' at all, was in reality only a negative system; in it, the attempt is made to comprehend the systematic unity of bourgeois, capitalist society, and, so to speak, to ask that society whether it really is the seamless unity which it pretends to be" (PT, vol. 2, p. 216).

It is this critical relationship to the categories of classical political economy which Adorno finds central to Marx's thought. Previous socialist efforts at political economy had usually begun by rejecting the premises of classical political economy outright. They provided alternatives of their own which were generally based on a dogmatic anthropology, that is to say, on a theory distinguishing natural needs from artificial wants. Their work thus tended to lose any explanatory grip on the reality of capitalism. It risked turning into a form of empty moralizing which insisted that things "ought" to be otherwise. The work of political economists such as Smith and Ricardo, by contrast, offered essential insights into capitalist society. Yet it confused the moral and political question of the justice of that society with something entirely different, the merely instrumental question of the continued functioning of that society, thus arriving at the result that, as it were, everything "is" just as it "ought" to be. What Marx did was to turn the buried normative elements of political economy's own concepts against itself: to ask, for example, whether the free and fair exchange which lay at the center of classical political economy really was free and fair. This was a critical and even philosophical task rather than a narrowly economic one in that it involved contesting the restrictedly technical redefinition of normative concepts – the redefinition of "free" to mean "contractually consenting," for example. This is an instance of the way in which, despite his farewell to philosophy, Marx's schooling in it nevertheless deeply fashioned the contours of his thought. The emergence of a body of thought shaped in this peculiar way, able to get past the bad choice between empty moral demands, on the one hand, and the complete liquidation of any moral or critical element, on the other, would have been unimaginable without the experience of Hegel's thought.

What Marx is thus able to uncover is the way in which a discourse with apparently exemplary liberal and enlightened credentials – classical political economy – in fact keeps relying on archaic and mythical categories which it cannot afford to question. It does this, not because it has simply got its facts wrong, but because it reproduces a logic of misidentification which is already present in capitalist exchange and production itself. An outstanding instance of this, and one of central importance for Adorno, is provided by Marx's analysis of "the fetishism of the commodity and its secret." For classical political economy, the exchange of commodities represents no kind of problem at all. Its fairness and freedom is guaranteed by the consent of the contracting parties.

For Marx, the identificatory judgement implicit in the exchange of commodities is from one point of view true. It states the exchange value of the items involved. Yet it is also, from another point of view, misleading, because of what it leaves out. What it leaves out is little less than everything: not only the nature and qualities of the objects involved (their "use value," as Marx puts it) but also the entire personal and social history which has led up to the exchange, including, crucially, the question of how each partner comes by what is exchanged. Marx's point is not restricted to particularly flagrant instances of monopolies but goes much further. Every time the exchange of commodities takes place, it implicitly represents heterogeneous objects, qualities, and histories as identical. What is really a relationship between people is represented as though it were a fact about a thing. The commodity exchange is thus at once an identification and a misidentification. *Capital* pursues the way in which this simultaneous identification and misidentification unfolds in all aspects of capitalist production, consumption, and exchange. It is in this sense that we have to understand Adorno's paradoxes, the idea that *Capital* is a "negative system," or that it is both a system and not a system (PT, vol. 2, p. 262). *Capital* does indeed unfold a systematic logic, the logic of the capitalist mode of production; yet at each stage it shows how this logic, however well it functions from its own point of view, carries with it a series of misrecognitions, concealments, and exclusions.

An especially important example is offered by Marx's theory of surplus value. Classical theories of surplus value such as Turgot's or Smith's were invented to deal with an ethical problem, the problem of how it came about that apparently fair exchange could yield a profit for one of the exchanging parties. Such profits appeared to suggest that the exchange in question was tilted in favor of one of the parties, and this apparent unfairness formed a central legitimating argument in medieval and later attacks on lending money at interest. For classical political economy, on the other hand, surplus value was not an ethical problem but the providential secret of social life itself: a "gift of nature,"[4] as Turgot put it, which would continue to be given only providing that no artificial obstacles were put in the way of free exchange.

The emergence of the theory of surplus value offers a key instance of the way in which the discourse of political economy is founded on the transformation of moral into technical problems. For Marx, surplus value arises by means of an especially critical instance of misidentification: the misidentification of human labor. From the point of view of the accounts, human labor is simply a commodity like any other. The capitalist contracts with workers to receive their labor and receives it. Unlike any other commodity, however, human labor is alive and is capable of producing further commodities, which, however, although produced by the workers, remain the property of the capitalist who has paid for the labor time. In one sense, therefore, the capitalist receives exactly what he or she has paid for: the labor time of the workers. In another sense, he or she receives more than was paid for, the further commodities produced because of the nature of living labor, which can never figure in the accounts. Marx's point, of course, is not that a better system of accounting would lead to more fairness but that, because of this systematic identification and misidentification, the crucial factor making surplus value possible – the capitalist's monopoly over the means of production – cannot be seen for what it is.

As will be evident, then, it is central to Marx's account that he neither returns to the simple moral attack on usury nor resigns himself to the transformation of surplus value into a technical economic problem. His thought simultaneously refuses not merely the empty *ought* but also, as it were, the empty *is*: the spurious deletion of the normative element from what will forever, unless it should be solved, remain both a descriptive *and* a moral problem.

Marx shows how such simultaneous identifications and misidentifications are at work in all the categories structuring capitalist society and are codified in classical political economy. They do not merely concern exchange but run right the way through to, for example, our very notion of what "production" itself might be. As Marx points out, the question of what constitutes productive labour is habitually decided from the standpoint of exchange value: "A singer who sells her song on her own behalf is an *unproductive worker*. But the same singer hired by an entrepreneur who has her sing in order to make money is a *productive* worker, since she produces capital."[5] As Adorno comments, "From these passages it actually follows that all the categories of bourgeois society, represented here by productivity understood in the sense of the principle of exchange, that is, in other words, the whole system which he is developing, is not a system of the absolute or of truth" (PT, vol. 2, p. 276). *Capital* does not pursue its purpose primarily by showing that classical political economy has made some particular crucial error – by showing, say, that it has "privileged" exchange over production. Rather it offers the phenomenology of a systematic illusion, an illusion whose every category is at once an identification and a misidentification.

This double structure of identification and misidentification causes particular problems for the critic of capitalism. The difficulty is that the identifications are not, from one point of view, *incorrect* at all. The critic is inside what he or she wants to criticize. If the critic tries simply to propose an alternative theory to the logic of capital, he or she is faced everywhere by categories which are already saturated by that logic. For example, one recurrently tempting alternative has been to offer a theory of economy based on a distinction between real and artificial needs. But the concept of "real" need is itself, as Marx himself showed, twinned indissolubly with that of profit. The notion of the bare minimum, the *strict nécessaire*, emerges coevally with that of surplus value as a "gift of nature." To found an economic anthropology on such a concept of absolute need, the bare minimum, is to mistake the bare existence of the wage laborer for the very model of life itself.

It is worth reflecting, then, on what kind of materialism such a critique presents. It is clearly not a materialist worldview in which the organization of the economy follows in a lawlike fashion from laws of nature; nor is it a materialist anthropology in which social structure is derived from a preestablished doctrine of natural human needs and interests; nor, in practice, is it a materialist method which would stand outside, preexist, and investigate its object, since its method unfolds only with the explication of its peculiar object. Instead, it is a materialism undertaken consciously from within the systematic illusion which it attempts to undo. It is clearly, then, in several ways distinct from a dogmatic naturalism. Yet at the same time, and perhaps no less importantly in the current climate, it is equally far from the cultural or economic idealism with which western Marxists have sometimes reacted. Adorno pays special attention to the way in which the category of nature appears in Marx (a topic on which one of his pupils wrote an important study which itself influenced Adorno's thinking on the topic). Nature is neither subjected, as it was later to be by Engels, to a full-blown exposition at the hands of "dialectical materialism," nor is the idea of nature placed under an embarrassed taboo, as is the case with much contemporary Marxism. Adorno remarks that "in the East something like a materialistic world-view has been made out of Marx's work, a worldview which the texts themselves strictly contradict. In the West, on the other hand ... the attempt has been made to get rid of the really materialist moment in Marx's thought" (PT, vol. 2, p. 256). Instead, we are given glimpses of what nature might be at the point where Marx's critical thinking breaks through the illusion of the self-sufficingness of human productivity. Perhaps the passage of Marx's work which Adorno most often cited was that in the "Critique of the Gotha Programme" in which Marx insists that "[L]abour is not the source of all wealth. *Nature* is just as much the source of use-values (and it is indeed of such that material wealth consists!) as labour, which is itself only the manifestation of a natural force, human labour power."[6] The true import of such a remark can only be measured if we remember that, despite all this, what Marx's chief work actually offers us is not a theory of how *use values* are produced, still less of how labor is "a manifestation of a natural force, human labour power," but rather a vast account of just that systematic illusion which is here abruptly dissented from. Far from believing that all human experience is culturally or economically constructed, Marx attempts to undo this illusion, but he knows that his work can best testify to the possibility of nature where such an illusion breaks down rather than by an immediate and dogmatic ontology of nature.

Adorno's undogmatic reading of Marx frees him from the need to swallow Marx whole or not at all. The truth content of Marx's thought is understood as something which is itself critical rather than dogmatically substantive and as something which is historical rather than invariant. Both these key features of Adorno's Marx are visible in his reassessment of the central themes of Marx's work. One example concerns an especially important issue in Marx's thought, the conflict between the forces and relations of production. Marx thought that a point was likely to be reached when the full development of the forces of production (that is, the total productive capacities available from living workers and technology combined) would be restricted by the existing relations of production (that is, the monopoly over the means of production by capitalists and the exclusion of workers from such means of production). Because Marx understood the forces of production as materially real and the relations of production, however apparently fixed, as in essence ideological, he anticipated that this conflict would be settled by the revolutionary overthrow of the existing relations of production, that is to say, by the ending of monopolies over the means of production.

Adorno regarded the fact that this had not happened as a highly significant one. He was heavily influenced in his own understanding of this question by the theory of "late" or "monopoly" capitalism developed by Friedrich Pollock and others amongst the political economists associated with the Institute for Social Research. According to Pollock, some kinds of productive forces – technologies such as railway networks or electricity grids, for example – far from being inhibited by monopolies, were only susceptible of full development on condition of monopoly ownership. Certainly Adorno was sometimes led to overstate the distinction between the "high" capitalism which Marx had analysed and the monopoly capitalism which Pollock believed current. But what is most of interest here is not any contribution to economic history on Adorno's part – there his work was necessarily largely derivative – but the way in which Pollock's idea prompted Adorno to reconsider the relation between economics and domination in Marx's thought. For Marx coercion and private property were coeval. As Adorno puts it, for Marx "economics has priority over domination; domination may not be deduced otherwise than economically."[7] If domination cannot be shown to be coeval with property relations, it becomes harder to argue that the end of those relations will also be the end of domination. Any such concession would appear to strengthen the conservative argument that domination is a "natural" and hence a legitimate feature of human societies. For Adorno, however, such a conclusion would be a non sequitur. The fact that domination has been a feature of all human societies to date tells us nothing at all about its legitimacy. There very well can be and has been domination without private property. Moreover, Adorno understood this less as an external criticism of Marx than as an extension of Marx's own central insight. For Adorno, as we have seen, the crucial motif of Marx's thought had always been the discovery of archaic monopoly and domination surviving within apparently liberal social arrangements.

One important result of this is that it changes the emphasis which is placed on the concept of capitalism itself. The collapse of capitalism would by no means be guaranteed to bring an end either to mystification or to domination; it might very well lead to much more direct forms of both. It is not that capitalism invents mystification but that in capitalism mystification presents itself, to an unprecedented extent, *as demystification.* Adorno's view is not that capitalism is too enlightened, disenchanted, or liberal but that it is not *even* enlightened, disenchanted, or liberal. The point is to turn capitalism's own norms against the experience of living with it. But to criticize capitalism by using norms which are at least partially its own of course implies, what Adorno repeatedly concedes, that it is capitalism which has in part made these complaints even possible.

The way in which this openness to historical change coincides with a rereading of Marx as a critic of capitalism and political economy rather than as the creater of a *Summa Economica* is visible in a significant but little discussed essay on the theory of class which Adorno wrote in 1942. The essay's central thought is an apparent paradox: *"So real die Klasse ist, so sehr ist sie selber schon Ideologie"* ("However real class is, it is itself, just as much, already ideology").[8] The claim is a good example of what is meant in practice by understanding Marx's materialism as critical and aporetic rather than dogmatic and positivistic. Marx understood class not as a quantitative concept denoting wealth or poverty but as a qualitative concept denoting the relation to the means of production. The owners of the means of production were to be understood as capitalists, wage laborers (whatever the wage in question) as workers. In the years leading up to Adorno's essay, liberal sociology had mounted a persistent critique of Marx's concept of class, pointing to its bluntness as a sociological instrument and the difficulty of understanding wage laborers of widely differing wealth as belonging to the same class. Adorno's response is not to resist this critique but to press it further: "The critique of liberal society cannot call a halt before the concept of class, which is as true and as untrue as the system of liberalism itself."[9] Instead, the concept of class is to be understood as an aporetic one, that is to say, a concept which designates not a real entity but rather a real illusion. There is clearly in one sense *no such thing* as a "class": in the sense that an attempt, precisely, to *classify* a diverse group of people under a single concept inevitably misleadingly identifies them. Yet, at the same time, this is not just *any* misidentification, one, for example, which could be dispelled just by noticing that it is a misidentification, but rather a misidentification which is daily performed in our lives. It is not, then, Adorno's aim to defend all concepts used by Marx to the last ditch, as though they were Marx's own invention, but to enable these misidentifications to be brought to an end, yet with the critical proviso that, because social process currently *consists* of these misidentifications, simply changing our terminology will only make it harder, not easier, to interpret and contest social illusion. It will give us the illusory idea that we ourselves, as "social scientists," for example, stand outside the illusions we wish to dispel.

It will be clear from this that the use which Adorno makes of Marx's thought in his social and cultural theory, whether in interpreting features of social experience or individual cultural artifacts, could not lead secondary or superstructural social or cultural symptoms back to fundamentally economic causes. The unscientistic, aporetic reading of Marxism already given has a deep impact on the relation between the critical theorist and systematic social illusion. Because the latter is thought of as something which the critical theorist is him- or herself inside of, interpreting cultural artifacts cannot simply be a matter of brusquely breaking their spell, of abruptly demystifying them by showing the elementary needs from which they have sprung. Any such procedure would only make it more difficult to see the spell in which such demystifying ideology critique itself remains caught. Instead, it requires understanding the way in which the "ideological" character of cultural artifacts and their possible truth content are deeply entwined. It may be precisely what at first makes a work of art look like a piece of mystification – for example, the difficulty which we might experience in deciphering its significance, its refusal readily to communicate with its audience – which enables such a work to resist the much more powerful mystification worked by the systematically repeated identifications and misidentifications of capitalist social process. It is in this spirit that Adorno refers to the work of art as a "fetish against commodity fetishism."[10] Works of art are fetishes insofar as they imply a claim to a value independent of human production and consumption. But when social process systematically appears as though it were a natural and inalterable set of givens, the fetish character of the work of art can, paradoxically, become the reverse of mystifying, a resistance to a systematically mystified social process.

MATERIALISM AND METAPHYSICS

Central to Adorno's rereading of Marx is a reassessment of the relationship between philosophy and social theory. It was no accident that Adorno so often cast his social thought as a critique of "positivism." For him it matters that the term recall the work of the founder of positivism and of sociology alike, Auguste Comte. Comte's idea of a scientific sociology is built on a unilateral declaration of independence from "metaphysics." But Adorno does not think that sociology really has become independent of metaphysics at all; critical philosophical questions have been repressed, rather than solved, in such a declaration, which is then fateful for the whole subsequent development of social science. The aspects of Marx's thought which cause Adorno most disquiet are the points at which Marx himself appears to declare an analogously abrupt farewell to philosophy; these moments in practice mean, not that philosophical problems have ceased to be problems, but only that they have ceased to be seen. As Adorno comments in *Negative Dialectics*, "Out of disgust at academic squabbling, Marx rampaged through the epistemological categories like a bull in a china shop" (ND, 206/206 translation altered). Against these positivistic moments, Adorno sets Marx's own understanding of social process as simultaneous identification and misidentification, an understanding which, for all Marx's criticisms of Hegel, would have been quite impossible without his experience of Hegelian logic. Adorno once remarked that Marx's analysis of the fetishism of the commodity ranked with the finest analyses of classical German philosophy. The praise is pointed because it directs attention to the extent to which, despite Marx's apparent materialist farewell to philosophy, the contours of his thought were permanently shaped by his experience of idealism.

Adorno's own nondogmatic materialism, especially as developed in his lecture courses of the late 1950s and 1960s, in his studies of Hegel, and, above all, in *Negative Dialectics*, is deeply formed by these lessons and in particular by his sense of the risk that supposedly materialist thinking will involuntarily turn into its opposite. The more literalistically materialism conceives itself – as, for example, a breaking of apparent idols such as subjectivity, spirit, or freedom – the more likely it is to fall captive to new mystifications of its own. For this reason, it is central to Adorno's materialism to understand his own thought as standing inside of, rather than outside of, the systematic identifications and misidentifications of which late capitalist social process and the philosophical thinking which goes on under late capitalism are alike composed. This means, not that the problems of understanding philosophical identification and misidentification are identical with, or merely a superstructural *result* of, those at work in a prior social process, but rather that the two are intimately connected. It also means that materialism cannot consist in a new method, or a new worldview, but must rather work as a reinterpretation of the social experience sedimented – now misleadingly, now revealingly – in the philosophical authorships which have come to dominate our understanding of cognition.

Despite this, *Negative Dialectics* is not restricted to an immanent critique of the philosophical tradition. Such critiques open out into a materialist reformulation of concepts and categories. Crucial here is the reinterpretation of the meaning of "thinking" itself. For Adorno, to think is always to think something. Even the most formal of formal logics would be unthinkable without the "something" to which it refers, and therefore an absolute separation of logic from ontology is impossible. Thinking necessarily contains within it a reference to something which is not thinking – something, that is, which is therefore transcendent with respect to thinking. In that respect, something like what is thought of as a "metaphysical" impulse – a drive to a knowledge of objects which would break the circle of logical immanence – is already implicit in thinking itself. At the same time, all thinking is always also bodily affectivity. There is no thought that is not also felt. This needs to be thought of not simply as an obstacle to thinking but also as a condition of its possibility. As Adorno remarks, "The thought without a need, the thought which did not wish for anything, would be nothing-like [*nichtig*] . . . " (ND, 100/93 translation altered).

This reexamination of the meaning of thinking, then, is not materialist in the sense of a dogmatic ontology stating that only matter is real. It is a nondogmatic materialism in the specific sense that it proceeds through a critique of thinking itself, a critique which understands thinking as always, necessarily, materially contaminated. It is always contaminated with a reference to an object; it is always contaminated with subjective affectivity. Thinking is not what we have when everything which might contaminate its "purity" has been gotten rid of; rather, it is only the supposed impurities that make thinking possible at all. Thinking would not be thinking, that is, if it were not thinking *of* something and *for* something.

For many, of course, this may no longer count as materialism at all. For Adorno, however, materialism was more a practice of thinking directed toward undeluded happiness, including bodily pleasure and freedom from physical suffering, than a peculiarly "materialist" set of ontological doctrines or methodological canons. What finally matters to Adorno is much less to define a checklist of characteristics for materialism and to measure up to them than to evolve a practice of thinking in which these impurities in thinking, the need in thinking and the reference in thinking, can be acknowledged rather than compulsorily suppressed.

It is for these reasons that the idea of philosophical artifice, the form which philosophical writing takes, becomes of such importance to Adorno's materialism. Philosophical materialism has usually been associated with a literal-minded bluntness, a determination to purge philosophical language of any delusive, especially figurative, component. For Adorno, on the other hand, materialism's repeated lapses against its will into idealism mean that more, not less, philosophical cunning is required if thought is ever to say what its object "is, rather than what it falls under" – if thought is to interpret rather than merely classify its objects.

Because such a materialism is neither a method nor a worldview, it cannot in the last analysis be satisfactorily paraphrased: "[I]t is essential to philosophy that it is not summarizable. If it were, it would be superfluous" (ND, 44/33 translation altered). This essay, I hope, is not a paraphrase but rather an introduction to an approach or an idiom of thinking about social experience. It is an idiom whose lack of a self-identical foundation will always render it vulnerable in the face of more methodologistic, idealist, or scientistic retranscriptions. Here I want simply to offer one thought about the subsequent fate of critical theory. Second-generation Critical Theory, even in its most philosophically nuanced forms, has habitually understood itself as rescuing central insights of Adorno's thought from a supposed aestheticism. What is notable, however, is the extent to which, perhaps surprisingly, what goes missing from critical theory when essayistic artifice is replaced by systematic theory is, precisely, *materialism*.

From Apel to Habermas to Wellmer to Schnädelbach, confidence that the outlines of a non-metaphysical theory of communicative action have been discovered means that the problem of materialist thinking drops out of view. Once we understand our own viewpoint as rather harder to free from metaphysical commitments than second-generation Critical Theory has wanted to admit, this step into the intersubjective becomes more problematic. The linguistic turn has been of such assistance to later critical theorists in making this step precisely because that turn was one of the salient means by which metaphysical problems were, not solved, but suppressed in the last century. Later Critical Theory has a powerful appeal to academic sociology departments partly because of its disconnection from the metaphysical problems posed by the philosophical tradition – partly because, that is, it repeats the unilateral farewell to metaphysics which inaugurates the discipline of sociology itself.

NOTES

1. Theodor W. Adorno, *Philosophische Terminologie* (Frankfurt am Main: Suhrkamp, 1974), vol. 2, 253. Hereafter cited as PT. All quotations from this text are given in my translation.
2. Max Horkheimer, *Between Philosophy and Social Science: Selected Early Writings*, trans. G. Frederick Hunter, Matthew S. Kramer, and John Torpey (Cambridge, Mass.: MIT Press, 1993), 242.
3. See Max Horkheimer, "Diskussionsprotokolle," *Gesammelte Schriften*, ed. Alfred Schmidt and Gunzelin Schmd Noerr (Frankfurt am Main: Fischer, 1990), vol. 12, 501.
4. Anne Robert Jacques Turgot, "Reflections on the Formation and Distribution of Wealth," in *Turgot on Progress, Sociology and Economics*, trans. and ed. Ronald L. Meek (Cambridge: Cambridge University Press, 1973), 158.
5. Karl Marx, *Theories of Surplus Value*, trans. Emile Burns (London: Lawrence and Wishart, 1969), vol. 1, 401 (translation altered).
6. Karl Marx, *Critique of the Gotha Programme* (London: Lawrence and Wishart, 1939), 3 (translation altered).
7. Theodor W. Adorno, *Negative Dialektik* (Frankfurt am Main: Suhrkamp, 1973), 315. Translated by E. B. Ashton under the title *Negative Dialectics* (New York: Seabury Press, 1973), 321 (translation altered). Hereafter cited as ND. German page number followed by English translation page number.

8. Theodor W. Adorno, "Reflexionen zur Klassentheorie," *Gesammelte Schriften*, ed. Rolf Tiedemann, vol. 8 (Frankfurt am Main: Suhrkamp, 1972) 379 (my translation).

9. Adorno, "Reflexionen zur Klassentheorie," 379 (my translation).

10. Theodor W. Adorno, *Aesthetic Theory*, trans. Robert Hullot-Kentor (London: Athlone Press, 1997), 227.

4   Leaving Home
On Adorno and Heidegger

Wer Keine Heimat mehr hat,
dem wird wohl gar das Schreiben zum Wohnen.
[For a man who no longer has a homeland,
writing becomes a place to live.][1]

Adorno
Minima Moralia

Taken from a text composed during the Second World War, the above epigraph is a formulation characteristic of Adorno. Aphoristically interweaving the personal and the philosophical, the particular and the universal, it consciously resists seamless integration into the totality of a philosophical system. Expressing his experience as an exile inhabiting what was for Adorno an especially strange life-world, and like many of the other reflections contained in *Minima Moralia*, it undermines the idea that Universal History could be construed in terms other than as a catastrophic logic stretching from the "slingshot to the megaton bomb."[2] In this sense, Adorno's writing constitutes the literary counterpart to atonal forms of the "New Music," whose partisan he undoubtedly was. For Adorno, who initially studied under Alban Berg in Vienna, New Music becomes not simply a mere analogue or trope but rather the concrete model for a writing that situates itself at the unstable boundary between art and philosophy. Existing precariously at this threshold, Adorno's writing is deeply suspicious of the impulse to communicate or reiterate a transparent content determined independently of its form of presentation. Yet, at the same time, it must avoid, lest it risk incoherence, a complete submersion in particularity.

Adorno's writing embodies the very paradox, then, of philosophy, on the side of the universal, and art, on the side of the particular: of "uttering the unutterable"(ND, 5). For this reason, and inasmuch as it is conscious of its own aporia, his writing, in the final instance, offers only cold comfort, for, as a place to live, it paradoxically takes its leave of the traditional idea of "homecoming." In this, it follows Schoenberg's undermining of the tonal system – the construction of music as a path or journey in which the destination is determined in advance as the return "home." Home in this sense becomes the point of arrival of the movement from a dominant to an "other" key, which serves as its negation, back to the "original key so that all *doubts* about where home is are dispelled."[3] As "atonal philosophy," therefore, Adorno's writing attempts to "do justice to all that the sharpened ear of the composer finds unresolved or antinomial in traditional music."[4] Such musical moments become ciphers for a happiness that was never realized. By emancipating the "unresolved" or "antinomial," writing intimates something of the "realm of freedom" suggested by Schoenberg's atonal compositions.[5] If New Music articulated a determinate negation of romanticism, then Adorno's atonal writing challenges the romantic conception of philosophy – understood by Novalis as a pervasive "homesickness," or "the urge to be at home everywhere."[6] Without a doubt, the most ambitious attempt to realize this conception of philosophy is Hegel's *Phenomenology of Spirit*. According to Hegel, while losing itself in moments of the most extreme forms of "otherness," Spirit nonetheless prevails in its drive, ultimately, to find its way back to itself. Indeed, Absolute Spirit is that which finds itself *at home* precisely in and through the conditions of it own exile. However, in the aftermath of the most horrific events of the twentieth century – for which the proper name "Auschwitz"[7] serves as the metonym – the Hegelian concept of experience, and with it the whole philosophical enterprise, enters into an irrevocable crisis.[8] As a German Jew, Adorno was precisely that "other" which Spirit must unburden itself of if it is truly to return home through the unfolding of Universal History; Spirit's triumphal homecoming is achieved, in other words, at the expense of the other who is forced to endure the privations of exile.

These reflections frame the following examination of the relation between Adorno and Heidegger in light of the much discussed parallels between negative dialectics and contemporary French thought.[9]

The latter has undergone a most significant transition from Hegel and Marx to Nietzsche and Heidegger that turns on the questions of "humanism" and the philosophical status of the subject.[10] Given that so much attention has been focused on this relation, it is unfortunate that comparatively little has been written on the complex and fraught question of Adorno's relation to Heidegger. In keeping with the spirit of Adorno's own antisystematic impulses, the aim here is not a comprehensive presentation, which would scarcely be appropriate in any case. Rather, what is proposed is a glimpse of the relation between the two thinkers through the specific constellation comprised of the problems of language, experience, and ethics embodied in the essay's epigraph. Such a reading seeks to lend a voice to an aspect of Adorno's work – what we might regard as its "silence" – that, in a manner of speaking, has been "drowned out" by the communication paradigm within the contemporary Critical Theory of Jürgen Habermas. Such a silence, which has an affinity with the silences of art, permits the often senseless prolixity of philosophical discourse to be heard.

That critical commentary on Adorno's relation to modern French thought has largely overlooked his connection with Heidegger is, itself, not entirely surprising, given what Herman Mörchen calls the "refused communication" [*Kommunikationsverweigerung*] between the two men after a brief meeting in 1929.[11] Indeed, it is appropriate that it is a refused communication that proves to be a vital, if mostly negative, link between these two most trenchant critics of communication.[12] Yet, in striking contrast to his friend and mentor Walter Benjamin[13] who, with Brecht, planned a reading group in the early 1930s oriented toward nothing less than the "destruction" of Heidegger's thought, Adorno addresses himself seriously to Heidegger throughout his career. From Adorno's inaugural lecture to the philosophy department at the University of Frankfurt,[14] the 1932 presentation to the Frankfurt *Kantgesellschaft*, "The Idea of Natural History," which draws Benjaminian and Lukácsian motifs into a dialectical negation of the categories of "Being" and "time,"[15] and the somewhat polemical *Jargon of Authenticity*[16] to radio addresses in the 1960s and his most important philosophical work, *Negative Dialectics*, Heidegger is the crucial interlocutor.[17]

Despite the importance of Heidegger's thinking as a foil for his own, Adorno's comportment toward Heidegger was occasionally abrasively polemical, even to the point of jeopardizing his stated

intention of providing an immanently critical reading of his philosophical adversary. While many of the recent discussions provoked
by the publication of Victor Farias's book *Heidegger and Nazism*[18]
have tried to be more or less delicate in characterizing the relation between philosophy and politics as that between "good" and "evil,"[19]
Adorno refused to mince words and, in the Frankfurt student newspaper *Diskus*, bluntly stated that Heidegger's thinking was "fascist
right down to its innermost components."[20] For his part, Heidegger
is alleged not to have been familiar with any of Adorno's writings –
a fact whose meaning, as Freud's active avoidance of Nietzsche
confirms,[21] is not unambiguous. His oblique references to the "reification of consciousness" in *Being and Time*[22] and his intriguing
remarks on Marx in the "Letter on Humanism" notwithstanding, Heidegger was largely indifferent to the materialist tradition.
Had he addressed himself to it in any thorough way, Heidegger no
doubt would have dismissed it as an exemplary manifestation of
Seinsvergessenheit [forgetfulness of Being] and the metaphysics of
subjectivity.[23]

I

The epigraph that begins this essay expresses in highly compressed
form Adorno's strange proximity to, yet fundamental distance from,
Heidegger. It is not difficult to hear in this formulation a kind of
anticipatory rejoinder to Heidegger's "Letter on Humanism." For
while Heidegger, too, emphasizes the necessary relation between
language and experience, his inflection is decidedly different. Such a
difference stems, I would suggest, from differences in the very concrete historical *experiences* of both thinkers, which, in turn, give rise
to divergent philosophical concepts of experience. It scarcely needs
to be remarked that Adorno, along with Horkheimer, Benjamin,
and Heidegger's own former students Herbert Marcuse and Hannah
Arendt, was among the legions of leftist and Jewish intellectuals who
were forcibly exiled or worse, whereas Heidegger, at least for a time,
viewed National Socialism as offering a solution to the looming crisis
of the West.[24]

As is well known, Adorno and Heidegger shared a particular affection for the German language. Heidegger believed that German
and Greek were the only authentic philosophical languages; one of

Adorno's principal reasons for returning to Germany after the war was a longing to write and speak in German. However, while Heidegger regarded the translation of Greek concepts into a corrupting Latin as an almost catastrophic moment in the forgetting of the primordial experience of Being,[25] Adorno viewed the spread of Latin as an important moment of genuine demythologization.[26] Indeed, the originality of both thinkers lies in their insistence on what is today, after the so-called linguistic turn, a commonplace: that philosophical discourse is bound by its own linguistic horizons. Heidegger effectively transformed phenomenology from a transcendental to a hermeneutic project by deconstructing the alleged purity of the transcendental ego by way of the existential analytic of *Dasein*. Far from being pure, according to Heidegger, every perception takes place in language qua interpretation. Similarly, Adorno argues that, its fetishization of "method" since Descartes notwithstanding, philosophy's tacit or overt dependence on texts confirms its inherently linguistic nature (ND, 55).

Taking this problem of language and reflection as their cue, then, Adorno and Heidegger pose the following question: How is it possible to think toward a form of experience that would not simply be the blind repetition of what "is"? Whereas Kant, upon entering his "critical" phase, sought to rethink metaphysics in such a way that it would not transgress the limit constituted by the realm of possible experience, Hegel famously argued that the identification of a limit is already a movement beyond it. Hegel therefore conceived the movement beyond the "Philosophy of Reflection" as, itself, the pathway of *experience*.[27] Hegel's solution was not, therefore, simply the sensuous intuition of a phenomenal object but a tracing of the unfolding of the subject-object relation itself. Experience becomes, for Hegel, a grasping of the identity of subject and object understood, in the final instance, as a mediation of Absolute Spirit; in the process, experience is rendered purely immanent. In opposition to Hegel, yet in a manner not entirely *unlike* him, Adorno and Heidegger aim at a form of experience that retraces, repeats, and ultimately pushes beyond the metaphysics of subjectivity in a way that breaks through such immanence and touches that which remains unthought.

As Shierry Weber Nicholsen has recently suggested, genuine experience, for Adorno, possesses three dimensions: "lived" particularity versus abstract repetition; accuracy, in as much as it is oriented specifically toward an object; and independence from a particular historical situation.²⁸ In Adorno's view, all three of these elements are simultaneously promised yet betrayed in the Hegelian concept of experience. Experience in the genuine sense is closed off by virtue of its reduction to philosophical concepts. According to Adorno, the traces of a mimetic loss of self in the other that were simultaneously present and forgotten in the dialectic could only be turned against the Hegelian concept (and thereby redeemed) by way of the experience of art.

In *Being and Time*, Heidegger likewise places the problem of experience at the heart of his project, though it must be remarked that this conception of experience was intended to be disorienting. Such a project was, of course, to engage in a *Destruktion* of Western metaphysics in such a way as to return to an allegedly more originary or authentic experience of the meaning of Being. Such an experience would displace and decenter its metaphysical reduction to "presence-at-hand" [*Vorhandenheit*].²⁹ After the so-called "turning" [*Kehre*] away from what he came to view as the subjectivistic starting point of *Being and Time*, experience could only be encountered in and through the enigma of a poetic language that simultaneously disclosed and concealed beings. Experience now came to be understood as an openness to precisely such a dynamic double movement.

That language lies at the heart of Adorno's concept of experience is clear in his repeated efforts to set into motion the dialectic between what he called "expression," or that which adheres to the particularity of the object almost to the point of incoherence, and "communication" through concepts that, ultimately, must sacrifice such particularity. Experience emerges from the "force field" constituted through these two moments of language. Such an intension is especially well captured in Adorno's portrait of Walter Benjamin: "He strove to give thought the density of experience without it having therefore lose any of its stringency."³⁰ Negative dialectics intends, in other words, to adhere as closely to the object as possible without relinquishing its conceptual moment (and hence philosophical truth claims). Significantly, the centrality of experience emerges in Adorno's immanent critique of Heidegger in *Negative Dialectics*, where he identifies in the latter's thought an essential moment of his own:

What is true in the concept of existence is the protest against a condition of society and of scientific thought that would expel *unregimented experience* [*der unregelmentierte Erfahrung*] – a condition that would virtually expel the subject as a moment of cognition. (ND, 123, emphasis added)

Adorno allies himself here with Heidegger and against "scientific thought," which we may read in this context as positivism. For both thinkers, positivism was premised on the reduction of language, as manifested, for instance, in the philosophy of the early Wittgenstein, to a transparent medium of representation.[31] Such a reductive understanding of language is the central premise of the correspondence theory of truth understood as the equivalence of thing and concept.[32] This conception of truth, which privileges the copula "is," leads to a violent negation of the historical dynamism of the object under the hegemony of a classifying, calculating gaze. Adorno calls such a conception of truth "identity-thinking," while Heidegger understands it as a metaphysics that has reached its "end" – in the sense of both culmination and exhaustion – in technology. For Adorno, identity-thinking results from the displacement of mimesis, understood as approximation, by a reductive form of pure imitation. For Heidegger, positivism represents the apotheosis of a philosophical tradition constituted in and through the "forgetting of Being" [*Seinsvergessenheit*]. This tradition precipitously reduces Being to what is enduringly present and in the process reifies and privileges the present over the past and the future. As we shall see, Adorno's and Heidegger's attempts to work free of such a reduction of experience move them down parallel paths toward a consideration of the intrinsic temporal dynamism of art.

It must be emphasized at the outset, however, that art – or, more properly, aesthetic experience – is not to be understood in the traditional way, as the subject's experience of an object, but rather as precisely that which constitutes the crisis of the identity of subject and object. For both Adorno and Heidegger, Kant's separation of art from science and morality constitutes what Jay Bernstein has called "aesthetic alienation," or the separation of the aesthetic from questions of cognition and ethics.[33] Inasmuch as they both seek to undermine this tripartite structure of critical philosophy, Adorno's and Heidegger's understandings of art are therefore properly thought of as "postaesthetic."[34] For both thinkers, it is by following the path opened up by the artwork that experience becomes possible. The imitation of what exists, as a hypostatization of the present, is transformed precisely by way of a repetition of imitation, but with a difference. Such a repetition comes about by way of the enigmatic manifestation of what Adorno calls the "truth content" of art and Heidegger calls the "setting to work" of truth. In other words, works of art repeat and retrace the reification of what "is" so as to break its spell.

II

Upon returning to Frankfurt in 1949, Adorno tried to persuade Horkheimer to review Heidegger's text *Holzwege*[35] for the journal *Der Monat*, stating that "Heidgger was *in favour* of false trails [*Holzwege*] that are not very different from our own."[36] It is in *Holzwege* perhaps more than any other text of Heidegger's that we find a thinking that shares a topos similar to that of Critical Theory, particularly in its attempt to lay bare the structure of the enframing (*Gestell*) that constitutes the essence of technology.[37] It is also where Heidegger engages in a close textual interpretation of the introduction to Hegel's *Phenomenology of Spirit* that runs parallel to yet (for obvious reasons) diverges from negative dialectics. We might say, then, that inasmuch as both seek to free experience from constitutive subjectivity in the direction of the "unthought," Adorno and Heidegger pursue *Holzwege*, pathless paths.

For Hegel, far from being pathless, the path of experience was, in contrast, *speculative* and therefore determined in advance as the self-unfolding of the Absolute – the repetition of beginning as end. The path of Spirit on the way back to itself as Absolute Knowledge is what is called "experience" [*Erfahrung*]. While characterized by moments of "doubt and despair," suffering, even death, experience is nonetheless "followed by a return to that truth again, after the doubt has been appropriately dispelled – so that at the end of this process the matter is taken to be what it was in the first place."[38] Decisive for this movement, at once forward and backward, is Spirit's achievement of being at home in its otherness; only through such a movement could Spirit, as Absolute Knowing or the subjectivity of the subject-object relation, be said to be truly at *home* in the world:

In pressing forward to its true existence, consciousness will arrive at a point at which it gets rid of its semblance of being burdened with something alien, with what is only for it, and some sort of "other," at a point where appearance becomes identical with essence, so that its exposition will coincide at just this point with the authentic Science of Spirit. And finally, when consciousness grasps its own essence, it will signify the nature of absolute knowledge itself.[39]

A *pathless* path, in contrast, is a path that resists such a determination, or more precisely a predetermination, and consequently seeks to open up a relation to the other that the philosophical tradition had always promised but repeatedly blocked. Such a path therefore has profoundly normative implications, not so much in the Kantian sense of morality but rather in the Hegelian sense of the relations of recognition constitutive of "ethical life." That is to say, the path opens up the possibility of a relation to the "nonidentical" that is based on the recognition of the cognitive limits of the compulsion to exhaust the other by way of its concepts in the interest of technological control and domination. Heidegger calls this kind of thinking *Gelassenheit* [releasement], a thinking that would open a relation toward the "earth" or matter in such a way that "sets it free to be nothing but itself."[40]

Adorno's and Heidegger's way of posing the problem of the relationship between language and experience might be illuminated through Nietzsche's early critique of truth. In "Truth and Lies in a Nonmoral Sense," Nietzsche argues that "truths are illusions which we have forgotten are illusions; they are metaphors that have become worn out and have been drained of sensuous force, coins that have lost their embossing and are now considered as metal and no longer as coins."[41] Intrinsic to the process of concept formation, then, is a certain kind of reification or forgetting. While originally signifying the experience of a particular, the word/concept then is extended to other particulars that might bear a superficial similarity to it. In the process, difference is sacrificed.

Every word instantly becomes a concept precisely insofar as it is not supposed to serve as a reminder of the unique and *entirely individual original experience* to which it owes its origin; but rather, a word becomes a concept insofar as it simultaneously has to fit countless more or less similar cases – which means, purely and simply, cases which are never equal and thus altogether unequal. Every concept arises from the equation of unequal things.[42]

Leaving aside the question of the possibility of an entirely original experience, Nietzsche's reflections provide a crucial framework for Adorno's and Heidegger's own engagement with metaphysics. As suggested above, Adorno roots the equation of what is unequal in the very structure of language, which is itself inextricable from the social *logic* in which it is embedded. The increasing fungibility of the signifier is the result of a historical process involving the progressive penetration of exchange value into ever remoter spheres of society qua *rationalization*.[43] Understood at the level of conceptual thought, such a process inverts the relation between "first" and "last" things. It is, put differently, the forgetfulness of that which makes thinking or identity possible in the first place, namely, what is nonidentical or what Adorno calls the "primacy of the object" [*Vorrang des Objekt*].

Heidegger also views the process of forgetting that constitutes Western metaphysics as reaching deeply into language. However, in contrast to Adorno, rather than rooting it in a distinctly *social* process, Heidegger understands such amnesia as the effect of particular interpretive practices, including the mistranslation of Greek words, and the experiences they name, into an alien Latin. Such translation is the first step on the catastrophic path toward the *subjection* of the question of Being to the categories of the subject. As we shall see, Adorno ultimately comes closer to Nietzsche, however, inasmuch as he undermines Heidegger's ontologization of language, the German language in particular, by showing how experience is made possible, not by a retrieval of the familiar in what has become unfamiliar, but rather by those moments of the strange, disclosed by foreign words, in what is familiar. Thus, if both Adorno and Heidegger contest Nietzsche's interpretation of truth as life's necessary illusion, they do so in opposite ways: While Heidegger returns to a future past in which a more primordial truth (as *aletheia*) displaces *adequatio*, Adorno makes truth conditional upon untruth, that is, upon a true society that "is" not yet.

III

Adorno and Heidegger take up Nietzsche's hermeneutics of suspicion vis-à-vis Husserl. The particular constellation of language and experience is therefore not simply fortuitous but stems from their individual critical encounters with transcendental phenomenology at the beginnings of their intellectual careers. The details of this relation lie beyond this essay's scope. However, it is appropriate to draw attention to the manner in which transcendental phenomenology represents for each the moment at which the edifice of the philosophical tradition begins to crumble and, in so doing, points beyond itself. Adorno wrote a dissertation on Husserl, with which he obtained his doctorate from the University of Frankfurt in 1924. This work presents a critique of Husserl from the standpoint of his teacher Hans Cornelius. Later, while in Oxford, he worked on the book that would later be published in 1956 as *Zur Metakritik der Erkenntistheorie*.[44] Heidegger's engagement with Husserl's *Logical Investigations* as a student played a central role in leading him away from theology in the direction of philosophy. It was in Husserl's seminars at the University of Freiburg, whose chair of philosophy Husserl assumed from Rickert in 1911, that Heidegger received a rigorous scientific [*Wissenschaftlich*] training in phenomenology. Heidegger later become Husserl's assistant and was to have coauthored the *Encyclopedia Britannica* entry on "Phenomenology" with him, but the plan never came to fruition.[45] As Robert D'Amico suggests, "The effect of Heidegger's break with traditional philosophical approaches, eventually including Husserl's own transcendental idealism, cannot be overestimated."[46] A glimpse at Adorno's and Heidegger's critiques of Husserl reveal that, while Husserl's thinking suggested a certain impulse in the direction of the "sensuous force" lying beneath concepts by way of the *epochē*, he failed to realize the extent to which it opened up the question of language.

Adorno transcribes Husserl's drive to achieve the "security" of the transcendental ego into signs and reads it allegorically as indicating the radical absence of such security. It is, in other words, an "unconscious transcription of history" inasmuch as the purportedly pure, unsullied contents of transcendental consciousness are suffused by the same social contents that it compulsively represses. Thus, "the real life-process of society is not something smuggled into philosophy through associates. It is rather the core of the contents of the logic itself" (ME, 26). Such a logic reveals the philosophical "need" for security amidst the antagonisms of a society in which just such security is absent. Husserl's attempt at making his philosophy concrete becomes illusory because he fails to reflect on this social logic.

The concrete was such by virtue of the history stored up in things which become objective through language.

Despite the devastating implications of his critique, Adorno recognizes the truth content of phenomenology. As a crystallizing moment of the dialectic of enlightenment – inasmuch as it pushes it to extremes as a form of thought that explicitly distills the contents of transcendental subjectivity *in the "things themselves"* – phenomenology represents a form of what Horkheimer and Adorno call "false projection."[47] In other words, it is a form of subjective projection on to the object, which nonetheless forgets itself qua projection. This is well captured in Adorno's reference to Benjamin's characterization, in a different context, of *Jugendstil* as "the dreamer who dreams he's waking up."[48] The task of a *materialist* philosophy, accordingly, is to rouse the dreamer from the dream that his projections are identical to the "things themselves."

This does not, however, amount to an abstract negation of projection per se, which Adorno regards as a necessary anthropological moment of cognition, but rather its reflective control. Controlled projection therefore involves reflection on the nature of this relation with the object. Such a form of projection is made conscious in the production and experience of the object in the realm of aesthetic experience. In other words, the truth content of phenomenology lies in the notion of "spontaneous receptivity,"[49] which can be achieved, not in an immediate way vis-à-vis nature qua imitation, but only in terms of the mimesis of the artwork – both in terms of its inner logic and the mimetic tracing of its unfolding.[50] Subject and object are inextricable moments within this dialectic, for it is precisely such a mimesis that makes genuine experience possible for the subject. We shall return to the significance of aesthetic experience for experience as such below. By displacing phenomenology in the direction of aesthetic experience, or what he calls "exact imagination," Adorno pushes it literally to the point of no return, that is, to the point where the structure of subjectivity is forced to open itself to what is not its own. Mimesis as the tracing of the object in figurative language, or "expression," forces the empty signifiers of "communication" to reveal those moments of nonidentity that they conceal.

The entire first division of *Being and Time* is an extended, if implicit, critique of the very transcendental phenomenology that makes Heidegger's project possible in the first place.[51] In establishing the "ontological difference" between Being and beings, Heidegger reaffirms phenomenology as transcendental, although in a way opposed to Husserl's positing of the purity of the transcendental ego. For Heidegger, the transcendental ego implies a "worldless subject," one that presupposes a particular interpretation of time as presence and is therefore extricated from the unique structure of temporality that, for Heidegger, constituted the essential, finite structure of *Dasein*. For Heidegger, far from being worldless, *Da*-sein was thrown into a world which was radically not of its own making and which, therefore, it could not fully thematize.[52] These worldly relations establish phenomenology as transcendental for *Dasein* (as the being for whom Being was a question) and as governed by the structure of "care" [*Sorge*]: It is thrown ahead of itself from the depths of the past toward the "possibility of its impossibility," toward the singularity of its own death.[53]

For Heidegger, the fundamental discovery of phenomenology is "categorial intuition" – the idea that the intuition of an object does not require, as is the case with Kant, the faculty of understanding to synthesize the manifold given in sensuous intuition but always already constitutes a nonsensuous categorial or "essential" unity. The interpretation that Husserl gives, failing of course to recognize it as an *interpretation*, follows the path laid out by the tradition. He reduces Being to the presence-at-hand or "object-thing," that which, as *Gegen-stand*, stands over and against a subject.[54] Heidegger's project, in contrast, aims at a purportedly more radical questioning, namely, at the *meaning* of Being. Therefore, the point of departure for *Being and Time* is that "the meaning of phenomenological description lies in interpretation."[55] With this shift, phenomenology is transformed from a "transcendental" to a "hermeneutical" enterprise. Thus, Heidegger's and Adorno's reading of Husserl converge precisely in their attempts to displace categorial intuition via an understanding of the necessarily temporal and linguistic character of experience that becomes explicit or thematic in the work of art.

IV

If Adorno and Heidegger begin with parallel engagements with Husserl, in particular with the concept of categorial intuition, they are repeatedly led back to the path that takes them to Hegel and, indeed, beyond. For if Hegel's concept of metaphysical experience is the richest, it is also the most problematic. The necessary forgetfulness of the concept unearthed by Nietzsche is exemplified in extreme form as Absolute Knowing. As suggested previously, Hegel conceives of the unfolding of the subject-object relation via the path of "doubt and despair" as re-collection [Er-innerung], the process by which what was externalized, made other, is reinternalized. However, such recollection is simultaneously a *forgetting* inasmuch as that which is not-Spirit, the "nonidentical" or the "thing," is transformed into a kind of mirror reflecting Spirit back to itself. Hegel's thinking is the apotheosis of the metaphysics of subjectivity and *in that very apotheosis* it points beyond itself. Just as Hegel had noted in discussing Kant's critical philosophy, the identification of a limit is always already a step beyond it (ME, 12).

For Adorno, the very end of philosophy that Hegel announces was delayed because its realization in the world was aborted. The belated existence of philosophy can no longer consign the truth of art to the past, as Hegel does in the introduction to his *Aesthetics*, for the latter becomes a crucial supplement in the wake of the collapse of metaphysical experience. Indeed, as in Adorno's reading of Beckett,[56] art plays a crucial role in making the collapse of metaphysical meaning *mean* not just nothing. For Heidegger, the end of philosophy in technological thinking points the way to a possible new beginning as the repetition of philosophy's primordial origins in the artwork. While Adorno (with Horkheimer) repeats the path of experience, which plays itself out in the cunning of mythological reason as the "dialectic of enlightenment," Heidegger refers to such a path of experience as the history of Western metaphysics, with its compulsive forgetting of Being.[57]

In *Dialectic of Enlightenment*, composed with Horkheimer during the war years, Adorno retraces and repeats Spirit's path of experience, the "ruse of reason," as a sacrificial logic. Adorno and Horkheimer's self-conscious repetition of Hegel's path of doubt and despair is undertaken with the aim of rescuing those moments within it that point beyond the repetition of constitutive subjectivity as mythology. The retracing of enlightenment as myth is undertaken therefore in the service of enlightenment itself. Shattering the theodicy of the concept, it shows that Spirit's return home to itself does not culminate in plenitude and fullness but rather in a living death. The dialectic of self-preservation at all costs, in other words, issues in the insane denial of the very life it seeks to preserve.

Such a dialectic is revealed through an allegorical reading of the *Odyssey* as the "primal history of subjectivity" in which "the self does not constitute the fixed antithesis to adventure, but in its rigidity molds itself only by way of that antithesis: being an entity only in the diversity of that which denies all unity" (DA, 47). Like Spirit on its path of "doubt and despair," Odysseus loses himself in order to find himself. However, rather than ultimately finding himself through the progressive subordination of nature to his own purposes, Odysseus loses himself by way of a repetition of blind nature:

The estrangement from nature that he brings about is realized in the process of the abandonment to nature he contends with in each adventure; and, ironically, when he, inexorable, returns home, the inexorable force he commands itself triumphs as the judge and avenger of the legacy of the powers from which he escaped. (DA, 48)

The very *inexorability* of the return, the fact of its being determined in advance, confirms not a break with but a repetition of the mythological "always-the-same" [*das Immergleiche*].

The sacrificial logic of the dialectic of enlightenment consists, then, in the repetition of sacrifice, by means of which external nature is mastered through *renunciation* or self-sacrifice. In other words, the control of external nature is paid for by an equivalent mastering of the spontaneous impulses of the subject itself. This is well exemplified by Odysseus's encounter with the Sirens, who signify the past as the promise of a future happiness. This episode allegorizes the detemporalization of time, its becoming increasingly abstract, and its reduction to the automatic repetition of the always-the-same. As suggested previously, this is conditional upon the progressive displacement of mimesis as approximation to nature, as manifested in magic, by a deathly form of imitation. The latter is a morbid imitation of, and consequent adaptation to, a nature that through its disenchantment has become lifeless. The speculative dialectic is thereby given an ironic turn: The mirror in which Spirit seeks to catch a glimpse of its own reflection reflects back not plenitude but death. Hence, "for the ego which sinks into the meaningless abyss of itself, objects become allegories of destruction which contain the meaning of its own downfall" (DA, 192).

This displacement results in the modern differentiation of language into expression and communication, which underwrites the modern separation of art from science [*Wissenschaft*],[58] as the former becomes the last refuge for a mimesis that undergoes destruction in the course of the dialectic of enlightenment. It is precisely because it becomes the repository for such mimetic behaviour that art is the place where enlightenment may, with the aid of philosophy, reflect upon itself. While expression permits the thing to be itself, "for itself," the progressively empty signifier, indifferent to any particular content, makes it available "for" others. Negative dialectics from one side and art from the other attempt to play this dialectic out by seeking to "utter the unutterable."

The archaic promise of the Sirens therefore lives on and makes a belated return, transfigured, in the "unresolved and antinomical" moments of the most advanced artworks, with their explosively Dionysian powers of dedifferentiation. Read through the allegorical structure of the chiasmus of natural history, Odysseus's journey becomes demythologization as the repetition of myth, and myth becomes the unfolding of enlightenment. Odysseus is compelled to repeat myth at the very moment that he believes himself to have broken with it. In the process, history is revealed as an enchanted "second nature" while nature is understood in terms of an all too historical disenchantment and domination.[59]

Where enlightenment and myth converge most explicitly is in the anthropomorphism culminating in Oedipus's answer to the riddle of the Sphinx: "It is man."[60] This is the philosophical gesture[61] *par excellence* inasmuch as it subsumes the particular beneath a universal concept, which enables the subject to see only his own image reflected back at him. For Hegel, this becomes the central moment of art as embodying Absolute Spirit, as the sensuous manifestation of the Idea. For the moment Oedipus solves the riddle of the Sphinx, he at the same time solves, once and for all, the problem of "unconscious symbolism," which leads directly to a privileging of art as the manifestation of Spirit over the beauty of nature.

The dialectic of enlightenment reaches its culmination in the culture industry, in which experience is effectively abolished since "every detail is so firmly stamped with sameness that nothing can appear which is not marked at birth, or does not meet with approval at first sight" (DA, 128). Thus, the Hollywood film, for example, provides the spectator with a "standardized echo of himself to which he hearkens."[62] The spectator becomes imprisoned as the object of the very spectacle he apprehends. As a repetition of Oedipus's fate, insofar as it seeks to be total, enlightenment's vision is ultimately self-revoking. It can only be rescued through a reflection on the finitude of the structures of its own cognition by way of the enigmatic play of the artwork, which affords a shimmering glimpse of the non-identical not yet drowned in the floodlight of subjective reason. In this way, art suggests the possibility of "the resistance of the eye that does not want the colours of the world to fade" (ND, 405).

V

For Heidegger, "Western metaphysics" is also a path characterized by a compulsive forgetting or *Seinsvergessenheit* – the forgetfulness of Being, understood as genitive subjective and objective. Heidegger's own path beyond it, his *Holzwege*, can be read as the gradual transition from the former to the latter. In *Being and Time*, Heidegger poses the question of Being through a *Destruktion* of the tradition. Such an engagement is not to be understood as a purely negative enterprise but as an enterprise that makes possible an allegedly more *primordial* experience of Being which remains inaccessible to the tradition. Heidegger's aim, of course, is to raise anew the question of Being through a thoroughgoing analysis of the existential situation, the throwness, of *Dasein* – the Being for whom being is a question.

In his later work, after the so-called turning, which some commentators have read as his attempt to distance himself from the susceptibility of his earlier writings to the seductions of National Socialism,[63] Heidegger's inflection is decidedly on the genitive objective. Otto Pöggeler has described Heidegger's turning as a shift from the interpretation of the meaning of Being, understood as *Dasein's* "elucidation" of this question, toward "emplacement." Emplacement is a kind of comportment towards Being that could not be simply understood as a "questioning." The shift from the former to the latter constitutes Heidegger's attempt to free his thinking from the subjectivism of the tradition which he believes himself to have uncritically repeated in his "existential analytic of *Dasein*." Thus, asks Pöggeler, "does not the analytic of the understanding of Being itself already stand under the destiny of the unconcealment of Being? Is not the entire approach (which begins with the subject as existence) determined by the way which the occurrence of truth has gone in the West?"[64] This questioning of his early work leads Heidegger to probe the question of "the occurrence of truth in the West." This is the shift from an interpretation of *Seinsvergessenheit* as *subjective* to *objective* genitive – that is, the pathway leading from the "being for whom Being is a question," namely, human *Dasein*, to Being per se, which, as a "destining" or a "sending," places man in question. Thus, elucidation

characterizes perhaps more precisely a thinking which belongs to that un-concealment whose appropriative occurring always situates Being as the openness of beings and of our questioning about Being. The task of the thinking which emplaces is to preserve elucidating from hypostatizing the elucidated essence into a constant presence. . . . Emplacement is thereby less of a doing of the thinking subject than a becoming emplaced through the tradition.[65]

With this transition from "thinking" to "emplacement," Heidegger's understanding of experience is correspondingly transformed. In the later works, as Pöggeler indicates, such as *On the Way to Language*, emplacement implies a concept of experience in terms of "going, to attain something underway, to achieve it by traveling upon the way." Crucially, experience is understood here as the leaving of one abode for a point of arrival that has yet to be determined, indeed, that is to a certain extent undeterminable, the "unthought." For Heidegger now displaces *Dasein* for Being itself.

Seinsvergessenheit thus becomes Being's forgetfulness of itself. Metaphysics, characterized as the reduction of Being to being, or en-during *presence*, culminates for Heidegger in a metaphysics of sub-jectivity. Indeed, like the formation of the subject allegorized by the *Odyssey*, Heidegger understands such a metaphysics as fundamen-tally anthropomorphic. In other words, it is a form of thought that forgets that Being lies outside of man and his attempts at revealing Being as a "challenging-forth" [*Herausfordern*] and that, like the cul-ture industry, it perpetuates the illusion that "man everywhere and always encounters only himself."[66] Modern humanity becomes so engrossed in challenging forth that this mode of revealing is no longer understood as one claim amongst others; it can scarcely be viewed as a *particular* comportment toward beings. Like Adorno, Heidegger views the metaphysics of subjectivity as inherently self-destructive:

As soon as what is unconcealed no longer concerns man even as object, but exclusively as standing-reserve, and man in the midst of objectlessness is nothing but the orderer of the standing-reserve, then he comes to the very brink of a precipitous fall, that is, he comes to the point where he himself will have to be taken as standing-reserve.[67]

The subject finds itself therefore sucked into the vortex of the ordering and manipulating of objects – a process that it believes itself to control. Nonetheless, if Adorno understands the logic of society as deeply penetrating precisely those forms of thought that most stubbornly insist on their own purity, then Heidegger views metaphysics as ultimately a destiny that discharges in modern technology. While fundamentally encompassing and determining the social, technology ultimately is "nothing technological" and is therefore nothing social. It is, rather, a destiny of Being itself. Adorno and Heidegger thus approach the same constellations of problems, though from opposite sides.

What we have been suggesting thus far is this: Adorno and Heideger repeat the Hegelian pathway of "doubt and despair," yet with a *difference*. They show that, rather than leading it back to itself, such a pathway does not constitute the negation of doubt and despair through which Spirit is formed. The path of experience, understood in terms of a metaphysics of the subject, is, in contrast, a pathway of self-destruction. Therefore, while it might be possible to argue that philosophy indeed has come to an end in the Hegelian system, in having come to such an end it paradoxically lives on. For Adorno, it lives on owing to the aborted realization of philosophy in the world – a failure which calls for a "conceptual" critique of the concept. For Heidegger, the "end," understood as the exhaustion of philosophy as technology, reveals philosophy's "essence," which is nothing other than a particular way of revealing beings – the repetition of a most primordial past, that is, the prehistory of philosophy itself, as future.

Inspired by Lyotard's reflections on the Kantian concept of the sublime, Tom Huhn provides a careful reading of Heidegger's understanding of the dynamic movement of the artwork, its setting truth to work, as the movement of "mimesis." The inherent dynamism of the artwork interrupts or forestalls the subject's mis-recognition of itself as something objective and static. The dialectic of enlightenment and the history of Western metaphysics represent two parallel ways of understanding the unfolding of such objective subreption: as repetitions of the process by which the subject mis-recognizes itself in a world thought to be totally of its own making. It is through the work of art that this process becomes available for reflection. Inasmuch as the artwork forestalls such a misrecognition, it has an effect running parallel to Kant's sublime. As the "refusal of displacement of subjectivity by objective subreption," the sublime becomes the "demand...for the actual *production* of the subject."[68]

The demand for the production of a subject is temporal at its very core in that it is a movement against *false* portrayal and imitation ("mimesis-unto-death") and the repetition of what "is" – as precisely that which underwrites such misrecognition. Instead, this movement anticipates the production of what "is" not yet.[69] The sublime therefore puts into play the aporia that lies at the heart of all thinking: that cognition is utterly dependent, not upon determinative judgment involving the subsumption of particulars under preexisting universals, but upon reflective judgment or the production of such universals in the first instance. We could say, then, that for both Adorno and Heidegger the experience of the work of art shatters or at least displaces the passive imitation of that which "is" and makes possible a different, nonreductive constellation in which the relation between the "identical and nonidentical," disclosure and concealment, is to be understood.

At the same time, however, it is not entirely clear that it is possible to understand both interpretations of the role of art as demanding the production of a *subject*. This becomes a crucial, if subtle, difference between Adorno and Heidegger, and according to Adorno himself, it is in philosophy where the nuances make all the difference.[70] While Adorno draws upon Wagner's *Parsifal* and argues that "only the spear that inflicted the wound can heal it,"[71] Heidegger, in contrast, suggests with Hölderlin that "Where the danger lies/Grows that which saves."[72] Thus, while Adorno insists on using the "strength" of the subject's own experience to move beyond constitutive subjectivity, Heidegger suggests that an understanding of the path beyond the metaphysics of subjectivity is itself a lineament of Being. Being therefore constitutes its own saving power. This becomes a fateful disclosure of *technē* as itself a way of revealing beings or the modern form of a primordial poiesis.

The differences between Heidegger and Adorno in their concepts of experience can, as I have suggested above, ultimately be traced back to their different social and historical conditions of possibility. Heidegger is led, again and again, to turn a blind eye to precisely this all too ontic realm of the social and the historical. This is exemplified by a passage appearing near the end of "Building Dwelling Thinking." There Heidegger proclaims,

> However hard and bitter, however hampering and threatening the lack of houses remains, the *real plight of dwelling* does not lie merely in a lack of houses. The real plight of dwelling is indeed older than the world wars with their destruction, older also than the increase in the earth's population and the condition of industrial workers.[73]

The real plight of dwelling, argues Heidegger, consists in humanity's fundamental homelessness, that is, its estrangement from language – the house of Being. Adorno, in contrast, turns the suffering that results from actual history – the very history which, as we have already remarked, turned Adorno into an exile – against the idea of Universal History. Thus, "[f]or he who no longer has a homeland, writing becomes a place to live"(MM, 87). However, in the end, one cannot seek refuge, as Heidegger does, in language: "In the end, the writer is not even allowed to live in his writing"(MM, 87). To seek refuge in language is to be an accomplice in reification, for it is to forget language's nonorganic nature. It is, then, to succumb to a "jargon of authenticity."

Drawing on his experience of exile, to which he returns repeatedly, Adorno argues that it is precisely the *Fremdwörter* (foreign words), exiles from other languages, that disenchant language by recalling the nonidentity between word and thing. In their interruption of the "the illusion that what is said is immediately equivalent to what is meant," foreign words "preserve something of the utopia of language, a language without earth, without subjection to the spell of historical existence, a utopia that lives on unawarely in the childlike use of language."[74] While the movement of truth in the artwork precipitously comes to a halt in a reenchanted language as the house of Being, Adorno takes leave of such a home by means of that which is irreducibly "other."

Referring to Nietzsche's remark in the *Gay Science* that it was his good fortune not to have been the owner of a house, Adorno remarked, "Today we should have to add: it is part of morality not to be at home in one's home" (MM, 39). There is, in other words, a profoundly ethical moment in the refusal to be at home, for when one finds oneself at home, all too at home, it often signifies a self-satisfied indifference to or at best a benign tolerance of the stranger. The moral content of not being at home is not far removed, then, from the thought of Emmanuel Levinas. Also profoundly marked by the experience of exile, dislocation, and the horror of Auschwitz, Levinas's own writings – writings that are simultaneously with and against Heidegger – suggest that the essence of the "ethical relation" is constituted by a welcoming of the other. In charting his own philosophical path, beyond both the metaphysical tradition and the fundamental ontology that seeks to "destroy" it, Levinas states that "the transcendence of thought remains closed in itself despite all its adventures – which in the last analysis are purely imaginary, or are adventures traversed as by Ulysses: on the way home."[75] In this, he is closer to Adorno than Derrida, with whom he has been most closely associated, inasmuch as alterity for him is not an effect of textuality, the differing, deferring play of signification; rather, it is reflected phenomenologically in the face of the other. In this respect, Levinas therefore would be in agreement, despite his differences – which it would be truly an act of violence to efface – with Adorno's comment that "good would be nothing but what has escaped from ontology"(ND, 122).

NOTES

I would like to thank John Abromeit, Raj Gandesha, Tom Huhn, Martin Jay, and Charles Reeve for helpful comments on previous drafts of this essay.
1. Theodor W. Adorno, *Minima Moralia: Reflexionen aus dem beschä-digten Leben* (Frankfurt: Suhrkamp, 1951), 152. Translated by E. F. N. Jephcott under the title as *Minima Moralia: Reflections from Damaged Life* (London: Verso, 1978), 87. Hereafter cited as MM. Page numbers refer to the English translation.

2. Theodor W. Adorno, *Negative Dialectics*, trans. E. B. Ashton (New York: Continuum Press, 1987), 320. Hereafter cited as ND.

3. Michael Hall, *Leaving Home: A Conducted Tour of Twentieth Century Music with Simon Rattle* (London: Faber and Faber, 1996), 25 (emphasis added).

4. Theodor W. Adorno, *Quasi una fantasia*, trans. Rodney Livingstone (London: Verso, 1992), 262. Hereafter cited as Q. "Atonal philosophy" is Martin Jay's formulation; see Jay, *Adorno* (Cambridge, Mass.: Harvard University Press, 1984).

5. Theodor W. Adorno, "Arnold Schoenberg, 1874–1951," in *Prisms*, trans. Samuel Weber and Shierry Weber (Cambridge., Mass.: MIT Press, 1981), 159.

6. Cited in Georg Lukács, *Theory of the Novel: A Historico-Philosophical Essay on the Forms of Great Epic Literature*, trans. A. Bostock (Cambridge, Mass.: MIT Press, 1971), 29.

7. For an examination of the role of the name in Heidegger and Adorno, see Alexander Garcia Düttmann, *Das Gedächtnis des Denkens: Versuch über Heidegger und Adorno* (Frankfurt: Suhrkamp, 1991).

8. This does not mean, however, that Adorno opts for an abstract negation of the concept; rather, he insists on an immanent critique of Hegel. This is what most sharply distinguishes him from the French reception of Hegel in the 1960s. See Theodor W. Adorno, *Hegel: Three Studies*, trans. Shierry Weber Nicholsen (Cambridge, Mass.: MIT Press, 1993).

9. For one of the few interpretations that engages Adorno's concept of mimesis with Heidegger's reading of the origin of the artwork framed by contemporary French thought, see Tom Huhn, "The Movement of Mimesis: Heidegger's 'Origin of the Work of Art' in Relation to Adorno and Lyotard," *Philosophy and Social Criticism* 22, no. 4 (1996): 45–69. For an interpretation of Adorno in relation to Derrida's critique of Husserl, see Sabine Wilke, "Adorno and Derrida on Husserl," *Telos* 84 (summer 1990): 177–3. For suggestions of parallels of a more general nature between Adorno and poststructuralism or postmodernism, see Jay, *Adorno*; Mark Ryan, *Marxism and Deconstruction* (Baltimore: Johns Hopkins University Press, 1982); Peter Dews, *Logics of Disintegration* (London: Verso, 1987); Christoph Menke, *The Sovereignty of Art*, trans. Neil Solomon (Cambridge, Mass.: MIT Press, 1998), Jay Bernstein, *The Fate of Art* (Oxford: Blackwell, 1992); Shierry Weber Nicholsen, *Exact Imagination, Late Work: On Adorno's Aesthetics* (Cambridge, Mass.: MIT Press, 1997); Eric Krakauer, *The Disposition of the Subject* (Evanston, Ill.: Northwestern University Press, 1998); Samir Gandesha, "The Theatre of the Other: Adorno, Poststructuralism and the

Critique of Identity," *Philosophy and Social Criticism* 17, no. 3 (1991): 243–63.

10. See Vincent Descombes, *Modern French Philosophy* (Cambridge: Cambridge University Press, 1980).

11. Herman Mörchen, *Adorno und Heidegger: Untersuchung einer philosophischen Kommunikationsverweigerung* (Stuttgart: Klett-Cotta, 1981), and Fred Dallmayr's extended review of the book in *Life-World, Modernity and Critique* (Cambridge: Polity Press, 1991), 44–71. Dallmayr's work represents a significant attempt to think Adorno and Heidegger together, albeit from a Heideggerian perspective. See also the insightful piece by David Michael Levin, "What-Is? On Mimesis and the Logic of Identity and Difference in Heidegger and the Frankfurt School," *International Studies in Philosophy* 28, no. 4 (1996): 41–60.

12. For Adorno, truth manifests itself not in the "discursive redemption" of validity claims but rather through failed communications. For instance, in *Negative Dialectics* (p. 48), he claims, "Only thoughts which cannot understand themselves are true." Similarly, Heidegger is sharply critical of what he calls the "idle chatter" [*Gerede*] of "*das Man*" for its instrumentalization of language. See *Being and Time*, trans. John Macquarrie and Edward Robinson (San Francisco: Harper and Row, 1962), pars. 34, 35.

13. Yet, Benjamin's and Heidegger's concerns remain strangely similar. See Rebecca Comay, "Framing Redemption: Aura, Origin, Technology in Benjamin and Heidegger," in *Ethics and Danger: Essays on Heidegger and Continental Thought*, ed. A. B. Dallery and C. E. Scott (Albany, N.Y.: SUNY Press, 1992), 139–69. For an interesting attempted synthesis of Heideggerian and Benjaminian motifs, see Peter Osborne's *Politics of Time* (London: Verso, 1995).

14. Theodor W. Adorno, "The Actuality of Philosophy," *Telos*, no. 31 (Spring 1977): 120–33.

15. Theodor W. Adorno, "The Idea of Natural History," trans. Robert Hullot-Kentor, *Telos*, no. 60 (Summer 1984): 111–24.

16. See Theodor W. Adorno, *The Jargon of Authenticity*, trans. Kurt Tarnowski and Frederic Will (Evanston, Ill: Northwestern University Press, 1973).

17. Indeed, Habermas states that Adorno's *Aesthetic Theory*, published posthumously, comes "shockingly close" to Heideggerian ontology; see *The Theory of Communicative Action*, vol. I, trans. Tom McCarthy (Boston: Beacon Press, 1984), 385.

18. Victor Farias, *Heidegger and Nazism*, ed. Tom Rockmore and Joseph Margolis (Philadelphia: Temple University Press, 1989). For the ensuing political and philosophical fallout, see Richard Wolin, ed., *The Heidegger*

Controversy (New York: Columbia University Press, 1991), and Tom Rockmore and Joseph Margolis, eds., *The Heidegger Case* (Philadelphia: Temple University Press, 1992).

19. See, for instance, Rüdiger Safranski, *Martin Heidegger: Between Good and Evil*, trans. Ewald Osers (Cambridge, Mass.: Harvard University Press, 1998).

20. Cited in Julian Young, *Heidegger, Philosophy, Nazism* (Cambridge: Cambridge University Press, 1997), 54.

21. See Peter Gay, *Freud: A Life for Our Time* (New York: Anchor, 1989), 45.

22. Lucien Goldmann argues that *Being and Time* can be considered as a rejoinder to Lukács's *History and Class Consciousness*, published in 1923, with "Being" as the counterpart to Lukács's concept of totality. While certainly thought provoking, Goldmann's interpretation is not always persuasive. See his *Lukács and Heidegger*, trans. W. Q. Boelhower (London: Routledge and Kegan Paul, 1977).

23. For Post-Heideggerian reflections along these lines, see Jean-Luc Nancy, *The Inoperative Community*, trans. Peter Connor et al. (Minneapolis: University of Minnesota Press, 1991), in which he argues against the notion that community can be understood as the work of collective production.

24. See Anson Rabinbach, "The Letter on Humanism as Text and Event," *New German Critique*, no. 62 (spring-summer 1994), 3–38.

25. See, for example, Martin Heidegger, "The Origin of the Work of Art," in *Poetry, Language, Thought*, trans. Albert Hofstadter (New York: Harper and Row, 1971), 23.

26. See Theodor W. Adorno, "Words from Abroad," in *Notes to Literature*, vol. 1, trans. Shierry Weber Nicholsen (New York: Columbia University Press, 1991).

27. For Hegel's critique of the "philosophy of reflection" see G. W. F. Hegel, *The Difference between Fichte's and Schelling's Systems of Philosophy*, trans. H. S. Harris and Walter Cerf (Albany, N.Y.: SUNY Press, 1977).

28. Nicholsen, *Exact Imagination, Late Work*, 51.

29. Heidegger, *Being and Time*, pars. 6, 7, 14.

30. Theodor W. Adorno, "A Portrait of Walter Benjamin," in *Prisms*, trans. Samuel Weber and Shierry Weber (Cambridge, Mass.: MIT Press, 1981), 240.

31. Ludwig Wittgenstein, *Tractatus Logico-Philosophicus*, trans. C. K. Ogden (London: Routledge and Kegan Paul, 1988).

32. For their respective critiques of truth as *adequatio*, see, for instance, Adorno's *Hegel: Three Studies*, esp. chap. 1, and Heidegger's "The

Meaning of Plato's Cave," *Great Thinkers on Plato*, ed. Barry Gross (New York: Putnam, 1968).

33. Bernstein, *Fate of Art*, 1–16. For an interpretation that seeks to show how questions of science and morality are inextricably bound up with aesthetic questions, see John Zammito, *The Genesis of Kant's Critique of Judgment* (Chicago: University of Chicago Press, 1992).

34. Bernstein, *Fate of Art*, 3.

35. Martin Heidegger, *Holzwege* (Frankfurt: Vittorio Klostermann, 1950).

36. Cited in Rolf Wiggershaus, *The Frankfurt School: Its History, Theories and Political Significance*, trans. Michael Robertson (Cambridge: Polity Press, 1994), 593 (translation amended).

37. See Krakauer, *Disposition of the Subject*.

38. G. W. F. Hegel, *Phenomenology of Spirit*, trans. A. V. Miller (Oxford: Oxford University Press, 1977), sec. 78.

39. Hegel, *Phenomenology of Spirit*, sec. 89.

40. Heidegger, "Origin of the Work of Art," 64.

41. Friedrich Nietzsche, *Philosophy and Truth: Selections from Nietzsche's Notebooks of the Early 1870's*, trans. David Breazeale (Atlantic Highlands, N.J.: Humanities Press International, 1979), 84.

42. Nietzsche, *Philosophy and Truth*, 83. See also Jay, *Adorno*, for Adorno's indebtedness to Nietzsche's understanding of reification.

43. See *Quasi una fantasia*, where Adorno argues that the New Music dissociates itself from the reified form of language, "which degrades the particular into a token, into the superannuated signifier of fossilized subjective meanings" (p. 2).

44. Translated by Willis Domingo under the title *Against Epistemology: A Metacritique* (Oxford: Basil Blackwell, 1982). Hereafter cited as ME.

45. Were it not for Heidegger's malicious treatment of Husserl after 1933, one would be tempted to say that Heidegger took to heart Nietzsche's dictum in *Thus Spoke Zarathustra* (trans. R. J. Hollingdale [London: Penguin, 1986] that "[o]ne repays a teacher badly if one remains only a pupil" (p. 103).

46. Robert D'Amico, *Contemporary Continental Philosophy* (Boulder, Colo.: Westview Press, 1990), 49.

47. Max Horkheimer and Theodor W. Adorno, *Dialectic of Enlightenment*, trans. John Cumming (New York: Seabury Press, 1972), 92–9. Hereafter cited as DA.

48. See Adorno, *Against Epistemology*, 138, and "Why Still Philosophy," in *Critical Models: Interventions and Catchwords*, trans. Henry Pickford (New York: Columbia University Press, 1998), 13.

49. Nicholsen, *Exact Imagination, Late Work*, 18.

50. See Nicholsen, *Exact Imagination, Late Work*, especially chap. 3.

51. See, for instance, Heidegger, *Being and Time*, par. 7, and D'Amico, *Contemporary Continental Philosophy*, chap. 2.
52. Heidegger, *Being and Time*, pars. 39, 40.
53. Heidegger, *Being and Time*, par. 41.
54. See Martin Heidegger, *The History of the Concept of Time*, trans. T. Kisiel (Indianapolis: Indiana University Press, 1992), esp. chap. 3.
55. Heidegger, *Being and Time*, par. 7.
56. Theodor W. Adorno, "Trying to Understand *Endgame*," *Notes to Literature*, vol. 1, trans. Shierry Weber Nicholsen (New York: Columbia University Press, 1991).
57. See David Roberts, "Art and Myth: Adorno and Heidegger," *Thesis Eleven* 58 (August 1999), 19–34.
58. See Bernstein, *Fate of Art*, 1–16.
59. See also Adorno, "Idea of Natural History."
60. See Robert Hullot-Kentor, "Back to Adorno," *Telos*, no. 81 (Fall 1989): 5–29, on the importance of Oedipus in the original conception of the text. See also Samir Gandesha, "Enlightenment as Tragedy: Reflections on Adorno's Ethics," *Thesis Eleven* 65 (May 2001): 109–30.
61. See Jean-Joseph Goux, *Oedipus: Philosopher*, trans. Catherine Porter (Stanford: Stanford University Press, 1993).
62. Theodor W. Adorno, *Aesthetic Theory*, trans. Robert Hullot-Kentor (Minneapolis: University of Minnesota Press, 1996), 17.
63. See, for instance, Phillippe Lacoue-Labarthe, *Heidegger, Art and Politics*, trans. C. Turner (Oxford: Basil Blackwell, 1990).
64. Otto Pöggeler, *Martin Heidegger's Path of Thinking*, trans. Daniel Magurshak and Sigmund Barber (Atlantic Highlands, N.J.: Humanities Press International, 1987), 221.
65. Pöggeler, *Heidegger's Path of Thinking*, 230–1.
66. Martin Heidegger, "The Question Concerning Technology," *Basic Writings*, ed. David Farrell Krell (New York: Harper and Row, 1977), 308.
67. Heidegger, "Question Concerning Technology," 308. Adorno comes extremely close to Heidegger's formulation when he states, in the context of addressing those hostile toward electronic music, "Nor should he be astonished to hear in tones of utter conviction that everything depends on people themselves, tones that set out to make us forget the extent to which people have become objects – namely, the objects of human relations" (Q, 266).
68. Huhn, "Movement of Mimesis," 50–1.
69. Huhn, "Movement of Mimesis," 55.
70. Theodor W. Adorno, "A Portrait of Walter Benjamin," in *Prisms*, trans. Samuel Weber and Shierry Weber (Cambridge, Mass.: MIT Press, 1981), 231.

71. Adorno, *Hegel*, 74.

72. Heidegger, "Question Concerning Technology," 316. Significantly, Horkheimer and Adorno quote this line in *Dialectic of Enlightenment* (p. 47) some five years prior to Heidegger, to refer to the manner in which Odysseus, like the Hegelian master, is able to turn danger to his own advantage.

73. Martin Heidegger, "Building Dwelling Thinking," in *Poetry, Language, Thought*, trans. Albert Hofstadter (San Francisco: Harper and Row, 1975), 161.

74. Adorno, "Words from Abroad," 192.

75. Emmanuel Levinas, *Totality and Infinity: An Essay on Exteriority*, trans. Alphonso Lingis (The Hague: Martinus Nijhoff, 1979), 27.

5   Is Experience Still in Crisis?

Reflections on a Frankfurt School Lament

Let me begin with two quotations:

> The identity of experience in the form of a life that is articulated and possesses internal continuity – and that life was the only thing that made the narrator's stance possible – has disintegrated. One need only note how impossible it would be for someone who participated in the war to tell stories about it the way people used to tell stories about their adventures.[1]

> [The war is] as totally divorced from experience as is the functioning of a machine from the movement of the body, which only begins to resemble it in pathological states. ... Life has changed into a timeless succession of shocks, interspersed with empty, paralyzed intervals. ... The total obliteration of the war by information, propaganda commentaries, with cameramen in the first tanks and war reporters dying heroic deaths, the mishmash of enlightened manipulation of public opinion and oblivious activity: all this is another expression for the withering of experience, the vacuum between men and their fate, in which their real fate lies.[2]

For those conversant with the history of Critical Theory, the lament expressed in these two citations will immediately sound familiar. If asked to identify their source, they would be likely to point to Walter Benjamin's celebrated essay of 1936, "The Storyteller," in which the First World War is blamed for starting a process that has impoverished something called experience (*Erfahrung*, not, for reasons to be discussed shortly, *Erlebnis*). It is here, after all, that one finds these now familiar lines: "For never has experience been contracted more thoroughly than strategic experience by tactical warfare, economic experience by inflation, bodily experience by mechanical warfare, moral experience by those in power."[3] Such an attribution would be logical but in fact wrong, for the first citation is from an essay written in 1954 by Adorno, entitled "The Position of the Narrator in the Contemporary Novel" and reprinted in *Notes to Literature*; the second comes from the aphorism "Out of the Firing Line," written in 1944 and published in *Minima Moralia* in 1951. The war in question is thus not the first World War but the second; the argument, however, is exactly the same. What Adorno has done is simply recycle Benjamin's claim that narrative continuity and with it a certain notion of experience have been shattered by the traumatic shocks and general unintelligibility of modern warfare.

I draw attention to this recycling, not to undermine any claim to Adorno's originality, an issue of no great significance, but rather to pose the question, when exactly did something called experience come into crisis? Was it an actual historical event or process, caused by a trauma like global warfare, or is something more ontological at issue? Is there, moreover, a coherent and unified notion of experience assumed by the lament, or does the word function in different ways in different contexts? And if different acceptations are to be discerned, can we say that all of them have withered to the same degree or even withered at all at the present time?

The assumption that something historical has indeed happened to undercut the possibility of experience would seem to inform many of the Frankfurt School's formulations of the problem. It is in the work of Adorno that they most frequently appear.[4] Thus, for example, in *Aesthetic Theory*, he would write, "The marrow of experience has been sucked out; there is none, not even that apparently set at a remove from commerce, that has not been gnawed away."[5] Likewise, in his 1960 essay "Presuppositions," he would claim that in the modernist writing of Joyce and Proust one can see "the dying out of experience, something that ultimately goes back to the atemporal technified process of the production of material goods."[6] And in an essay of the previous year, "Theory of Pseudo-Culture," he would complain that experience, which he defined in almost Burkean terms as "the continuity of consciousness in which everything not present survives, in which practice and association establish tradition in the individual," has now been "replaced by the selective, disconnected, interchangeable and ephemeral state of being informed which, as one can already observe, will promptly be cancelled by other information."[7]

Attempts to revive a robust variety of experience in the present, Adorno would moreover argue, are doomed to failure, especially when they seek to recover an alleged ur-experience that is somehow deeper than the mediations of culture and society. In *The Jargon of Authenticity*, he would mock efforts by latter-day adepts of *Lebensphilosophie* to reenchant the world:

The contrast between primal experiences and cultural experiences, which [Friedrich] Gundolf invented *ad hoc*, for [Stefan] George, was ideology in the midst of superstructure, devised for the purpose of obscuring the contrast between infrastructure and ideology. . . . [Ernst] Bloch rightfully made fun of Gundolf for his belief in today's primal experiences. These primal experiences were a warmed-over piece of expressionism. They were later made into a permanent institution by Heidegger. . . . In the universally mediated world everything experienced in primary terms is culturally preformed.[8]

Here experience is understood more in terms of *Erlebnis* than *Erfahrung*, as prereflective immediacy without narrative continuity over time, but the point is the same: It is no longer available to us. As Adorno wrote in a 1967 essay on the poetry of Rudolf Borchardt, "[T]he poetic subject that did not want to give itself over to something alien to it had become the victim of what was most alien of all, the conventions of the long exhausted *Erlebnislyrik* [poetry of experience]. . . . The ideology of primal experience that Gundolf promulgated on George's behalf is refuted by Borchardt's poetic practice."[9]

There is, in short, an implied sense of loss of something that once existed and has been seriously damaged, if not entirely destroyed, in the present. Variously attributed to the traumas of world war, modern technologies of information, and the "atemporal, technified process of the production of material goods," which seems another way to say capitalist industrialization, the decay of something called experience is for Adorno an index of the general crisis of modern life. How far back the roots of the crisis may go will be clearer if we turn briefly to the even more frequent bemoaning of the decay of experience in Benjamin, who provided, as we have seen, an inspiration for many of Adorno's own ruminations on this theme. There is an enormous literature on the question of experience in Benjamin, which has culminated, at least for the moment, in Howard Caygill's recently published *Walter Benjamin: The Colour of Experience*.[10]

Drawing on the hitherto ignored fragments of Benjamin's earliest writings on perception, visuality, and color, Caygill has constructed a carefully nuanced account of his lifelong preoccupation with the possibility of reviving a lost experience. Prior to the articulation of that project in linguistic terms, in such essays as "On Language as Such and the Language of Man" of 1916 and "On the Program of the Coming Philosophy" of 1918, Benjamin, he shows, experimented with expressing it in visual terms.[11] Reaching back behind Kant's restriction of experience to merely what is filtered through the synthetic a priori function of the understanding, the young Benjamin sought a frankly metaphysical alternative in the more immediate perception of prereflective intuition. According to Caygill,

Benjamin's speculative recasting of Kant's transcendental account of experience involves the introduction of the absolute or infinite into the structure or forms of intuition – space and time – and the linguistic categories [*logoi*] of the understanding. Benjamin sought to avoid both Kant's scission of experience and the absolute and what he regarded as Hegel's "mysticism of brute force" which for him reduced the absolute by expressing it in terms of the categories of finite experience.[12]

Color as opposed to form was particularly important in this quest because of its infinite divisibility, which eludes the categorizing reifications of a merely epistemological relation to the world based on the rigid distinction of subject and object. In a fragment written in 1914–1915, entitled "A Child's View of Color," Benjamin contended that "color is something spiritual, something whose clarity is spiritual, so that when colors are mixed they produced nuances of color, not a blur. The rainbow is a pure childlike image."[13] Benjamin's subsequent valorization of Romantic aesthetic criticism, in particular the work of Schlegel and Novalis, is foreshadowed here in his celebration of childlike vision and the spiritual presence of infinity in color. When in his later work he turned toward modern, urban experience, largely characterized in negative terms as a fallen realm of shocklike, discontinuous *Erlebnisse*, he still sought traces or prefigurations of the redeemed *Erfahrung* which he had glimpsed in his earliest ruminations on visual intuition. Never abandoning his quest for what Caygill rightly calls "a non-Hegelian account of speculative experience,"[14] Benjamin believed that the absolute could somehow be revealed through an immanent critique of even the most mundane of phenomena. Thus, he avoided the paralysis of nostalgia based on a simple inversion of the model of unidirectional progress he so tellingly criticized.

How successful Benjamin's quest actually was is, of course, a matter of some dispute, as many of Benjamin's redemptive readings, like his political commitments, seem more like wishful thinking than anything else. So too the precise chronology of the fall from grace with which he tacitly worked is not fully coherent. At times, it seems as if Benjamin was making a typical Romantic argument about the loss of childhood innocence that would have done Wordsworth proud, an argument that is inherently ahistorical. At other times, he seemed to be saying that the fall came when the world of mimetic similarities, in which nature was a legible text, was supplanted by a dead world of de-animated objects to be scrutinized by the scientific gaze and given philosophical justification by Kant's desiccated epistemology. Here his celebrated argument about the Baroque as a period of mourning for the lost wholeness represented in Greek tragedy, a period of allegorical rather than symbolic representation, suggests that the absolute had already been driven out of experience and the infinite abjected from the finite by the seventeenth century. The technological transformations of more recent years, leading to the loss of the ritual, cultic aura around earlier art, thus merely continued and intensified a change that had begun much earlier. The unevenness of the process is shown, however, by his claim in "The Storyteller" essay that Nikolai Leskov, a writer of the nineteenth century, was still able to convey genuine *Erfahrungen* in his tales in a fashion no longer available in the modern novel. Perhaps Russia was still the site of a ritualized communal life allowing the narrative transmission from one generation to the next that was one expression of genuine *Erfahrung*. If so, Benjamin would not have been alone in finding an exception to the rule in Russian literature, another obvious example being the Dostoyevsky extolled by Lukács in his *Theory of the Novel*.

Be that as it may, Benjamin bequeathed to Adorno a strong belief in the importance of experience, once freed from its empiricist and Kantian limitations, as a locus of possible redemption, a place in which something called "the absolute" might make an appearance. His exaltation of color even found an occasional echo, as in Adorno's remark in *Negative Dialectics* that "the resistance to the fungible world of barter is the resistance of the eye that does not want the colors of the world to fade."[15] Benjamin also gave Adorno, as we have seen, an unexamined assumption that, at some indeterminate time in the past, actual lived experience came closer to this condition than it does today. Since that time, a kind of fall from grace had occurred, causing experience in this metaphysical sense to "decay" or "wither." Such a fall needed, to be sure, to be read dialectically in the hope that something of what was lost might still be lurking in the debris, or even brought into the world anew with the fresh vision of every child.

Where Adorno, however, moved away from Benjamin was in his greater sympathy for Hegel's conceptualization of experience, which demonstrated his links with the other philosophers at the Frankfurt Institute. Perhaps the difference is best shown in his defense of Hegel against the attack launched by Martin Heidegger in the latter's *Holzwege* of 1950.[16] Without wanting to conflate Benjamin and Heidegger, who were in many respects very different, on the issue of experience they shared certain similar inclinations.[17] Both were, for example, hostile to the privileging of immediate "lived experience" [*Erlebnis*] in *Lebensphilosophie*, both were against the reduction of experience to an epistemological category in the Kantian or empiricist sense, and both were anxious to transcend psychologistic subjectivism and restore a notion of experience prior to the split between subject and object. Heidegger, like Benjamin, was determined to return to more fundamental levels of truth, whether they be called the metaphysical absolute or the ontological real, than the tradition of disenchanted secular humanism had allowed.

In *Holzwege*, Heidegger juxtaposes passages from Hegel's *Phenomenology of Spirit* with extended commentaries on their significance. He highlights the fact that Hegel had first called the work "Science of the Experience of Consciousness" and argues that his version of phenomenology is still deeply indebted to that project. Heidegger foregrounds Hegel's noncommonsensical definition of experience, which reads as follows: "This *dialectical* movement, which consciousness exercises on itself – on its knowledge as well as its object – is, *in so far as the new, true object emerges to consciousness* as the result of it, precisely that which is called *experience*."[18] Glossing this passage, Heidegger claims that Hegel means by "experience" the "Being of beings.... Experience now is the word of Being, since Being is apprehended by way of beings *qua* beings."[19] Here he seems to be assimilating Hegel's position to his own.

But then Heidegger adds that for Hegel "[e]xperience designates the subject's subjectness. Experience expresses what *'being'* in the term 'being conscious' means – in such a way that only by this 'being' does it become clear and binding what the word 'conscious' leaves still to thought."[20] Thus, Hegel's notion of experience remains hostage to that fateful privileging of the subject that Heidegger found so distressing in modern metaphysics. This bias is revealed, Heidegger continues, because experience for Hegel involved the presentation of an appearance for a consciousness, a manifestation of being to a subject in the present. In fact, Hegel's dialectical method is itself grounded in a still subjective view of experience. "Hegel does not conceive of experience dialectically," Heidegger writes, "he thinks of dialectic in terms of the nature of experience. Experience is the beingness of beings, whose determination, *qua subjectum*, is determined in terms of subjectness."[21] The ultimate subject for Hegel is, of course, the Absolute Spirit. Thus, for Hegel "experience is the subjectness of the absolute subject. Experience, the presentation of the absolute representation, is the *parousia* of the Absolute. Experience is the absoluteness of the Absolute, its appearance in absolving appearance to itself."[22]

Heidegger concedes that Hegel understood that natural consciousness lacks this more exalted metaphysical notion of experience because it ignores the deeper question of Being. But the way in which the Hegelian Absolute exteriorizes itself and re-collects itself at a higher level produces the questionable claim that the experience of consciousness lends itself to a post facto scientific recapitulation. Significantly, Heidegger points out, "experience" occupies the middle position between "science" and "consciousness" in the title "Science of the Experience of Consciousness," which indicates that for Hegel "experience, as the being of consciousness, is in itself the inversion by which consciousness presents itself in its appearance. That is to say: in making the presentation, experience is science."[23]

Heidegger concludes by speculating on the reasons Hegel dropped this original title shortly before the book was published and substituted "Phenomenology of Spirit" instead. Noting that for Kant "experience" had merely meant "the only possible theoretical knowledge of what is," Heidegger hazards the guess that Hegel had found it too daring to restore an earlier meaning: "a reaching out and attaining, and attaining as the mode of being present, of ειγαι, of Being."[24] Perhaps because of this failure of nerve, Hegel had not quite attained the level of insight into Being Heidegger ascribed to his own thought. His sympathetic interpreter Robert Bernasconi summarizes the essential differences between the two thinkers in the following terms:

"Experience" in Heidegger does not have the sense of a progressive development as it has in Hegel. For Heidegger, experience almost always takes place in the face of a lack.... For the phenomenological thinking of Heidegger, a lack or default gives access to Being.... The difference between Hegel's concept of experience and Heidegger's is that the former is tied to the rule of presencing and the latter commemorates it. Phenomenology for Hegel is a *parousia*, whereas for Heidegger it is letting the nonapparent appear as nonapparent.[25]

Commemorating what has been lost – the oblivion of Being in Heidegger's case – rather than celebrating presence as the cumulative realization of a successful dialectical process is reminiscent of Benjamin's critique of Hegelian memory as *Er-innerung*, a too harmonious re-membering in the present of what had been sundered in the past. A commonality between Heidegger and Benjamin might also be found in the recognition in both their work of the etymological link between *Erfahrung* and *Gefahr*, the danger that must be encountered in the perilous journey that is experience ("experience" derives from the Latin *experiri*, as does the English word "peril"), a danger that in the modern period is perhaps best revealed in the context of technology, with its destructive as well as emancipatory potential. And both thinkers were arguably at one in their dissatisfaction with Hegel's contention that knowledge or science [*Wissenschaft*] can be perfectly reconciled with experience, an assumption that rests, as Hans-Georg Gadamer was to claim in *Truth and Method*, on the solipsistic nature of the Hegelian subject, who ultimately absorbs into himself the object and never really has an encounter with what is truly different from and alien to him.[26]

Such an encounter was, of course, also the earmark of Adorno's *Negative Dialectics*, which sought to avoid idealism's coercive sublation of difference and to preserve the nonidentity of subject and object. His own interpretation of Hegel's notion of experience was designed, however, to resist the ontological interpretation of

Heidegger's *Holzwege* and brush Hegel against the grain, finding in him what both Heidegger and Benjamin had claimed he denied. Adorno deliberately began the essay entitled "The Experiential Content of Hegel's Philosophy," first published in 1959 and included in the 1963 collection *Hegel: Three Studies*, by distancing himself from Heidegger's reading:

> The concept [of experience] is not intended to capture phenomenological "ur-experience"; nor, like the interpretation of Hegel in Heidegger's *Holzwege*, is it intended to get at something ontological.... His thought would never have ratified Heidegger's claim that "The new object that arises for consciousness in the course of its formation" is "not just anything that is true, or any particular being, but is the truth of what is true, the Being of Beings, the appearance of appearance." Hegel would have never called that experience; instead for Hegel, what experience is concerned with at any particular moment is the animating contradiction of such absolute truth.[27]

If experience for Hegel is more than the presubjective "event" or "appropriation" (*Ereignes* in Heidegger's special lexicon) of Being, it is also not the unmediated sense perception assumed by empiricists like Hume. Experience is not for Hegel something undergone by the isolated individual but entails the interdependency of subjects with each other and with the world. Nor, and this is even more important, is it equivalent to the science of knowledge, the *Wissenschaft*, that was its tombstone: "By no means does the experiential content of idealism simply coincide with its epistemological and metaphysical positions" (H, 61). Tacitly respecting the limits on knowledge placed by his predecessor Kant, even as he ultimately hoped to overcome them, Hegel identified experience precisely with the obstacles to full transparency presented by the contradictions in reality, not merely in thought. According to Adorno, Nietzsche's claim that "there is nothing in reality that would correspond strictly with logic" (H, 76) captures Hegel's notion of experience better than attempts, such as those of orthodox dialectical materialists, to impose dialectical reason on the world without remainder. In fact, it is the recognition of contradiction in society, the idea of antagonistic totality, which allows Hegel to move beyond absolute idealism.

Hegel, to be sure, had wrongly thought his philosophy could encompass the whole and reveal its truth. However, as Adorno argued,

[E]ven where Hegel flies in the face of experience, including the experience that motivates his own philosophy, experience speaks from him.... the idea of a positivity that can master everything that opposes it through the superior power of a comprehending spirit is the mirror image of the experience of the superior coercive force inherent in everything that exists by virtue of its consolidation under domination. This is the truth in Hegel's untruth. (H, 87)

Another unintended truth, one with a very different implication, is revealed, according to a later essay by Adorno on Hegel's opaque style,[28] in the tension between his desire to work entirely with concepts adequate to their objects and the linguistic medium through which he necessarily expressed them:

In Hegel the expressive element represents experience; that which actually wants to come out into the open, but cannot, if it wants to attain necessity, appear except in the medium of concepts, which is fundamentally its opposite.... The whole of Hegel's philosophy is an effort to translate intellectual experience into concepts. (H, 138)

But the medium of its expression inevitably interferes with this goal, for

thought, which necessarily moves away from the text, from what is said, has to return to it and become condensed within it. John Dewey, a contemporary thinker who for all his positivism is closer to Hegel than their two alleged standpoints are to one another, called his philosophy "experimentalism." Something of this stance is appropriate for the reader of Hegel. (H, 144)

Adorno's surprising reference to Dewey, whose pragmatism the Frankfurt School often disparaged, suggests a certain countercurrent in Adorno's thought to the lament about the virtually complete withering of experience, for Dewey was cautiously optimistic about the possibilities of genuine experience at the present time. Adorno, to be sure, resisted Dewey's identification of experiment with its scientific variety, preferring instead the literary essay, which "invests experience with as much substance as traditional theory does mere categories."[29] But that substance, he claimed, involves an opening to what is new rather than a ratification of what has been:

What Kant saw, in terms of content as the goal of reason, the creation of humankind, utopia, is hindered by the form of his thought, epistemology. It does not permit reason to go beyond the realm of experience which, in the mechanism of mere material and invariant categories, shrinks to what has always already existed. The essay's object, however, is the new in its newness, not as something that can be translated back into the old existing forms. (NL, vol. 1, p. 21)[30]

If Adorno shared with Dewey a belief that some sort of experimentation pointing toward the renewal of experience was possible even in the totalizing system of domination that he saw as the sinister reversal of Hegel's dictum that the "whole was the true," he also agreed that aesthetic experience in particular was its privileged laboratory. In such works as *Art as Experience*, published in 1934, "the unique and truly free John Dewey," as Adorno once called him, had ruminated on the significance of aesthetic experience as a model for a more general mode of unalienated existence (AT, 335).[31] Although it has sometimes been argued, most notably by Hans Robert Jauss,[32] that Adorno's own understanding of aesthetic experience was too negatively ascetic and lacked an appreciation of the communicative function of art even in the present "administered world," it is clear that he shared with Dewey an appreciation of the utopian moment in that experience.

This is not the place to attempt a full-fledged analysis of what Adorno meant by aesthetic experience, but several points warrant emphasis.[33] First of all, it should be understood that, contrary to the image of him as a mandarin elitist, Adorno never considered aesthetic experience, even that engendered by the most advanced modenist art, to be an entirely protected sphere in which the horrors of modern life were somehow successfully kept at bay. As he once wrote in an essay on the great nineteenth-century realist novel *Lost Illusions*, "Balzac knows that artistic experience is not pure, official aesthetics to the contrary; that it can hardly be pure if it is to be experience."[34] Aesthetic experience, at least in this usage, which we might call descriptive rather than normative, is necessarily impure because it is damaged by the changes outside art to which we have already alluded: modern warfare, the replacement of narrative by information, alienating technology, and capitalist industrialization. By itself, it cannot bring back the world of Benjamin's storyteller. Its truth content, Adorno always emphasized, thus had to be brought out by an accompanying philosophical cum social theoretical analysis that provided the critical discursive tools that art inevitably lacked.

But it is also the case that for Adorno aesthetic experience, however maimed, can preserve a certain trace of what existed before, which somehow has not been completely obliterated. Here he employed "experience" in an explicitly normative sense. Proust, Adorno claimed, was able to provide an almost Hegelian model of that preservation, for in his work "undamaged experience is produced only in memory, far beyond immediacy, and through memory aging and death seem to be overcome in the aesthetic image. But this happiness achieved through the rescue of experience, a happiness that will not let anything be taken from it, represents an unconditional renunciation of consolation."[35]

Genuine experience, experience worth rescuing from the damaged variety of modern life, is thus closely tied to the memory of happiness, whose faint promise to return is what art is able to offer, as Stendhal, Nietzsche, and Marcuse had argued. Significantly, when Adorno answered his own question "What is metaphysical experience?" in *Negative Dialectics*, he fell back on Benjamin's argument about an Adamic, prelapsarian language of mimesis before the fall into arbitrary language:

If we disdain projecting it upon allegedly primal religious experiences, we are most likely to visualize it as Proust did, in the happiness, for instance, that is promised by village names like Applebachsville, Wind Gap, or Lords Valley. One thinks that going there would bring the fulfillment, as if there were such a thing.... To the child it is self-evident that what delights him in his favorite village is found only there, there alone and nowhere else. He is mistaken; but his mistake creates the model of experience, of a concept that will end up as the concept of the thing itself, not as a poor projection from things. (ND, 373)

Although necessarily a semblance of such a mimetic paradise and not the real thing – indeed precisely because it is such a semblance and knows itself as such – art gestures toward the happiness of genuine metaphysical experience, which is precisely what the current world denies and which the merely epistemological concept cannot even envisage. It does so paradoxically through its mimesis of the other, which resists reduction to subjective constitution.[36] Experience, as many commentators have used the term, comes only with an encounter with otherness in which the self no longer remains the same. Adorno would add that to be undamaged, experience must treat the other in a nondominating, nonsubsumptive, nonhomogenizing manner.

Can such an encounter, however, be with what Benjamin called "the absolute" in his earliest writings on colors? Certainly, some of the pathos of that claim clings to many of Adorno's statements about experience and its decay, which are written from what the famous last aphorism in *Minima Moralia* called "the standpoint of redemption" (MM, 247). We have already noted the claim in *Negative Dialectics* that resistance to the world of exchange "is the resistance of the eye that does not want the colors of the world to fade." As a result, some commentators have ignored Adorno's attempts to distance himself from "allegedly primal religious experiences" and decried what they see as the "mystical" underpinnings of his concept of experience.[37]

But what perhaps indicates the inadequacy of such a reading, and by extension suggests that Adorno was not entirely happy with Benjamin's formulation of the problem, is his unwillingness to go all the way toward what can be called "experience without a subject," that moment of equiprimordiality prior to the split between self and other. Giorgio Agamben has noted in his book of essays on the destruction of experience, *Infancy and History*, that "in Proust there is no longer really any subject. . . . Here the expropriated subject of experience emerges to validate what, from the point of view of science, can appear only as the most radical negation of experience: an experience with neither subject nor object, absolute."[38] Adorno, as we have seen, may have approvingly invoked Proust's preservation of childhood happiness through memory, but he did not, I want to argue, embrace this notion of absolute experience in which neither subject nor object was preserved. As his disdain for Heidegger's appropriation of Hegel's "science of the experience of consciousness" for his own project of the recollection of Being illustrates, Adorno was loath to short-circuit a negative dialectic that preserved some distinction between the two. The unsublatable dialectic of art and philosophy, like that between mimesis and construction or concept and object, suggests that even the most metaphysical of experiences for Adorno could not be reduced to perfect reconciliation or the restoration of equiprimordiality. Thus, even the Benjaminian rhetoric of a child's perception of color is inadequate to his position, for color is precisely that aspect of visual experience that resides in the subjective response to objects, not in material objects in themselves. Despite his occasional mobilizing of the rhetoric of Adamic names, as in the passage cited from *Negative Dialectics* above, Adorno never relied on mimesis alone to provide the model of realized utopia.

Such an acknowledgment still does answer the question we posed at the beginning of this essay: Is there a crisis of experience that can be understood in historical terms, involving a loss of something that once actually existed? Ruminating on the work of Benjamin more than Adorno, Agamben presents a challenge to the implied assumption that such a condition has ever really obtained in some prior Golden Age. He notes that a robust notion of experience, which puts us in touch with the absolute and is prior to the alienations of damaged life, ultimately derives from a fantasy of recovered infancy, which he defines as the period of human existence before language and before history. "In this sense," he writes,

to experience necessarily means to re-accede to infancy as history's transcendental place of origin. The enigma which infancy ushered in for man can be dissolved only in history, just as experience, being infancy and human place of origin, is something he is always in the act of falling from, into language and into speech.[39]

That fall is the source of the split between subject and object, because only grammar produces a strong sense of the autonomy of the first person singular, the "I" who is apart from the world. If this is true, then authentic experience, at least as a metaphysical possibility, was not destroyed by the depredations of war or the reifications of capitalism but was always already undone by the fall into language, the primal alienation that defines us as human. The alleged "memory" that we have of a lost happiness is thus of a condition that can never be regained short of the death that reunites us with a mute world prior to our insertion into language. Even as sympathetic a reader of the Frankfurt School tradition as Albrecht Wellmer could extend this skeptical conclusion beyond Benjamin, claiming that Adorno too, "like Schopenhauer, conceives aesthetic experience in ecstatic terms rather than as a real utopia; the happiness that it promises is not of this world."[40]

What, however, may allow us to salvage a less impotent reading of Adorno's lament about the loss of experience is the recognition of his subtle movement away from the more intransigently absolutist position of Benjamin and the Heidegger of *Holzwege*. For Agamben's rebuke only draws blood if we understand his description of absolute experience, prior to the fall into language, anterior to the split between subject and object, as in fact converging with what is normally understood as experience's most charged antonym: total innocence. Although Adorno does have positive things to say about childhood and the memory of happiness, he shows little real nostalgia for any historical time of alleged prelapsarian grace. Witness the following passage from *Negative Dialectics*:

The meaningful times for whose return the early Lukács yearned were as much due to reification, to inhuman institutions, as he would later attest it only to the bourgeois age. Contemporary representations of medieval towns usually look as if an execution were just taking place to cheer the populace. If any harmony of subject and object should have prevailed in those days, it was a harmony like the most recent one: pressure-born and brittle. The transfiguration of past conditions serves the purpose of a late, superfluous denial that is experienced as a no-exit situation; only as lost conditions do they become glamorous. Their cult, the cult of pre-subjective phases, arose in horror, in the age of individual disintegration and collective regression. (ND, 191)

In his studies of Hegel, it will be recalled, the experience he claims shines through the *Phenomenology* is that of the inability of life to be subsumed entirely under concepts and the extent of the present order's totalizing power to compel a social equivalent of that outcome. It is the tension between these two insights, which Adorno called Hegel's depiction of the antagonistic totality, that is forgotten in idealism and *Lebensphilosophie*. Despite his borrowing of Benjamin's rhetoric of loss and decay in the passages cited at the beginning of this chapter, Adorno understood, as he put it in *Negative Dialectics*, that

the concept of metaphysical experience is antinomical, not only as taught by Kantian transcendental dialectics, but in other ways. A metaphysics proclaimed without recourse to subjective experience, without the immediate presence of the subject, is helpless before the autonomous subject's refusal to have imposed upon it what it cannot understand. And yet, whatever is directly evident to the subject suffers from fallibility and relativity. (ND 374, translation emended)

In short, redeemed experience, undamaged experience, authentic experience, if indeed such a condition can ever be attained, would not mean a restoration of innocence before the fall into language or a harmonious reconciliation in a utopian future but rather a non-dominating relationship between subject and object. It would paradoxically retain at least some of the distinctions felt as alienated diremptions by what Hegel had called "the unhappy consciousness," but now in such a way that they no longer frustrate the subject's desire to master the world through conceptual and practical activity. Instead, the experiential happiness that is promised by works of art restores one of the fundamental senses of "experience" itself: a passive suffering or undergoing through an encounter with the new and the other, which moves us beyond where we, as subjects, were before the experience began. It is for this reason, as J. N. Bernstein has noted, that "the image of life without experience is finally the image of life without history, as if the meaning of life were in its eternal cessation: death. There cannot be historical life without experience; only lives articulated through experience can be fully and self-consciously historical."[41] Here the conclusion is precisely opposite that of Agamben, who identifies history with the fall out of the pure experience that is prelinguistic infancy or postlinguistic death.

Adorno himself, we have to admit in conclusion, never fully sorted out the welter of denotations and connotations that cling to the numinous word "experience." At times he expresses an apparent nostalgia for a lost undamaged experience; at others he mocks romanticizations of an alleged state of prelapsarian bliss. While invoking the rhetoric of a progressive loss, he only vaguely hints at the existence of an actual historical time before the decay. Accepting Benjamin's critique of empiricist or Kantian notions of experience, he nonetheless resists accepting the maximalist notion of absolute experience that also infuses, as we have seen, Heidegger's reading of Hegel in *Holzwege*. Looking for traces or prefigurations of undamaged experience in aesthetic experience, he clearly knows that semblance is not reality and that a gap looms large between works of art and redeemed life, which may never be as close to the absolute as Benjamin in his more metaphysical moods had hoped. In short, the experience of reading Adorno on experience is itself one of nonidentical refusals of easy consistencies, producing the realization that experience is an openness to the unexpected, with its dangers and obstacles, not a safe haven from history but a reminder of the encounters with otherness and the new that await those who, despite everything, are willing and able to embark on the voyage.

In this sense, it may be premature to write the epitaph of experience as such, for, paradoxically, it will only be when the crisis itself ends and a deadly calm settles over the world that the perilous journey that is experience will no longer be a human possibility.

NOTES

1. Theodor W. Adorno, "The Position of the Narrator in the Contemporary Novel," in vol. 2 of *Notes to Literature*, trans. Shierry Weber Nicholsen (New York: Columbia University Press, 1992), 31. Hereafter cited as NL.

2. Theodor W. Adorno, *Minima Moralia: Reflections from Damaged Life*, trans. E. F. N. Jephcott (London: New Left Books, 1974), 54–5. Hereafter cited as MM.

3. Walter Benjamin, "The Storyteller: Reflections on the Work of Nikolai Leskov," in *Illuminations*, trans. Harry Zohn, ed. Hannah Arendt (New York, Schocken, 1969), 84.

4. There is, in fact, a considerable discussion in German of Adorno's concept of experience. See, for example, Hans-Hartmut Kappner, *Die Bildungstheorie Adornos als Theories der Erfahrung von Kultur und Kunst* (Frankfurt: Suhrkamp, 1984); Peter Kalkowski, *Adornos Erfahrung: Zur Kritik der Kritischen Theories* (Frankfurt: Suhrkamp, 1988); Anke Thyen, *Negative Dialektik und Erfahrung: Zur Rationalität des Nichtidentischen bei Adorno* (Frankfurt: Suhrkamp, 1989).

5. Theodor W. Adorno, *Aesthetic Theory*, trans. Robert Hullot-Kentor, ed. Gretel Adorno and Rolf Tiedemann (Minneapolis: University of Minnesota Press, 1997), 31.

6. Theodor W. Adorno, "Presuppositions: On the Occasion of a Reading by Hans G. Helms," in NL, vol. 2, p. 101.

7. Theodor W. Adorno, "Theory of Pseudo-Culture," *Telos*, no. 95 (Spring 1993): 33.

8. Theodor W. Adorno, *The Jargon of Authenticity*, trans. Knut Tanowski and Frederic Will (Evanston: Northwestern University Press, 1973), 99. Whether or not Adorno was accurate in characterizing Heidegger's notion of experience in these terms is debatable.

9. Theodor W. Adorno, "Charmed Language: On the Poetry of Rudolf Borchardt," in NL, vol. 2, p. 205.

10. Howard Caygill, *Walter Benjamin: The Colour of Experience* (London: Routledge 1998). For references to earlier literature on the question and

my own attempt to make some sense of it, see "Experience without a Subject: Walter Benjamin and the Novel," in Martin Jay, *Cultural Semantics: Keywords of the Age* (Amherst, Mass.: University of Massachusetts Press, 1998).

11. The relevant essays are now available in Walter Benjamin, *Selected Writings*, vol. 1, ed. Marcus Bullock and Michael W. Jennings (Cambridge, Mass.: Harvard University Press, 1996).

12. Caygill, *Walter Benjamin*, 23.

13. Walter Benjamin, "A Child's View of Color," in *Selected Writings*, 50.

14. Caygill, *Walter Benjamin*, 8.

15. Theodor W. Adorno, *Negative Dialectics*, trans. E. B. Ashton (New York: Seabury Press, 1973), 405. Hereafter cited as ND.

16. The relevant section is translated as Martin Heidegger, *Hegel's Concept of Experience* (New York: Harper and Row, 1970). For a suggestive commentary, see Robert Bernasconi, *The Question of Language in Heidegger's History of Being* (Atlantic Highlands, N.J.: Humanities Press International, 1986), chap. 6.

17. All of Benjamin's recorded reactions to Heidegger were critical; Heidegger seems to have been unaware of Benjamin's work. Nonetheless, similarities between Heidegger and Benjamin were first stressed by Hannah Arendt in her controversial introduction to Benjamin, *Illuminations*. For more recent attempts to see parallels, as well as some distinctions, see Howard Caygill, "Benjamin, Heidegger and the Destruction of Tradition," and Andrew Benjamin, "Time and Task: Benjamin and Heidegger Showing the Present," in *Walter Benjamin's Philosophy: Destruction and Experience*, ed. Andrew Benjamin and Pete Osborne (London: Routledge, 1994). For discussions of the differences between the two, see Richard Wolin, *Walter Benjamin: An Aesthetic of Redemption*, 2nd ed. (Berkeley: University of California Press, 1994), 102, and Beatrice Hanssen, *Walter Benjamin's Other History: Of Stones, Animals, Human Beings, and Angels* (Berkeley: University of California Press, 1998), 2.

18. Heidegger, *Hegel's Concept of Experience*, 112.

19. Heidegger, *Hegel's Concept of Experience*, 114.

20. Heidegger, *Hegel's Concept of Experience*, 114.

21. Heidegger, *Hegel's Concept of Experience*, 119.

22. Heidegger, *Hegel's Concept of Experience*, 120–1.

23. Heidegger, *Hegel's Concept of Experience*, 139.

24. Heidegger, *Hegel's Concept of Experience*, 143.

25. Bernasconi, *Question of Language*, 83–5.

26. Hans-Georg Gadamer, *Truth and Method* (New York: Crossroad, 1986), 318–9.

27. Theodor W. Adorno, *Hegel: Three Studies*, trans. Shierry Weber Nicholsen (Cambridge, Mass.: MIT Press, 1993), 53. Hereafter cited as H.
28. Theodor W. Adorno, "Skoteinos, or How to Read Hegel," in *Hegel: Three Studies*.
29. Theodor W. Adorno, "The Essay as Form," in NL vol. 1, p. 10.
30. In this passage, Adorno seems to forget the redemptive notion of experience he inherited from Benjamin and uses the term instead to refer only to the epistemological synthetic a priori judgments of Kant's first *Critique*.
31. John Dewey, *Art as Experience* (New York: Minton, Balch and Co., 1934).
32. Hans Robert Jauss, *Aesthetic Experience and Literary Hermeneutics*, trans. Michael Shaw (Minneapolis: University of Minnesota Press, 1982), 13–22.
33. For helpful recent discussions, see Shierry Weber Nicholsen, *Exact Imagination, Late Work: On Adorno's Aesthetics* (Cambridge, Mass.: MIT Press, 1997), and Tom Huhn and Lambert Zuidervaart, eds., *The Semblance of Subjectivity: Essays on Adorno's Aesthetic Theory* (Cambridge, Mass.: MIT Press, 1997).
34. Theodor W. Adorno, "On an Imaginary Feuilleton," in NL, vol. 2, p. 33. In *Aesthetic Theory*, he makes a similar point: "[N]o particular aesthetic experience occurs in isolation, independently of the continuity of experiencing consciousness.... The continuity of aesthetic experience is colored by all other experience and all knowledge, though, of course, it is only confirmed and corrected in the actual confrontation with the phenonmenon" (AT, 268–9).
35. Adorno, "On Proust," in NL, vol. 2, p. 317.
36. I have attempted to explore some of the implications of mimesis in his work in "Mimesis and Mimetology: Adorno and Lacoue-Labarthe," in Huhn and Zuidervaart, *Semblance of Subjectivity*.
37. Kalkowski, *Adornos Erfahrung*, 110–1.
38. Giorgio Agamben, *Infancy and History: Essays on the Destruction of Experience*, trans. Liz Heron (London: verso, 1993), 42.
39. Agamben, *Infancy and History*, p. 53.
40. Albrecht Wellmer, *The Persistence of Modernity: Essays on Aesthetics, Ethics, and Postmodernism*, trans. David Midgely (Cambridge, Mass.: MIT Press, 1993), 12.
41. Bernstein, "Why Rescue Semblance? Metaphysical Experience and the Possibility of Ethics," in Huhn and Zuidervaart, *Semblance of Subjectivity*, 203.

6 Mephistopheles in Hollywood
Adorno, Mann, and Schoenberg

At the end of 1947, *Dialectic of Enlightenment* was published by Querido Verlag. Written with Max Horkheimer, the book was the most important product of Theodor Adorno's exile in the United States. While its significance for Adorno's subsequent work has long been recognized, less attention has been paid to its relationship to two other works, both of which appeared at about the same time: Thomas Mann's *Doctor Faustus* and Arnold Schoenberg's *Survivor from Warsaw*.[1] The three share a good deal more than their common birthdate. Brought together, they form a triptych in which each offers a different perspective on the themes addressed by the others. Produced by refugees from Hitler's Germany, all three were responses to the diabolical force that had driven their creators into exile; in differing ways, all three explored the intertwining of enlightenment and myth, reason and barbarism, civilization and cruelty; and all three were produced by men who knew one another and lived within a few miles of each another, just outside Hollywood.

IN THE GARDEN OF EARTHLY DELIGHTS

It is difficult to think of a less likely spot from which to contemplate the collapse of European culture. But Adorno, Mann, and Schoenberg were hardly unique in their residence. Throughout the 1930s and early 1940s a steady stream of German exiles in flight from the Third Reich traveled from the East Coast to settle in Los Angeles.[2] As if by magic (albeit the blackest of magics), a substantial portion of the Weimar intelligentsia found itself transplanted along a line running from the oceanside community of Pacific Palisades through Brentwood, Bel Air, and Beverly Hills to Hollywood.[3] Thomas Mann

148

was joined by his brother Heinrich and by such fellow writers as Bertolt Brecht, Franz Werfel, Lion Feuchtwanger, Alfred Döblin, and Leonhard Frank. In addition to Schoenberg, the composers Hanns Eisler, Erich Wolfgang Korngold, and Ernst Toch as well as the conductors Bruno Walter and Otto Klemperer settled in the area. And in the spring of 1941, Max Horkheimer (former professor of social philosophy at the University of Frankfurt and director of its Institute for Social Research, which had moved to Columbia University in 1934), seeking a respite from his administrative responsibilities, journeyed west, bringing with him, for shorter or longer stays, his associates Herbert Marcuse, Leo Löwenthal, and Theodor Adorno. The displacement was so massive that, in an oddly optimistic note to the Hungarian classicist Karl Kerényi, Mann wondered whether it even made sense to call it an exile:

"Exile" has become something wholly different than in the past; it is no longer a condition of waiting oriented for a home-coming but a foretaste of a dissolution of nations and a unification of the world.[4]

Others, however, viewed their situation with a good deal more ambivalence.

Shortly after his arrival, Brecht wrote to an East Coast friend, "I feel here as if I were in Tahiti, surrounded by palm trees and artists, it makes me nervous, but there you are."[5] He explained to another, "Custom here demands that you try to 'sell' everything, from a shrug to an idea, and so you're always a buyer or a seller."[6] A poem entitled simply "Hollywood" made it clear which role he preferred:

> Every day, to earn my daily bread
> I go to the market where lies are bought.
> Hopefully
> I take up my place among the sellers.[7]

His best-known poem about the city in which he found refuge (and let us pause to reflect on the curiosity that the most famous poem about Los Angeles is written in German) began with an even more disturbing prospect:

> On thinking about Hell, I gather
> My brother Shelley found it was a place
> Much like the city of London. I

> Who live in Los Angeles and not in London
> Find, on thinking about Hell, that it must be
> Still more like Los Angeles.[8]

Brecht's faux paradise of monstrous flowers (guzzling alarming quantities of water) and relentlessly happy people (gliding down the boulevards in massive automobiles) struck Schoenberg, in contrast, as heaven itself.[9] Shortly after arriving in Los Angeles, he contrasted his fate to that of the serpent in Genesis, which, "driven out of paradise," was condemned "to go on its belly and to eat dust all the days of its life." He, however, had the good fortune to be banished to a land

where neither dust nor better food is rationed and where I am allowed to go on my feet, where my head can be erect, where kindness and cheerfulness is dominating, and where to live is a joy and to be an expatriate of another country is the grace of God. I was driven into paradise.[10]

But eventually he too had misgivings. "You complain of lack of culture in this amusement-arcade world," he wrote Oskar Kokoschka in 1946. "I wonder what you'd say to the world in which I nearly die of disgust." He described a magazine advertisement he had seen:

There's a picture of a man who has run over a child, which is lying dead in front of his car. He clutches his head in despair, but not to say anything like: "My God, what have I done!" For there is a caption saying: "Sorry, now it is too late to worry – take out your policy at the XX Insurance Company in time."

"And these are the people," he observed, "I'm supposed to teach composition to!"[11]

By the end of 1947, the first inquiries into the role of Communists in the film industry had begun, with a particular interest in Hanns Eisler, who was a former student of Schoenberg (he managed to include a tribute to his teacher in his testimony before the House Un-American Activities Committee), Brecht's favorite collaborator (among the works he composed in America was a setting of Brecht's "Hollywood Elegies"), and the coauthor, with Adorno, of *Composing for Films* (though Adorno withdrew his name from the title page when Eisler's political troubles began).[12] Within the next few years, Brecht would acquire an Austrian passport and a West German publisher, put on a bewildering performance before an investigating committee, and join Eisler in East Berlin;[13] Mann would be called before a congressional committee as an "unfriendly witness" and be attacked in the right-wing journal *Plain Talk* as America's "fellow traveler No. 1";[14] and the ever-cautious Max Horkheimer would put the finishing touches on arrangements to return the Institute for Social Research to Frankfurt.

Doctor Faustus, Dialectic of Enlightenment, and *A Survivor from Warsaw* thus appeared at a moment when old horrors were giving way to new uncertainties. Walter Benjamin's much overworked but still irresistible image of the angel of history might be pressed into service once more:

His face is turned toward the past. Where we perceive a chain of events, he sees one single catastrophe which keeps piling wreckage upon wreckage and hurls it in front of his feet. The angel would like to stay, awaken the dead, and make whole what has been smashed. But a storm is blowing from Paradise; it has got caught in his wings with such violence that the angel can no longer close them. This storm irresistibly propels him into the future to which his back is turned, while the pile of debris before him grows skyward. This storm is what we call progress.[15]

Dialectic of Enlightenment, Doctor Faustus, and *A Survivor from Warsaw* stared resolutely at the past even as they were wrenched backwards into an uncertain future. They gasped in horror at what had been destroyed and sought to fathom the dimensions of the catastrophe. Every panel in this triptych offers a different perspective on hell.

ENTER MEPHISTOPHELES

When Adrian Leverkühn, the composer-protagonist of Thomas Mann's *Doctor Faustus,* finally meets the Devil face to face, he finds that the Father of Lies cannot hold to one shape. He appears initially as "a *strizzi,* a pimp master," recalling the figure who led Adrian to the prostitute from whom he contracted the syphilis that will eventually render him insane. Thus, by the time Mann's Faust is formally introduced to his Mephistopheles, the demonic pact has already been inscribed in his own blood, granting him, in the years before his collapse into madness, "great time, mad time, the most devilish time, in which to soar higher and higher still."[16] Leverkühn has also already begun to reap the rewards of the pact, discovering a radical new method of musical composition which subjects the composer to the most extreme technical constraints while unleashing unparalleled expressive possibilities. Encoded in a recurring six-note phrase in the first of his compositions to exploit this new method is the pet name he bestowed on the one who infected him, *Hetaera esmeralda*, the Latin name of a butterfly whose pink and violet wings resemble the prostitute's garish makeup.[17]

As the conversation proceeds, the Devil begins to change his shape, gradually taking the form of "an intellectualist, who writes of art, of music, for vulgar newspapers, a theorist and critic, who is himself a composer."[18] The physical appearance of this "better sort of gentleman" – "spectacles rimmed in horn atop his hooked nose, behind which somewhat reddened eyes shine moist and dark; the face a mingling of sharpness and softness;...pale and vaulted the brow, from which his hair indeed retreats upward, whereas that to the sides stands thick, black, and woolly" – has struck some readers as bearing an uncanny resemblance to Theodor Adorno, Mann's neighbor and advisor on musical matters.[19] Lest this sly in-joke be missed by those likely to get it, Adorno's patronym "Wiesengrund" [meadowland] had already been used in Chapter 8 of the book during a lecture delivered by Adrian's composition teacher, Wendell Kretschmar. Kretschmar employed the word as an illustration of the rhythmic structure of the *Arietta* of Beethoven's piano sonata, op. 111.[20] The wink at Adorno was an obscure acknowledgment of a far deeper debt. In writing Kretschmar's lecture, Mann had taken more from Adorno than just his father's name: Much of Kretschmar's argument was lifted from a talk Adorno had given on the sonata at an October 1943 musical gathering in his home.[21]

Shortly before the close of the conversation, the devilish musical theorist sprouts a "small forked beard" and a "mustache ending in stiff twirled points." Restored to his more traditional guise, the Devil exits, but not before disavowing any knowledge of, or responsibility for, his appearance. He credits it all to "[c]onformation, mimicry,...the mumchance and conjuring of Mother Nature, who always keeps her tongue in her cheek."[22] Like the *Hetaera esmeralda* – whose colorful wings resemble, in flight, a windblown petal, thus allowing it to outwit its predators – the Devil's performance is one more manifestation of nature's unsettling capacities for mimicry. Years earlier, Jonathan Leverkühn had initiated his son into these mysteries, leading him into a world where frost on windows resembles the veins of tree leaves, where music becomes visible in the fine sand spread on a vibrating glass plate, and where patterns on shells form the letters of an alphabet that Jonathan tries in vain to interpret. Everywhere it is as if nature, "in her creative dreaming, dreamt the same thing both here and there, and if one spoke of imitation, then certainly it had to be reciprocal."[23]

As with nature, so with Mann's art. Writing to Karl Kerényi in 1934, he confessed that

there is something marvelously enticing and mysterious in the world of "correspondences" [Beziehungen]. The word itself has for a long time enchanted me, and what it signifies plays a pre-eminent role in all my thinking and artistic activity.[24]

Doctor Faustus is, if nothing else, a phantasmagoria of correspondences, imitations, resemblances. Begun on May 23, 1943, two months after Mann had returned to an outline he had drafted in 1901 for a short story based on the Faust legend, the novel is narrated by Adrian Leverkühn's life-long friend Serenus Zeitblom, who, like Mann, begins his narrative on May 23, 1943.[25] As he recounts the story of Leverkühn's life against the background of the steadily worsening situation within Germany during the last years of the Third Reich, there are times when Zeitblom – a self-proclaimed humanist who makes it clear from the start that he is uncomfortable with the demonic and has nothing but disgust for the Nazi regime – cannot be sure whether his hand is shaking because of his horror at what he is recounting or because of the vibrations from Allied bombs that are flattening nearby cities.

In the novel, Leverkühn faces the problem of how to go on composing in an age when, as the Devil, echoing Kretzschmar (whose words were taken from Adorno), explains, "the historical movement of musical material has turned against the self-contained work."[26] His solution came in the demonic gift of a technique of musical composition in which the twelve notes of the music scale are related only to each other and not to the conventional rules and expectations associated with tonal music. With this method Leverkühn composes a series of works, culminating in The Lamentation of Dr. Faustus, a cantata that achieves the one thing in music that "is not fictitious, not a game": "the unfeigned and untransfigured expression of suffering."[27]

Mann likened the technique of *Doctor Faustus* to a "montage" in which the fictional narrative constantly draws upon "factual, historical, personal, and even literary data."[28] Thus, actual historical figures, such as Mann's friend Bruno Walter, appear by name in the narrative, while other figures appear in the most meager of disguises. Mann modeled Leverkühn's descent into madness on the fates of Friedrich Nietzsche and the German composer Hugo Wolff and patterned Leverkühn's method of composition on that of Arnold Schoenberg.[29] Less obvious – and for the book's first readers, impossible to recognize – was the degree to which much of the discussion of music in the book had been taken verbatim from Adorno's unpublished manuscript "The Philosophy of New Music."[30]

In July 1943, while working on Chapter 7 of *Doctor Faustus*, Mann began reading and taking notes from Adorno's manuscript, which struck him as "something important."[31]

The manuscript dealt with modern music on both an artistic and on a sociological plane. The spirit of it was remarkably forward-looking, subtle and deep, and the whole thing had the strangest affinity to the idea of my book, to the "composition" in which I lived and moved and had my being. The decision was made of itself: this was my man.[32]

During the writing of *Doctor Faustus*, Mann met regularly with Adorno, read passages of the novel to him, and sought his help in the daunting task of providing descriptions of the music that Leverkühn allegedly wrote.[33] In December 1945, Mann gave Adorno a copy of all that had been written thus far in order, as he later explained, "to give him a complete insight into the unfolding of the novel's ideas, to acquaint him with my intentions, and to cajole him into helping me with impending musical problems."[34]

In a letter to Adorno written at the end of December, Mann discussed his use of "the principle of *montage*, which peculiarly and perhaps outrageously runs through this entire book," and somewhat sheepishly raised the touchy problem of his wholesale pilfering from Adorno's unpublished manuscript. Noting that his description of Leverkühn's illness employs "Nietzsche's symptoms word for word as they are set forth in his letters," he explained that it was his practice to take documents such as this and "drop it into the story as if

it were a mythic theme there for the taking, in the public domain."
Finally coming to the "more difficult – not to say more scandalous"
case of his "brazen – and I hope not altogether doltish" appropriation
of Adorno's "Philosophy of New Music," a work which, still unpublished, could hardly be considered part of the "public domain," Mann
confessed,

These borrowings cry out all the more for apology since for the time being the
reader cannot be made aware of them; there is no way to call his attention to
them without breaking the illusion. (Perhaps a footnote: "This comes from
Adorno-Wiesengrund"? It won't do!).[35]

One is tempted to ask, Why not? The answer leads us to one of the
more peculiar features of *Doctor Faustus*.
    In his letter to Adorno, Mann attributed his penchant for such
uncredited borrowings to his inclination to view life "as a cultural
product, hence a set of mythic clichés."[36] Art mimed life, constructing a fictional world composed of these same mythic clichés but
rearranged to suit the purposes of the artist. Within the artistic creation, these borrowings "acquire a symbolic life of their own – while
at the same time continuing to exist *intact in their original places* in
works of criticism."[37] It is as if both Mann's novel and the real world
were the product of the same slumbering nature, which "dreamt
the same thing both here and there."[38] Between the symbol and the
original there can be no lines of communication. Hence, as Mann
explained, since the story of Leverkühn is so completely at one with
that of Nietzsche, Nietzsche's name cannot appear in the narrative
(as Mann put it, "because the euphoric musician has been made so
much Nietzsche's substitute that the original is no longer permit-
ted a separate existence").[39] It can hardly be accidental, then, that
among the many names of composers in *Doctor Faustus* one will
search in vain for that of Arnold Schoenberg. In the face of that absence, Mann's later assertion that "[t]he figure of Adrian Leverkühn
has nothing whatsoever to do with Arnold Schoenberg in character, fate, circumstances" is true only in the narrowest of senses.[40]
The "character, fate, circumstances" of Adrian Leverkühn may have
more to do with Friedrich Nietzsche than with Arnold Schoenberg,
but the artistic crisis faced by Adrian Leverkühn and his resolution
of it so perfectly mirrors Adorno's account of the situation Arnold
Schoenberg confronted that to allow Schoenberg into the narrative

would be to introduce a *Doppelgänger* whose very presence would break the spell and bring the entire fiction crashing to the ground.

THE NIGHTMARE OF REASON

While Mann was assembling his montage in the office of his home on San Remo Drive, an even more baffling construction was nearing completion a few blocks away: Max Horkheimer's long-planned book on "dialectical logic." Adorno was called to Los Angeles in November 1941 to assist in the writing of what Horkheimer had once characterized as the work "for which all my earlier studies, published and unpublished, have been merely the groundwork."[41] Initially conceived as an examination of the categories of "causality, tendency, progress, law, necessity, freedom, class, culture, value, ideology, dialectic" which would combine a "determination of philosophical concepts" with "a presentation of human society in its historically given constitution,"[42] what Horkheimer wound up writing with Adorno was *Dialectic of Enlightenment*, a book that wove Homer, Immanuel Kant, the Marquis de Sade, the Hollywood studio system, and the psychological mechanisms that produced anti-Semitism into a montage that more than matched *Doctor Faustus* in its flair for uncovering unexpected correspondences.

Adorno was not the only collaborator Horkheimer considered.[43] At one point or another, Herbert Marcuse, Karl Korsch, and Franz Neumann were mentioned as possible coauthors.[44] In the spring of 1941, an exasperated Leo Löwenthal, hoping to clarify Horkheimer's intentions, summarized the confusion about the project that reigned in New York:

First you told Neumann and also Marcuse that you wanted to write your book with them; now Teddie explains that the book will be written with him. In response to Neumann's question, whether Teddy would be going west, I have presented the true state of affairs to him. In a further conversation with Neumann, you had said that, on the one hand, Marcuse should work with you on the book and, on the other, he should concern himself with his lectures and then that you had even said that he should look around for another position.[45]

Matters were eventually straightened out. By the end of 1941, Adorno was in Los Angeles and Marcuse was headed back to New York.

Within a year, Neumann and Marcuse would be in Washington, working for the Office of Strategic Services, and Horkheimer's "dialectical logic" was beginning to resemble what would ultimately be published under the title *Dialectic of Enlightenment*.[46]

As early as the spring of 1941, Horkheimer's focus had begun to shift from the laundry list of categories he had broached in his letters from the late 1930s to the themes that were to dominate *Dialectic of Enlightenment*. He explained to his friend Friedrich Pollock that he intended to explore the "breakdown of 'culture'" by developing three theses: (1) that culture itself was "duplicitous, full of contradictions, fragile" (an insight that he credited to de Sade and Nietzsche); (2) that there was a link between contradictory conceptions of truth and contradictions in actual forms of social existence (an insight he attributed to Hegel and Marx); and (3) that the concept of truth is "critical, negative" (which he saw as Schopenhauer's crucial insight). He observed, somewhat cryptically, "Perhaps the notion that one can 'make use of the truth' (Hitler) instead of fulfilling it (Jesus) is the secret conflict of modern society." Philosophy and art take on particular importance in this "secret conflict" because only they remain faithful to the mission of "fulfilling" the truth; science, in contrast, has bound itself to a project of dominating nature in which truth is equated with instrumental efficiency.[47]

The emphasis placed on the problem of truth in this sketch was in keeping with Horkheimer's concern from at least the mid-1930s.[48] In a series of articles in the *Zeitschrift für Sozialforschung*, he argued that scientistic positivism and irrationalist metaphysics "have both assumed the function of accommodating human beings to things as they are."[49] A 1939 letter characterized the situation in this way:

If one had to give a quick rough characterization of the complicated process of the breakdown of culture in recent decades – its ultimate causes in every field will be found to go back to the Renaissance – one might say that passionate and unconditional interest in truth has been replaced by an interest in "success."[50]

Even language had not escaped unscathed. Listening to one of Hitler's speeches on the radio, Horkheimer was overwhelmed by the feeling that what he was hearing was no longer language but instead "a force of nature." "The word is concerned with truth," he explained to Löwenthal, "but this is a means of war, it belongs to the glistening armaments of the inhabitants of Mars."[51] Nor was Horkheimer sanguine about his own ability to find words that were equal to the task of comprehending the horrors that engulfed Europe. "Language, and in a certain sense even thinking," he wrote Harold Laski, "are powerless and inadequate in face of what appears to be in store for mankind."[52] If Adrian Leverkühn faced the problem of how to write music when the means of musical expression had been exhausted, the challenge Horkheimer faced was even more daunting: How could one make sense of the world when language, the vehicle of thought itself, was steadily decaying into an instrument of domination?

He found a way forward in the very same work that had so excited Thomas Mann; at the end of August 1941 he read the manuscript of Adorno's "Philosophy of New Music." "If I have ever in my life experienced enthusiasm," he wrote Adorno, "it was in this reading. If there are literary documents in which hope finds a basis, your work belongs to them."[53] What Adorno's manuscript offered him was nothing less than the key to deciphering the process by which culture had collapsed into barbarism. Reflecting on developments in music since the turn of the century, Adorno concluded that the integrity of the musical work itself had been called into question: "Today the only works which really count are those which are no longer works at all."[54] Having brought music to a level of expressivity that threatened to destroy the very possibility of a finished work of art, Schoenberg sought to "reconstitute the lost totality – the lost power and responsibly binding force of Beethoven."[55] He attempted to achieve this through a domination of nature that, in the end, deprives the composer of the subjective freedom that had been the means by which Beethoven had given meaning to tonality.

Twelve-tone technique is truly the fate of music. It enchains music by liberating it. The subject dominates music through the rationality of the system, only in order to succumb to the rational system itself.[56]

In Adorno's account of rationality turning against itself – seeking a liberation from old forms but succeeding only in undermining the autonomy of the subject – Horkheimer found an image for the course of Europe from the Enlightenment onward. "Enlightenment... has always aimed at liberating human beings from fear and installing them as masters," the book he wound up writing with Adorno began, "yet the wholly enlightened earth is radiant with triumphant clarity."[57]

An explanation for this fatal trajectory of enlightenment could be found in the intertwining of myth and enlightenment that lay at the heart of what Horkheimer and Adorno came to call the "dialectic of enlightenment": "[M]yth is already enlightenment and enlightenment reverts to mythology."[58] The goal of enlightenment, as they understood it, was "to dispel myths and to overthrow fantasy with knowledge."[59] Yet, "the myths which fell victim to enlightenment were themselves its products."[60] Enlightenment's attack on mythology presses forward until even its own normative commitments are themselves denounced as mythical. Reason is now reduced to a strategy of self-preservation which, in the end, "boils down to an obstinate compliance as such" that is "indifferent to any political or religious content."[61] All thought that does anything other than make its peace with existing powers stands condemned as "poetry" or empty "metaphysics."

It is possible that Horkheimer could have elaborated this much of the argument of *Dialectic of Enlightenment* without Adorno's aid. The transformation of reason into a mechanism for self-preservation that paradoxically requires individuals to sacrifice themselves to the demands of the collectivity had been a persistent theme in Horkheimer's work since the end of the 1930s.[62] Taken by itself, this argument would have resulted in a book that repeated the argument that defenders of traditional values had long marshaled against the Enlightenment: The grand project of freeing mankind from illusion ultimately culminates in nihilism. What set *Dialectic of Enlightenment* apart from arguments such as these was the other half of the chiasmus around which the plot of the book unfolded: "Mythology is already enlightenment." This was the crucial insight that Horkheimer owed to Adorno.[63]

The argument had first been broached by Adorno in a January 1939 discussion with Horkheimer in which he "improvised" a "historico-philosophical theory of the individual" which saw Oedipus as standing at the threshold of mankind's progress towards "maturity."

Oedipus' answer to the question of the mythical Sphinx, which causes its demise, constitutes the identity of man against the diversity of the ages of his life. In the same moment in which the Sphinx is driven into the abyss by the word "man," the vagrant gains possession of wife and property. In the moment in which he banishes mythical multiplicity, it falls to him as what he possesses.[64]

With a single word, then, Oedipus reduces a baffling multiplicity to a coherent unity (whether it crawls on four legs, walks on two, or hobbles on three, it remains "a man") and establishes his sovereignty: Jocasta and Thebes are now his. His solution to the Sphinx's riddle – "It is man!" – provides later enlighteners with a paradigm for bringing a diversity of mythical figures under a common denominator and thus depriving them of their power: Everything turns out to be an alienated projection of human powers.[65]

Mythology thus begins a process which ultimately severs all magical/mimetic relations with nature. Magic presupposed neither a unity of nature nor a unity of the subject: Deities are local and specific, and the shaman must take up various cultic masks in order to imitate the objects over which mastery is to be gained.[66] Mythology, in contrast, represents an attempt both "to report, to name, to tell of origins" and "to narrate, record, explain."[67] With the breaking off of magical/mimetic relations, language renounces the claim to be like nature and limits itself to the tasks of calculation and control.[68] To the extent that it is not simply repressed, mimesis can now be exploited instrumentally. The unmoved countenance with which "practical men, politicians, priests, managing directors, and racketeers" carry out the tasks that assure the smooth functioning of society has its mirror image in the bellowing of fascist orators and concentration camp guards. Their howl, Horkheimer and Adorno observed, is "as cold as business"; like the noise generator on a flying bomb, it is something that can be switched off or on as the need requires.[69] Nazi anti-Semitism must be understood, then, not as a regression behind what civilization had achieved but rather as a further ratcheting up of its attempt to rationalize mimesis: "Fascism is also totalitarian in seeking to place oppressed nature's rebellion against domination directly in the service of domination."[70] Fascism perfected the black art of miming mimesis in the interest of domination.

Banished from rational thought, mimetic forms of behavior exact a terrible revenge. All the "irrational" trappings of fascism – the uniforms, symbols, drums, torches, repetitive speeches, and night rallies – are "so many organized imitations of magical practices, the mimesis of mimesis."[71] Adorno's studies of anti-Semitic agitators led him to the surprising conclusion that "there is no anti-Semite who does not feel an instinctive urge to ape what he takes to be Jewishness" – which, for the anti-Semite, ultimately boils down to a collection of mimetic ciphers: particular hand movements, a tone of the voice, a shape of the nose. In gathering together, anti-Semites celebrate the moment when authority permits what had been forbidden: The galvanizing moment in their rallies comes when the speaker, at long last, mimics the Jew.[72] The third panel of our triptych recorded, with frightening intensity, the violence such moments unleash.

IMPENDING DANGER, ANXIETY, CATASTROPHE

A Survivor from Warsaw, Arnold Schoenberg's cantata for narrator, male chorus, and orchestra, was composed in August 1947 and premiered the next year. Its text recounts a survivor's memories of the liquidation of the Warsaw ghetto.[73] The narrator, employing Schoenberg's technique of pitched speaking (*Sprechstimme*), recalls how a stumbling mass of workers aroused from uneasy sleep by reveille (announced by the trumpets, playing a theme that recurs throughout the piece) are repeatedly beaten over the heads with rifle butts because they are moving too slowly to suit the sadistic sergeant who is in charge of their fate. Those surviving the onslaught are then ordered to count off; their initial halting attempt (imitated by pizzicato strings) is interrupted by the sergeant's bellowed command to begin again so that he may know how many are to be delivered to the gas chambers. The counting commences once more, accelerating until it sounds like "a stampede of wild horses" (a triplet figure in the woodwinds, harp, and violins), when "all of a sudden, in the middle of it, they began singing the *Sh'ma Yisroel*." At these words, a unison male chorus enters, reenacting "the grandiose moment when they all started to sing, as if prearranged, the old prayer they had neglected for so many years – the forgotten creed!"

Hear, O Israel, the Lord is our God, the Lord is one. Thou shalt love the Lord thy God with all thy heart, and with all thy soul, and with all thy might. And these words which I command thee this day shall be upon thy heart. Thou shalt teach them diligently to thy children, speaking of them when thou sittest in thy house and when thou walkest by the way, when thou liest down and when thou risest up. (Deut. 6)

The effect of these seven minutes of music is shattering. Reviewing a 1951 broadcast of the work, Hans Keller wrote, "What higher praise can the *Survivor* receive than a musician-survivor's confession that never since his escape from the Nazis did he feel, at the same time, so terrifyingly near and so redeemingly far from the memory of his experiences?"[74]

Schoenberg had long anticipated the catastrophe that *A Survivor from Warsaw* depicted. In a 1923 letter to Wassily Kandinsky, he asked, "What is anti-Semitism to lead to if not to acts of violence. Is it so difficult to imagine that?"[75] As a soldier during the First World War, he quickly recognized that the war was "being conducted not merely against enemies from abroad but at least as vigorously against those at home," a group that included, "besides all those interested in liberal and socialist causes, the Jews." Several years later, he and his family were compelled to leave an "Aryan-only" vacation spa near Salzburg; he later noted sarcastically that this experience entitled him to claim the distinction of being "one of the first Jews in Central Europe to become the victim of an actual expulsion."[76] When he was appointed to the Prussian Academy of the Arts in 1925, he was denounced in the *Zeitschrift für Musik* as a "Jew who relies only on himself, is no longer rooted in any soil, and consciously denies tradition."[77] He left Germany shortly after Hitler came to power, and in Paris, with Marc Chagall as his witness, he formally renewed his ties to Judaism.[78]

In October 1933 he arrived in America, shuttling between Boston, where he held a position at the Malkin Conservatory, and New York. Finding Boston winters unbearable, he moved to Los Angeles in 1934, eventually obtaining a position as professor of music at UCLA. He had known Mann in Germany, and the two met from time to time during the early stages of the writing of *Doctor Faustus*.[79] But their relationship was never particularly comfortable. Schoenberg had sought Mann's support in 1938 for a plan he had drawn up in response to the desperate situation faced by European Jews. Much in Schoenberg's proposal was remarkably prescient; he saw, far more clearly than others, the likelihood of mass slaughter unless an evacuation of Jews was organized quickly, and he recognized the political difficulties of resettlement in Palestine.[80] But his call for a suspension of the boycott against Germany on the grounds that the principal aim should be, not a "fight against anti-semitism or nazism," but a struggle to create a separate Jewish state, and his demand for a united Jewish party that rejected democratic procedures and internal dissent disturbed Mann, who responded with a letter critical of Schoenberg's "fascist" and "terrorist" tactics.[81]

Schoenberg also had known Adorno in the days before exile. Adorno studied composition in Vienna during the 1920s with Schoenberg's disciple Alban Berg and had written criticism for the journal *Anbruch*.[82] But this relationship had also become strained by the time the two settled in Los Angeles,[83] and the discovery that Adorno had collaborated with Mann on a book which credited its protagonist with the invention of the system of twelve-tone composition did little to improve matters.[84] Though a "nervous eye-affliction" prevented Schoenberg from reading *Doctor Faustus*, his assistant Richard Hoffmann recorded the sections of the book dealing with musical matters on a Dictaphone.[85] Schoenberg was amused by the novel's descriptions of musical compositions but baffled by the expertise displayed in the book's account of the method of twelve-tone composition, which he recognized as beyond Mann's competence. Disturbed by the prospect that Mann had somehow succeeded in presenting a readable and accurate description of his method of composition to a mass audience (*Doctor Faustus* was, unlikely as it may now seem, a Book-of-the-Month Club selection) without giving proper credit to its creator, in February 1948 Schoenberg fired off a letter to Mann which contained a bizarre document entitled "A Text from the Third Millennium."[86] Allegedly written by an author in the year 2060, the text reports that a search through a 1988 American musical encyclopedia reveals that a man named "Arnold Schoenberg" – a teacher and writer of theoretical works on music who, according to the fictitious article, left behind no compositions – appears to have gotten into "a kind of a battle with the well-known German writer Thomas Mann." Mann, the author explains, was "clearly the inventor of the method of composing with twelve tones, based on the emancipation of dissonance," and after devising the method sometime around 1933 he allowed Schoenberg – "an unscrupulous exploiter of other people's ideas" – to take credit for the invention of the system. In the last years of their lives, the article explains, Mann and Schoenberg became bitter enemies, and Mann "took his property back and attributed its origin to a person whom he had created himself." In Schoenberg's imaginary encyclopedia article, Mann's montage has been accepted as historical truth, while "Arnold Schoenberg" survives only as the mirror image of Schoenberg's angry portrait of Mann: a man who exploits the ideas of others.[87]

The more Schoenberg came to see Leverkühn's "creation" as his own "intellectual property," the more troubled he became by the eventual fate of the novel's protagonist.[88] For Schoenberg, the method of composition in twelve tones was charged with a deeply spiritual significance. By subjecting music to a single unifying idea which, nevertheless, allowed for an astounding variety of compositional possibilities, it offered an "absolute and unitary perception" that opened up a musical space in which "as in Swedenborg's heaven...there is no absolute down, no right or left, forward or backward."[89] This description, which echoes the imperative delivered by the Archangel Gabriel at the start of Schoenberg's unfinished oratorio Die Jakobsleiter, suggests the unique mission that Schoenberg ascribed to his music. In the face of the temptations of materialism and idolatry, it held fast to the task assigned to the Jewish people: "to think the thought of the one, eternal, unimaginable, invisible God through to completion."[90] An approach to composition which, for Schoenberg, represented "the lone prophetic voice of morality in a world of rampant materialism" had been transformed, in Mann's novel, into the product of a pact with the Devil that culminated in syphilitic paralysis.[91]

The publication in 1949 of Adorno's Philosophy of Modern Music elicited an equally bitter response from Schoenberg:

The book is very difficult to read, for it uses this quasi-philosophical jargon in which modern professors of philosophy hide the absence of an idea. They think it is profound when they produce lack of clarity by undefined new expressions.[92]

Granting that Adorno "knows all about twelve-tone music," Schoenberg insisted that he nevertheless had "no idea of the creative process":

He, who...needs an eternity to compose a song, naturally has no idea how quickly a real composer writes down what he hears in his imagination....He seems to believe that the twelve-tone row, if it doesn't hinder thought, hinders invention.[93]

Composing in twelve tones was a "secret science," Schoenberg maintained, not because it was "what an alchemist would have refused to teach you," but rather because "it is a science which cannot be taught at all." What Mann's Leverkühn knew of this art was what he had been told by Adorno, "who knows only the little I was able to tell my pupils."[94]

Schoenberg had accurately discerned the provenance of *The Lamentation of Dr. Faustus*. Mann cribbed much of the description of Leverkühn's cantata for chorus and orchestra from a detailed description of the work that Adorno had drawn up for him.[95] While Schoenberg dismissed the imaginary work – suggesting that it should bear the subtitle *Leverkühn's Twelve-Note Goulash*[96] – it is difficult to read the description of its impact and not think of what Schoenberg actually accomplished in *A Survivor from Warsaw*. Toward the end of *Doctor Faustus*, Zeitblom reflects on Leverkühn's cantata and observes,

> There were years when we children of the dungeon dreamt of a song of joy – *Fidelio*, the Ninth Symphony – with which to celebrate Germany's liberation, its liberation from itself. But now only this work can be of any use, and it will be sung from our soul: the lamentation of the son of hell, the most awful lament of man and God ever intoned on this earth.[97]

With *The Lamentation of Dr. Faustus*, Leverkühn honors his pledge to "take back the Ninth Symphony." Shattered by the death of his beloved nephew Echo, the composer had vowed to replace Beethoven's song of joy and brotherhood with an ode to sorrow. But a personal loss, however shattering, hardly seems to justify so drastic a step as the revoking of the Ninth Symphony – the grounds for that demand have more to do with Mann than with his protagonist.

Early in his exile Mann himself had suggested that Beethoven's *Fidelio* was "virtually made to be the festival opera for the day of liberation from the second-rate Pizarros under whom we now groan."[98] But Hitler proved to be something more serious than a "second-rate Pizarro," and Mann came to regard the crimes of the Third Reich as so monstrous – and the complicity of the German people so complete – as to rule out any thought of celebration.[99] Faced with a catastrophe so total, he sought Adorno's aid in imagining a composition that would return music to what Adorno's manuscript had argued was its primal function: lamentation.

Its origin is gesticulative in nature and closely related to the origin of tears. It is the gesture of release. The tension of the face muscles relaxes; the tension which closes the face off from the surrounding world by directing the face actively at this world disappears. Music and tears open the lips and set the arrested human being free.[100]

It is tempting to see *A Survivor from Warsaw* in the light of the *Doppelgänger* Adorno constructed for Leverkühn. Here too is a work that puts into question the optimism of Beethoven's Ode to Joy. The baritone recitative that opens Beethoven's choral finale turns us away from the sounds of sorrow, but Schoenberg's narrator leads us into a world of almost inconceivable suffering.

Yet, as Reinhold Brinkmann has suggested, this analogy does not quite hold. With the entry of the chorus in Schoenberg's cantata – reenacting the "grandiose moment" when those who are about to be slaughtered break into a forgotten prayer and affirm a solidarity with their tradition – victims are suddenly turned into victors who even in the face of death remain true to the vow that Schoenberg had uttered a quarter of a century earlier in his letter to Kandinsky: "to survive in exile, uncorrupted and unbroken, until the hour of salvation comes!" At this moment, Brinkmann argues, *A Survivor from Warsaw* becomes "a modern 'Ode to Joy,' born out of the deepest desperation and terror."[101] It portrays a scene of utter horror but promises redemption. As Adorno observed shortly after Schoenberg's death,

in this piece, Schoenberg . . . suspends the aesthetic sphere through the recollection of experiences which are inaccessible to art. Anxiety, Schoenberg's expressive core, identities itself with the terror of men in the agonies of death, under total domination. . . . Horror has never rung as true in music, and by articulating it music regains its redeeming power through negation.[102]

Even so, something remains terribly unsettling about this work, and as Adorno later noted, the unease does not reside simply in the desire of audiences not to be reminded of events they would rather forget.

The victims are turned into works of art, tossed out to be gobbled up by the world that did them in. The so-called artistic rendering of the naked physical pain of those who were beaten down with rifle butts contains, however distantly, the possibility that pleasure can be squeezed from it.[103]

Thus, what makes *A Survivor from Warsaw* so difficult to bear is that, ultimately, it is not at all difficult to bear.

Like all of Schoenberg's works, there are unexpected beauties in an aural landscape that, on first survey, seems to offer only utter terror – in that sense, it is at one with Schoenberg's great expressionist masterpiece *Erwartung*. Snatches of woodwind phrases recall not scenes of horror but favorite moments from Mahler's symphonies. The triplet figures that accompany the counting off of the bodies can be anticipated with pleasure in later listenings; the accelerando that leads up to the entry of the chorus is riveting. Perhaps no work is more effective in refuting the notion that Schoenberg wrote dry and cerebral music that only other musicians can appreciate. At the European premier of *A Survivor from Warsaw*, an audience that had only moments before attempted to stop a performance of a piece by the Venetian serialist Bruno Maderna with hissing and mock applause responded to Schoenberg's work with such enthusiasm that it had to be repeated.[104]

Yet the more *A Survivor from Warsaw* takes its place among the masterpieces of twentieth-century music, the more disturbing it becomes. For what can it mean when music can be made from suffering of this sort? Schoenberg bemoaned the tendency of contemporary composers to "care so much about style and so little about idea."[105] For him, composition was concerned, above all else, with the musical idea – "immutable and Platonic" – which "rises above historical contingency."[106] Viewed strictly in musical terms, the entry of the chorus at the end of *A Survivor from Warsaw* demonstrates how it is possible to stabilize an apparently chaotic musical field – the musical material that accompanies the opening narration – without the conventional resources of tonality.[107] But to see the work in this way borders on the obscene; it turns an historical atrocity into the "style" best suited for the presentation of a musical idea. Across the score of *A Survivor from Warsaw* eternal musical ideas collide with historical fact. "An idea," Schoenberg wrote in 1946, "can never perish."[108] The text of *A Survivor from Warsaw* reminds us that people do: painfully, brutally, and senselessly.

Shortly after Schoenberg's death, Adorno hailed the concluding chorus of *A Survivor from Warsaw* as "the protest of mankind against myth."[109] A decade later he was not so sure what to make of it. He wondered whether the solemn prayer at the conclusion served to "make the unthinkable appear to have some meaning" and in this way effaced "something of its horror."[110] Adorno found no way out of the dilemma. An art that remained deaf to the cries of the slaughtered could not "stand up to the demands of justice." Yet, at the moment when art gives voice to their cries of desperation, it runs the risk of replacing their suffering with a song of affirmation.[111] For the rest of his life, Adorno kept pulling at this same knot. After announcing (famously) that "[t]o write poetry after Auschwitz is barbaric,"[112] he had second thoughts and granted that he might have been mistaken: "Perennial suffering has as much right to expression as a tortured man has to scream."[113]

"Art," he observed in *Minima Moralia*, "is magic delivered from the lie of being truth."[114] The fascist demagogue imitated the Jew, pressing the forbidden power of mimesis into the service of rationalized domination. Within the magic circle of *A Survivor from Warsaw*, the tables turn: Struggling to remember, a Jewish survivor imitates a Nazi camp guard and releases a prayer that promises redemption. It is a testimony to the unmasterable ambivalence this work cannot help but unleash that, at recent performances, audiences have been directed *not* to applaud. Such strategies are probably not enough to keep the Devil from getting his due. Perhaps Mann was on to something. Even when it is serves enlightenment, there is something diabolical about the act of mimesis.

NOTES

1. Perhaps it is not entirely out of place for the author to note that he, too, entered the world at about this time. Nor, he hopes, would it be inappropriate for him to place a note of thanks here to his son, Benjamin MacDonald Schmidt, whose interest in Schoenberg and enthusiasm for *Doctor Faustus* spurred his father to reflect on the curious trinity of works whose birth year he shares. Thanks are also due to the National Endowment for the Humanities, which supported the seminar that I organized on these works during the summer of 2000, and to the members of the seminar, who helped me to clarify many of the points discussed here. Finally, I am indebted to Lydia Goehr for a number of helpful comments on this essay and to Leslie Epstein for his unique understanding of the world explored in this essay and his unfailing kindness to its author.

2. For general discussions of the "intellectual migration," see Franz Neumann et al., *The Cultural Migration: The European Scholar in America* (Philadelphia: University of Pennsylvania Press, 1953); Donald Fleming and Bernard Bailyn, eds., *The Intellectual Migration: Europe and America, 1930–1960* (Cambridge, Mass.: Harvard University Press, 1969); Laura Fermi, *Illustrious Immigrants: The Intellectual Migration from Europe, 1930–1941*, 2nd ed. (Chicago: University of Chicago Press, 1971); Anthony Heilbut, *Exiled in Paradise: German Refugee Artists and Intellectuals in America, from the 1930s to the Present* (Boston: Beacon, 1983); Jarrell Jackson and Carla M. Borden, eds., *The Muses Flee Hitler: Cultural Transfer and Adaptation, 1930–1945* (Washington, D.C.: Smithsonian Institution Press, 1983); Martin Jay, *Permanent Exiles: Essays on the Intellectual Migration from Germany to America* (New York: Columbia University Press, 1985); and Reinhold Brinkmann and Christoph Wolff, eds., *Driven into Paradise: The Musical Migration from Nazi Germany to the United States* (Berkeley, Los Angeles, and London: University of California Press, 1999). Brinkmann's contribution to *Driven into Paradise*, "Reading a Letter" (pp. 3–20), provides a helpful overview of this literature and a thoughtful discussion of the issues at stake in the choice of terms – "migration," "immigration," and "exile" – used to describe the event. For a general survey of Hollywood in the 1940s, see Otto Friedrich, *City of Nets: Hollywood in the 1940's* (New York: Harper and Row, 1987).

3. For a guide (originally written for German tourists making the pilgrimage), see Cornelius Schnauber, *Hollywood Haven, Homes and Haunts of the European Émigrés and Exiles in Los Angeles*, trans. Barbara Zeisl Schoenberg (Riverside, Calif.: Ariadne Press, 1997).

4. Letter to Karl Kerényi of February 18, 1941, in *Mythology and Humanism: The correspondence of Thomas Mann and Karl Kerényi* (Ithaca: Cornell University Press, 1975), 101. Likewise, Ludwig Marcuse, reflecting on his exile in Los Angeles, observed, "One is not such a foreigner when one is surrounded by friendly foreigners.... I hardly realized there were any Americans here" (*Mein zwanzigstes Jahrhundert* [Munich: Paul List, 1960], 266).

5. Bertolt Brecht, *Letters 1913–1956*, trans. Ralph Mannheim (New York: Routledge, 1990), 116.

6. Ronald Hayman, *Brecht: A Biography* (New York: Oxford University Press, 1983), 257.

7. Bertolt Brecht, *Poems 1913–1956* (New York: Routledge, 1987), 382.

8. Brecht, *Poems 1913–1956*, 367.

9. See Brinkmann's insightful discussion of their differences in "Reading a Letter," 4–7.

10. Arnold Schoenberg, "Two Speeches on the Jewish Situation," in *Style and Idea*, ed. Leonard Stein, (Berkeley and Los Angeles: University of California Press, 1975), 502.

11. Letter to Oskar Kokoschka of July 3, 1946 (Arnold Schoenberg, *Letters*, ed. Erwin Stein [Berkeley and Los Angeles: University of California Press, 1987], 242).

12. On Eisler's appearance before HUAC, see Heilbut, *Exiled in Paradise*, 270–4. In the 1969 afterword to the German edition of *Composing for Films*, Adorno explained that he and Eisler had long-standing political disagreements, and he withdrew his name from the title because he had no interest "in becoming a martyr to a cause that was not mine and is not mine" (Theodor W. Adorno and Hanns Eisler, *Komposition für den Film* in Theodor W. Adorno, *Gesammelte Schriften*, vol. 15 [Frankfurt: Suhrkamp, 1976], 144). For a detailed discussion of government surveillance of the exile community that draws on recently obtained documents, see Alexander Stephan, *Communazis: FBI Surveillance of German Émigré Writers* (New Haven, Conn.: Yale University Press, 2000). For an account of the contents of Adorno's FBI file, see Andrew Rubin, "The Adorno Files," in *Adorno: A Critical Reader*, ed. Nigel Gibson and Andrew Rubin (Oxford: Blackwells, 2002), 172–90.

13. Hayman, *Brecht*, 299, 308–10, 313–4.

14. Donald Prater, *Thomas Mann: A Life* (New York: Oxford University Press, 1995), 403, 424.

15. Walter Benjamin, *Illuminations*, trans. Harry Zohn (New York: Schocken, 1969), 257–8.

16. Thomas Mann, *Doctor Faustus*, trans. John E. Woods (New York: Knopf, 1997), 246.

17. Mann, *Doctor Faustus*, 165–6.

18. Mann, *Doctor Faustus*, 253–4.

19. The resemblance was noted in Hans Mayer's 1950 study, *Thomas Mann: Werk und Entwicklung* (reprinted, with additional material, as *Thomas Mann* [Frankfurt: Suhrkamp, 1980]). Adorno called the work to Mann's attention in his letter of July 6, 1950 (Theodor W. Adorno and Thomas Mann, *Briefwechsel 1943–1955*, ed. Christoph Gödde and Thomas Sprecher [Frankfurt: Suhrkamp, 2002], 72). In his response of July 11, Mann described Mayer's claim as "entirely absurd" and denied that the Devil resembled Adorno at all, asking Adorno incredulously, "Do you actually wear horn-rims?" (*Briefwechsel*, 76). Adorno (who did in fact wear horn-rims, something which could hardly have escaped Mann's attention) was less emphatic in denying the connection and, Mayer suggests, rather liked the idea. A year later, Adorno presented Mayer with a copy of *Minima Moralia* inscribed with the words "For

Hans Mayer, with best wishes, from his old devil" (see Mayer, *Thomas Mann*, 25–7).

20. Mann discussed this reference to Adorno in his account of the writing of *Doctor Faustus*, *The Story of a Novel: The Genesis of Doctor Faustus*, Richard and Clara Winston, trans. (New York: Knopf, 1961), 48. Mann's earliest letter to Adorno (dated October 10, 1943) was a request for a few notes on the Arietta theme (see *Briefwechsel*, 9); in response, Adorno sent Mann a transcription of the relevant passage (see *Briefwechsel*, 156). In his 1949 polemic with Mann, Schoenberg observed that Mann failed to get the phrasing of the passage right. See Arnold Schoenberg, "Further to the Schoenberg-Mann Controversy," *Music Survey* 2, no. 2 (1949), pp. 77–80.

21. Mann, *Story of a Novel*, 47–8. See Mann's diary entry for October 6, 1943, in Mann, *Tagebücher 1940–1943*, ed. Peter de Mendelssohn (Frankfurt: Fischer, 1982), 635. Just as Mann was alluding to Adorno's patronym, Adorno himself was getting rid of it: About this time, Adorno, whose name had been registered as "Wiesengrund-Adorno" on his birth certificate, legally dropped the first part of his name. See Rolf Wiggershaus, *The Frankfurt School: Its History, Theories, and Political Significance*, trans. Michael Robertson (Cambridge, Mass.: MIT Press, 1994), 66.

22. Mann, *Doctor Faustus*, 244.

23. Mann, *Doctor Faustus*, 21.

24. Letter to Kerényi of March 24, 1934, in *Mythology and Humanism*, 46.

25. Mann, *Story of a Novel*, 30; *Doctor Faustus*, 5.

26. Mann, *Doctor Faustus*, 256. Cf. Adorno, *Philosophie der neuen Musik*, in *Gesammelte Schriften*, vol. 12 (Frankfurt: Suhrkamp, 1975), 36–8; translated by Anne G. Mitchell and Wesley V. Blomster under the title *Philosophy of Modern Music* (New York: Seabury Press, 1973), 29–32.

27. Mann, *Doctor Faustus*, 256.

28. Mann, *Story of a Novel*, 32.

29. There are, however, important differences, which Schoenberg attributed to Mann's failure to understand his approach. For a discussion of the differences, see Patrick Carnegy, *Faust as Musician: A Study of Thomas Mann's Novel* Doctor Faustus (London: Chatto and Windus, 1975), 37–54.

30. Adorno had completed the manuscript – which corresponds to the first chapter of his *Philosophie der neuen Musik* – by the summer of 1941; see Max Horkheimer's letter to Theodor Adorno of August 28, 1941 (Horkheimer, *Gesammelte Schriften*, vol. 17, *Briefwechsel 1941–1948*, ed. Gunzelin Schmid Noerr [Frankfurt: Fischer, 1996], 146). The manuscript, which is chiefly concerned with Schoenberg's work, was

coupled with a discussion of Stravinsky and published in 1948. Mann's reliance on Adorno's discussions of Schoenberg's work was first pointed out by John L. Stewart, "On the Making of *Doctor Faustus*," *Sewanee Review* 59 (1951) 329–42, an article that appeared shortly after the publication of Adorno's *Philosophy of New Music* and attributed the divergence between Schoenberg and Leverkühn's approaches to twelve-tone composition to Mann's overly condensed summary of Adorno's argument. Mann also acknowledged reading Adorno's still unpublished book on Wagner, which eventually appeared in 1952 (translated by Rodney Livingstone under the title *In Search of Wagner* [London: New Left Books, 1981]); see Mann, *Story of a Novel*, 94–5. But as Rolf Tiedemann has documented, Mann's reading of Adorno's work was even more extensive than he acknowledged: Mann also had access to Adorno's essay *Spätstil Beethovens* and to Willi Reich, *Alban Berg* (Vienna, Leipzig, and Zürich: Herbert Reichner, 1937), a volume which included a number of contributions by Adorno. See Rolf Tiedemann, "Mitdichtende Einfühlung: Adornos Beiträge zum *Doctor Faustus* – noch einmal," *Frankfurter Adorno Blätter* 1 (1992): 11–13. The recently published exchange of letters between Mann and Adorno indicates an even more extensive acquaintance, which includes the manuscript of *Dialectic of Enlightenment* (see Mann's letter to Adorno of September 7, 1944 [Adorno and Mann, *Briefwechsel*, 12]) and Adorno's essay "Spengler Today" (see Mann's letter of December 13, 1944 [*Briefwechsel*, 14]).

31. The two had met as early as the end of 1942 at Max Horkheimer's house, but Mann did not appear to develop an interest in Adorno's work until after hearing his lectures on Beethoven's op. 111. For a discussion of the revelant documents, see the editorial note in Adorno and Mann, *Briefwechsel*, 10–11.

32. Mann, *Story of a Novel*, 43. Adorno's manuscript is first mentioned in Mann's diary entry for July 21, 1943; see Mann, *Tagebücher 1940–1943*, 603. Mann probably met Adorno a month earlier; his diary entry for June 26 reports that he had lunch at "Horckheimers Social Scienze [sic]" (*Tagebücher*, 445). Mann had known Horkheimer for some time. A diary entry from 1940 (prior to his move to California) reports that he is reading "Horkheimer's arrogant *Zeitschrift für Sozialforschung*" (*Tagebücher* 41) and that he attended a housewarming party when Horkheimer moved into his neighborhood in Pacific Palisades (*Tagebücher* 293). Horkheimer and his wife served as witnesses for Mann and his wife when they applied for citizenship. See Katia Mann, *Unwritten Memoirs*, trans. Hunter Hannum and Hildegarde Hannum (New York: Knopf, 1975), 122.

33. Mann's account of their collaboration may be found in *The Story of a Novel* (see, esp. 42–8, 102–3, 150–6, 221–3), a book which Mann

described as having been motivated "by the moral obligation to give Dr. Adorno *credit*, to use the American phrase, for what I brazenly took from him and which he gave me in collaborating on the musical aspects of *Faustus*" (letter to A. M. Frey of January 19, 1952, in *Letters of Thomas Mann*, trans. Richard Winston and Clara Winston [New York: Vintage, 1975], 448). See also the letter to Jonas Lesser of October 15, 1951, in Mann, *Briefe*, ed. Erika Mann (Frankfurt: Fischer, 1961–1965) vol. 3, 225–6. Mann's diaries for the period 1944–8 confirm that Mann met regularly with Adorno. For Adorno's account of the collaboration, see "Toward a Portrait of Thomas Mann" in *Notes to Literature*, vol. 2, trans. Sherry Weber Nicholsen (New York: Columbia University Press, 1992), 12–9. The descriptions of Leverkühn's works that Adorno produced for Mann are reprinted in Adorno and Mann, *Briefwechsel*, 158–61.

34. Mann, *Story of a Novel*, 150.
35. Letter to Theodor Adorno of December 30, 1945 (Mann, *Letters*, 361–2; (for the German, see Adorno and Mann, *Briefwechsel*, 118–22).
36. Mann, *Letters*, 361.
37. Mann, *Letters*, 362.
38. Mann, *Doctor Faustus*, 21.
39. Mann, *Story of a Novel*, 32.
40. Letter to Alberto Mondadori of June 19, 1950 (Mann, *Letters*, 429). See also Mann's exchange of letters with Arnold Schoenberg in *Saturday Review*, which contains a similarly specific denial of parallels: "There is no point of contact, not a shade of similarity, between the origin, the traditions, the character, and the fate of my musician, on the one hand, and the existence of Arnold Schoenberg, on the other" (Letter to the Editor, *Saturday Review*, January 1, 1949, p. 23).
41. Letter to Juliette Favez of February 17, 1939 (Horkheimer, *Gesammelte Schriften*, vol. 16, p. 561). For the connection between the proposed "Dialectical Logic" and *Dialectic of Enlightenment*, see Schmid Noerr's discussion in Horkheimer, *Gesammelte Schriften*, vol. 5, pp. 431–2 (translated as "Editor's Afterword" in Max Horkheimer and Theodor W. Adorno, *Dialectic of Enlightenment*, trans. Edmund Jephcott [Stanford: Stanford University Press, 2002], 225–6).
42. Max Horkheimer, "Idee, Aktivität und Program des Instituts für Sozialforschung," in Horkheimer, *Gesammelte Schriften*, vol. 12, p. 156. See also Max Horkheimer, "Notes on Institute Activities," *Studies in Philosophy and Social Science* 9, no. 1 (1941): 121–2.
43. The earliest evidence of collaboration came in a letter from Adorno to Horkheimer of March 2, 1937, which spoke of plans for "our common book on dialectical materialism" (Horkheimer, *Gesammelte Schriften*, vol. 16, p. 68).

44. Horkheimer discussed a possible collaboration on a book on "Dialectics" in a letter to Karl Korsch of August 31, 1938 (Horkheimer, *Gesammelte Schriften*, vol. 16, pp. 467–8); see also Wiggershaus, *Frankfurt School*, 177–8, 260. As early as 1936, Horkheimer and Marcuse had begun soliciting suggestions for a textbook on "materialist doctrines" from antiquity to the nineteenth century that would address such topics as "suffering and poverty in history, meaninglessness of the world, injustice and repression, critique of religion and morality, the connection of theory and social practice, demands for the better organization of society, etc." See the letter of May 6, 1936, from Herbert Marcuse and Max Horkheimer to Theodor Adorno, Walter Benjamin, Ernst Bloch, Eduard Fuchs, Henryk Grossman, Paul Honigsheim, and Hans Mayer (Horkheimer, *Gesammelte Schriften*, vol. 15, pp. 517–8). In a letter to Benjamin on April 13, 1937, Horkheimer mentioned that he and Marcuse would be bringing out a textbook on "dialectical materialism" in "about two years" (Horkheimer, *Gesammelte Schriften*, vol. 16, p. 113). In a letter to Friedrich Pollock of April 27, 1941, Horkheimer states that he was anticipating Marcuse's arrival and looking forward to working with him on a book which is now described as encompassing such themes as the "breakdown of culture" and the link between science and the domination of nature (Horkheimer, *Gesammelte Schriften*, vol. 17, p. 24). As late as July 6, 1942, Horkheimer explained to Otto Kirchheimer that the work in which he was engaged – which he now described as centered on "the theory of language and of enlightenment" – was being undertaken in collaboration with "Adorno and Marcuse" (Horkheimer, *Gesammelte Schriften*, vol. 17, p. 309).

45. Letter of Leo Löwenthal to Max Horkheimer, May 1, 1941 (Horkheimer, *Gesammelte Schriften*, vol. 17, p. 31). It appears that Löwenthal himself hoped to play a role in the writing of Horkheimer's magnum opus. In a letter to Horkheimer of February 3, 1942, discussing the work in which Horkheimer and Adorno were engaged, Löwenthal quipped, "It is – to repeat it again – against reason, justice, and (my) happiness that, so far, it is happening without me but with Teddie!" (Horkheimer, *Gesammelte Schriften*, vol. 17, p. 256). Widening the circle of possible collaborators still further, Horkheimer's March 10, 1942, letter to Felix Weil expressed the hope that both Weil and Friedrich Pollock could come to Los Angeles for six months to work on the "economic and political parts" of the book (Horkheimer, *Gesammelte Schriften*, vol. 17, p. 274).

46. An initial version of the book was circulated to friends and associates of the Institute for Social Research in mimeographed form under the title *Philosophische Fragmente* late in 1944. For a discussion of the

differences between this manuscript and the final version, see my article "Language, Mythology, and Enlightenment: Historical Notes on Horkheimer and Adorno's *Dialectic of Enlightenment*," *Social Research* 65 (1998): 810–12. Thomas Mann read the manuscript in October, prior to its circulation, see Mann, *Tagebücher 1944–1946*, ed. Inge Jens (Frankfurt: Fischer, 1986), 110–11.

47. Letter to Friedrich Pollock, April 27, 1941 (Horkheimer, *Gesammelte Schriften*, vol. 17. pp. 24–5).

48. See, for example, his 1935 essay, "The Problem of Truth," translated in Max Horkheimer, *Between Philosophy and Social Science* (Cambridge, Mass.: MIT Press, 1993), 177–216.

49. Horkheimer, *Between Philosophy and Social Science*, 260.

50. Letter to Robert Maynard Hutchins of January 7, 1939 (Horkheimer, *Gesammelte Schriften*, vol. 16, pp. 536–7).

51. Letter to Leo Löwenthal of July 21, 1940 (Horkheimer *Gesammelte Schriften*, vol. 16, p. 731).

52. Letter to Harold Laski of March 10, 1941 (Horkheimer, *Gesammelte Schriften*, vol. 17, p. 18 [written in English]).

53. Horkheimer, *Gesammelte Schriften*, vol. 17, p. 146.

54. Adorno, *Philosophie der neuen Musik*, 37 (*Philosophy of Modern Music*, 30).

55. Adorno, *Philosophie der neuen Musik*, 69–70 (*Philosophy of Modern Music*, 30).

56. Adorno, *Philosophie der neuen Musik*, 68 (*Philosophy of Modern Music*, 67–8).

57. Max Horkheimer and Theodor W. Adorno, *Dialektik der Aufklärung*, in Horkheimer, *Gesammelte Schriften*, vol. 5 (Frankfurt: Fischer, 1987), 25 (Dialectic of Enlightenment, 1). See also Theodor W. Adorno, *Minima Moralia*, trans. E. F. N. Jephcott (London: New Left Books, 1974), 140.

58. Horkheimer and Adorno, *Dialektik der Aufklärung*, 21 (*Dialectic of Enlightenment*, xviii).

59. Horkheimer and Adorno, *Dialektik der Aufklärung*, 25 (*Dialectic of Enlightenment*, 1).

60. Horkheimer and Adorno, *Dialektik der Aufklärung*, 30 (*Dialectic of Enlightenment*, 5).

61. Max Horkheimer, "End of Reason," in Andrew Arato and Eike Gebhart, eds., *The Essential Frankfurt School Reader*, (New York: Urizen, 1978), 34.

62. See particularly Horkheimer's articles "The Latest Attack on Metaphysics" (1937) in *Critical Theory* (New York: Herder and Herder, 1972), (pp. 142–3 no. 165) and "Montaigne and the Function of

Skepticism" (1938) in *Between Philosophy and Social Science* (pp. 271, 292, 294).

63. This distinction is mirrored in the division of labor that marked the composition of *Dialectic of Enlightenment*. Surviving drafts suggest that the opening chapter, which examined the intertwining of the two theses, was the result of an intense collaboration between Horkheimer and Adorno. In contrast, the first excursus, an account of the *Odyssey* that stresses the extent to which myth already is a process of enlightenment, was written by Adorno, while the second excursus, which uses de Sade and Nietzsche to show how enlightenment collapses into myth, was written by Horkheimer. For a discussion of the composition of *Dialectic of Enlightenment*, see Gunzelin Schmid Noerr, "Nachwort," in Horkheimer, *Gesammelte Schriften*, vol. 5, 427–30 (*Dialectic of Enlightenment*, 219–24).

64. "Diskussionen über die Differenz zwischen Positivismus und materialischer Dialektik," in Horkheimer, *Gesammelte Schriften*, vol. 12, p. 453.

65. Horkheimer and Adorno, *Dialektik der Aufklärung*, 28–9 (*Dialectic of Enlightenment*, 4).

66. Horkheimer and Adorno, *Dialektik der Aufklärung*, 31–4 (*Dialectic of Enlightenment*, 5–7).

67. Horkheimer and Adorno, *Dialektik der Aufklärung*, 30 (*Dialectic of Enlightenment*, 5).

68. Horkheimer and Adorno, *Dialektik der Aufklärung*, 40 (*Dialectic of Enlightenment*, 13).

69. Horkheimer and Adorno, *Dialektik der Aufklärung*, 212 (*Dialectic of Enlightenment*, 150).

70. Horkheimer and Adorno, *Dialektik der Aufklärung*, 215 (*Dialectic of Enlightenment*, 152).

71. Horkheimer and Adorno, *Dialektik der Aufklärung*, 212–6 (*Dialectic of Enlightenment*. 150–3). The awesome power of this organized regression to forbidden magical practices was not lost on Mann's friend Kerényi. In the summer of 1934, he wrote to Mann, "The German 'intelligentsia' *has* already collapsed.... The youth in Germany today are being reared in the atmosphere of this insanity.... I have watched this youth – a *whole* city – march out one Saturday evening in Heidelberg, in long columns, under flags and in uniforms marked by symbols of death; I was forced to listen to their battle songs and combat games the whole night through; this was perhaps the most sorrowful moment of my life.... " (letter to Mann of August 13, 1934 [*Mythology and Humanism*, 58–9]).

72. Horkheimer and Adorno, *Dialektik der Aufklärung*, 213 (*Dialectic of Enlightenment* 151). See also Theodor W. Adorno, "Anti-Semitism and

Fascist Propaganda," in *Anti-Semitism: A Social Disease*, ed. Ernst Simmel (New York: International Universities Press, 1946), 125–37, and "Freudian Theory and the Pattern of Fascist Propaganda," in Andrew Arato and Eike Gebhart, eds., *The Essential Frankfurt School Reader* (New York: Urizen, 1978), 118–37.

73. Earlier accounts of this work alleged that Schoenberg based his text on an eyewitness account by a survivor of the uprising; for example, see René Leibowitz, "Arnold Schoenberg's *Survivor from Warsaw* or the Possibility of 'Committed Art,' " *Horizon* 20, no. 1 (1949): 126. But more recent discussions have emphasized the lack of fit between the narrative, with its references to conditions in extermination camps, and the crushing of the uprising in the Warsaw ghetto. See especially Michael Strasser, " 'A Survivor from Warsaw' as Personal Parable," *Music and Letters* 76, no. 1 (1995): 52–64; Camille Crittenden, "Texts and Contexts of *A Survivor from Warsaw*, op. 46," in Charlotte M. Cross and Russell A. Berman, eds., *Political and Religious Ideas in the Works of Arnold Schoenberg* (New York: Garland, 2000), 231–58; and David Isadore Lieberman, "Schoenberg Rewrites his Will: *A Survivor from Warsaw*, op. 46," Ibid., 212–13.

74. H. K. [Hans Keller], "A Survivor from Warsaw," *Music Survey* 3, no. 4 (1951): 279.

75. Letter to Wassily Kandinsky of May 4, 1923 (Schoenberg, *Letters*, 90). For a discussion of Schoenberg's exchange of letters with Kandinsky regarding anti-Semitic views among members of the Bauhaus, see Peg Weiss, "Evolving Perceptions of Kandinsky and Schoenberg: Toward the Ethnic Roots of the Outsider," in *Constructive Dissonance: Arnold Schoenberg and the Transformations of Twentieth-Century Culture*, ed. Juliane Brand and Christopher Hailey (Berkeley: University of California Press, 1997), 48–51.

76. See Schoenberg's letter of May 12, 1934, to Jacob Wise, translated in Alexander L. Ringer, *Arnold Schoenberg: The Composer as Jew* (Oxford: Clarendon Press, 1990), 153.

77. See Alfred Heuss, "Arnold Schönberg – Prussian Teacher of Composition," translated in Alexander L. Ringer, *Arnold Schoenberg*, 224–6.

78. H. H. Stuckenschmidt, *Arnold Schoenberg: His Life, World, and Work*, trans. Humphrey Searle (New York: Schirmer, 1978), 368. Schoenberg had become a Lutheran in 1898, a religion which in Catholic Vienna, as Alexander Ringer observes, was looked upon "with only slightly less suspicion than Jews" (Ringer, *Arnold Schoenberg*, 26).

79. Mann borrowed Schoenberg's copy of *The Theory of Harmony* (Schoenberg's article "Further to the Schoenberg-Mann Controversy," *Music Survey* 2, no. 2 [1949]: 79, describes it as "one of the few extant copies of the work"), which he used in certain of the book's technical

discussions (see *Mann, Story of a Novel*, 29, 51–2, 67, 217). Stuckenschmidt (*Arnold Schoenberg*, 456) reports that in July 1942 Mann
attended some of Schoenberg's lectures at UCLA (which were also attended by Eisler and Brecht), though there is no mention of this in
Mann's diaries.

80. See Arnold Schoenberg, "A Four-Point Program for Jewry," in Ringer,
Arnold Schoenberg, 230–1, 241–4. For a discussion, see Ringer, *Arnold
Schoenberg*, 138–49.

81. See Schoenberg, "A Four Point Program," 231–41. For a discussion of
the exchanges between Schoenberg and Mann, see E. Randol Schoenberg's introduction to his edition of the correspondence between
Thomas Mann and Arnold Schoenberg, *A proposito del Doctor Faustus:
letterre 1930–1951*, ed. E. Randol Schoenberg (Milan: Rosellina Arch-
into, 1993). For a criticism of Schoenberg's "authoritarian propensities"
that parallels Mann's comments, see Ringer, *Arnold Schoenberg*, 131.

82. For a discussion, see Max Paddison, *Adorno's Aesthetics of Music*
(Cambridge: Cambridge University Press, 1993), 5–7, 22–5, 37–52, and
Susan Buck-Morss, *The Origin of Negative Dialectics* (New York: The
Free Press, 1977), 11–17.

83. Stuckenschmidt reports that "at meetings in the houses of common
friends there were battles of words between them" (*Arnold Schoenberg*, 495). Schoenberg found Adorno's mode of expression preten-
tious and was disgusted by his "oily pathos," his "pomposity," and
his intrusive attempts to solicit Schoenberg's advice on his own compositions. Schoenberg found the latter particularly offensive because
when Schoenberg had sought a contribution from Adorno in the early
1930s for a lexicon of concepts in compositional theory, Adorno had
rebuffed him with the explanation that he was "not a musician,
but a philosopher." See Jan Maegaard, "Zu Th. W. Adornos Rolle
im Mann/Schönberg-Streit," in Rolf Weicker, ed., *Gedenkschrift für
Thomas Mann, 1875–1975* (Copenhagen: Text und Kontext, 1975), 216–
7, which quotes extensively from a fragment written by Schoenberg in
December 1950.

84. Schoenberg credits Alma Werfel-Mahler as his source of information
in his letter to the *Saturday Review* (January 1, 1949, p. 22). In a rather
transparent reference to Alma, Mann expresses regret that Schoenberg's
acquaintance with the work was "based exclusively on the gossip of
meddling scandal mongers." The portrait of Alma that emerges from
Katia Mann's memoirs is not an attractive one: "She always drank far
too many sweet liqueurs and was rather malicious by nature. She loved
to start gossip, and it was she who got Arnold Schoenberg going on the
business of the twelve-tone system in *Faustus*" (*Unwritten Memoirs*,

123–4). For Alma's (rather unreliable) account of the affair, see Alma Mahler-Werfel, *And the Bridge Is Love* (London: Hutchinson, 1959), 275.

85. See Richard Hoffmann, "Der Roman eines 'Roman eines Romans,'" *Publikationen der Internationalen Schönberg Gesellschaft* 2 (1986): 234–41.

86. The text is translated in Stuckenschmidt, *Arnold Schoenberg*, 547–8.

87. Mann eventually added a note to *Doctor Faustus* informing the reader that the method of composition discussed in the book is "in truth the intellectual property of a contemporary composer and theoretician, Arnold Schoenberg." In his letter to the *Saturday Review*, Schoenberg accused Mann, once again, of having "taken advantage of my literary property" and criticized him for having "hid" his explanation "at the end of the book, on a place on a page where no one ever would see it." Schoenberg further complained that the explanation belittled him by referring to him as "*a* [a!] *contemporary* composer and theoretician." In "two or three decades," Schoenberg wrote, "one will know which of the two was the other's contemporary" (*Saturday Review*, January 1, 1949, p. 22).

88. See Hoffmann, "Der Roman eines 'Roman eines Romans,'" 238.

89. Arnold Schoenberg, "Composition in Twelve Tones (1)" in *Style and Idea*, 223. See the discussion in Ringer, *Arnold Schoenberg*, 74–5.

90. Ringer, *Arnold Schoenberg*, 36; see also p. 40.

91. Ringer, *Arnold Schoenberg*, 40; Stuckenschmidt, *Arnold Schoenberg*, 495.

92. Letter to Joseph Rufer of December 5, 1949, quoted in Stuckenschmidt, *Arnold Schoenberg*, 508. Schoenberg's disgust with what he regarded as the unnecessarily labored style of Adorno's texts dates back to his reading of Adorno's contributions to the journal *Anbruch*. See Arnold Schoenberg, "Glosses on the Theories of Others" (1929), in *Style and Idea*, 315.

93. Letter to Joseph Rufer of December 5, 1949, quoted in Stuckenschmidt, *Arnold Schoenberg*, 508.

94. Arnold Schoenberg, "The Blessing of the Dressing" (1948), in *Style and Idea*, 386.

95. Adorno's description of the piece is reprinted in Adorno and Mann, *Briefwechsel*, 160–1.

96. Schoenberg, "Further to the Schoenberg-Mann Controversy," 78.

97. Mann, *Doctor Faustus*, 509.

98. Letter to Alfred Knopf, November 8, 1935 (Mann *Letters*, 202).

99. These views placed him in opposition to Brecht and others on the question of forming a German government in exile. For a discussion, see

Herbert Lehnert, "Thomas Mann, Bertolt Brecht, and the 'Free Germany' Movement," in *Exile: The Writer's Experience*, ed. John M. Spalek and Robert F. Bell (Chapel Hill: University of North Carolina Press, 1982), 182–202.

100. Adorno, *Philosophie der neuen Musik*, 122 (*Philosophy of Modern Music*, 128).

101. Reinhold Brinkmann, "Schoenberg the Contemporary: A View from Behind," in *Constructive Dissonance*, 211–14. For some reservations about this line of interpretation, see Steven J. Cahn, "Variations in Manifold Time: Historical Consciousness in the Music and Writings of Arnold Schoenberg" (Ph. D. diss., State University of New York, Stony Brook, 1996).

102. Theodor Adorno, *Prisms*, trans. by Samuel Weber and Shierry Weber (London: Neville Spearman, 1967), 172.

103. Adorno, "Engagement," in *Notes to Literature*, vol 2, p. 88.

104. See the review by Christina Thorseby in *Music Survey* 3, no. 2 (1950): 116–7.

105. Schoenberg, "New Music, Outmoded Music, Style and Idea," in *Style and Idea*, 123.

106. These characterizations are taken from Murray Dineen, "Adorno and Schoenberg's Unanswered Question," *The Musical Quarterly* 77, no. 3 (1993): 417, 421. For the development of Schoenberg's notion, see Patricia Carpenter and Severine Neff, "Schoenberg's Philosophy of Composition: Thoughts on the 'Musical Idea and Its Presentation,'" in *Constructive Dissonance*, 146–59.

107. For a discussion of how Schoenberg accomplishes this, see Christian M. Schmidt, "Schönbergs Kantate 'Ein Überlebender aus Warschau' op. 46," *Archiv für Musikwissenschaft* 33, no. 4 (1976): 174–88, 261–77.

108. Schoenberg, "New Music, Outmoded Music, Style and Idea," 123.

109. Adorno, *Prisms*, 172.

110. Adorno, *Notes to Literature*, 88.

111. Adorno, *Notes to Literature*, 88.

112. Adorno, *Prisms* 34.

113. Theodor Adorno, *Negative Dialectics*, trans. E. B. Ashton (New York: Seabury, 1973), 362.

114. Adorno, *Minima Moralia*, 222.

7 Right Listening and a New Type of Human Being

Adorno's *Aesthetic Theory* is currently the object of considerable interest in this country.[1] This is a good thing, but puzzling as well. And it is this puzzle that I want to address. The book is more distant from us than might be indicated by the immediate response its new translation has engendered. It, along with Adorno's philosophy as a whole, involves a way of making distinctions, types of distinctions, and experiences that are inimical to us; in our heart of hearts, down home, they rub us the wrong way. If Adorno's pronouncements on jazz have notoriously aggravated many, by the power of hearsay alone, without almost anyone having read the relevant essays or wondered what exactly he was criticizing, this is only the barest indication of his capacity to bother us. Of the musical compositions that might spontaneously occur to the inner ear of the overwhelming majority of the American readers of this essay – themselves an educated elite – there might not be a single song that would not have resounded in Adorno's own ear as "trash" and so stereotypical in its construction that the puzzle for him would have been how anyone could parse one such tune from another. To our minds, this must represent some special grudge Adorno held against all things popular.

Yet this was not at all the case. For neither did Adorno like Dvořák, Hindemith, Elgar, Debussy, Stravinsky, or Sibelius, among many, many others. And there was much he found wanting in Schoenberg as well. Adorno may have been as dissatisfied with each and every composition – of whatever art form – as anyone has ever been. This dissatisfaction has an implication that is so remote from us that it is hardly to be intuited this side of the Atlantic: For if Adorno was dissatisfied with all existing art, it was because he was intent on finding the *one* right artwork, the one that would be *the* artwork. In other words – and this is the thought that more than any other in all of aesthetics has the ability to grasp the mind of our commercial tribe between thumb and forefinger and squeeze – Adorno thought not just that one artwork may be liked better than another but that this one work would be, in itself, better than another.

This was not momentary bad manners that slipped into an otherwise distinguished philosophy, any more than St. Augustine absentmindedly lost track of the main point of his theology when he admonishes us that one can love the wrong thing. Adorno's philosophy conceived as a whole seeks the primacy of the object. His critique of the judgment of taste is inextricable from this central philosophical intention, not as a part that had to conform to an overriding thesis but as the originating impulse of that thesis. His philosophy of the primacy of the object has its source in the experience of one artwork as superior to another. It could not be otherwise. There is no other basis, this side of the moon, on which to understand or sympathize with the intensity of his thought. And without an ear for emphatic music, for music that means to be *the* music, every line Adorno wrote echoes hollowly convoluted or blindly exaggerated. The philosophy of the primacy of the object itself derives from the audibly urgent primacy of one artwork over another in a mind that is prepared to hear it.

Not to be pugnacious, but to be a little blunt: Our minds, in general, would rather not hear this primacy; even when we sense it, we do not know what to make of it. Though we insist on having our preferences and consider the freedom to like and dislike inherent in democracy, these preferences are limited to the judgment itself. Whatever we find to like in an art gallery, we assume someone else might, with equal justification, dislike. Conversely, what someone else likes, we might just as well, and with equal justification, dislike. In the morality of our everyday aesthetics, what is important to us is that we have our likes and dislikes, and at any moment be ready to call a truce over the objective claim of a distinction in value rather than insist that we have put our hands on what all the world must acknowledge as the *one* right thing. We are sure that any person who would argue that taste should subserve the object – that the object itself wants to be the one and only right thing, that if seen or heard "correctly," the correct object would be chosen and the "wrong" one dismissed – is streaked with authoritarianism.

For us, in our everyday aesthetics, the coauthor of the *Authoritarian Personality* would be an autocrat, and when he lived in the United States, he was experienced as that by many. This is so plausible to us – to those of us who are certain that many paintings are required to cover our many walls – that something must be said at the outset to make Adorno's position even momentarily worth considering. On this score, though Adorno will not find many allies among art consumers, he does have many among artists. Here is what Francis Bacon, the painter, has to say on the topic of what one might have a taste for: "Of course what in a curious way one is always hoping to do is to paint the one picture which will annihilate all the other ones, to concentrate everything into one painting. . . . I've got an obsession with doing the one perfect image."[2] And, in fact, at the Centre Pompidou, one wall is reserved for each of his paintings, as if neighbors in any proximity, even framed and under glass, might be eaten alive. It should not, however, be supposed that such a claim to being the only artwork is exclusive to artworks with explicitly ferocious imagery. Even Wallace Stevens, who thought that modern poetry must "speak words that in the ear/In the delicatest ear of the mind, repeat,/Exactly, that which it wants to hear,"[3] had tolerance exclusively for one poem. Thus, in "Credences of Summer," he wrote, "One day enriches the year. One woman makes the rest look down,"[4] only because that poem tests itself, as a credence of poetry, by its capacity to transmute these ultimate elements of natural beauty – one woman, one day – into its claim to being the one poem. But why then, if there is only to be one work, are there so many artworks? From the perspective of art – from the perspective of a genuinely monstrous productive energy such as, say, Picasso's – the answer is that there is a multiplicity of works only out of wanting the one artwork.

If this is enough to grant Adorno's position, provisionally, a degree of tolerance, still we are hardly ready to accept it. It is not ours. And if, as claimed, Adorno's position is central to his aesthetics, and to his philosophy as a whole – and if we still want to have much to do with either – we must come to terms with the foreignness of his critique of taste. It will not, however, help this discussion to focus immediately on this question of taste for the one right artwork. This would involve us just as quickly in a narrowly tangled dispute. The aim, rather, is to sketch the foreignness of Adorno's aesthetics in several dimensions, including national levels, and then come back to this specific problem. We cannot approach it meaningfully until we have collided as openly with Adorno's thought as we do implicitly. This antagonism is worth investigating. If the interest in Adorno's *Aesthetic Theory* is puzzling, it is just as certain that there is an urgency right now to understand the work correctly – to find out what it really has to say. This goal will not be realized by pretending that *Aesthetic Theory* is waiting to embrace us at the gate.

I

Let's begin then to notice how foreign to ourselves Adorno's work is by seeing why the current interest in *Aesthetic Theory* is puzzling. The first, broadest reason is just that the book is an utterly speculative work, an aesthetics. Aesthetics is itself the most remote region of philosophy, and in that remote philosophical region of aesthetics, *Aesthetic Theory*, if one went to look for it, would be found at the vanishing point, the distant limit. In its complexity, in its sometimes hermetic, Pythian expression, the book stands at the philosophical maximum. In its very tone, as is well known, the book portrays itself as a philosophy, which to be philosophy at all would need to be the only philosophy. And while *Aesthetic Theory* is located at that philosophical maximum, in absolute distance and tone, we are located at the other extreme, at the philosophical minimum. We would not only shy away from the warmonger aesthetics of a Francis Bacon, we would not even join in a thumb wrestle over the difference between stoicism and skepticism. What would bother us, on the contrary, is if we learned that some contemporary of that seminal third-century Greek skeptic, Sextus Empiricus, had been denied "the right to say it," whatever it might have been. Then we are ready to go to war, and not with paint either. It is this mix of avoidances and proclivities that marks us, under the banner of civilization, as the least philosophical people that ever walked the earth. If this is not self-evident, if you doubt it, notice how right this second, in your own reading sensorium, just this mention of the word "civilization" – an irredeemably philosophical concept – may already have caused the inner hackles to stir. "What do you mean," the inner voice of the inner hackles asks, "by 'civilization'? Who is 'civilized' and who is not? And who are you to say which is which?" But whatever the answers to this string of questions, whatever "civilization" may mean, my main point, that we are the unphilosophical, is hardly unprecedented. To Tocqueville, for instance, it was preeminently obvious. "Americans have no school of philosophy peculiar to themselves," he wrote. And later added, "Less attention is paid to philosophy in the United States than in any other country of the civilized world."[5]

Let's let Tocqueville's pronouncement antagonize us a bit so we can overhear the inner voices of the lurking national audience in us all get mad and, though basically disinterested in philosophy, demand this: "Who is to say who is philosophical and who is not?" Tocqueville, who certainly considered himself a philosophical man, apparently thought he could make the distinction. And his answer is valuable to us because, as will be seen, it helps differentiate the tradition in which Adorno worked from the one in which we live. Thus, when Tocqueville distinguishes the philosophical from the unphilosophical, it is as a distinction between the philosophical ideal and its opposite – the thought of an American.

And how, if we follow up on Tocqueville, does the philosophical ideal think? As does the deity. And how does the deity think? I hesitate to report on it. It is hard for the likes of ourselves, unspeculative people that we are, to consider this sort of thing, but here it is: When the deity thinks, says Tocqueville, he does not, for instance, view the human race collectively. Rather, he sees individuals, each separately, each in the resemblances that make him like his fellows and in the differences that make him unlike his fellows.[6] The thinking of the deity, in other words, is the utterly articulated perception of the one and the many. The deity is not ever obliged to make unlike like, or to subsume the particular to the general in order to know it, but thinks emphatically only, so that in place of concepts there would effectively be proper names: In such a mind, a painting perceived as a painting would have to be *the* painting as nothing else made of paint and canvas would be.

The deity, therefore, has no need of normative or general ideas. General ideas are, rather, the necessary instruments of the frail human mind; they are what the mind has recourse to when it has no other way to grasp reality. And this frailty, says Tocqueville, is the exaggerated characteristic of the unphilosophical American mind. It is the fate of the mind most exclusively shaped by the pressure of equality. For under this pressure, every mind is necessarily suspicious of every other mind, with which it is necessarily in competition, and thus no mind can accept anyone else's judgment as its own. Rather, each seeks to control each of its judgments with the tenacity of a hermit. This narrow type of intelligence, out of its weakness, must insist on wanting to answer every question on the basis of its own self, which – since it has been deprived of any historical resonance by the democratic break from tradition – it takes to be a general self. Therefore, the American has a strong propensity for general ideas.[7]

Even without taking time here to examine Tocqueville's analysis step by step, most any of us – one by one, of course, and reviewing this, right this moment, in the privacy of our own particular reading cave – will recognize enough of ourselves in it to see that Tocqueville has put his finger on our special capacity: It is the capacity of the principle of equality as it shapes our minds to produce general ideas. Thus, what the likes of us most want to do, when we think, is to come to the conclusion that things are the "same." Nothing is more obvious to us, for instance, than that all that sounds might as well be called music; that every ragged list of words might as well be called a poem; that wherever people congregate, there is a civilization. We are obliged to insist, and are most proud of ourselves when we insist, and feel the power of being a certain kind of nation when we insist, for instance, that everyone who thinks is already a philosopher, to the extent that anyone might want to bear that appellation. It is the power we consider "transgressive" and the pursuit of "difference" when the Guggenheim Museum mashes together a display of Armani suits and Cezannes, flatware and motorcycles.

II

The tradition of thought that appears in Tocqueville is one that – in the choice between thinking like the deity and thinking like an unphilosophical American – makes its preference plain. Not only might Americans, in confronting it, suspect Tocqueville of being anti-American, but even nonreligious Americans may intuit a heretical bent in Tocqueville's own intellectual aspirations. It is, actually, just this suspiciousness, a sense of religious heresy in a philosophical undertaking, that is needed here if we are to be able to study

Adorno in self-consciousness of our own national comprehension. In this frame of mind, look at the following passage from *Minima Moralia*, for instance. I have chosen it because it is so regularly and self-evidently quoted that anyone familiar with the literature will be ready to groan with recognition:

The only philosophy which can be responsibly practised in face of despair is the attempt to contemplate all things as they would present themselves from the standpoint of redemption. Knowledge has no light but that shed on the world by redemption.... Perspectives must be fashioned that displace and estrange the world, reveal it to be, with its rifts and crevices, as indigent and distorted as it will appear one day in the messianic light.[8]

The urgency of this passage, which to this moment can be felt in our throats, is just that what has been may never be known for what it has been. These lines have been much quoted only because one can hardly help but quote them. All the same, it is not sure that, this side of the Atlantic, we realize what we are dealing with. And if the passage is indeed greeted by some with an ache of recognition, the aim here is to show that this is an ache of false recognition. Notice that, even though the passage does not seem complicated, it is not obvious how to understand it. Clearly, Adorno insists that the one, the only possible, philosophy must aspire to a divine vantage as a surrogate for a messianic light to come. But if we try to take Adorno at his word, if, for instance, we start to conclude that he held that philosophy must entrust itself to the light shed by some messianic plenipoteniary on the order of John the Baptist, the glare of misinterpretation becomes too intense to continue. The passage is obviously not a work of theological fervor. It does not want us to bend at the knee. On the contrary – and here we have arrived at a set of boundary lines that are not always so available to the eye – Adorno can invoke the messiah qua philosopher just because as a philosopher Adorno was not a religious man. He was not a believer but a philosopher. Though he had the bearing of a priest back of the lectern, it was a philosopher's lectern he stood back of. Thus the passage should be interpreted, not as a demand that philosophy take up the stance of John the Baptist, but as a demand that John the Baptist should be a philosopher. And Adorno was only able to urge this by having confidence that as a philosopher he would not invoke the magical contents of what he named. This prerogative was his as a capacity that he inherited, as did the whole of European philosophy, Tocqueville included, as it came into receipt of a theology shaped by the thought of antiquity and transmuted by the Enlightenment. The turning point in that secularization was, of course, Romanticism, that profane mysticism, which, as we can now see in Adorno's passage, wanted to conjure the image of divine light, not in order to behold the deity as its source above, but to illuminate a damaged nature below. The passage exhorts us to the secular act of a genuinely isolated, elite individual who without a doubt seeks another world, but not that recommended by any church.[9] Adorno's philosophy thus was able to be as full of theology as Kierkegaard's without his being any more a believer than Kierkegaard – the single distinction being that Kierkegaard wanted to be a believer and Adorno did not.

III

Adorno was only able to write that much quoted passage because he had no need to worry, as would an American, that at dawn on the day of publication a millenarian congregation would be there to greet him in his kitchen for prayers, cookies, and a march on the canyon – to view the rifts and the crevices – in expectation of the messianic light. It is striking, in fact, that any effort to situate Adorno's passage in an American context causes comic ironies to fan out in every direction. For instance, a rigorously trained American philosopher, in scrutinizing Adorno's passage, might conceivably reject it out of hand as full of hocus pocus and hardly philosophical. But this would only be because the magical intensities presumed of Adorno might verily be the beam in the beholder's own eye. For it is on this side of the Atlantic, not on Adorno's side, that the magical claim of these theological concepts has remained undiminished. And to bring the American situation more into focus, this same philosopher-reader (who on the job, back of the lectern, might look like a dentist), having made short shrift of Adorno on the grounds of symbolic logic, could well lock up his professional office for the week, looking forward to joining the chorus at church on Sunday. American philosophy, in contrast to European philosophy, is shaped by the ramifications of a national order which, in its primary desire to protect religious freedom, established religion as the truth of the private sphere, thus isolating religious thought from the process of enlightenment.

This is why, statistically, by documented sightings alone, the Virgin Mary, in any given year, spends more time on American shores than in Italy or the whole of western Europe.

IV

For us, aesthetics is the most remote dimension of philosophy. When he was a preeminent American Kant scholar, Robert Paul Wolff, for instance, was proud to say that he had never read the third *Critique*. It did not matter, and anyway he preferred lying on the sofa watching James Bond movies. In the German tradition, by contrast, aesthetics inevitably becomes the keystone of any philosophical construction. Thus, Adorno necessarily stood at the apex of his intellectual ecclesia as a priest of art. This is not a metaphor. And here, however much the problem is to make Adorno as foreign as possible to us, described as a priest of art he will necessarily become inscrutable. For without special study, the office – a priest of art – is unknown to us. These words are not combined in our language. In German thought, however, intimations of the office go back as far as Cusanus, and the institution emerges full blown in Wackenroder and Tieck's seminal Romantic work, *Outpourings of an Art-Loving Friar*. Notice that the title of this book must catch the American ear entirely off guard. And to read the book is to encounter the vision of art taking the place of divine mediation. Art, the good friar explains, "must come before love . . . for art is of heavenly provenance." And again: "Art must become a sacred love or a loved religion. . . . Earthly love may then take its place after art."[10] Theologically, art has here taken the place of Christ, by whose sacrifice human love becomes possible.

It must be emphasized that in the whole of American thought there is nothing like this. In the first place, there are simply no similar philosophical speculations on the topic. And if one consulted the epochly correlative volumes of American romanticism, one would discover that the American movement is in fact distinct from the European movement specifically by virtue of the hesitant, muted presence of any kind of art religion. Adorno illuminates this difference when he writes, in his *Beethoven*, that in the nineteenth century the European middle class prayed while listening to Beethoven.[11] In those concert halls, the magical aspect of religion was preserved as a kind of aesthetic ecumenicalism that provided a foundation for a solution to the wars of religion. In its ideal of a person of taste, the middle class was united, beyond the bloody nation-mangling struggles of the reformation. For Europe, the greatest hopes became lodged in aesthetics. By contrast, Americans simply pray when they pray, and that is often. Though they may sing in church, they have never experienced music as a secularization of the divine. Indeed, for their historiographical imagination, because it postdates the division of art into high and low, art does not originate, as it does obviously for all Europeans, in religious imagery. Otherwise the United States would not have been so able to become the primary world purveyor of industrial literary and musical entertainment.[12] And for the same reason, an Americanist who sought an elite intellectual to compare directly with the aesthetical elites of European Romanticism would otherwise be able to find someone closer than Thoreau, who would listen to Bach in ecstasy and then get drunk.

When Adorno informs us on European habits of aesthetic prayer, there is no doubt that he himself prayed in this fashion. As proof, the whole of *Aesthetic Theory* could be cited. For a more concise piece of evidence, we may note that in his view Hitlerism was partly caused by the loss of the experience of emphatic art: "It is the lack of experience of the imagery of real art, partly substituted and parodied by the ready-made stereotypes of the amusement industry, which is at least one of the formative elements of that cynicism that has finally transformed the Germans, Beethoven's own people, into Hitler's own people."[13] However much one wishes the thesis were true, it is well known that any number of SS officers were as proud of their ability to play Mozart on the pianoforte as of their cruelty in the bunker. But it is the starkness of the contrast that is at issue here: For Adorno, and out of a centuries-long European development, the most profound human hopes, theological hopes, took shape as aesthetic hopes. Only in this context could his challenge to the possibility of "poetry after Auschwitz" hit so central and common a European nerve that ever since the whole of his philosophical writings – in newspapers, journals, and many books – has been known by that one maxim. *Aesthetic Theory* itself is nothing but an extended meditation on that question and the implications of an envisioned catastrophic end to art. In the United States, however, if one wanted to formulate an even vaguely compelling equivalent of that maxim, a saying that risked something comparable, it might appear on a Holiday Inn marquee along a Georgia highway: "Is there Jesus after Auschwitz?"

V

If Adorno's thinking can now be recognized as alien to our own, it is worthwhile to turn attention to the obverse issue and recognize our foreignness to him. When he came to the United States in 1938, roughly a century after Tocqueville and very much in the same tradition (for example, they engaged in a similar critique of equality and both had a high regard for the idealist concept of truth), Adorno found himself involved in a study of how music is transformed when it is mass reproduced by radio transmission. In these decades, most of the American democratic left hoped that radio would finally lift the stain of privilege from cultural treasure so that, along with the mink-clad and chaufferred urbanites arriving at Carnegie Hall for a performance of Beethoven, the farmer's wife in Iowa would also be able to attend, just by being at home next to her radio receiver. Adorno, however, dissented from the democratic left's hopes. He saw that subordinating important music to the principle of equality would not universalize cultural treasure but neutralize it. After he completed what he could of this study, *Current of Music*, he turned his attention from how music is transformed by radio transmission to the recipients of the music, the inhabitants of this country. And here he discovered that, in fact, the effects of radio transmission on serious music were relatively a matter of indifference. A "new type of human being" had emerged in the United States for whom, no matter what the manner of performance, serious music had become inapposite.[14] Indeed, Adorno wrote, given this new type of human being, the fiction could no longer be maintained that it was progressive and humanistic for men and women to hear Beethoven symphonies, read Milton, and contemplate Raphael's madonnas. Culture itself had entered into such opposition to the real conditions of life that it could no longer fulfill its age-old task of humanizing the individual.

Adorno was aware that these observations, though in some regards they begin where Tocqueville left off, were in their extremity unprecedented. No one had previously considered that the nature of the person could be so transformed historically that culture would become inadequate to humanity. Adorno goes on to describe who he thought we are, these people who are beyond culture's power to cultivate. Whereas culture presupposed an autonomous individual, the contemporary American has been so overwhelmed by real and constant anxiety, has been so broken in on by heteronomous forces, that this autonomy and its capacity for involvement with extramental reality could no longer be presumed. Adorno thought that this incapacitation of the person began in earliest childhood, and he noted several aspects of what had happened. First, the world no longer provides actual images to the American child but only images that arrive with the insignia of their own untruth stamped on them. Second, the objects of action have all become technical objects that primarily demand adaptation to their own instructions. Third, the collapsed family no longer provides a buffer between society and person, which partly explains why the American child is flooded with anxiety. Fourth, the traditional language of people has been supplanted by a language of advertisement that does not fulfill people but instead leaves them speechless. Fifth, libido is directed toward tools so that the world of things becomes a substitute for images. And sixth (the factor Adorno thought the most important),the relation of people to their own nature, their own bodies, has been transformed. A sports culture had developed, he found, that had suspended the longstanding taboo on naked physical power, and this was responsible for efforts to translate cultural objects into categories of physical performance. The translation of novels into films would, for instance, be a variant of this.

If Tocqueville's analysis of the style of American thinking obviously hit the nail on the head in various particulars, Adorno's description of this new type of human being, of ourselves, pounds the nail deep into the plank. This muscle-for-mind image is used here advisedly, with the alacrity of our tribe, to conjure up the relevance of Adorno's description. Likewise, the efforts earlier in this chapter to engage the "inner hackles" of the reader have similarly been used as intellectual sport, on the assumption that intellectual concentration alone would not draw thought through. And it might be worthwhile to continue in this style, for just a moment, as it will allow us to check a main point in Adorno's description of the ontogeny of this new type of human being: that we are not to become cultured individuals, people capable of being much involved in what is other than ourselves, because we have been broken in on too many times. Confirmation is actually not hard to find, though the following miniature psychological test for regression – which would be the overarching tendency of such a self – requires at least that each reader find some equivalent to a phrase like "the Lone Ranger" to experiment with. These words alone may do the trick and will be used here for demonstration. But if these do not work, you the reader, of whatever generation, will not have to look much farther than, for instance, a fragment from that first popular song that you heard and hated but then heard repeated so many times that you started singing it yourself, an event that is now probably a definitive marker in this country of the initiation into adolescence. Take that rhythmical fragment or the phrase "the Lone Ranger" and feel how it works back of your eyes and along the cheekbones and wonder where it got its familiarity with you. And wonder also, what of this sense of familiarity – as if it would be the basis of familiarity with most anyone – actually exists? And if there is no real familiarity in that fragment, if there would be nothing much to say to someone else to follow up on the clue "Remember the Lone Ranger" or "Remember that song" – how it was this way, how it was that way – then what is being perceived as "familiarity" is just the memory trace of regression; the familiarity is only that of a moment when the self could no longer hold out against the pressure of what was being forced on it. Most of what we have in our heads at this point – regardless whether the reader is in a group that in this country would be considered an intellectual elite (for example, professors, deans, or graduate students) – turns out to have this quality rather than any quality at all of being "our memories." And if the test is over now, we can conclude that what might just have been felt – including the sideways grin, the sense of something yellow on the face, or anger at the childishness of the test – is how Adorno thought that that "new type of human being," who is not to become a cultured individual, feels.

VI

Adorno would not have minded this way of making a sport of regression. He was not a rigorist. He did not conclude his reflections on the new type of human being by insisting that some way must be found to return these miscreants to culture. On the contrary, his approach to this, as to any situation, was to try to discover what new powers the transformed moment might be able to release. For Adorno, the only way out was through. Thus, he concluded his essay on "A New Type of Human Being" by listing what new powers this new type of being might have, among which he mentions the following: a cold readiness for sacrifice, a cleverness in the struggle with mega-organizations, a speechless preparedness to do what is decisive.

Perhaps in the war years, many of these powers became actual. But whatever came of that, whatever of those powers may indeed be ours, this discussion has now come around to consider more closely Adorno's *Aesthetic Theory*. For his approach to the capacities of the new type of human being closely parallels what he considered to be the fundamental capacity of art: It is the possibility of turning the powers of the world against itself. This is a dialectical way of putting something that fits our (genuinely undialectical) ears better as Wallace Stevens would put it, talking of poetry, when he wrote that poetry is a "violence from within that protects us from a violence without."[15] It could not be more obvious than that there are no powers adequate to reality other than reality's own powers; they are the only *modus operandi*. Thus, just as in his study of the new type of human being Adorno tried to discern a way to direct its powers against those in which they originated, in his aesthetics he thought similarly that art itself must turn the violence against the violence, but in the realm of illusion. For it is only in the realm of illusion that the violence against the violence could be free of violence. Only there could it be shaped as the articulation of the one and the many, an articulation in which what is brewing in us all – which is for sure, if not only, a disaster – could possibly appear in such a way that whoever was capable of concentrating on it would rightly exclaim, "If only it were." Art is the conceivable point at which the brewing disaster becomes inextricable from "if only it were," the image of reconciliation. Or to condense it again, art is the effort to shape the truth in the form in which it can rightly be longed for, in that moment when the body is covered with goosebumps. And it is because there is a discernible difference between the false shudder and the true shudder that an aesthetics devoted to the primacy of the object claims that one artwork can be, and absolutely must seek to be, better than any other artwork. The process of each and every artwork that emphatically undertakes to be art is the process by which the work destroys its own illusion.[16] In Benjamin's terms, certainly the origin of Adorno's aesthetics, every work ruins itself for the truth. Even the most stereotypical tune, by bringing itself to a close, however predictably, insists that there should only be one artwork. Because art seeks what is utterly real, no artwork can tolerate any other work, let alone its illusion-bound self. To presuppose many works, a diversity of artworks, is to assume that art is finally no more than an illusion, good at best for covering our walls. Thus Adorno's dissatisfaction with each and every artwork was his alliance with each one as it seeks to be the only artwork. If there is anything despotic in this intention, it is a despotism of the desire for the particular and real in opposition to what simulates it.

VII

In conclusion, it is worth thinking back to Adorno's list of the powers apposite to a new kind of person who is not to be cultured. Note that he did not enumerate probable powers of patient translation or a discernible eagerness to study *Aesthetic Theory*. But he might have seen this coming had he thought about it. In his own genuinely haughty, uncompromising style, shaped by a complete disdain for the philistine, he could, for instance, have written, "Textbook dialectics – only the excluded can be needed." *Aesthetic Theory* could only have been written on the basis of Adorno's return to Germany from the United States. The book is written in utter opposition to what we are. This formed the potential for the book to become more important here than in Germany, a potential that is now urgent. This is not to say that we need *Aesthetic Theory* so we can pretend to be priests of art or speculative philosophers. That is not, to my sense, in the offing. Rather, at this moment *Aesthetic Theory* could give us a basis on which to figure out in what way taste can be disputed and the correlative impulse to develop an exactitude in listening, what Adorno called "adequate listening." As he wrote, "It is more essential for the listeners to please the Beethoven symphony than for the Beethoven symphony to please him."[17] Ears that were keyed to this level of differentiation, that would listen for what is emphatic in art and take its side against all that is not, that could even tolerate for a moment such arch apothegms as "Right listening means above all the overcoming of the current false listening"[18] might discover that jazz as Adorno knew it, then synoymous with Sweet and Swing, was the reggae of the thirties and forties. And they also might discover that the howl today over his antipathy to that bland music obscures the aversion of most people to advanced contemporary jazz, which is a genuinely marginal music that has internalized the entire development of the twelve-tone music that Adorno once championed, is in fact hardly played on "all jazz" radio stations, and has a miniscule listenership more restricted than that of so-called classical music. *Aesthetic Theory* could become a power of differentiation allowing us to let things drop; dig in our heels with a willful disinterest in amusement; let the many movies spool silently elsewhere without worrying that we are being left behind by having missed them; protect the museums from the Armani and bake shops; notice that what now makes our toes tap, and our faces light up miscellaneously, is no one's memory; and act on the impulse to protect ourselves, or our imagination anyway, as the power over possibility, from what otherwise uses that power, second by second almost, to break in on us and to defeat that possibility.

NOTES

1. Theodor Adorno *Aesthetic Theory*, trans. Robert Hullot-Kentor (Minneapolis: University of Minnesota Press, 1997).
2. David Sylvester, *The Brutality of Fact: Interviews with Francis Bacon* (New York: Thames and Hudson, 1987), 22.
3. Wallace Stevens, "Of Modern Poetry," in *Collected Poetry and Prose* (New York: Library of America, 1997), 219.
4. Wallace Stevens, "Credences of Summer," in *Collected Poetry and Prose* (New York: Library of America, 1997), 324.
5. Alexis de Tocqueville, *Democracy in America*, trans. George Lawrence (New York: Harper Collins, 2000), 429.
6. Tocqueville, *Democracy in America*, 437.
7. Tocqueville, *Democracy in America*, 439.
8. Theodor W. Adorno, *Minima Moralia*, trans. E. F. N. Jephcott (London: New Left Books, 1974), 247.
9. Cf. Erich Kahler, *Man the Measure* (New York: Meridian, 1967), 488.
10. Wilhelm Heinrich Wachenroder and Ludwig Tieck, *Outpourings of an Art-Loving Friar*, trans. Edward Mornin (New York: Frederick Ungar, 1975), 26.

11. And as Walter Benjamin points out, even in the film age European critics aspired to pray to these images: "Alexandre Arnoux concludes his fantasy about the silent film with the question: 'Do not all the bold descriptions we have given amount to the definition of prayer?'" Walter Benjamin, "The Work of Art in the Age of Mechanical Reproduction," in *Illuminations*, trans. Harry Zohn (New York: Schocken, 1969, 227). Benjamin quotes Arnoux from *Cinema pris*, 1929, p. 28.

12. Again, Tocqueville was the first to document this, and – in a chapter entitled "The Industry of Literature" – did so a full century before Adorno wrote on the "culture industry." In that chapter, Tocqueville writes, "Democracy not only gives the industrial classes a taste for letters but also brings an industrial spirit into literature" (*Democracy in America*, 475).

13. Theodor W. Adorno, "What National Socialism Has Done to the Arts," in *Gesammelte Schriften*, vol. 20, pt. 2, ed. Gretel Adorno, Susan Buck-Morss, and Klaus Schulz (Frankfurt: Suhrkamp, 1986), 419.

14. Theodor W. Adorno, "Problem des neuen Menschentypus" (June 23, 1941), Adorno Archive, Frankfurt.

15. Wallace Stevens, *Collected Poetry and Prose*, 665.

16. Adorno, *Minima Moralia*, 75–76.

17. Theodor Adorno, *Nachgelassene Schriften*, vol. 3, *Current of Music*, ed. Robert Hullot-Kentor (Frankfurt: Suhrkamp), forthcoming.

18. Adorno, *Current of Music*.

8 Authenticity and Failure in Adorno's Aesthetics of Music

> Scars of damage and disruption are the modern's seal of authenticity.[1]
>
> Adorno
> *Aesthetic Theory*

What does Adorno mean by 'authenticity'? The concept undoubtedly occupies an important place in his aesthetics and pervades his thinking to a remarkable degree, even when the term itself is absent. But as is the case with much of his conceptual framework, his notion of authenticity is never directly defined or addressed, and its meaning has to be inferred from its relation to other concepts. This apparent fuzziness makes it prone to dismissal as mere rhetoric and lays it open to the accusation that it serves no other purpose than to conceal summative and unsubstantiated value judgments on artworks under a cloak of unattributed authority.[2] It can appear to lack a clear identity. Its dependency on its relation to clusters of other concepts becomes obvious enough when one considers claims like the following in *Ästhetische Theorie* (1970): 'The seal of authentic artworks is that what they appear to be appears as if it could not be prevaricated, even though discursive judgment is unable to define it' (AT, 199). This does not mean that the concept of authenticity lacks a strong focus in Adorno's aesthetics, however, and I suggest that it is precisely through the exploration of its 'force field' of related concepts – what Adorno calls, borrowing a favourite term of Walter Benjamin's, its constellation – that light can be shed on this complex and value-loaded term.

In his well-known discussion of the music of Schoenberg and Stravinsky in *Philosophie der neuen Musik* (1949) Adorno identifies the accepted notion of authenticity as 'being-so-and-not-being-able-to-be- otherwise'.[3] However, it is clear that he is not using the concept in any of its more familiar senses when he maintains that, after Auschwitz, the authentic works are the failures and that 'the authentic artists of the present are those in whose works there shudders the aftershock of the most extreme terror'.[4] Revealed here are the polarities we come to expect in Adorno: On the one hand, authenticity concerns the way a work appears to be what it is because it can be no other way, an idea which contains a range of related concepts, including those of self-contained structural consistency and of totality; on the other hand, pitted against this is the idea that the authentic modernist work is characterized by failure in these terms and that the social and the historical impinge on the apparently autonomous world of the work of art, fracturing its integrity and making its consistency look suspect and ideological in the face of the horrors of the real world which culminate in Auschwitz. Authenticity for Adorno is therefore also associated with a modernist, fractured relationship between the individual and the social, the internal structure of the artwork and the external conditions within which it functions, a relationship which imputes a high degree of self-consciousness and self-reflexivity to the work of art at a structural, technical level. At the same time, it is also necessarily posited on a concept of *inauthenticity*, that is, on the notion that there are works which do not internalize this fractured relationship, which are not self-reflexive, and which remain content to comply with the traditional stereotypes – what Adorno calls 'resigned art'. What is decisive for Adorno is the relationship of art to the 'crisis of meaning'. Authentic art rejects handed-down meaning through negation, to the effect that it appears to elevate meaninglessness itself in place of meaning, thereby becoming meaningful in spite of itself; resigned art affirms accepted meaning as if it were unproblematic, becoming itself the embodiment of reified consciousness. Adorno formulates this division in *Ästhetische Theorie* in terms that can serve as a point of reference for the ensuing discussion:

The dividing line between authentic art that takes on itself the crisis of meaning and a resigned art consisting literally and figuratively of protocol sentences is that in significant works the negation of meaning itself takes shape as a negative, whereas in the others the negation of meaning is stubbornly and positively replicated. Everything depends on this: whether meaning inheres in the negation of meaning in the artwork or if the negation conforms to the status quo; whether the crisis of meaning is reflected in the works or whether it remains immediate and therefore alien to the subject. (AT, 154)

While the concept of authenticity has a broad application within his aesthetics and his philosophy in general, it has a special focus for Adorno in relation to music. It is this focus I shall examine here. The concept is complex because, if one may risk such a metaphor, it is multidimensional. Keeping its different and opposing aspects in view at any one time is difficult, as one is compelled always to view the whole from a particular perspective, like walking around a large three-dimensional object where the experience of the totality is always partial and restricted and where a conception of the whole can only be pieced together later. Furthermore, there is also a historical dimension to the concept which demands attention, because here is to be seen the dynamic impulse of the concept of authenticity and its relation to Adorno's theory of the historical dialectic of musical material. What I am attempting to describe here is, of course, nothing more than the Hegelian underpinning to all Adorno's thinking – how to deal with contradiction in a manner which does not simply reduce it to a static formula but which also avoids losing a sense of the dynamic totality of Adorno's thought. To attempt to reveal this underlying dynamic structure of Adorno's thinking on authenticity, I first address the more familiar understandings of the term 'authenticity' in music through considering his critique of the historical performance and early music movement, then go on to what I see as the main topics of this essay: the concept of technical consistency as one cornerstone of Adorno's dialectical notion of authenticity; the ideological aspect of authenticity and consistency as false consciousness; and, finally, authenticity as self-reflexion, critique, and ultimately failure.[5]

I. AUTHENTICITY, HISTORICISM, AND ONTOLOGY

The term 'authenticity' has been hijacked in music by the historical performance movement in a manner that has all but obliterated any other understanding of it within musicology. While the focus of this essay is not on early music, there is nevertheless a need to reforge the link present in Adorno's thinking between the positivistic notion of authenticity associated with the historical performance movement and the ontological concept of authenticity [*Eigentlichkeit*] associated in the first place with Heideggerian phenomenology.

In its most straightforward and everyday sense, the term 'authenticity' refers to 'the real thing', the original, the unique, as opposed to the illusory, the imitation, the reproduction, the fake, the counterfeit, or the mass produced. It is also associated with the authority that comes from the real as opposed to the illusory or fake. These everyday meanings are also part of Adorno's use of the term *Authentizität* but are given a turn toward conceptions of 'truth' and 'untruth' which are critical in orientation. In everyday terms, 'truth' can, of course, be taken reasonably simply as 'true to' something outside itself, loosely along the lines of correspondence theories of truth. This raises the question: true to what? One version is 'true to self', in the sense of inner expression of 'true identity', as implied in the aesthetics of expression. Another is 'true to roots', or 'true to origins', in the sense of 'This Delta blues player is authentic'. If understood in the purely positivistic sense of 'This painting is authentic, it is a genuine Chagall, it's not a fake', it boils down to a version of 'true to itself' as that unique material object that can be authenticated by subjecting it to scientific tests to prove that it is what it purports to be. More contentiously, the historical performance movement claimed, at least in its most fanatical years, that 'early music', to be authentic, must be performed on the original instruments with original tunings and performance conventions and using historically-researched performing editions to produce the sound as it would have been heard at the time of its composition – in brief, according to the composer's intentions. The contradictions arising from this position in relation to historical performance have been pretty thoroughly debated over the last half of the twentieth century and are now sufficiently well known not to require rehearsing here. The critiques of the movement have been particularly well represented in Richard Taruskin, Laurence Dreyfus, Joseph Kerman, and Peter Kivy.[6]

Adorno's 1951 essay 'Bach gegen seine Liebhaber verteidigt' ('Bach Defended against his Devotees') represents one of the earliest and most influential of the critiques of the historicizing tendency in the performance of early music. In it he argues that the positivism which characterizes the historical performance movement (and lays claim to an objectivity of method reminiscent of the natural sciences) is combined with adherence to an ontology which gives to the object an aura of 'pure Being' [Sein] and has much in common with the phenomenology of Husserl, Heidegger, and Jaspers. This means that the notion of authenticity promoted by the early music movement (Adorno uses the aftermath of the bicentenary of Bach's death as the obvious occasion for his essay) has two aspects to it. The first, and perhaps most obvious, is the focus on authentic performance at the expense of the work itself. Adorno's critique of this tendency is polemical:

Historicism has excited a fanatical interest that no longer concerns even the work itself. At times one can hardly avoid the suspicion that the sole concern of today's Bach devotees is to see that no inauthentic dynamics, modifications of tempo, oversize choirs and orchestras creep in; they seem to wait with potential fury lest any more humane impulse become audible in the rendition.[7]

Adorno is not seeking to defend the performance excesses of the Romantic rediscovery of Bach in the mid-nineteenth century and its consequences in the first half of the twentieth century (although he clearly has some sympathy for Schoenberg's remarkably opulent and 'inauthentic' orchestral arrangements of the master). His criticism is directed at what he sees as the spurious claim to objectivity and the identification of this with the original performance of the work at the time:

What calls for refutation...is that of which the purists are most proud – their 'objectivity'. The only objective representation of music is one which shows itself to be adequate to the essence of its object. This, however, is not to be identified – as Hindemith, too, took for granted – with the idea of the historically first rendition. (P, 143)

He argues that the composer's view of his work cannot be taken as final and that it cannot be reconstructed. Furthermore – and this is very much part of Adorno's larger argument throughout his writings on music – he maintains that works cannot be identified with the limitations of particular performances or indeed with the conscious intentions of the composer. He writes, 'Authentic works unfold their truth content, which transcends the scope of individual consciousness, in a temporal dimension through the law of their form' (P, 143). Adorno shifts the emphasis, therefore, from historical performance practice to the work itself and to what he calls its 'law of form' – that is, he moves from a discussion of authenticity of performance practice to authenticity of the work as a form of cognition. I shall return to a discussion of Adorno's concept of form in later sections. For the moment, however, it needs to be emphasized that he is proposing the idea of the work, not as static Being [*Sein*] outside history, but instead as an historical unfolding, as a Becoming [*Werden*]. This crucial distinction brings us on to the second aspect of Adorno's reading of the historicist approach to performance: the concept of Being.

Adorno argues in his Bach essay that, through an emphasis on its objectivity, Bach's music is elevated by the historicists to an abstract principle which transcends the individual subjectivity and which serves to close off any possibility of understanding the participation of his music in his time. By this Adorno means that Bach was also, in spite of his Pietism, a man of the Enlightenment who, through his music, took part in the rationalizing impulses of the Age of Reason. This contrasts with the historical performance movement's reduction of Bach to the status of a provincial church composer–craftsman. Adorno – in the context of the fashion for Heidegger in the 1950s – suggests that

[t]he present function of his [Bach's] music resembles the current vogue of ontology, which promises to overcome the individualistic condition through the postulation of an abstract principle which is superior to and independent of human existence and yet which is free of all unequivocally theological content. They enjoy the order of his music because it enables them to subordinate themselves.... Bach is degraded by impotent nostalgia to the very church composer against whose office his music rebelled and which he filled only with great conflict. (P, 135)

According to Adorno's reading, therefore, the historicists have secularized Bach, then promptly elevated him to the status of 'universal Being' in a manner which bestows on him a theological authority to which they then subordinate themselves. This process reifies Bach and prevents the dynamic and progressive features of his music being understood. His music, reduced to static Being, represents the security of a bolthole from a threatening modern world and is correspondingly mystified and becomes ideology in the sense of false consciousness. It is interesting to compare this interpretation with a section in *Negative Dialektik* (1966) which formulates the contradictory characteristics of the Heideggerian concept of *Eigentlichkeit*, normally also rendered in English as 'authenticity': '[T]he authenticity Heidegger misses will promptly recoil into positivity, into authenticity as a posture of consciousness – a posture whose emigration from the profane powerlessly imitates the theological habit of the old doctrine of essence.'[8] Adorno's critique of German Existentialism is to be seen in his book *Jargon der Eigentlichkeit* (1964; *Jargon of Authenticity*) as well as *Negative Dialektik*. While the fundamentals of this debate go right back to Adorno's work on Kierkegaard and Husserl in the 1930s, it is particularly in his critique of Stravinsky in *Philosophie der neuen Musik* that its relevance to music becomes apparent and that the two 'objectivities' of neo-classicism and historical performance can be seen to share a common ideology. This is not to say that Adorno regards Stravinsky as emulating Bach in any naïve way. In fact, the reverse is the case, as he portrays Stravinsky as the urbane and sophisticated manipulator of style, arguing that he 'succumbed to the temptation of imagining that the responsible essence of music could be restored through stylistic procedures', and that his intention was 'emphatically to reconstruct the authenticity of music – to impose upon it the character of outside confirmation, to fortify it with the power of being-so-and-not-being-able-to-be-otherwise' (PM, 136). Schoenberg's music, in contrast, is interpreted by Adorno in *Philosophie der neuen Musik* as, in a sense, provincial when compared to Stravinsky's urbanity, but at the same time radical in the manner in which it relates to the historically handed-down musical material. Schoenberg, in this interpretation, renounces the external gestures of 'authenticity' (that is, the attempt to stamp musical gestures with the authority of the past) and instead, through responding to the immanent demands of the material, achieves an 'authenticity of structure' characterized by what Adorno terms, significantly, 'immanent consistency' [*immanente Stimmigkeit*]. As he puts it,

In so doing, this school [Schoenberg and the Second Viennese School] endangers almost every one of its own structures, but at the same time it gains, on the other hand, not only a more cohesive and instinctive artistic view, but also a higher objectivity than that objectivism – an objectivity, namely, of immanent consistency – and, further, of the undisguised appropriateness to the historical situation. (PM, 214, translation amended)

2. AUTHENTICITY, AUTONOMY, AND CONSISTENCY

Thus Adorno identifies authenticity with the concept of consistency [*Stimmigkeit*] in connection with the way a work of art is structured. A work is structurally consistent [*stimmig*] to the extent that its structure is the full realization of its dominating idea (*Gedanke*, as Schoenberg uses the term). Adorno argues that 'the more authentic works of art are, the more closely do they follow the objective re-quirements of internal consistency'.[9] The 'truth' of a work in this sense corresponds to the philosophical conception of truth discussed by Adorno in *Negative Dialektik* as 'identity theory': That is to say, the idea of the work is identical to its structure, just as form is in-separable from content. In effect, the notion of consistency belongs at one level to that category of truth theories characterized by the coherence of a system consistent within itself rather than by cor-respondence to something outside itself. However, as we shall see, Adorno also goes on to disrupt this self-contained notion of authen-ticity as consistency to include a combination of both (that is, to incorporate also a version of the correspondence theory).[10]

The concept of consistency goes back a long way in the develop-ment of Adorno's thinking, and it played an important part in the debates he had with the composer Ernst Křenek in the late 1920s and early 1930s on musical material. In brief, these debates con-cerned the nature of the composer's relation to musical material: Křenek took the line that the composer was the sovereign creator who selected the material as needed from among all available possi-bilities, whereas Adorno's position was that the composer's choice was severely limited by the historical stage reached by the mate-rial and that not all possibilities were actually available. Indeed, he insisted that the material itself made historical demands on the com-poser to which the composer had no choice but to respond. Adorno also linked the concept of consistency to the idea of progress and progressiveness in relation to musical material – that is to say, those composers who responded to the objective demands of the handed-down material were progressive and, by implication, their music was 'authentic' (at this period he employed the term *echt*). In an article from 1930 which grew out of this debate, 'Reaktion und Fortschritt' ('Reaction and Progress'; Křenek wrote a companion article entitled 'Progress and Reaction'), Adorno argued that 'it is only in its immanent consistency that a work proves itself as progressive. In each work the material registers concrete demands, and the movement with which each new work manifests these is the sole obligatory shape [*Gestalt*] of history for the author. A work that meets these demands completely is consistent [*stimmig*].'[11] A further issue debated by Adorno and Křenek is whether musical material is to be regarded as of natural or of historical/cultural origin. Adorno argues that all that is meaningful in musical material is historical and social in origin and that indeed musical material is not 'nature' but is culturally preformed; thus, what the composer engages with when composing is sedimented history and society. He writes, 'Whatever nature might be to start with, it receives the seal of authenticity [*Echtheit*] from history. History enters into the constellation of truth.'[12]

All this has to be understood within the context of the notion of the fully autonomous work in Western art music, Carl Dahlhaus's 'idea of absolute music',[13] historically liberated from its functional origins. The work is 'true' to the extent that it is true to its structuring idea (that is, consistent) and to the extent that it is a response to the demands of the historically handed-down musical material. This is what constitutes the work's authenticity *at this level* – its genuineness, its truth to itself and to its material, given these terms of reference.

These are, of course, very different notions of authenticity and truth from those which occupy analytic philosophers. There, the main concerns are with authenticity and performance practice; composers' intentions and expression; the distinctions to be made between sincerity and authenticity; and the problem of originals, fakes, and copies. The concept of consistency receives scant attention. For the Hegelian Adorno, however, it provides an obvious starting point for a concept of truth, one which he sees as fundamental to any notion of authenticity. The concept of consistency is derived from Hegel's system of logic as put forward both in his *Wissenschaft der Logik* (1812) and in *Logik* (part 1 of the *Enzyklopädie*). Hegel writes, 'The study of truth, or, as it is here explained to mean, consistency [that is, the agreement of an object with our conception of it], constitutes the proper problem of logic'.[14] It is a deceptively small step for Adorno to understand this in musical terms, given the longstanding conviction throughout the nineteenth century in German aesthetics and writing on music – from Wackenroder and the Schlegels through to Hanslick and Nietzsche – that music was itself a mode of cognition, a form of knowledge, albeit non-conceptual. At the same time, nevertheless, there are obvious problems with employing a notion like consistency, dependent as it is in Hegel's system on conceptualization, to account for a non-conceptual mode of experience like autonomous instrumental music. What would constitute 'truth' in such music and how would we recognize the 'authentic' work which embodied this truth? Hegel's account of 'truth' in his *Wissenschaft der Logik* makes the matter clear enough in relation to conceptual thought through emphasizing the inseparability of the act of thinking from truth: 'Truth is the agreement of thought with the object, and in order to bring about this agreement – for it does not exist on its own account – thinking is supposed to adapt and accommodate itself to the object.'[15] How can music achieve this? Hegel himself, like Kant, had no doubt that it could not, and he considered that 'independent music' without a text risked becoming empty and devoid of meaning because of its identity of form and content. In his *Vorlesungen über die Ästhetik* (1835; *Aesthetics: Lectures on Fine Arts*), he writes,

The composer for his part can of course put into his work a specific meaning, a content consisting of ideas and feelings and their articulated and complete succession, but, conversely, he can also not trouble himself with any such content and make the principal thing the purely musical structure of his work and the ingenuity of such architecture. But in that case the musical production may easily become something utterly devoid of thought and feeling, something needing for its apprehension no previous profound cultivation of mind or heart.[16]

Hegel, like Kant, had little understanding of autonomous music – indeed, he happily acknowledged his limitations in this field – and never once mentioned anywhere in his writings the obvious paradigm case for such music: that of his exact contemporary, Beethoven. At the same time, both Hegel and Kant, through their immense joint influence on the thought of the nineteenth century, serve as a catalyst – one could even say a provocation – for the development of an autonomous music which sees itself also as a form of cognition on a par with philosophical speculation. A brief excursus into the musical aesthetics of the nineteenth century will help provide the essential historical dimension at this point. The question is this: How does a mode of art like Western art music, regarded as a form of cognition *without concepts* and characterized by a condition of extreme autonomy, come to be the focus for a discussion of what it means to establish an authentic (that is, true) relation to the world?

Excursus 1: Art Music, Consistency, and the Autonomy Aesthetic

I suggest that this question has two aspects which can be usefully illuminated by juxtaposing certain ideas of Hanslick and Nietzsche. On the one hand, Eduard Hanslick, in his carefully argued *Vom Musikalisch-Schönen* (1854; *On the Musically Beautiful*), sought to refute the dominant expression aesthetic and to justify a self-contained musical logic as meaningful and consistent in itself (that is, without reference to anything outside itself and dispensing with metaphysical explanations). Hanslick's argument has had an enormous influence, not least on Adorno. His position, which, like Adorno's own, owes much to Hegel's logic but little to his thoughts on music as put forward in his *Vorlesungen über die Aesthetik*, is clearly stated in Chapter 3 of *Vom Musikalisch-Schönen*:

In music the concept of 'form' is materialized in a specifically musical way. The forms which construct themselves out of tones are not empty but filled; they are not mere contours of a vacuum, but a mind [*Geist*] giving shape to itself from within.... Music has sense and logic – but musical sense and logic. It is a kind of language which we speak and understand yet cannot translate. It is due to a kind of subconscious recognition that we speak musical 'thoughts' and, as in the case of speech, the trained judgment easily distinguishes between genuine thoughts and empty phrases. In the same way, we recognize the rational coherence of a group of tones and call it a sentence [*Satz*], exactly as with every logical proposition we have a sense of where it comes to an end, although what we might mean by 'truth' in the two cases is not at all the same thing.[17]

Hanslick's position offers the possibility of understanding the concept of consistency in relation to music through emphasizing the concept of form as the shaping of musical material by the mind

[*Geist*]. There is an emphasis on the 'rational coherence' of a work and on the idea of a purely immanent musical logic, all of which ties in well with the music theory and music pedagogy of the middle and second half of the nineteenth century.[18]

On the other hand, the problem of music's referentiality remains an issue with formalism and is not satisfactorily dealt with simply by arguing that musical works refer only to themselves in their unity of form and content and that they are meaningful because they are products of a mind shaping musical material. It can also be argued that the vestiges of music's preautonomous referentiality still remain and have themselves, with their extramusical origins, given shape and form to what Hanslick and his followers regarded as purely musical figures and gestures. Indeed, Richard Wagner calculatedly used the contrived conjunction of musical motif and extramusical gesture to develop the central structural feature of his music, the theory and practice of the leitmotif. Furthermore, this is clearly the origin of the position put forward by Friedrich Nietzsche in *Menschliches, Allzumenschliches* (1878), where in aphorisms 215 and 216 he argues for a recognition of the historical process through which musical figurations, conventions, gestures acquire their apparently immanent musical meanings – that is, largely through former, but now naturalized, associations with drama, poetry, dance, and physical gesture:

'Absolute music' is either form in itself, at a primitive stage of music in which sounds made in tempo and at varying volume gave pleasure as such, or symbolism of form speaking to the understanding without poetry after both arts had been united over a long course of evolution and the musical form had finally become entirely enmeshed in threads of feeling and concepts.[19]

Adorno, who was greatly influenced by Nietzsche (to such an extent that he cited the whole of aphorism 215 in a lengthy footnote in *Philosophie der neuen Musik*),[20] had acknowledged this tendency as an aspect of the language character of music. For him it also encompassed the previous social function of music, now sublimated within the autonomous work and manifesting only as residual gestures. In *Versuch über Wagner* (1952), he considers the gestural dimension of absolute music:

It is no doubt true that all music has its roots in gesture and harbours it within itself. In the West, however, it has been spiritualized and interiorized into expression, while at the same time the principle of construction subjects the overall flow of the music to a process of logical synthesis; great music strives for a balance of the two elements.[21]

While this repressed heteronomy does not affect the capacity of the work to achieve consistency of form, it is a factor which nevertheless constantly threatens the self-enclosed autonomy of absolute music with the danger of disintegrating into its heteronomous elements. Adorno has Wagner in mind here when he argues that the very strategy which was designed to give the music dramas their large-scale sense of unity, coherence, and consistency – that is, the technique of the leitmotif – also threatens disintegration through too great an emphasis on the constant identity of the leitmotifs in spite of their constant transformations.

Thus the consistency of the work is achieved through domination of material which itself has a tendency to revert to its heteronomous origins. This negation of origins is one aspect of the ideological character of the technical consistency of the work. The other is that, as music achieved its historical autonomy through ever increasing rationalization of its material and its procedures toward total consistency, it also retreated from the outside world into its own inner, closed world. The epitome of this process for Adorno is the music of Brahms.

3. AUTHENTICITY, INAUTHENTICITY, AND IDEOLOGY

In *Philosophie der neuen Musik*, Adorno expands on the extreme consistency of Brahms's music, including its principle of economy, the derivation of a multiplicity of ideas from a minimum of basic motivic material, and the inheritance of these processes by Schoenberg and the Second Viennese School: 'There is no longer anything which is unthematic, nothing which cannot be understood as derived from the identity [of the basic thematic material], no matter how latent' (PM, 57; translation amended). In *Einleitung in die Musiksoziologie* (1962), however, he offers an ideology critique of these same features in the following terms:

That Brahms – like the entire evolution since Schumann, even since Schubert – bears the mark of bourgeois society's individualistic phase is indisputable enough to have become a platitude. In Beethoven the category of totality still preserves a picture of the right society; in Brahms it fades increasingly into a self-sufficiently esthetic principle for the organization of private feelings. This is the academic side of Brahms. His music beats a mournful retreat to the individual, but as the individual is falsely absolutized over society Brahms's work too is surely part of a false consciousness – of one from which no modern art can escape without sacrificing itself.[22]

Thus Adorno's notion of authenticity can be understood as incorporating a further stage, a critique of self-enclosed consistency which opens it to that which lies beyond its autonomous sphere. Adorno writes, 'The consistency of art works is the aspect that enables them to share in the truth, but it also implicates them in falsehood' (EMS, 242). The notion of authenticity as consistency is also inadequate – indeed, it is ideological. As we have seen, the term 'ideology' is here to be understood both in the Hegelian sense of illusion or semblance (Schein) and in the Marxian sense of 'false consciousness' (that is, as referring to cultural forms which express the material relations of society in a way which embodies the interests of a dominant class while simultaneously concealing them). So at this level the consistency of the work and its integrated totality, its truth and authenticity, put forward initially as universal principles, are seen as false, as illusory, as inauthentic. However, read in a certain way, even the ideological moment of all art can also be seen as 'authentic', in that it acts as a critical commentary on the real material relations of society, whether it wishes to or not. As Adorno puts it in Ästhetische Theorie, 'A critical concept of society is inherent in all authentic art works and incompatible with how society conceives of itself' (AT[L], 335). This is because, in Adorno's terms, music contains social relations within its material and its structure, but unconsciously, so to speak, while at the same time positing an ideal set of relationships, instances of the relationship of part to whole, which is utopian and therefore acts as a criticism of the excluded real world. In this, I suggest, can be seen a juxtaposition rather than a combination of the coherence and the correspondence theories of truth. Furthermore, the autonomous musical work is ideological in another sense: Its autonomy is an illusion, given the commodity character of all art today as a result of the effects of the culture industry. Wagner is a good example here, and Adorno's critique of Wagner's music also attempts to discuss the composer in relation to commodity fetishism and the Hollywood movie. Similarly there is the example of his much maligned and misunderstood critique of popular music and mass culture. A second brief excursus is relevant at this point to discuss the emergence of notions of authenticity, autonomy, and consistency in rock music and the discourses around it since Adorno and to see these in the context of an ideology critique.

Excursus 2: Rock Music and the Rise of Ideologies of Authenticity and Consistency

In spite of appearances, there are also moments when Adorno concedes that popular music contains a utopian 'promise of happiness', however much a product of the culture industry. Indeed, it is clear that a notion of authenticity underlies all value judgments in spite of current claims in cultural theory to have dispensed with the need for it by dismissing it as part of the mythologizing of the rock auteur by rock criticism. This has become particularly noticeable in discussions concerning rock music versus pop music, whether among rock academics, rock journalists, or rock fans. Not unexpectedly, the Adornian claim that authentic music resists commodification while inauthentic music embraces it plays a part here too and has become assimilated and internalized within the culture of rock music itself since the 1960s (in the 1950s, rock 'n' roll showed no interest in issues of authenticity, stars, fans, and music press alike happy to accept the music as entertainment). As Michael Coyle and Jon Dolan have observed,

> The concern to distinguish authentic rock from industry pabulum developed from sources antithetical to all that rock 'n' roll represented to its early audiences. On the one hand, the notion of authenticity derived from fiercely intellectual objections to the very nature of consumer culture. In particular, the attacks of German critical theorists Theodor Adorno and Walter Benjamin provided a rhetoric whereby to imagine a preindustrial, precommercial pastoral: to imagine forms of artistic expression that were the genuine expression of total forms of life. This rhetoric has been and remains broadly compelling.[23]

But in one very important respect, Coyle and Dolan seriously misrepresent Adorno when they suggest that his notion of authenticity depends on the image of 'a preindustrial, precommercial pastoral'. In fact, Adorno locates authenticity in the unflinching encounter with the fragmentation and contradictions of modernity – that is, with the industrialized, rationalized urban world. Authenticity in rock music has certainly attached itself to the idea of 'roots' and, in particular, of 'folk', especially, as Coyle and Dolan have pointed out, through the intermediary of the college scene of the late 1950s and the early 1960s. In this respect, the so-called folk movement, with its legacy to rock music, has features in common with the search for 'rootedness' in tradition, folk, and community which characterized tendencies in the art music of the early twentieth century and the version of continuity and imposed consistency which went with them. I suggest that Adorno's ideology critique of this version of authenticity applies as much to popular music as it does to the 'early music' movement and to neoclassicism and folklorism. Furthermore, in the light of notions of authenticity which appeared during the 1960s, rock music has developed its own understandings of progress and reaction, of modernism and neoclassicism, of an avant-garde (dadaism, surrealism) and anticommodity aesthetic, and of a relation to a tradition of expectations and generic norms to be subverted. It is no exaggeration to suggest that rock music in this sense has risked retreating into its own form of autonomy as a consequence of growing older, coming of age, losing its exclusively youthful audience, and becoming one of a number of competing style-systems. It is in this context that one dares talk of 'consistency' as well as authenticity in relation to rock music. In support of this contention, I draw on the central argument put forward by Allan Moore in his book *Rock: The Primary Text*: 'What does serve to separate rock from other sorts of music is a degree of consistency which can be found within its musical rules and practices. This consistency can most clearly be discussed by invoking the concept of "style."'[24]

Simon Frith, in addressing the problem of value in rock aesthetics, attempts to step round the issue of authenticity while in the process paying his respects to Adorno:

Rock music depends on myth – the myth of the youth community, the myth of the creative artist. The reality is that rock, like all twentieth-century pop musics, is a commercial form, music produced as a commodity, for a profit, distributed through mass media as mass culture. It is in practice very difficult to say exactly who or what it is that rock expresses or who, from the listener's point of view, are the authentically creative performers. The myth of authenticity is, indeed, one of rock's own ideological effects, an aspect of its sales process: rock stars can be marketed as artists, and their particular sounds marketed as a means of identity. Rock criticism is a means of legitimating tastes, justifying value judgments, but it does not really explain how those judgments came to be made in the first place. If the music is not, in fact, made according to the 'authentic' story, then the question becomes how we are able to judge some sounds as more authentic than others, what are we really listening for in making our judgments? ... The question of the value of pop music remains to be answered.[25]

Frith attempts to answer this question by assuming that the notion of authenticity in popular music is founded on the myth of expression – the expression of 'the "real" artist, emotion or belief lying behind it'.[26] He suggests that 'the question we should be asking is not what does popular music *reveal* about "the people" but how does it *construct* them.'[27] But this gets us only halfway toward an answer, because it uses a very limited concept of authenticity which does not recognize the extent to which the idea that music is exclusively about expression had already been seriously questioned in the 1850s. Moreover, Frith always considers 'music' in the most general and generic terms, never asking more detailed questions about the way in which music itself is also *constructed*. This unwillingness, or perhaps inability, to make a thoroughgoing connection between the constructedness of people and the constructedness of music is a weakness in his position, as it is also in other sociological approaches which ignore the fact that, whatever else it might be, a rock song is also a musical structure. The relation to commodification is itself a material one, inherent in the structure of the music, and not merely a matter of lyrics or function as social cement.

Rock academics, including Frith, who take an exclusively sociological perspective on popular music rightly criticize the tendency of musicologists and, in particular, music analysts to fetishize the musical object itself at the expense of its role as part of the context of identity construction. Consistency, the focus of technical analysis, *is* ideological, dependent as it is on a questionable autonomy aesthetic. At the same time, it is also significant: The technical makeup of the musical object, as well as its relation to other musical objects and to currently available musical material and technical means, is also an indicator of social relations mediated as musical-technical relations.

To ignore this is to place the music itself at the periphery as the mere occasion for the construction of identity rather than within the nexus of social relations.

I argue that Adorno's use of the term 'authenticity' focuses the tension between *consistency as truth* and *consistency as ideology*, an antagonistic relationship of opposites to which there can be no resolution at the level of the musical object and which leaves its traces as fractures in the structure of the work. The authentic work at this level manifests its truth content, to use Adorno's loaded term, as the objective problems of its form:

In works of art immanent consistency and meta-aesthetic truth go to make up truth content. . . . Art works pose the problem of how the truth of reality can become the truth of art. . . . Society's discontinuities, its untruths and ideologies, emerge in the work as structural discontinuities, as deficiencies. This is so because the orientation of works of art, their 'stance towards objectivity', remains a stance towards reality. (AT[L], 395–6)

4. AUTHENTICITY, SELF-REFLECTION, AND CRITIQUE

At this level of the authenticity of a work as the sublation of its immanent structural consistency and of its ideological moment as the excluded, repressed social other, there is the further important feature already noted: The work functions also as a form of critique, as critical reflection. The question is, to what precisely does art address this critique? To society or to musical material? The answer is *both*. On the one hand, Adorno considers that 'authentic modern works are criticisms of past ones', and indeed he suggests that 'aesthetics becomes normative by articulating these criticisms' (AT[L], 492). But lest we mistake this as an argument for formalism pure and simple, Adorno also argues that society appears in musical material immanently. As he puts it in *Ästhetische Theorie*, 'The unresolved antagonisms of reality appear in art in the guise of immanent problems of artistic form. This, and not the deliberate injection of objective moments or social content, defines art's relation to society' (AT[L], 8). What this reading attempts to clarify is a complex problem in Adorno's aesthetics: that the autonomous, individual work of art can be simultaneously ideological (i.e., a manifestation of false consciousness, illusion, self-deception) and authentic (in the sense of being a form of critical cognition, of critical reflection). Adorno formulates the problem thus: 'The fact that society "appears" in works of art both in an ideological and a critical manner is apt to lead to historico-philosophical mystification. Speculative thought is easily duped into thinking there is a pre-established harmony between society and works of art, courtesy of world spirit. Their true relation is different, however' (AT[L], 335). That is to say, their true relation is antagonistic, fragmented, and critical. The case of Mahler comes to mind here as an example of this problem and of Adorno's dialectical interpretation of it.

Autonomous artworks, according to Adorno, are like windowless monads in the Leibnizian sense. They contain society but are blind to their social content. Social forces and relations of production 'crop up in art because artistic labour is social labour and because an artistic product is a social product' (AT[L], 335). The difference between artworks and society lies in the way in which artworks turn away from society and operate with a different form of rationality even while being part of the dominant social forces and relations of production. Authentic works, in Adorno's terms, use extreme rationalization to dominate the handed-down material yet do so in a way which allows the repressed social content of the material to speak again, but now in purely musical terms within the closed world of the work. Such a notion of authenticity, however, whereby a work attempts to achieve consistency of form (which implies integration) through a critical relationship to the handed-down material (material which, since the period of the late Beethoven and Berlioz, has tended increasingly toward fragmentation and disintegration), leads to failure, according to Adorno – a kind of failure which is not simply the result of technical inadequacy on the part of the composer but rather comes from the impossibility of succeeding in the task to be faced, a task which must be undertaken nevertheless. This is what could be called 'truth to the historical demands of the material', in Adorno's terms, and it is an aspect of what he calls the 'truth content' of a work. The handed-down forms and schemata begin to lose their binding power. The historical thrust toward integration within autonomous music in the Western art tradition is taken to extremes – versions of it at different stages are to be seen in, for example, Beethoven, Wagner, Brahms, Schoenberg, and, of course, the multiple serialism of the 1950s as its *telos*, which also sees its final collapse. In the process, total integration, indeed, autonomous music itself as a cultural form which grew up with and came of age in the 'bourgeois period' from the eighteenth-century Enlightenment to the mid-twentieth century and the end of aesthetic modernism, becomes revealed and is seen as illusion. Adorno attempts to formulate this dilemma as follows:

Extreme integration is illusion pushed to the extreme. But there is a possibility of a reversal of the process: ever since the late Beethoven, those artists who had gone farthest along the road to integration were able to mobilize disintegration eventually. At this point in the career of an artist, the truth content of art whose vehicle was integration turns against art. It is precisely at these turning points that art has had some of its greatest moments. (AT[L], 67)

It is interesting to consider two examples of what Adorno means here in relation to authenticity and failure. First, in Adorno's book *Mahler: Eine musikalische Physiognomik* (*Mahler: A Musical Physiognomy*, 1960) we find the following remarkable passage: '[I]t is only in the moment of inauthenticity, which unmasks the lie of authenticity, that Mahler has his truth.... Objectively Mahler's music knows, and expresses the knowledge, that unity is attained not in spite of disjunction, but only through it.'[28] Adorno argues that Mahler's music reveals consistency as integration (which, as we have seen, is what can be regarded as constituting authenticity at the level of the autonomous work as an 'in-itself') to be an illusion – that is, as inauthenticity. And furthermore, through his structural, critical relationship to 'inauthentic', commodified, second-hand materials, he achieves a different level of authenticity.

   The second example is from Adorno's unfinished Beethoven book, *Beethoven: Philosophie der Musik*, the fragments of which were first published in German in 1993:

Art works of the highest rank are distinguished from the others not through their success – for in what have they succeeded? – but through the manner of their failure. For the problems within them, both the immanent, aesthetic problems and the social ones.... are so posed that the attempt to solve them must fail, whereas the failure of lesser works is accidental, a matter of mere subjective incapacity. A work of art is great when it registers a failed attempt to reconcile objective antinomies. That is its truth and its 'success': to have come up against its own limit. In these terms, any work of art which succeeds through not reaching this limit is a failure.[29]

And he continues: 'This theory states the formal law which determines the transition from the "classical" to the late Beethoven, in such a way that the failure *objectively* implicated by the former is disclosed by the latter, raised to self-awareness, cleansed of the appearance of success and lifted, for just this reason, to the level of philosophical succeeding' (BPM, 100). A more polished version of these fragments appears in the essay 'Verfremdetes Hauptwerk: Zur *Missa Solemnis*' (1959; 'Alienated Masterpiece: the *Missa Solemnis*'):

The late Beethoven's demand for truth rejects the illusory appearance of the unity of subjective and objective, a concept practically at one with the classicist idea. A polarization results. Unity transcends into the fragmentary. In the last quartets this takes place by means of the rough, unmediated juxtaposition of callow aphoristic motifs and polyphonic complexes. The gap between both becomes obvious and makes the impossibility of aesthetic harmony into the aesthetic content of the work; makes failure in a highest sense the measure of success. In its way even the *Missa* sacrifices the idea of synthesis.[30]

What is ultimately significant for Adorno is the nature of the subject-object relation within musical works. This is, of course, a dominant theme running through *Philosophie der neuen Musik* and is the decisive factor in Adorno's assessment of Schoenberg in relation to Stravinsky in that book. Music, as a particular version of the externalization and objectification of subjectivity, is seen as a sublimated, or repressed, relation to society in its interaction with its material. The historical grounds for such an alienated relationship, where art ends up both as an unconscious recording of history and as an attempt to escape it through positing a utopian alternative, provide the poles for Adorno's field of enquiry. In the fragmented work, the work whose self-reflexivity is a result of 'coming of age', Adorno sees authenticity in the failed attempt to achieve coherence, integration, and consistency in a fractured world.

NOTES

1. Theodor W. Adorno, *Aesthetic Theory*, trans. Robert Hullot-Kentor (London: Athlone Press, 1997), 23. Hereafter cited as AT.
2. Trevor Wishart, for instance, insists that 'the use of the words "authentic" and "true" simply imply an evaluative position for Adorno as critic

which transcends the social situation' ('On Radical Culture', in John Shepherd et al., *Whose Music? A Sociology of Musical Languages* [New Brunswick and London: Transaction Books, 1977], 235).

3. Theodor W. Adorno, *Philosophy of Modern Music*, trans. Anne G. Mitchell and Wesley V. Blomster (London: Sheed and Ward, 1973), 136. Hereafter cited as PM.

4. Theodor W. Adorno, 'Jene zwanziger Jahre,' in *Eingriffe, Gesammelte Schriften*, vol. 10, pt. 2 (Frankfurt: Suhrkamp, 1977), 506 (my translation). English translation on p. 48 of Theodor W. Adorno, *Critical Models: Interventions and Catchwords*, trans. Henry W. Pickford (New York: Columbia University Press, 1998).

5. In sections of this essay, I elaborate and extend a theoretical model developed in my books *Adorno's Aesthetics of Music* (Cambridge: Cambridge University Press, 1993), 52–64, and *Adorno, Modernism and Mass Culture* (London: Kahn and Averill, 1996), 71–80; the model has its origins in a review article, 'Adorno's *Aesthetic Theory*', *Music Analysis* 6, no. 3 (1987): 355–77.

6. Richard Taruskin, 'On Letting the Music Speak for Itself', *Journal of Musicology* 1 (1982): 338–49; Laurence Dreyfus, 'Early Music Defended against its Devotees', *Musical Quarterly* 69, no. 3 (1983): 297–322; Joseph Kerman, 'The Historical Performance Movement', in *Musicology* (London: Fontana/Collins, 1995), 182–217; Peter Kivy, *Authenticities: Philosophical Reflections on Musical Performance* (Ithaca, N.Y., and London: Cornell University Press, 1995).

7. Theodor W. Adorno, 'Bach Defended against his Devotees', *Prisms*, trans. Samuel Weber and Shierry Weber (London: Neville Spearman, 1967), 142–3. Hereafter cited as P.

8. Theodor W. Adorno, *Negative Dialectics*, trans. E. B. Ashton (London: Routledge and Kegan Paul, 1973), 113.

9. Theodor W. Adorno, *Aesthetic Theory*, trans. Christian Lenhardt (London: Routledge and Kegan Paul, 1984), 288. Hereafter cited as AT[L].

10. Mattias Martinson has characterized these theories as follows: 'The spectrum of truth-theories can be characterized as having one extreme point in the notion of correspondence and the other extreme point in coherence. Truth then becomes a function of (1) thought's correspondence to objects, (2) the coherence of a system of thought, and (3) combinations of these two options' (*Perseverance without Doctrine: Adorno, Self-Critique, and the Ends of Academic Theology* [Frankfurt: Peter Lang, 2000], 65).

11. Theodor W. Adorno, 'Reaktion und Fortschritt,' in Theodor Adorno and Ernst Křenek, *Briefwechsel* (Frankfurt: Suhrkamp, 1974), 176 (my translation).

12. Adorno, 'Reaktion und Fortschritt', 179 (my translation).

13. Carl Dahlhaus, *The Idea of Absolute Music*, trans. Roger Lustig (Chicago: University of Chicago Press, 1989).

14. G. W. F. Hegel, *Encyclopaedia of the Philosophical Sciences*, pt. 1, *Logic*, trans. William Wallace (Oxford: Clarendon Press, 1975), 41.

15. G. W. F. Hegel, *Science of Logic*, trans. A.V. Miller (London: George Allen and Unwin, 1969), 44.

16. G. W. F. Hegel, *Aesthetics: Lectures on Fine Art*, vol. 2, trans. T. M. Knox (Oxford: Clarendon Press, 1975), 954.

17. Eduard Hanslick, *On the Musically Beautiful*, trans. Geoffrey Payzant (Indianapolis, Ind.: Hackett Publishing, 1986), 30.

18. A. B. Marx, a central figure in the development of music theory in the nineteenth century and a fervent Hegelian in his thinking, wrote in his essay 'Form in der Musik' (1856), '[A]bove all, then, let us hold fast to this: even in music, form is a necessary thing; it is...the expression of the rational spirit coming to consciousness and elevating itself to reason – and it is not something arbitrary, not something that imposes itself from without' ('Form in Music', in *Musical Form in the Age of Beethoven: Selected Writings on Theory and Method*, ed. and trans. Scott Burnham [Cambridge: Cambridge University Press, 1997], 62).

19. Friedrich Nietzsche, *Human, All Too Human; A Book for Free Spirits*, trans. R. J. Hollingdale (Cambridge: Cambridge University Press, 1986), 99.

20. See Adorno, *Philosophy of Modern Music*, 138–9 n. 3.

21. Theodor W. Adorno, *In Search of Wagner*, trans. Rodney Livingstone (London: Verso, 1981), 34–5 (translation amended).

22. Theodor W. Adorno, *Introduction to the Sociology of Music*, trans. E. B. Ashton (New York: Seabury Press, 1976), 63–4. Hereafter cited as EMS.

23. Michael Coyle and Jon Dolan, 'Modelling Authenticity', in *Reading Rock and Roll: Authenticity, Appropriation, Aesthetics*, ed. Kevin J. H. Dettmar and William Richey (New York: Columbia University Press, 1999), 26.

24. Allan F. Moore, *Rock: The Primary Text* (Buckingham, England: Open University Press, 1993), 1.

25. Simon Frith, 'Towards an Aesthetic of Popular Music', in *Music and Society: The Politics of Composition, Performance and Reception*, ed. Richard Leppert and Susan McClary (Cambridge: Cambridge University Press, 1989), 136–7.

26. Frith, "Towards an Aesthetic of Popular Music," 137.

27. Frith, "Towards an Aesthetic of Popular Music," 137.

28. Theodor W. Adorno, *Mahler: A Musical Physiognomy*, trans. Edmund Jephcott (Chicago and London: University of Chicago Press, 1992), 32–3.

29. Theodor W. Adorno, *Beethoven: The Philosophy of Music*, trans. Edmund Jephcott, ed. Rolf Tiedemann (Cambridge: Polity Press, 1998), 99–100 (translation amended). Hereafter cited as BPM.

30. Theodor W. Adorno, 'Verfremdetes Hauptwerk: Zur *Missa Solemnis*', *Gesammelte Schriften*, vol. 17 (Frankfurt: Suhrkamp, 1982), 159 (my translation). English translation: 'Alienated Masterpiece: The *Missa Solemnis*', *Telos*, no. 28 (summer 1976): 113–24.

9 Dissonant Works and the Listening Public

What Odysseus hears is without consequence for him; he is able only to nod his head as a sign to be set free from his bonds; but it is too late.[1]

Adorno and Horkheimer
Dialectic of Enlightenment

I. THE ANXIETY OF LISTENING

This chapter is about what happens, according to Adorno, to the production of music under the modern condition of oppressed or improper listening and why he locates resistance to this condition in an aesthetic or dialectic of loneliness [*Dialektik der Einsamkeit*].[2] I present two models of musical listening: Arnold Schoenberg's, then Adorno's. Each is motivated, not by acoustic or physiological studies of the ear, but as a response to the charge that music of a dissonant character, particularly Schoenberg's, is unlistenable. So motivated, these models of listening are better conceived as models of reception, and of the reception particularly of what Adorno calls New Music.

The chapter has two parts: first, a presentation of the two models; second, a detailed expansion and commentary on Adorno's model. I set Adorno's model in detail and dialectically (as Adorno did himself) against a sketch of Schoenberg's. My interest is in Adorno and why he focused on Schoenberg. To explain this, we must immerse ourselves in Adorno's general philosophical engagement with music. My first objective is to show that there is nothing isolated or merely preferential about Adorno's focus. He uses Schoenberg to articulate his own profound pessimism regarding the condition of his times and the response his own philosophy can have to it. He sees New Music's radical task to be at one with his philosophical task, namely, to challenge what we take in experience to be most self-evident. He uses Schoenberg to show how we rationalize and traditionalize our listening habits and deal with the music that challenges them.

My reading of Adorno focuses on something others have not, namely, how much Adorno's philosophy is concerned with exposing, via works of New Music and our modern experience of them, the ideological or deceptive character of self-evidence. For Adorno, the construction of purported self-evidence arises out of a compulsion for sameness. This unity is then destabilized by the need for, and fact of, difference. Difference is the appropriate philosophical response to the overwhelming sameness he takes to characterize modern times. 'What we differentiate', he writes in *Negative Dialectics*, 'will appear divergent, dissonant, negative for just as long as the structure of our consciousness obliges it to strive for unity.'[3]

Schoenberg's own model of listening or reception is conservative, both in aesthetic terms and as a model for the philosophy of history – specifically regarding the relation of 'the new' to 'the tradition'. He denies what in his compositions Adorno sees to be their new or radical potential. His 1937 essay 'How One Becomes Lonely' tells a long and sad history of complaints about his music.[4] He tells his listening public to be patient because their ears will soon adapt. Adorno is not convinced they will adapt to what Schoenberg wants them to and fears they will instead adapt to miss the music's challenge. Adorno employs many of the same principles as Schoenberg, derived from an established formalist aesthetic, but reconfigures them to produce a philosophical-sociological model of critique. This critique establishes a dialectical relation between the way we listen and the works we listen to, or, more specifically, between the general condition of oppressive reception and the anxiety of loneliness to which Schoenberg's works give expression. This dialectic reveals the confrontation between the desire for sameness and the challenge of difference.

In his *Philosophie der neuen Musik* of 1948, Adorno discusses a piece of text by John Henry Mackay that Schoenberg uses in an early tonal song, '*Am Wegrand*' (op. 6), and then by brief quotation at the end of the latter's 1909 monodrama *Erwartung*.[5]

Thousands of people march past, / The one for whom I long, / He is not among them! / Restless glances fly past / And ask the one in haste, / Whether it is he... / But they ask and ask in vain. / No one answers: / "Here I am. Be still." / Longing fills the realms of life, / Left empty by fulfillment, / And so I stand at the edge of the road, / While the crowd flows past, / Until – blinded by the burning sun – / My tired eyes close.

Herein, Adorno claims, lies the formula of the style of loneliness [*die Formel des Stils der Einsamkeit*] (PM, 46–51), a formula the expressionist uses to reveal the pervasiveness of loneliness through the individual gesture of the lonely person. I shall say a little more about this since it introduces the way one thing, for Adorno, is shown indirectly and often with social contortion by opposite or opposing thing. Lonely discourse [*einsame Rede*] is about individuals isolated or separated from a society of enemies. More deeply, it is about advanced capitalist society that has itself become alienated. As this isolation is universalized, so is the loneliness [*Einsamkeit als Allgemeinheit*]. The loneliness does not receive its general expression but is returned by the society, which does not or cannot face it directly, to the individuals. Thus the individuals express a condition for which they are not responsible but for which they are made to assume guilt. Society's universal loneliness is expressed in displacement, in the victimized gesture of the lonely person. Adorno writes of Schoenberg's *Die Glückliche Hand* as the work that most significantly dramatizes in musical terms this dialectic of lonely expression. However, it is *Erwartung* that provides him his more usual example (PM, 51).[6]

Schoenberg was never convinced by Adorno's reading of his works, especially not by Adorno's judgment that the works themselves actually belied Schoenberg's own justifications for them. Adorno called these justifications 'hapless' (P, 150). But against what theoretical background did Adorno make this call? Certainly his philosophical use of the works put them at the center of the modernist project of critical theory, but only because he separated the works from Schoenberg's understanding of them. This chapter is also about how Adorno refuses Schoenberg's own model and instead finds in and for his works a radical, social function. No wonder Schoenberg was annoyed. Once mockingly he asked a friend, 'Was', according to Adorno, 'tut die Musik?' and then answered himself: 'Sie philosophiert.'[7] Had he asked Adorno directly, he might have heard this response: Yes, 'music philosophizes' and it is the philosophical critic's role to show how it does, though how it does might contradict what the composer thinks he is doing. It was not only an anti-intentionalism that inspired Adorno but also his belief that the modernist role of the philosophical critic was to interpret and articulate for music a meaning (a social and philosophical one) that would otherwise remain enigmatic or unarticulated in its purely musical form. This was not a self-serving doctrine. It picked up on the thought that philosophy as a conceptual language stood in a necessarily interpretative relation to languages, like music, that were not primarily conceptual or conceptual at all. It was a view further derived from Adorno's conception of modernity in crisis – where music no longer fitted generally known and accepted compositional rules and public demands but had retreated into a lonely place, the social significance of which even the modernist composer might not be able to grasp. In this relation between philosophy and music, Adorno saw how to make explicit New Music's critical epistemological potential, its involvement with truth and opinion. Adorno also saw the way for himself to be Schoenberg's exemplary philosophical critic.

Adorno stood to Schoenberg as dialectical critic to conservative composer. This relation is important because many readers of Adorno seem to acquire the impression that he simply followed Schoenberg in endorsing a conservative and elitist model of autonomous and formalist work-production. But in so reading him, they miss his critique precisely of Schoenberg's model. In missing this, they also miss a fundamental claim made within his infamous critique of 'popular music', that whatever is wrong with 'popular music' is also wrong with 'serious music', though the wrong is shown differently in different musics as two sides of a dialectical development. The responsibility for these wrongs lies not so much in any music per se but in the society that produces and petrifies the categories of the serious and popular. Adorno's critique both of popular and serious music is a modernist critique of social administration and the categorical thought – the 'overwhelming striving towards sameness' – he thinks it shapes.

Schoenberg's Model

Schoenberg never had a very happy relationship with his listeners. In 1918 he wrote to Alexander Zemlinsky, '[As for] the consideration for the listener, I have exactly as little of this as he has for me. All

I know is that he exists, and in so far as he isn't "indispensable" for acoustic reasons (since music doesn't sound well in an empty hall), he's only a nuisance.'[8] But he adds, from the avenging perspective of the listener, the listener will do with the music whatever he wants.

For Schoenberg, atonal music stands in a continuous relation to the tonal tradition primarily of the Austro-Germans (Bach, Beethoven, Brahms). The tradition develops logically according to eternal aesthetic laws dictating principles of form, unity, coherence, comprehensibility, and beauty. Further, atonal music is a natural development out of tonality: It solves all the problems – harmonic, formal, orchestral, and emotional – tonality created (SI, 49). It shows the progress that can be made within tonality. But Schoenberg asks, what is the use of telling the listener all this 'if he does not feel it'? (SI, 50).

Schoenberg asks that words such as 'atonal' and 'dissonant' be used with caution. Though descriptively accurate, perhaps, to mark the musical development beyond tonality, they should not be used as slogans to encourage the thought that his music is negative: 'not tonal' or 'not what tonal music was'. He also demands that these terms be denied use as slogans of revolution or radicality (cf. SI, 263). Music's development demonstrates principles of evolution, 'not revolution' (SI, 50). Still, if evolution explains the path of music's development, then someone's music must be determined to constitute the next step: '[S]omeone had to be me' (SI, 104).

Schoenberg conceives music's evolution in terms of a series of styles, each of which represents a historical presentation of the eternal 'idea' [Gedanke] (SI, 123). Suffice it to say here that the idea is conceived along Hegelian lines as the idea sensuously embodied in an artwork, also along Schopenhaurean lines as purely musical expression, though it also comes to have for Schoenberg significant theological connotations. For Schoenberg, the idea is grasped by a 'genius', a composer who comes to know it 'compositionally' but not 'cognitively'. It is grasped as a musical thought or as a 'tone-row' (or 'theme, melody, phrase, or motive' [SI, 122]). Here is the point: That the composer can grasp the idea compositionally enables him to 'speak ahead of his time', to stand in an evolutionarily more advanced position than the general public. This advanced stand explains the embattled position in which the composer finds himself; hence his loneliness.[9] But Schoenberg's own extreme loneliness leads him to wonder whether he should not just give the public what they want to hear. No, he feels a moral duty to do otherwise.

I knew I had to fulfil a task: I had to express what was necessary to be expressed and I knew I had the duty of developing my ideas for the sake of progress in music, whether I liked it or not; but I also had to realize that the great majority of the public did not like it. However I remembered that all my music had been found to be ugly at first; and yet . . . there might be a sunrise such as is depicted in the final chorus of my *Gurrelieder*. (SI, 53)

Schoenberg underscores this promise of sunlight with a view about the musical listener. There is a direct adaptive line from the composer's to the public's ear. The principle of adaptation has a basis in human nature; musical nature must naturally accord with our nature (SI, 253). Thus the listener should come to hear the work the way the composer hears it. Schoenberg further presumes that if atonal works conform to the same aesthetic principles as traditional ones, then, because the ear has adapted to those, it will in time adapt to his. Given the adaptation principle, the lonely composer just has to wait for the public to catch up. 'I can wait' (SI, 264).

Yet listening to music with pleasure does not amount to getting used to dissonances. The main purpose is rather to grasp the structural working out of the idea within a particular composition. The feeling of beauty is closely related to the satisfaction of a listener who can follow 'the idea, its musical unfolding, and the reasons for such' (SI, 215). Listening is a contemplative (focused and concentrated) act in which listeners put aside their feelings and tastes to grasp the musical object directly.

If listening requires an advanced ability to follow structure, it cannot, Schoenberg next says, be an activity suitable 'for the common folk' but is appropriate only for those with education in the principles of composition or instrumental playing. One reason the contemporary public does not appreciate his music, he surmises, is that in his lifetime there has been a noticeable decline in amateur music-making (SI, 382). Still, he is adamant about giving listeners the responsibility to educate themselves. Listeners must work at their listening. Music is always hard to understand, whether tonal or atonal (SI, 103). On the other side, he feels the comparable duty to make his music comprehensible. 'Comprehensible' does not mean easily accessible or fashionable but 'coherent and consistent' in purely musical or formal terms. The beauty of form that results will be truthful, sincere, and lasting – and that should satisfy listeners.

This commitment to beauty and coherent form in no way distinguishes his music, in his view, from the 'masterpieces' of the tradition. What then is the difference? The language or style used to express the work's idea. Recall, it is the languages and styles that show the stages of evolution, not the idea, which runs its course 'absolutely'. From his contemporary standpoint, Schoenberg thus concludes, the new might look very different from the old, but the difference should not be exaggerated. To exaggerate the newness of the new is usually done for the most suspect reasons, most usually to 'épater le bourgeois' (SI, 88).

Adorno's Model

Adorno denies the adaptive, linear, and progressivist assumptions of Schoenberg's model. He agrees that the history of Austro-German music follows an internal, purely musical logic of development, yet the development is also mediated, and hence challenged, by the society in which the music is composed, performed, and received. Music's history, the relation of the new to the old, is also dialectical. One way to describe this history is by reference to its complex strands of continuity and discontinuity and to its moments of rupture, radicality, and regression. It is, Adorno writes, 'quite mistaken to insist...on the essential unity and continuity of all music', (Q, 253), but it is 'no less true that the elements and problems of the New Music are all rooted in the musical tradition' (Q, 251).

Listeners do not stand in an immediate, pure, or merely contemplative relation to the musical work. Their listening is influenced and conditioned by the society within which they live and within which the works are produced. Just as there is no innocent eye, there is no pure listening ear. But how does society intervene in our listening?

The model both with which and against which Adorno operates is Schoenberg's – where listening is assumed ideally to be an auditory activity in which one devotes one's attention to the structural unfolding of the work's idea. The ear focuses on the work via a performance that strives to present the work's meaning as faithfully as possible.

This is a listening mode suitable for the serious music of the last two centuries associated with the concert hall, a modern and bourgeois listening mode stripped of premodern occasional and ritual associations (dance, religious service, and social entertainment), a passive activity in which listeners sit silently and motionlessly absorbing the information given them. But Adorno denies this passivity. What we do not see are all the expectations met and thwarted, preferences expressed, fetishes formed, indeed all the behavioral habits socially and historically connected with presenting and packaging music in this concert hall way.[10]

For Adorno, to listen properly to music is spontaneously to compose the music's inner movement, acutely to attend to its 'simultaneous multiplicity', and intensively to hear its unique and specific qualities often 'changing in the smallest space'. Such listening demands 'not mere contemplation, but praxis', an educated form of 'active and concentrated participation' (P, 150). Yet it does not come naturally or easily. Why? Because part of this education also involves an explicit renunciation of our more 'customary crutches of listening', the sort of listening where we already know what to expect and which already pleases. Indeed, the renunciation of our habits meets with extreme resistance. When we first listen to Schoenberg's music, we are struck by its 'seriousness, richness, and integrity', but rather than those qualities arousing our interest and appreciation, they arouse resentment (P, 149). We respond unequivocally by declaring the music 'too difficult'.

Why the resentment? Because, Adorno says, the more Schoenberg's music gives the listeners, the less it offers them. Thinking of all that mediates the listening experience, he finds a regressive and infantile need for ease and comfort (EFS, 286). A work is rarely listened to in itself but rather listened to as conforming to the principle of sameness (or self-sameness)[11] – sameness of genre perhaps, but more importantly for this argument, sameness of tonal system. When listening, we exhibit a strong tendency to make works familiar by making them fit what we already know and like. Consider the familiarity we feel when listening to the warhorses of nineteenth-century music, typically a Beethoven symphony (and it does not matter which one). This familiarity is built on a spurious reductive ability we have to hear all these works in the same way under the 'veneer' or apparent 'gravitational pull of tonality'. We thus ignore the differences and the details of the work by denying our attention to the work even while we are listening to it (EFS, 271).

But though we tend toward this kind of regressive experience, Adorno thinks it nonetheless does not satisfy. It bores us by demanding too much sameness. The satisfaction it yields is only apparent. Indeed, the only way we experience it as satisfying is by suppressing that side of our experience that requires more effort: 'Pleasure hardens into boredom because, if it is to remain pleasure, it must not demand any effort and therefore moves rigorously in the worn grooves of association. No independent thinking must be expected from the audience: the product prescribes every reaction' (DA, 137).

Schoenberg also argues against sameness: A composer cannot simply repeat things over and over again, as a tennis player or boxer cannot (SI, 102). But why, one might then ask, does he stress the sameness of his music to that which preceded it rather than its difference? Perhaps, by stressing the sameness, he actually undermines what listeners really want, namely, the thought that his music is different from what they already know, even though they recoil from this difference when they actually experience it as such. Listeners, Adorno observes, genuinely want the new but not somehow the 'too new'.

With what does the 'too new' confront them? Adorno says, with a concretely experienced strike against 'conformity' and 'affability' (P, 150). Schoenberg's works 'blaspheme' precisely against the listener's expectation of 'pleasurable sensations.' They challenge the 'natural preserve of infantility' that 'demands a quota of juvenile happiness'. They sin against 'the division of life into work and leisure' by insisting that one work for one's leisure. They cater to the mature needs of the mind. These 'too new' works, Adorno observes, produce in listeners 'the primordial shudder' – a shudder of the Muse – in the age of reification (AT, 51, 79).

Why do we balk at that which might meet our mature needs? Because, though we say we want music that requires our effort, we get from it no pleasure. So we return to the 'predigested' music which we already like and which reestablishes itself as preferred every time we confront indigestable music. Music as 'babyfood', with listeners driven by an 'infantile compulsion' to satisfy the needs 'easy music' created in the first place (CI, 58).

Obviously, Adorno will not be convinced by any simple adaptive ability of the ear to get used to Schoenberg's music. Listeners, he writes, experience New Music only 'as something which deviates from their fixed notions as to what constitutes music. Their listening habits, which suffice in their view to enable them to deal with everything from Monteverdi to Richard Strauss, do not give them access to Schoenberg, Webern, or Boulez' (Q, 252). He thinks the very idea of adaptation twists the demand around. To adapt to Schoenberg's music does not require the listener to listen with the devoted musical attention this particular music demands. Rather, so to adapt demands this music be brought into the sphere of what listeners already know and like. What we already know, or think we already know, is tonal music. And what we already mistakenly believe is that tonality corresponds to our natural condition of hearing (Q, 263). This is our starting presumption when we enter the concert hall.

But what happens when we find we cannot adapt to Schoenberg's music, or, better, when we cannot adapt Schoenberg's music to our listening habits? In answering, Adorno highlights the radical potential of Schoenberg's music to break these habits. Precisely in our inability to adapt or, better, in our inability to make Schoenberg's music fit, we make audible to ourselves (through 'reflection') the 'sensuous' differences or particularities of the work at hand, those differences hidden by 'the tonal veneer'.

To make these differences audible is to make explicit our failure to subsume atonality under tonality as a general concept.[12] In other terms, this dialectic of differentiation confronts us with our most deceptive assumptions. So consider those times when we anxiously ask whether New Music will ever feel natural or become popular. In making the differences of atonality audible, Adorno says, we suddenly understand this question to be 'hypocritical' (Q, 263). Where is the hypocrisy? Not in our noticing that atonality is different from tonality because tonality is natural and popular and atonality is not, but in our assuming tonality's naturalness and popularity in the first place. What we learn vicariously (or again by displacement) when we begin to see how different and difficult atonality is is that tonality is different and difficult too. Our deception thus resides in thinking that tonality has flowed harmoniously and naturally through history in a way atonality never has. Tonality too, he remarks, has its own history of acceptance and rejection.

Adorno next rejects our attempt to set New Music aside as a category distinct from the tradition we all know and love. To do this encourages us to accept and thereby ignore New Music simply as incomprehensible. We say dismissively, 'We do not attend concerts of that sort – those concerts of New Music' (historically, concerts of the International Society for Contemporary Music [ISCM]).[13] Yet to travel the other route and assert New Music's sameness to the tradition does not convince either. 'Just the same' or 'too different', either rationalization allows us to turn a deaf ear to the potential of New Music to challenge our most habituated modes of reception.

But if the way to avoid either route is to treat New Music as a category neither distinct from nor identical to the tradition, why does Adorno speak apparently so categorically of New Music? He answers by saying that he is not designating strict categories, only registering tendencies. Dialectical critique makes explicit the way society organizes itself by registering tendencies that produce deceptive categories. Similarly, at this sociological level, Adorno says he also wants to register the social tendencies of atonal music, even though he worries, as Schoenberg did, about using so loaded a term (Q, 253).

What tendency does atonal music then register? 'Shockwaves', Adorno often says, in 'an ocean of new sounds', even if, he adds, these shockwaves increasingly cease to shock as they become the effects composers aim for (Q, 253). At first, shock was integral to new works, emerging out of their internal construction. (He speaks of montage technique.) The point was not to shock but that the works shocked. Gradually, when shock became imposed on the work as an application of method or as a way to shock (he mentions Stockhausen and Cage), the contemporary works ceased to be new. Given all contemporary works (and here he includes some of Schoenberg's middle-period serialist compositions), few are in fact new.

But what is social about shock? One aspect is that the shock that registers the tendency of the new in New Music also registers the tendency of the new, by extension, in the music of the tradition, say, in a late Beethoven string quartet. What the sociological registering of shock does here is undermine our attempt to quarantine New Music as a way to show our loyalty to the tradition. It subverts the conservative rationalization. Not only do we recognize our deception in thinking the tradition never presented anything new. We also come to see the illusion in claiming that, because it is natural, true, and immutable, our tradition could not be other than it is (Q, 254, 260).

What is the consequence of thinking that listening to Beethoven properly or structurally is as hard as listening to Schoenberg properly? Consider the apparent familiarity we feel when listening to Beethoven. Is our familiarity based on the fact that our ears have simply gotten used to Beethoven's dissonances? Are our ears simply outdated? Are we just waiting for them to catch up with contemporary forms? Turn the thought around. Is it not odd to think that our ears find something that is already two centuries old easier to listen to than music composed in our own time? Do we not generally assume we know best what we are closest to, that which is contemporary? Are not our ears utterly familiar with Schoenberg's sounds: Are they not the sounds of our world? Perhaps not. Perhaps our contemporary sounds are not our new sounds. Adorno poses these sorts of questions to undermine our confidence in familiarity.[14] So consider what we do to Beethoven's music to make it cozy and comfortable, a 'feast for the ears' (AT, 98). Do we really make Beethoven's music familiar? Or do we form for ourselves out of this music a comfortable, familiar, and contemporary Beethoven-like music? The potential of New Music lies here, in refusing to give us the comfort we seek (K, 34). The focus of the argument is now clear. Rather than thinking our ears are lagging behind contemporary times and we just have to wait for them to catch up, Adorno is asking us to recognize through New Music the disciplined deceptions to which our ears (and minds) are purportedly so subject (EFS, 272).

2. EXPANSION AND COMMENTARY

Adorno's philosophical engagement with music is evident in at least a third of his extensive writings and implicitly in almost every sentence he ever wrote. Music provides him his prototypical example, his prime exemplar, in the most and least obvious ways (AT, 23, 122). But rarely does he treat music as an example made to fit a predesigned philosophical method. He denies his philosophy this traditional sort of systematicity. For this reason we should not blindly call his philosophical engagement with music 'a philosophy *of* music'. How better we ought think about it is a question Adorno hopes will perpetually preoccupy us as it so preoccupies him. So when he opens his *Aesthetic Theory* (1970) with the sentence 'It is self-evident that nothing

concerning art is self-evident any more, not its inner life, not its relation to the world, not even its right to exist', he sets the stage for
a thorough critique of self-evidence, specifically of what might once
have been well-held opinions but now no longer are.

Adorno thinks the rationalization behind Schoenberg's model
draws too naïvely on two commonplaces of modern society, on a
conservative tendency nostalgically to bemoan the loss of a bourgeois musical world and on a utopian tendency to paint an alternative and future world as a way to criticize the present one. Adorno
unsettles both. Though he also looks back to the nineteenth century, to what then was still possible, he rejects the desirability of
its return. He rejects nostalgic, backward-faced longings. After all,
that world led through one of its dialectical tendencies precisely to
the hell, the rationalized hell, of Auschwitz.[15] He also rejects painting alternatives to the world as futile. He thinks our condition so
ideologically petrified that we can no longer envisage ourselves as
different from how we presently are. The most the critical theorist
can do in this crisis is discern social patterns in hindsight or engage
critically in the concrete condition of the present to motivate the
thought that the present condition is not necessarily so. What the
theorist can no longer do is produce a total philosophical system (as
Hegel purportedly once did) in which all things fit. The modernist
is concerned with what does not fit and is intent on subverting the
modern culture industry's attempt to make everything fit – falsely
and deceptively. For Adorno, the whole *now* is untrue.

His negative dialectic criticism emerges usually out of the way
that it confronts conservative criticism, or, more specifically, ex-
poses the contradictions of the existing order that he thinks conservative criticism masks. He asks us to think of conservative criticism
as holding ideology in place by portraying a life that is true and immutable, or by affirming an appeal to a separate high culture or to a
natural or fixed tradition (say, of tonality), to show the satisfaction
that can be gained through the existing order. Dialectical criticism
then turns this claim back on itself by showing how the existing
order not only fails to provide this satisfaction but does so precisely
when and because the 'guardians of culture' appeal to a separate high
culture to do the job or look back to a past tradition they claim already has (DA, 127).[16] As before, this argument is directed against
claims about the traditionalizing, say, of tonality that help produce

the apparently unchanging standard of what, say, music is and should be.

Adorno thinks one of the most hellish aspects of the existing order is that it sustains itself by making people think their society has assumed the only possible and best form, that their interests and desires are being fully satisfied. 'The schema of mass culture', he writes, 'prevails as a canon of synthetically produced modes of behavior' (CI, 78). It provides the crutches for listening, as for many other kinds of activity; it 'channelizes audience reaction' and social participation (CI, 142). Part of the hope he places in New Music is that it will help us see through established patterns of socially-formed expectations and that we will come to comprehend that our society, the existing order, is not necessarily so. Any activity or form of expression that pricks through the ideological web of familiarity is, for Adorno, already radical in the deepest sense and sustains the only hope possible. For radical does not mean revolutionary; more deeply, it implies the sort of reflection that cracks established patterns of self-evidence.

Consider, now, Schoenberg's claim that each great composer solves the problems raised by the previous composer. Adorno suggests contrarily that a work makes transparent the problem a previous work tried to hide behind the aesthetic appearance of a solution. Tradition, he writes, 'is not imitation, regression or straightforward continuation, but the ability to gain insight into challenges which remained unresolved and which left flaws behind in the music. The New Music faces up to these challenges' (Q, 262). Adorno then offers the dialectical twist of the conservative assumption by claiming that each work, or each composer, stands (or may stand) to a previous one as an enemy,[17] or that '[t]radition is far more present in works deplored as experimental than in those which deliberately strive to be traditional' (P, 155). For what the experimental does at best is overturn aesthetic laws as received laws and give them new material and formal expression. What we see here is Adorno finding in New Music a challenge to tradition qua received or inherited law comparable to his own new philosophical challenge to Schoenberg's received justification for his own new music.

Consider, next, Adorno's remark that Schoenberg's music honours listeners precisely by making no concessions to them. Adorno thinks their expectations will be shattered. The music will deny them their comfort or easy pleasure, a denial he now associates, as Schoenberg also associates though with different intent, with the prohibition in Jewish law against graven images. Think of Schoenberg's opera *Moses und Aron* and of Moses' displeasure in Aron's offering of deceptive pleasure through the Golden Calf. Adorno sees the denial of real or mediated pleasure (sensuality mediated by cognition) as triggering a displeasure in merely apparent or mere pleasure (mere sensuality). To explain this, he draws upon a remarkable resemblance he sees between Schoenberg's music and popular songs, since both make transparent 'their refusal to be enjoyed' (EFS, 274). Yet the resemblance is just that, a resemblance, not an identity. The refusal of popular songs is based on their preventing the possibility of real pleasure by offering an all-consuming apparent or superficial pleasure (Aron's gift to the people). The refusal of Schoenberg's music is based on the denial of a real pleasure without any promise that a superficial pleasure will be offered in its place. The musical occasions, when listeners expect pleasure, are thus transformed either into bacchanalian frenzies ('ecstasy without content' [EFS, 292]) or into occasions of anxiety and terror (or, for Moses, a profound but anxious silence), to which New Music gives unmitigated and unconsoling form and expression (EFS, 298).[18]

Although he thinks his opera does give form to this resemblance between the new and the popular, Schoenberg nonetheless worries about linking its truthfulness to denying listeners their comfort. Adorno thinks the link crucial if one wants to show through New Music the deceptions of the society in which this music is so deeply entangled. One might suggest that in failing to articulate Moses' final anxiety (the opera is left deeply unresolved) Schoenberg is left to fall into the same trap as his resistant listeners. He is left only with the option of saying that for the time being his music is too difficult or that Aron was justified in offering the Golden Calf to the people, and the listeners are happy to agree. So Adorno believes he has Schoenberg's opera on his side. More than once he writes that even if Schoenberg does not understand his music, his music understands us. His music does not lie.

I have focused on Adorno's model of listening against the background of Schoenberg's. However, I have not yet acknowledged that focusing on listening is not the straightforward route for understanding either theorist. Both give priority to the works themselves. Why my focus? Because keeping our attention on the socially disciplined deceptions to which our listening is purportedly so subject reveals the thoroughly dialectical character of Adorno's turn to radical works.

Consider how persuasively Rose Rosengard Subotnik has shown the overdependence of Adorno's conception of educated, structural hearing on the serious production of musical works and hence his failure to acknowledge that different sorts of music production might require different, not merely less adequate, forms of listening.[19] Nonetheless, I think the defense of the 'classical' or 'serious' form of listening is not his point, even if it serves as a dialectical (Subotnik says 'utopian') point of reference. His interest, rather, is in providing in concrete terms a critique of the administration of technology; its deceptive ways of stereotyping, streamlining, standardization, and simplification; its deceptive support of easy listening. His interest in listening always reflects his concern with the present state of society's exchange categories, its totalizing form. To provide a concrete critique, one has to engage in the actual practice of music that exists. And no practice apparently reveals the dialectical play between truth and deception better than that of serious music. However, that this practice developed in a society that required and allowed other practices to develop alongside means a resembling dialectic will be found in them too.

In other words, Adorno does not isolate serious music from the society that contains also other practices, say, of jazz, light, mass, popular, and/or entertainment music. Why then does he distinguish them? For the critical theorist, to describe these categories, their function and division, is to see 'the truth about society'. The very division is 'incorporated into the almighty totality', even if the two sides 'do not add up' (CI, 58). But to see this truth is to see how society itself tries to disguise it. How does the deception work? By the culture industry's assuming control of the age-old division between serious and popular music to render both sides socially impotent. First it tries to make serious music conform to what it produces as popular entertainment. Either it succeeds at the expense of the music (favorite hits from Beethoven) or it fails. When it fails, it markets the music as incomprehensible and avant-garde and so reestablishes the division for its own purposes. Adorno traces how the avant-garde has bought into the story. Retreating willingly into isolation, it has assumed with increasing contentment the deception of being socially irrelevant. But social irrelevance is exactly what the culture industry wants in order to obliterate the music's challenge (AT, 254).

On the other side, popular art has played into the deception of being socially legitimate. Why the deception? Because the terms on which society has allowed it to be socially legitimate have also been those rendering it harmless. It has looked as if the music has communicated to the people as music, as it apparently once did, but really its effect has been soporific and innocuous.

Adorno's point is that if the culture industry has won on one side, it has won on both. The industry has shaped both sides of the schema and encouraged retreat into one or both precisely to disempower any actual music that has been produced. This is crucial: Retreating to the category of the popular to look for resistance to the establishment proves no more effective than retreating into the elite. The mistake is to look on either side instead of to particular instances of music that might, in their particularity, subvert the social categorization. It is the deception of categorical thought – the logic of sameness and satisfaction upon which the culture industry survives and deceives – that is the target of the critique, not any given piece or type of music per se.

Yet some music has played willingly into society's categorizations – many examples of jazz and light music, but many of Stravinsky's works too.[20] Regressive tendencies toward standardization, repetition, and conciliation are found in any music that sacrifices integrity of structure in favor of affirming the status quo. The music proves 'insufficiently dialectical', a fact seen both in formal features and dialectically in the conformity the form shows to already established patterns of easy listening. The music might offer immediate gratification, but it does not last (remember Aron's gift) (Q, 261). 'To be sure', Adorno writes, 'dissonances occur in jazz practices, and even techniques of intentional misplaying have developed. But an appearance of harmlessness accompanies all these customs' (EFS, 289).[21] The dissonance is too easily put aside. Or, of serious works: 'The repugnance aroused by these insinuating, ingratiating gestures, which have wormed their way into even the greatest works, forms part of the pathos of the qualitatively New Music' (Q, 261). Not incidentally, if there is elitism here, it is expressed not in preferences but in expectations. Adorno is much harder on Stravinsky's purported failings than on any jazz musician's. It is as if he expects far less from the music he associates (and we would say too readily) with the sphere of the popular.

Why does Adorno choose Schoenberg's music to do the work of resistance? Adorno is trying to display a dialectic within the history of music equivalent to the one he and Horkheimer describe for enlightenment. He interprets the serious and popular forms as emerging in the nineteenth-century and then in more troubling ways in the early twentieth-century European and American world of the culture industry. Against this background, he sees the Beethoven to Schoenberg line as similar to the Hegel to Adorno line. 'In a similar sense to that in which there is only Hegelian philosophy, in the history of music there is only Beethoven.'[22] And if, at the other end, Schoenberg is producing dissonant works in music, Adorno is aiming for the same in philosophy. For, as he argues, it is philosophy's task to enunciate, as it is New Music's task to express, the distinction between truth and opinion when society no longer does.

On the other side, he sees the folk-song to popular-song line as similar to the 'Wagner to Hollywood' line,[23] and these lines as similar, in their developmental tendencies, to the totalizing 'isms' of philosophy (idealism, scientism, positivism) that extended from the nineteenth-century into the twentieth. What the 'ism' represents is similar to what mass culture represents: 'an organized mania for connecting everything with everything else, a totality of public secrets' (CI, 72).[24] One might think Adorno falls prey to the same tendency. Yet, when critically exposing and thus demystifying the tendency toward organization, the dialectic of enunciation demands that one of its sides not merely represent but also embody this tendency.

I mentioned earlier that, for all Adorno's interest in listening, he objects to focusing our attention here. The place where aesthetic theory should begin, and indeed also end, is the produced musical work. Here he shows a formalist commitment. Yet it is not like Schoenberg's commitment or the traditional formalist line in which the work's significance or beauty is contained completely within its formed content (the unfolding of the musical idea). That's only half the story. Adorno's commitment is dialectical: He is a critical formalist. He conceives of the work doubly as aesthetic form and social fact (AT, 5).

However, he does not reject listening as the focus because listening fails to exhibit a double character: It does not so fail. He rejects the focus because of the methodological tendency to then overencourage feeling theories. Witness, he says, the history of aesthetic theory. The problem with feeling theories is less that they usually ignore the role feelings play in fostering illusions and more that they encourage subjectivism, a subjectivism that isolates feelings from objects. Reiterating his argument against conservative criticism, he says that isolating feelings disempowers the truth potential of art. Instead of revealing the truth content of the social processes in which feelings are entangled, the isolation allows those processes to remain in place. It is not that feelings assume their own independent significance from being so isolated. Rather, just because of their assumed isolation, they end up conforming (like the avant-garde) to the shape the society imposes upon them when it co-opts their isolation for its own purposes. Society, Adorno claims, trades on the claimed purity of aesthetic experience, on aestheticist disavowals of social character, to maintain its present form. Aesthetic theory should not play so easily into society's hands. Indeed, it should expose the illusion that the isolation of the aesthetic is 'an isolated matter'.[25]

In a similar vein, Adorno argues that autonomy does not amount to a freedom from or isolation from social process. Recall his claim that isolating concerts of New Music undermines the potential of this music to challenge the belief that it is incomprehensible. It serves society but not individuals to have this belief so uncritically held. Comparably, defensive isolation and retreats by aesthetic theorists into the purely subjective or purely aesthetic do not constitute, but in fact undermine, the real autonomy Adorno believes music can have to emancipate listeners from the social confines of the ideologically self-evident. Wherein lies this autonomy? Here Adorno shows his (mediated) objectivist commitment when he answers: in the works themselves.

Yet not every work challenges our listening habits, only autonomous ones do. Despite suggestions sometimes to the contrary, it is not aesthetic theory, the domain of art, or even all works that are autonomous. Only some works are. Consistently and unflaggingly he picks atonal and dissonant works, particularly some of the works of Schoenberg. However, autonomous works are such not because they have dissonant or atonal formed content per se but because with this sort of formed content (construction) they have proved (the claim is historical) most resistant to incorporation into administered society.

Not every resistant work need necessarily have dissonant content of the Schoenbergian sort (this is not a claim about correct musical content). However, it does need to stand in a certain relation to the social patterns of listening in relation to which it is produced. What is the relation? This resistance?

Certainly, for Adorno, it is nothing to celebrate. Autonomy is not a naïve assertion of aesthetic or artistic freedom. On the contrary, resistant works at most show that there exist oppositional elements (spaces, fractures, or gaps) within administered society that might give listeners the opportunity to tear the ideological web (AT, 98). Yet these works are always also commodities, as much implicated in society's packaging of music as opposed to such patterns of organization in their aesthetic mode. In this sense, their autonomy is relative and mediated.

The mediation takes the historical condition of society into account, and society now is in very, very bad account. Autonomy, accordingly, is at its most extreme. In this extremity we finally find Adorno's reason for focusing on Schoenberg's early expressionist works. In them, he says with increasing pessimism, we find a truthful expression of resistance to a world that has increasingly less freedom to celebrate. As society's condition becomes more administered, musical expression becomes more futile. Schoenberg's works show this futility to the extreme. Content to suffer, to weep, to declare their social 'impotence', they paradoxically 'represent the liquidation of every last trace of resistance' (CI, 67).[26] They no longer represent feelings, passions, as traditional works did, but are just expressions in themselves of extreme anxiety. No longer fulfilling the traditional function of works (the unfolding of the idea), they move increasingly toward brevity and instantaneous gestures and cease to be works. Equally as paradoxically, Stravinsky's works prove socially deceptive just because they fail to register such impotence and offer the too affirmative illusion that art and work production are still possible. Recalling a Hegelian option, Adorno takes Schoenberg to be stoical and Stravinsky cynical.

Adorno takes literally Schoenberg's techniques of dissonance and atonality to argue for a metaphorical (social and philosophical) dissonance that can be identified in any work that has alienated or mutilated form relative to the social conditions of production pertaining to it (AT, 75, 84). Hence his description also of Beethoven's

Missa Solemnis as an 'alienated masterpiece'.[27] Dissonance does not result from an application of atonal method. It results from a quality of works that, even if and because they appear as perfectly formed totalities, suggest there is also a moment of something more (that resistant moment) that subverts that unity (AT, 85–6). If Beethoven's symphonies appear formally consonant with the scheme of early nineteenth century bourgeois culture, the late string quartets begin to reveal, through their internal fractures, a growing deception of wholeness that bourgeois culture was beginning to provide. The dissonant form implicated by the work concept, despite the appearance of total and harmonious form, is made fully explicit in Adorno's historical scheme by Schoenberg.

Adorno chooses particular works to do the wretched work of autonomy because they exhibit the same kind of character of totalizing form as society in its developing form of administration. As aesthetic totalities, as constructions, works serve as the most appropriate dialectical opposition to, but then also as exemplars of, the present commodified and contradictory shape of administration. As objects with commodity and aesthetic character, these works assume the adequate shape to reflect, in their own resistance or truthfulness, the untruth of the social totality. Works that truthfully show the untruth of society are those that have dissonant or mutilated form. If 'dissonance shows the truth about harmony', then dissonant elements in society show the untruth of its apparent harmonious administration (AT, 110).

Schoenberg's works reveal a world of fragmentation, suffering, and loneliness but also the suppression of seeing this world through the dominant drives of late capitalism. 'Anxiety, Schoenberg's expressive core, identifies itself with the terror of men in the agonies of death, under total domination' (P, 172). At their most extreme, most historically-advanced position, the works produce terror. They show through their (mediated) form the antagonisms society bears itself but does everything to hide. That the suppression is so complete explains why New Music's expressivity is so futile. Recall *Erwartung's* nightmare. The music does not show the nightmare by offering a hopeful alternative vision. To produce such a vision now would be to capitulate to a modernity that is fascist or totalitarian. New Music expresses no solace and no hope, its beauty 'no longer beautiful' (AT, 53).

'And yet' – Adorno often uses this expression to show a dialectical reversal – there are in these works flashes of hope of 'a world that is not yet', a world, he also says, that carries the residue of resistant subjectivity. 'Only by ceasing to be "lovely"' (a term he uses in English) can these works provide 'an intimation of beauty' (Q, 257). Art is the last refuge for uncompromised subjects. Does this look like utopianism after all? Adorno takes this thought away. Radical works fulfill their promise to offer sanctuary from horrifying norms by denying what is expected of them (that is, real pleasure). They offer aestheticization without gratification or enjoyment. Listeners who listen thus appreciate them in truth only for their sincerity.

Radical music shows a damaged world by pulling listeners in two directions, toward the social surface of comfort and toward loneliness and suffering. Here I think is atonal music's radical potential within the schema of mass culture made fully explicit – to maintain the conflicted character of that experience. Experienced as conflicted, society fails to 'have it all its own way' (CI, 170). Audiences 'force their eyes shut and voice approval', Adorno remarks of movie audiences, 'in a kind of self-loathing'.[28] So too, by extension, with the listening public for New Music: listeners play into the music's isolation and incomprehensibility; they play into its futility. But they also demonstrate on occasion that they have real interests and are not entirely content with their response and thus that they are 'still strong enough to resist, within certain limits, total inclusion' into the purportedly totalized form of administration.

There is another reason Adorno pays attention to Schoenberg's works. He wants to distance himself from a view held by many of his contemporaries (notably Brecht), that the emancipatory or political potential of music lies in music's content rather than in its form. His argument against content is an argument against tendentious music or music with messages (political songs with political messages).[29] (He also identifies this position with the claims of popular music.) He denies that music's political potential lies in its didactic content or specified social use. Rather, it lies in the indirect, unseen, even disguised function of works, in those that assume the appearance of purely aesthetic and internally motivated structural form. We have already seen this in his argument for the resistance or autonomy given in Schoenberg's mutilated or dissonant form. The form registers the social relation. Here Adorno shows a commitment to so-called pure works of music, though 'purity' is anything but pure.

Adorno distinguishes the communicability of form from the communication of content or statements. Music underscores the communicative potential of form by resisting 'reduction to statement' (to concept) (Q, 255). Communicability captures what he otherwise describes as New Music's ability to 'communicate through non-communication: it aims to blast away the things blocking mankind's ears which they themselves hasten to close once more' (Q, 265). Now we know why Adorno focuses not only on works but also on musical works, then not only on musical works but also on radical musical works. Radical musical works are like 'messages thrown into the sea, such is the extremity of their alienation. They tell the truth about our predicament in the world, but do so indirectly, in cipher form' (P, 21). Why cipher form? Because it reflects the 'history of man' more truthfully [gerechter] than the document (PM, 47).

I end simply with a question regarding Adorno's commitment to New Music. Can it be untethered from his social critique so that the latter can find application to the music of our now rather than his? Or is his critique merely a product of his times? Here we might consider whether his dissonant philosophy is as futile and lonely, even if historically necessary, as he sees Schoenberg's music to be. Adorno thinks it is, but he thinks this thought so dark that we will deny it. As with Schoenberg's music we seek redemption in it but not an explanation of it. Adorno decries this search for redemption for the same reason he decries easy listening. 'The darkness must be interpreted, not replaced by a clarity of meaning' (AT, 27). But philosophy, like music, does not face darkness head on but confronts it only in cipher form.

Adorno's thought is so deeply dialectical that any mere extension of it or simple adoption of his principles for contemporary purposes is likely to assume the character of a reified or organized deception. He is not the first philosopher to refuse mere disciples. In this respect, I think he interestingly continues a Socratic tradition of philosophical pursuit of unremittingly offering us a glove we can never make perfectly fit. He does not give answers but tries through his interpretations to undermine our most cherished assumptions about how things are in the world. His close friend Horkheimer once wrote, 'Socrates died because he subjected the most sacred thoughts to dialectical thought.' We might add that, for Adorno, dialectical thought replaced a deceptive sacredness for another more worthy of the name.

NOTES

1. Theodor W. Adorno and Max Horkheimer, *Dialectic of Enlightenment*, trans. J. Cumming (New York: Continuum: 1996), 34. Hereafter DA.
2. Cf. Theodor W. Adorno, *Philosophie der neuen Musik* (Tübingen, Germany: J. C. B. Mohr, 1949), 28–9. Hereafter cited as PM. (Translated by Anne G. Mitchell and Wesley V. Blomster under the title *Philosophy of Modern Music* [London: Sheed and Ward, 1973].) Adorno's use of '*neuen Musik*' corresponds to the more common use of 'modern music', though for the sake of accurate translation I use 'New Music' (capitalized). More importantly, the quality of the new takes on special significance in Adorno's theory; see his 'Music and New Music', in *Quasi una fantasia*, trans. Rodney Livingstone (London: Verso, 1992), 249–68. Hereafter cited as Q. Also see his *Aesthetic Theory*, trans. Robert Hullot-Kentor (Minneapolis: University of Minnesota Press,1997), 19 ff. Hereafter cited as AT.
3. Theodor Adorno, *Negative Dialectics*, trans. E. B. Ashton (New York: Seabury Press, 1973), 5.
4. *Style and Idea: Selected Writings of Arnold Schoenberg*, ed. Leonard Stein (Berkeley and Los Angeles: University of California Press, 1975), 30–53. Hereafter cited as SI. See also Adorno's 'Arnold Schoenberg', in *Prisms*, trans. Samuel Weber and Shierry Weber (Cambridge, Mass.: MIT Press, 1981), 149–72. Hereafter cited as P. And on the accusation that New Music is chaotic, ugly, and meaningless, see 'New Music, Interpretation, Audience', (in *Sound Figures*, trans. Rodney Livingstone (Stanford: Stanford University Press, 1999), 29. Hereafter cited as K.
5. The libretto by Marie Pappenheim refers only to the clause 'Thousands of people march past'.
6. Adorno was not impressed by the libretto of either work, so sought their dramatic and radical potential in the musical form or in the composer's innovative uses of inherited musical material.
7. Unpublished manuscript 'Wiesengrund' and letter to Kurt List, 1949.
8. *Arnold Schoenberg: Letters*, ed. E. Stein (London, Faber: 1964), 54.
9. Contrast Nietzsche: 'The progress from one level of style to the next must be so slow that not only the artists, but also the listeners and spectators participate in it and know exactly what is taking place. Otherwise, a great gap suddenly forms between the artist, who creates his works on remote heights, and the public.... For when the artist no longer lifts

this public, it sinks quickly downwards and falls, in fact the deeper and more dangerously the higher a genius had carried it; like the eagle, from whose talons the turtle, carried up into the clouds, drops to disaster' (*Human All Too Human*, trans. M. Faber (Lincoln, Neb.: University of Nebraska Press, 1986), aphorism no. 168.

10. Cf. Theodor W. Adorno, 'On the Fetish-Character in Music and the Regression of Listening', in *The Essential Frankfurt School Reader*, eds. A. Arato and E. Gebhart (New York: Continuum: 1995), 270–99. Hereafter cited as EFS.

11. Theodor W. Adorno, 'The Schema of Mass Culture', in *The Culture Industry*, ed. J. M. Bernstein (London: Routledge, 1991), 57. Hereafter cited as CI.

12. Cf. DA, 145: 'The perfect similarity is the absolute difference. The identity of the category forbids that of the individual cases'.

13. Q, 249; cf. also Theodor W. Adorno, 'On the Social Situation of Music', trans. W. Blomster, *Telos*, no. 35 (spring 1978): 153–4.

14. Cf. Theodor W. Adorno, *Minima Moralia: Reflections from Damaged Life*, trans. E. F. N. Jephcott (London: Verso, 1974), 80: '[T]he value of thought is measured by its distance from the continuity of the familiar.'

15. Cf. DA for the thesis of enlightenment become anti-enlightenment; also Theodor W. Adorno, 'The Culture Industry Reconsidered', in *Critical Theory and Society*, ed. S. E. Bronner and D. Kellner (London: Routledge, 1989), esp. 135.

16. This point is also made well by Jay Bernstein in his introduction to CI.

17. Adorno, *Minima Moralia*, 52.

18. 'The terror which Schoenberg and Webern spread, today as in the past, comes not from their incomprehensibility, but from the fact that they are all too correctly understood. Their music gives form to that anxiety, that terror, that insight into the catastrophic situation which others merely evade by regressing' (EFS, 298).

19. Rose Rosengard Subotnik, 'Toward a Deconstruction of Structural Listening: A Critique of Schoenberg, Adorno, and Stravinsky', in *Deconstructive Variations: Music and Reason in Western Society* (Minneapolis: University of Minnesota Press, 1996), 148–76.

20. Cf. PM for the most extreme version of his Schoenberg-Stravinsky opposition.

21. For the classic and most extreme version of his views on popular music, see 'Perennial Fashion – Jazz', in *Prisms*, 119–32.

22. Theodor W. Adorno, *Beethoven: The Philosophy of Music*, trans. Edmund Jephcott (Stanford: Stanford University Press, 1998), 10.

23. Theodor W. Adorno and Hanns Eisler, *Composing for the Films* (New York: Oxford University Press, 1947), 7. See also Andreas Huyssen,

'Adorno in Reverse: From Hollywood to Richard Wagner', in *After the Great Divide; Modernism, Mass Culture, Postmodernism* (Bloomington: Indiana University Press, 1986), 16–43.

24. On 'isms', see AT, 25.

25. Adorno, 'On the Social Situation of Music', 129.

26. Cf. also Adorno, 'On the Social Situation of Music', 130.

27. Theodor W. Adorno, 'Verfremdetes Hauptwerk: Zur *Missa Solemnis*', in *Moments Musicaux* (Frankfurt: Suhrkamp, 1964). Translated into English as 'Alienated Masterpiece: The *Missa Solemnis*', *Telos*, 28 (summer 1976): 113–24.

28. Adorno, 'Culture Industry Reconsidered', 132.

29. Theodor W. Adorno, 'Commitment' in *Aesthetics and Politics*, ed. Ronald Taylor (London: Verso, 1977); also AT, 104, 123.

ANDREW BOWIE

10 Adorno, Heidegger, and the Meaning of Music

I

In an outline of ca. 1949 for a never-written work on *The History of German Music from 1908 to 1933,* Adorno remarks that, when the Nazis took over, they hardly needed to suppress 'cultural-bolshevist' music – that is, 'new music', such as that of Berg or Schoenberg – because the suppression had already largely taken place within the realm of 'so-called new music' itself, so that 'certain late forms of new music (Weill's *Bürgschaft*) could be taken over almost un-changed by fascist composers (Wagner-Régeny)'.[1] Adorno continues,

In the historical analysis of this section [of the proposed book] the idea is to be developed via the model of music that the decisive changes, whose drastic expression is the seizure of power by fascism, take place in such a deep stratum of social life that the political surface does not decide at all, and that these experiences of the depths, as they are connected to the problem of unemployment and the elimination of the rising bourgeoisie (crisis of the opera), are strikingly expressed in an apparently as derivative area of culture as that of music.[2]

Understandably, many approaches to the philosophy of music or to musicology are liable to treat such statements with more than a hint of scepticism. Is it possible to legitimate an approach to music which thinks it is more likely, as Adorno claims in a related context, that one will arrive at historical insight by 'a really technically strict in-terpretation of a single piece like the first movement of the *Eroica* that makes its discoveries transparent as discoveries about society' than, for example, by looking at the broad history of musical styles[3] or, indeed, at the social and economic conditions of musical produc-tion and reproduction?

248

How might one move from 'technically strict interpretation' to discoveries about society without either failing in musical terms or failing in sociological terms? Now there are no easy answers to these questions, but Adorno's aims should not, despite the fact that some of them are patently unfulfillable, simply be dismissed. Are we happy to think that the *Eroica* is, as Peter Kivy claims, a 'beautiful noise, signifying nothing',[4] in order to avoid making statements which, given that the *Eroica* does not strictly refer to anything, cannot claim to be about what the *Eroica* refers to, let alone about its 'truth'? If the *Eroica* indeed means more than Kivy suggests – and even his suggestion that it means nothing depends on the emergence of the notions of aesthetic autonomy and of 'absolute music' in the eighteenth century which supplanted the notion that music represented feelings – how is its meaning to be approached without the approach just being dictated by the assumptions made before engaging with the music itself? One is evidently confronted here with a hermeneutic circle that affects any attempt to explore the meaning of a largely non-semantic form of articulation with semantic means. However, as we shall see, this circularity may not be quite as destructive as it first appears. It should already be obvious that what is at issue leads to a whole series of revealing philosophical questions about the nature of 'meaning' – in the broad sense of that which human beings can understand – in relation to music.

Before getting to these philosophical questions, let us, though, briefly consider an extreme example of Adorno's attempts to see the meaning of music in sociopolitical terms (an example which makes the dangers of such approaches all too clear). In 1963, a Frankfurt student newspaper reprinted an unfortunate 1934 review by Adorno of works for male choir with texts by Baldur von Schirach.[5] The review at times uses the Nazi jargon of the day, but it does also try to give an analysis of the music, suggesting, with only slightly disguised critical intent, that the successful pieces 'are not concerned with patriotic mood and vague enthusiasm, but with the question of the possibility of new folk-music'.[6] In response to the re-publication of the review, Adorno, while freely admitting he had made a serious error of judgement, rightly asserts that the rest of his life's work contradicts this misguided attempt at a tactical accommodation with a régime which he at the time, like many others, thought had no chance of lasting. He then insists that 'whoever has an overview of the continuity of my work could not compare me with Heidegger, whose philosophy is fascistic in its innermost cells'.[7] When asked in 1939 to address the question 'What is music?' Adorno maintained,

> If the question wanted to be understood as an ontological one and was directed at the 'being' of music as such, then I believe it would move at a level of abstraction which would offer the occasion for 'radical' questions in the dubious Heideggerian sense.[8]

The radical questions about music in which Adorno is interested are, then, supposed to be wholly different from the kind of 'radical' questions asked by Heidegger. But are they really?

From the examples cited above, it is patent that a lot must be going on under the surface for Adorno even to begin to contemplate such links between music and society. Despite his refusal to engage in an 'ontological' approach – by which he means one that would try to establish the essence of what music is – Adorno has to entertain at least some heuristic notions concerning what it is about music that allows it to be interpreted as an indication of fundamental social issues. At the same time, some of Adorno's suspicions of 'ontological' accounts of music are plainly valid in relation to approaches to music which try to convert a phenomenon that can only be understood as a historical manifestation of human imagination – something which is therefore irredeemably 'intentional' – into something akin to a part of nature that would be accessible to scientific investigation. As Adorno argues, 'compositional material' is as different from what is described in a physicalist or psychological account of acoustic phenomena 'as language is from the store of its sounds'.[9] Carl Dahlhaus makes the essential point:

> Instead of beginning with the rules of the musical craft and – for the sake of their theoretical legitimation – looking for illusory causes of historically based norms in a fictive nature of music, theory of music would have to ask about the categories via which a collection of acoustic data could be constituted as music at all.[10]

The real question, then, is the status of the categories via which something is apprehended as music.

Looking at music in terms of meaning is already less problematic in this respect: In order to regard something as music at all, one must assume that there is something to be understood in ways

not possible for non-music. The question is how this understanding relates to the understanding of language. The ways in which
we come to understand something 'as' something are, of course, as
Heidegger shows, the bread and butter of any hermeneutic enterprise. Given the shifting historical boundaries of the musical and the
non-musical, musical understanding cannot be reduced to a series of
methodological rules of the kind that might apply to the scientific
classification of sounds, not least because a major factor in the development of music is *disagreement* over whether something is music
or not. (Something analogous applies, at least in the modern period,
to literature and other forms of art.) Despite Adorno's strictures concerning 'ontology', Heidegger explicitly linked his reflections on the
issue of 'seeing as' to a vital aspect of the philosophical tradition
to which Adorno also regards himself as being an heir – an aspect
which Adorno also uses to interpret the meaning of music. It is here
that there will be some significant mileage in bringing these two
approaches together.

II

Adorno's unfinished book on Beethoven contains remarks that make
it fairly easy to establish a link to the tradition to which Heidegger's hermeneutics also belongs. However, before looking at these
remarks, we need first to consider other remarks Adorno makes,
both about his aims in the Beethoven book – whose subtitle, *Philosophy of Music*, suggests, in a manner which I shall investigate
more fully at the end, that Beethoven is the paradigm of 'music' –
and about philosophical problems involved in understanding music. In the introductory material to the book, Adorno asserts that
'one of the basic motives of the book' is that Beethoven's 'language,
his content, tonality as a whole, i.e. the system of bourgeois music,
is irrevocably lost for us'.[11] This remark is explained by his more
general comments about the 'affirmative' – and therefore 'ideological' – nature of music. Music's ideological character is present in
the very fact 'that it *begins*, that it *is* music at all – its language is
magic in itself, and the transition into its isolated sphere has an a
priori transfiguring aspect' which is the result of music's setting up a
'second reality *sui generis*' (B, 25/6–7). Because of its inherently con-
soling aspect, music as a whole is 'more completely under the spell of

illusion (*Schein*)', which means that it contributes to existing injustices by reconciling listeners to reality as it already is. (By this time, after all, the reality in question does include what leads to Nazism.) However, in terms of what Adorno calls its 'immanent movement', music's 'lack of objectivity and of unambiguous reference' make it '*freer* than other art' (B, 26/7). It is less bound to reproducing determinate aspects of existing reality and is therefore able to perform a critical role in keeping alive an awareness of how things could be transformed. Consequently, 'it may be that the strict and pure concept of art can only be derived from music', because great literature and painting necessarily involve material which cannot be 'dissolved into the autonomy of the form' (B, 26/7).

This latter remark might appear to locate Adorno in Kivy's camp. The dissolving of the material of the *Eroica* into the 'autonomy of the form' would seem to be what renders it free of the convention-bound meanings of a 'reified' reality of the kind Adorno thinks invade 'significant' [*bedeutend*] literature via the representational aspect of verbal language (B, 26/7).[12] However, far from making autonomy the basis of music's *lack* of meaning, Adorno's approach to the philosophy of music is distinguished by the fact that it is precisely the great autonomous works which are supposed to communicate the important truths, especially, as we saw, about society and history. In order to be able to make such connections between music and society Adorno initially relies on the idea of a reconciliation between compositional freedom and technical necessity in the great works and, as we shall see, on the assumption that this reconciliation relates to a key aspect of modern philosophy. This connection between music and society does, though, entail some very questionable presuppositions.

The concept of 'technique' in art is, for example, related to, but vitally different from, what is involved in technology in the more usual sense. Adorno thinks that the subject of 'instrumental reason' contributes to the delusions characteristic of 'bourgeois society which has been driven towards totality and is thoroughly organised' (PM, 28/25). Instrumental reason, like the commodity structure, imposes forms of identity onto nature of the kind whose effects are now apparent in the ecological crisis. The artist's products, on the other hand, offer a model of what an emancipated employment of historically developed 'technical' resources in other spheres might achieve.

Because it requires freedom from instrumental ends for it to be aesthetic at all, aesthetic production does not necessarily involve the kind of repression Adorno regards as definitive of the 'universal context of delusion' of which modern technology is a part.[13]

However, Adorno's account of the utopian aspect supposedly inherent both in modern art's refusal to ignore the need for innovation and in its resistance to being used for instrumental ends relies on an indefensible equation of two different senses of 'techne', the one instrumental, the other not. Furthermore, 'advanced' has a different sense in relation to problem-solving technology from the sense it has in relation to the choice of possibilities in musical composition. These objections are pretty damning, and they might seem to invalidate much of Adorno's approach. However, a passage from *Philosophy of Modern Music* on the idea that 'the confrontation of the composer with the material is the confrontation with society' does offer some hints as to how Adorno's conception may involve more than just dubious analogies:

> The demands which go from the material to the subject derive...from the fact that the 'material' is itself sedimented spirit, something social, which has been preformed by the consciousness of people. As former subjectivity which has forgotten itself this objective spirit of the material has its own laws of motion. What seems to be merely the autonomous movement of the material, which is of the same origin as the social process and is always once more infiltrated with its traces, still takes place in the same sense as the real society when both know nothing of each other and mutually oppose each other. (PM, 36/33–4)

Unfortunately, despite involving some persuasive ideas, this position, which is based on Hegel's notion of objective spirit, is also questionable.[14]

Adorno is too reliant on his version of a Hegelian-Marxist-Weberian idea of the totalized nature of 'modern society' that results from the commodity structure's reduction of all value to exchange value. In the present-day world of transnational capitalism, such a view should not just be dismissed, but it leaves too little room for crucial discriminations between the functioning of musical material in societies with differing histories and thus with differing forms of 'sedimented spirit'. What can in one context be the emancipatory adoption of previously ignored compositional means may in another context be a clichéd abdication of the autonomy of the artist. This levelling of discriminations can, for example, explain why Adorno fails to do justice to composers like Sibelius who, whatever their faults may be, cannot be adequately understood or appreciated in terms of the aspects of central European musical modernism which Adorno uses to criticize them. Adorno's conception also fails to deal with the idea, later developed by Gadamer, that what makes art 'true' is something that cannot be located in one particular historical perspective but results rather from interactions between different historical horizons. This is why Adorno has to claim that when Beethoven's historical constellation – the constellation in which new kinds of social freedom and integration seemed possible[15] – no longer pertains, the music is 'lost' to us because what it meant is no longer available to us. But what if the survival of Beethoven's music is not a timeless survival but depends rather on the way in which his music may continue to reveal *different* things to different musicians and audiences? There is too little in Adorno's perspective to enable one to understand why this might be the case, so concerned is he with the undeniable fact of reactionary appropriations of bourgeois culture in his own historical context.

The universalizing perspective which leads Adorno to the assertion that there is an 'advanced state of the musical material' requires precisely the final Hegelian overcoming of the subject-object split in the 'concept' which elsewhere is often the justified target of his philosophical criticism. How are we supposed to *identify* this most 'advanced state' without already possessing a totalizing insight into the historical significance of music? The fact that *in some contexts* certain kinds of conventional employment of musical material, like the diminished seventh chord, can indeed be said to become 'false' does not allow one to infer that this falsehood reveals the total state of the 'technique' with which the composer must work. All that can be established by such facts is the need for a critical vigilance which takes seriously the social significance of aesthetic forms and practices. Too much of Adorno's position with regard to Western music depends, as we shall see, upon the viability of his interpretation of the link between Hegel's claim to achieve the final philosophy and Beethoven's establishing of new forms of integration for musical material. The link is the source both of some significant insights and of Adorno's ultimately ethnocentric perspective.

Adorno's further esoteric claim in the passage cited above, that precisely because it is most isolated from contamination by existing meanings in society, the 'advanced' work of art will, by freely making the same sort of demands on itself that technology forces upon those developing the means of production, articulate otherwise inaccessible truths is never substantiated in this text; nor, for that matter, is it in *Aesthetic Theory*. The claim ultimately has to rely on a notion either of repression or of Sartrean bad faith on the part of members of modern societies, who are supposedly reconciled to existing injustices. Adorno's reliance on such notions is apparent in his remark that the technically advanced dissonances in new music, which result from a composition's adequacy to the history to which the music is a response, 'horrify' the concert-going public and 'speak of their own state: only for this reason are they unbearable to them' (PM, 15/9). This judgement from above is simply not adequate to the complexity of the phenomenon in question. As Nicholas Cook points out, the same dissonant music that elicits a negative response in the concert hall or on the radio can, for example, become acceptable to the same people if it is heard first as the accompaniment to a film.[16] There is little doubt that a frequent link *can* be established in some contexts between an antipathy to aesthetic modernism and political reaction, as Nazi cultural politics makes very clear, but this fact is not sufficient to establish the position Adorno proposes as the basis for his overall assessment of aesthetic modernism.

However, despite all these problems, the idea of a tension between the 'consciousness of people' and the objectifications, be they musical, linguistic, or visual, which can both constrain individuals and yet also enable them to articulate meanings, must be part of any serious attempt to understand modern art's role in society. The sense that Schoenberg exemplifies a crisis in music that results from a disintegration of a shared 'language' of tonality, the seeds of which are sown in the deconstruction of forms in Romantic music from Schubert to Mahler, is undeniable, as is the fact that the development of this music is connected to the social and political crises of modern Western history. Although his evidence and his interpretation of the significance of this disintegration may be flawed, Adorno's ways of trying to understand it are still important. The question to be answered here is how an account of the relationship between 'material' which is pre-given in the social world and what the artist can spontaneously achieve with this material can be made to work as an approach to the understanding of music and society.

Adorno rightly argues that it is no good using examples of music to illustrate 'something already established' (PM, 30/26) about society: The meaning of the music qua music would be irrelevant because the ascribed meaning would be merely the circular consequence of a prior interpretation of society. Instead, he maintains, the aim is 'social theory by dint of the explication of aesthetic right and wrong in the heart of the [musical] objects' (PM, 30/26). This is because 'All forms of music . . . are sedimented contents. In them survives what is otherwise forgotten and can no longer speak in a direct manner' (PM, 44/42). Tempting as this claim might sound, it involves a further problem, namely, a kind of 'aesthetic antinomy' of the kind Kant identified in his 'antinomy of taste', which demanded that the aesthetic object be both uniquely particular and yet universally significant. If the piece of music, which must be in some way unique if it is to be aesthetically significant, is the only means of articulating what has been forgotten, any verbal attempt to say what this is must necessarily fail. Of course, if only the music says it, we will never be able to recover it in conceptual form anyway. Adorno begins his remarks on 'Music and Concept' in the Beethoven book with a reflection on precisely this dilemma: 'That music can only say what is proper to music: that means that word and concept cannot express its content *immediately*, but only mediately, i.e. as philosophy' (B, 31/10). But what does 'philosophy' mean here? It is at this point that the link to Heidegger's hermeneutics and to the Romantic philosophical tradition adumbrated above can be very revealing. The link can also suggest how many existing philosophical conceptions of meaning, particularly within the analytical tradition, fail to come to terms with vital dimensions of what human beings can understand.

III

How, then, does Adorno see the 'mediation' of music by philosophy? The Beethoven book, he claims, must 'decisively determine the relationship of music and conceptual logic' (B, 31/11), and he embarks on an intriguing initial attempt to do so:

The 'play' of music is play with logical forms as such, of positing, identity, similarity, contradiction, whole, part, and the concretion of music is essentially the power with which these forms articulate themselves in the material, in the notes. ... The threshold between music and logic does not therefore lie with the logical elements, but rather with their specific logical synthesis, the *judgement*. Music does not know judgement, but rather a synthesis of a different kind, a synthesis which constitutes itself purely from the constellation [i.e., the particular configuration of musical material], not from the predication, subordination, subsumption of its elements. The synthesis also stands in relation to truth, but to a completely different truth from apophantic truth ... The reflections would have to terminate in a definition like *Music is the logic of judgementless synthesis.* (B, 32/11)[17]

In *Aesthetic Theory*, Adorno extends this latter idea to art in general: 'In the work of art judgement as well is transformed. Art works are analogous to judgement as synthesis; but the synthesis in them is judgementless, one could not say of any of them what it judges, none of them is a so-called proposition [*Aussage*]'.[18]

As we saw above, Adorno claims that there is an important link between music and language, because no form of articulation can be understood either as music or as language if all that is at issue are the objectifiable phenomena in which it is instantiated. What makes music into music and language into language is therefore connected, and in a way which relates to what makes art into art. Crucially, whatever the conditions of the existence of music, language, and art may be, they are prior to what we can subsequently analyse in propositions, involving what Adorno talks of in terms of 'the mimetic ability'. This is the ability of

the musician who understands his score, follows its most minute movements, and yet in a certain sense does not know what he is playing; it is the same for the actor, and for this reason the mimetic ability manifests itself most drastically in the praxis of artistic representation, as imitation of the curve of movement of what is represented. (AT, 189/125)

The 'logical' aspect of works of art is, he maintains, most closely related to inference, by which he seems to mean, for example, the way in which the resolution of dissonances in tonal music is, to listeners used to the conventions of Western music, like the conclusion of an argument from premises. This claim becomes comprehensible when Schumann, for example, does *not* resolve the dissonance at

the end of the first song of *Dichterliebe*. We are left with the sense
that an expected 'conclusion' is lacking, as it would be in an incomplete inference. What is lacking is therefore not just the resolution of
the dominant seventh chord – that would be to confuse the material
with its contextual significance. The point of this piece of music's
'saying' what it does is not grasped by making a general point about
resolved and unresolved chords. What we say propositionally about
the music is not inherently 'false' but points rather to dimensions of
meaning – dimensions, often relating to the mood or feeling revealed
by the music – which are not reducible to how we talk about them
by employing general terms.[19]

The point which interests me here is that philosophical concern
with what is not encompassed by 'apophantic' truth, which Adorno
sees as central to music, is also central to Heidegger's examination
of the question of 'being'. One of Heidegger's major insights, which
also brings him close to the later Wittgenstein, who connected much
the same idea to music, is that what we understand when we understand is the world we inhabit rather than just propositions about
states of affairs, which are in fact only part of what we employ to
bring that understanding about. Wittgenstein says, for example, that
'[u]nderstanding a sentence in language is much more akin to understanding a theme in music than one thinks', and he links poetry to
music via the idea of there being 'something which only these words
in these positions express'.[20] Implicit in the view shared by Heidegger and Wittgenstein is the reason why, as Hilary Putnam suggests,
analytical philosophers have been so signally unable to *state* in what
the understanding of the meaning of 'Snow is white' consists, even
though we understand what it means in most contexts. In Heidegger's terms, the 'proposition is not the locus of truth, rather truth is
the locus of the proposition' – by 'truth' he means here the fact of
the world's being disclosed as intelligible at all.[21] Thus, propositions
about what is the case are 'derivative': Without prior understanding
of a world which concerns us, there would be no way of understanding how words, as Heidegger acutely puts it, 'accrue' to meanings,
or, for that matter, of understanding how children can acquire language. 'Meanings' therefore need not be conceived of as inherently
verbal, which is precisely what opens the path to seeing music as
having meaning. Heidegger himself, despite occasional hints in its

direction, such as later references to the 'singing' of true *Dichtung*, says nothing directly about the significance of music. However, a pupil of Heidegger's did, the musicologist Heinrich Besseler, one of the key figures in the formulation of the idea of *Gebrauchsmusik* (music for use), which informed the compositional practice of Eisler, Hindemith, and others.

Besseler's essential insight is contained in his wonderful dictum, in an essay of 1925, that '[m]usic originally becomes accessible to us as a *manner/melody of human being* [*Weise menschlichen Daseins*]'.[22] The play on the sense of the word *Weise*, which by Besseler's time generally just meant 'manner' or 'way' but which in a musical context could still have the traditional sense of 'melody' or 'tune', suggests that our ways of being in the world can be 'melodic'. The point of the dictum is to resist music's becoming a simple object of analysis and to suggest how it is actually constitutive of our 'being in the world'. How would melody ever come to seem significant to us in the first place if it had no connection to our ways of being? Roger Scruton talks, in much the same vein, of music as 'the universal idiom which, being "free from concepts", can be understood by anyone who is open to the influence of the surrounding world'.[23] 'Melody' is, of course, also present in patterns of speech, of the kind that children often pick up, precisely for their 'musical' aspect, without necessarily grasping their sense. In such a view, we do not live in a world merely of 'representations' and 'propositional attitudes', in which we function in terms of beliefs, doubts, and so forth, and of the relation of these attitudes to our actions (that is, the world as too often seen in analytical philosophy). We actually live in a world whose meaningfulness lies not only in what we can articulate in propositions but also, for example, in moods, memories, and presentiments which may not reach the level of verbal articulation. These can involve structures of coherence and sources of pleasure in making connections, without which life becomes intolerable. Such structures are evidently linked to non-verbal forms of articulation and thus to the meanings music can have for us.

Charles Taylor has argued that our linguistic activity has its roots in the need to articulate our being in the world and cannot be understood just in terms of representing objects and states of affairs.[24] Taylor claims, in line with Heidegger, that the 'expressive', 'constitutive' dimension of language is prior to its 'designative' aspect, because the 'expressive' activity of using language to communicate cannot be convincingly explained as being generated just by the need to exchange information.[25] Without already living in a 'disclosed' world that we try to share with others by articulating ways of being in it, not least as a means of reassuring others of our social intentions, we could not even come to the point where the idea of exchanging information dominates the way language is conceptualized. 'Nice day today' cannot be understood as telling someone something about the weather – as though saying it arose out of the need to communicate a piece of information that would otherwise be hidden to one's interlocutor – and when it is said ironically on an awful day, it is only the expressive *tone* of the utterance, or an accompanying gesture or look, rather than what the utterance supposedly 'represents' that allows us to understand it at all. Taylor argues that the explicit *theoretical* understanding of language in disclosive terms, as part of our being in the world, only becomes a possibility with the beginning of modernity. The vital fact in the present context is that it is at the moment in eighteenth-century Europe when the notion of the divine origin of a language of names comes into question that the link between language and music becomes a central philosophical issue. This is evident in the rise of the idea of 'absolute music', in the elevation of music by many thinkers to being the highest of the arts rather than the lowest, and in the emergence of questions about what language really is – questions of the kind explored by Rousseau, Herder, Hamann, Humboldt, the early romantics, and Schleiermacher, all of whom connect language to music.[26]

The question here is, therefore, how the borderline between language and music is to be understood in the light of these historical changes. The logical forms of 'positing, identity, similarity, contradiction, whole, part' which Adorno sees as constitutive of music as 'judgementless synthesis' are evident in a claim like Besseler's that 'musical rhythm' – itself dependent on identity, similarity, and so forth – 'would generally relate to the manner in which we "are there at all" and "move", to a certain "temporal" basic character of our existence'.[27] Lest these claims about music and logic still seem rather vague, we need to trace their philosophical pedigree somewhat more precisely.

IV

For Besseler, as for Heidegger, the forms of logic must be dependent on the prior nature of our 'being in the world'. This is, as we shall now see, because the forms of differentiation which are the basis of logic are dependent on temporal disclosure. What, then, is the 'certain "temporal" basic character of our existence' and why does it play the role it does in Heidegger? This question is decisive in considering the meaning of music because Heidegger wants to argue that time is the 'meaning of being', and music is, of course, generally regarded as the most 'temporal' art. Heidegger relies for important parts of his account of the meaning of being on a rethinking of the 'schematism chapter' of Kant's first *Critique*. In his account of schematism, Heidegger characterizes the schema as 'the making-sensuous of concepts'.[28] The pure geometrical concept of a triangle and the empirical image of a triangle are topically different, so we need a bridge between them if we are to use geometry to judge the spatial nature of real objects. Kant calls the schema a 'rule of the synthesis of the imagination' that can connect a pure notion in the understanding and an empirical one in 'sensibility'. The schema, then, overcomes the divide between the 'sensuous' and the 'intelligible', the receptive and the spontaneous aspects of the subject. J. G. Hamann, who thought the first language was music, already points out in 1784 that language, as sensuous sign and non-sensuous meaning, would seem to involve the same bridging of the two realms, and in 1800 Schelling sees the schema as the basis of the whole of language because it enables the establishing of conventions. The schema, which Schleiermacher terms a 'shiftable image', also overcomes the gap between an empirical concept and any example of the concept: The same concept of 'dog' must apply to the Great Dane and the Chihuahua if we are to see them both as dogs. Although schematism is clearly germane to the ability to use both pure and empirical concepts, which is Kant's main contention in the first *Critique*, it actually is the basis of forms of *any* kind that could be recognized. This recognition can take place even without concepts, as Kant will suggest in the *Critique of Judgement* by the notion of the aesthetic idea, 'that representation of the imagination which gives much to think about, but without any determinate thought, that is, *concept* being able to be adequate to it, which consequently no language can completely attain and make comprehensible'.[29] The notion of aesthetic idea is one of the key sources of the romantic attention to the 'language of music'.[30]

Most fundamentally – and this is what draws Heidegger to the notion – Kant's schema is the ground of identity in temporal difference that allows the object world to become intelligible at all. Kant terms schemata in this respect 'nothing but *determinations of time* a priori according to rules'.[31] These determinations enable us to apprehend things in terms of the categories of, for example, causality, which relies on temporal succession; reality, which relies on presence at a specific time; necessity, which relies on presence at all times, and so forth. The same schemata of time are, of course, necessary for hearing music as music.

Kant famously grounds *both* logic and time in the 'synthetic unity of apperception' of the I, which binds together the different moments of the presence of things to myself that would otherwise disintegrate into chaotic multiplicity. Heidegger suggests, though, that if the I is the 'correlate of all our representations,' it is 'almost literally the definition of time, which, according to Kant, stands absolutely and persists and is the correlate of any appearances at all'.[32] Without the prior temporal opening up of the world into a world of differences, then, the activity of synthesis, in which identity is made from difference, could not occur at all. As such, the synthesizing spontaneity of the I, which Kant is forced implausibly to exclude from time altogether in order to prevent it from being part of the world of causality, is secondary to the happening of time itself, in which the world is disclosed as an object of our concern:

It is not that an I think is first given as the purest a priori and then a time and this time as the mediating station for a coming-out to a world, but the being of the subject itself *qua* Dasein is being-in-the-world, and this being-in-the-world of Dasein is only possible because the basic structure of its being is time itself, in this case in the modus of presenting (*des Gegenwärtigens*).[33]

In this perspective, Kant's schema, when temporalized in the manner Heidegger suggests, plays something like the role of Heidegger's 'as-structure' of understanding, which is 'pre-predicative' and makes predication possible, though it does not necessitate it. Apprehending things 'as' what they are is a basic manner of our being in the world, and this apprehension need not be essentially conceptual. Heidegger talks of Dasein's speaking, walking, and understanding, such that '[m]y being in the world *is* nothing but this already understanding moving myself in these ways [*Weisen*] of being'.[34]

Although Heidegger shows no awareness here of the dual sense of '*Weise*' as 'manner' and 'melody', it is not difficult to make a connection between unconceptualized but meaningful ways of being, such as certain kinds of movement or moods, and Adorno's 'judgementless synthesis'. This, as we saw, involved 'identity, similarity, contradiction, whole, part', and music is the 'logic' that renders it intelligible. What is at issue here are precisely the prepredicative, non-subsumptive, but intelligible ways of being in the world that Bertrand Russell might also be seen as pointing to in his idea of 'knowledge by acquaintance'. Scruton talks in this connection of 'a peculiar "reference without predication" that touches the heart but numbs the tongue' in our hearing of music,[35] and Wolfram Hogrebe suggests, linking the idea to music, that 'in feelings ... everything is already wordlessly full of meaning'. Hogrebe characterizes this kind of meaning in terms of a 'pre-linguistic existential semantics' that is present in '*Stimmung*', 'mood', or 'attunement' to the world.[36] Without the prepropositional capacity to apprehend and establish identities, neither repetition nor rhythm (which Schelling termed the 'music in music') would come to be significant at all. Indeed, the very ability to arrive at conventions – be they linguistic, musical, or both, as in 'tone of voice' – that can sustain socially established meanings would become incomprehensible. The idea that music can have more immediately universal significance than natural languages relates in this view to the claim that there is a kind of being in the world which precedes any insertion into a specific 'symbolic order'.[37]

Adorno, of course, is suspicious of Kant's schematism and of Heidegger's revision of it. He regards schematism as echoing the reduction of difference to identity characteristic of the commodity structure and of the aesthetic conventions of the culture industry. His suspicion, though, results from a tendency to conflate different senses of identity. The notion of identity involved in identifying something *as* something cannot simply be equated with that involved in identifying something *with* other things.[38] The former can involve identifying something as unique and irreplaceable, when we, for example, identify thematic material in a Mahler sonata recapitulation as related to previous material, even though the context, the significance, and the manner of appearance of the material is different. The latter can, most obviously in the workings of the commodity structure but also in certain kinds of musical analysis, have potentially negative implications, when unique value or significance is obscured in the name of exchange value or of mere classification of musical material without proper regard for its value within what Adorno terms its constellation. Taking this proviso into account, certain aspects of Adorno's view of music can be illuminated by a central consequence of what we have investigated in terms of schematism. This will eventually take us back to the questions with which we began.

V

One revealing way of considering what is at issue in the idea of schematism and its relationship to music is apparent in the question of metaphor. Metaphor, which evidently relies on schematism, is arguably a form of 'judgementless synthesis'. If I say 'You are a pig!' I do not tend to mean it as a truth-determinate literal judgement (though I suppose I could if you had the requisite real porcine attributes). Donald Davidson claims that 'the endless character of what we call the paraphrase of a metaphor springs from the fact that it attempts to spell out what the metaphor makes us notice, and to this there is no clear end. I would say the same for any use of language'.[39] If one does not assume that one can only notice states of affairs that can be represented in propositions, it seems plausible to claim that music can make one notice aspects of moods, feelings, temporality, landscape, or, even, in some cases, states of affairs – for instance via the effects of film music on what one understands in a film – that may not be adequately expressible in judgements. Indeed, music may first enable certain ways of being to become accessible to us at all: The successes of music therapy indicate just how important this might be. Music can, therefore, be understood to be what Heidegger terms 'world-disclosive', both in the sense that it is part of what renders the world intelligible and in the sense that it can render the world meaningful by offering ways of inhabiting the world which *feel* 'right'. Confirmation of the world-disclosive nature of music is evident in the need to have recourse to metaphor in order to try – and fail – to communicate what music actually says. Metaphors in this sense have the form of a judgement (that is, 'a is b'), but they only function as imaginative syntheses, not as truth-determinate judgements. Despite this necessary failure, it is clear that the best metaphors employed to talk about music do make us understand music better and that, conversely, great music can reveal aspects of verbal art which may otherwise remain concealed. What this suggests is that there cannot be a final boundary between the musical and the linguistic, given that they can each affect the other and that there is no decisive way in which the boundaries of either can be established.

There is no space to do justice to this issue here, but the interplay between music and language can be used to question the claim in some analytical philosophy that a firm line can be drawn between metaphor and literal meaning, a line which means that it is invalid to talk of music having meaning.[40] The usual strategy here, whose employment in some ways weakens Scruton's otherwise perceptive account of musical meaning, is to maintain that the literal meaning of a word is established by identifying its truth-conditions or the rules for its correct use. What, though, *is* the literal meaning, for example, of the word 'music'? As I have shown elsewhere, any attempt to specify definitive truth conditions for a word or utterance leads to a regress, because the statements which give the conditions or rules must themselves then be analyzed in terms of statements of their conditions or rules, and so on ad infinitum, which renders meaning incomprehensible.[41]

If one makes the hermeneutic assumption that what we understand is the living, changing historical world that we articulate in language and not just statements that are supposed to represent that world, the distinction between metaphor and literal meaning ceases to be absolute, and we also become able to understand how music can affect our understanding of verbal language. As Rom Harré suggests in relation to Susanne Langer's idea that words have 'fixed connotations': '[T]he contextuality of the significance of the musical sign is not enough sharply to distinguish language from music', because context, which precludes fixed connotation, is vital to the functioning of both words and music.[42] If context is inseparable from meaning, music can even be said to 'refer' when it signals a conventionally accepted significance or practice, though this might be likely, as Adorno suggests, to make music liable to function as ideology.[43] Furthermore, the resistance to paraphrase or literalization of living metaphor, in poetry, for example, is importantly related to our inability to specify a semantics of music.

This fact seems to me to affect a recent further way in which one might approach the music-language relationship, namely, Robert Brandom's inferentialist semantics.[44] Brandom separates the conceptual aspect of language from what is involved in mere differential responses to stimuli of the kind animals are capable of, which might therefore seem to place the language of music at the level of mere response to affective stimulus. Brandom's separation relies on the claim that inferential knowledge of a concept's relations to other concepts is required to know when a concept is applicable. This seems highly plausible until one comes to certain aesthetic issues, where the limitations of this model become apparent. The knowledge required to make a note into part of a piece of *music* is surely not adequately grasped either by the idea that we know the inferential significance of saying that it is such because it relates to other notes in a rule-governed manner (say, in terms of its harmonic relations), or, for that matter, by the idea that we know what the note belongs to is music because we grasp the conceptual content of the term 'music' – can *that* content really be arrived at by music's being sound, not being painting, and so forth? There seems therefore to be a dimension involved in such aesthetic claims which is not exhausted by Brandom's model of making things explicit.[45] This dimension is not, as it might appear, simply 'immediate', in the manner of what is involved in a case of simple stimulus and response. Musical judgement, of the kind involved both in production and reception, requires its own kind of knowledge, but this cannot be wholly conceptual, even in the sense Brandom develops. Stanley Cavell suggests the kind of immediacy involved here when he claims that '[i]t is essential in making an aesthetic judgement that at some point we be prepared to say in its support: don't you see, don't you hear, don't you dig. ... Because if you do not see something, *without* explanation, then there is nothing further to discuss'.[46] It is at this point that we can rejoin Adorno once again.

VI

In the essay 'On the Present Relationship between Philosophy and Music' of 1953, Adorno maintains, in a manner not so far from

Besseler, 'In music it is not a question of meaning but of gestures. To the extent to which it is language it is, like notation in its history, a language sedimented from gestures'.[47] His claim can be elucidated by Scruton's remark that 'the formal organisation of music can be understood only by the person who relates it, through a metaphorical perception, to the world of life and gesture'.[48] Gestures are inherently contextual and are often established by convention: This is evident in the use of music as a signifying practice for certain kinds of social function. At the same time, gestures can also be a form of communication giving rise to a unique directness and a 'rightness' which in some contexts words may not – one thinks again of the successes of music therapy.[49] However, Adorno then claims that the attempt to establish the 'meaning [Sinn] of music itself is...a deception' that results from music's similarity to language,[50] a similarity which he regards, for reasons to be considered in a moment, as increasing during the history of Western music.

Following questionable ideas adopted from the early Walter Benjamin – can we really assert there ever was a time when signifier and signified were not arbitrarily linked? – Adorno then asserts,

Qua language music moves towards the pure name, the absolute unity of thing and sign, which is lost in its immediacy to all human knowledge. In utopian and at the same time hopeless exertions to achieve the name lies the relationship of music and philosophy, to which for this reason music stands incomparably more close than every other art.[51]

This is problematic for a variety of reasons,[52] but the defensible part of the argument is apparent when Adorno insists on the historicality of this pursuit of a utopia. By doing so, he adverts to the ways in which music can become part of a particular society's ways of articulating its aspirations. When music becomes subordinated to exchange value rather than resisting subsumption into established conventions, it can, in this perspective, rightly be criticized for merely conforming to an already existing reality rather than trying to transcend it. Precisely because what music says 'offers much greater resistance to translation into other media than other art',[53] it is, he asserts, able to convey a meaning that has claims to its own truth. Other forms of articulation may lack such truth by being too closely bound to already established forms of understanding.

However, this idea can involve a further problem. In the Mahler book, Adorno maintains that 'for the person who understands the language of music what music means becomes obscured: mere meaning would just be an image of that subjectivity [i.e., of instrumental reason] whose claim to omnipotence is destroyed by music' (M, 39/25). At one level, this just repeats the questionable idea that predicative language – which involves 'mere meaning' – is inherently a form of repressive identification. This idea neglects the fact that music's being understood as significant at all is evidence of a complex history of subjectivity which is linked to the Romantic idea that what we can determinately say is not enough to articulate a sufficiently diverse understanding of our being. One obvious location of such a sense of verbal inadequacy lies, as Adorno himself suggests, in the experience of time. He uses the example of differing forms of temporality in Palestrina, a fugue of the Well-Tempered Clavier, the first movement of Beethoven's Seventh,[54] a prelude of Debussy's, and twenty bars of Webern to suggest how the need for musical rather than discursive articulation may be generated.[55] There clearly are ways in which the differences in the articulation of temporality in these examples can illuminate approaches to the meaning of time in ways that words cannot, from a theological sense of timeless order to the crucial example of the dynamic totality of a Beethoven sonata movement, which Adorno links to Hegel's philosophy, and thence to Max Weber's dynamic of rationalization in the modern world.

It is here, though, that the decisive questionable assumption in Adorno's linking of philosophy to music will be located. In the Beethoven book, Adorno asserts that '[i]n a similar sense to the one in which there is only Hegel's philosophy, there is only Beethoven in the history of Western music', and he insists this link should not be just an analogy but rather the 'thing itself [*die Sache selbst*]' (B, 31/11). Thinking of the kind Adorno relies upon here about the relationship between music and philosophy actually belongs to the tradition of early Romantic philosophy, which first tried to come to non-theological terms with 'the unsayable', and it is by no means inherently implausible. The problem lies in the consequences Adorno draws from this particular link. Friedrich Schlegel had already asked in 1800, writing about pure instrumental music that actually sounds as though it could have been Beethoven's, 'Is the theme in it not as developed, confirmed, varied and contrasted as the object of meditation in a sequence of philosophical ideas?'[56] Adorno's idea is that in Hegel and Beethoven both philosophy and music are 'self-grounding' because the organization of their elements does not follow from anything external to those elements; thus, 'the sonata is the [philosophical] system as music' (B, 231/160). What is arguably the first fully autonomous music and the most complete attempt at a self-grounding system of philosophy do, of course, emerge at the same time in much the same cultural location – and, incidentally, do not in fact communicate with each other.

In the same way as Hegel begins his *Logic* with the indeterminate particular concept of 'being', Adorno argues, Beethoven often uses thematic material which has no value in itself for his most successful sonata movements. The contingent particular beginning in both only transcends its nullity by being taken up into contexts which make it determinate as part of a whole. It does so, though, at the expense of its having to appear to contradict the other particulars in the process, so that 'only the whole proves its identity, as particulars they are as opposed as the individual to the society that is opposed to it' (B, 35/13). In this sense, the musical 'subjects', thematic material whose 'history' occurs in the music, are analogized to the moments of *Geist* in the *Phenomenology of Spirit*, whose implicit 'immediate' truth at the beginning is made explicit at the end of the process of mediation. At the same time, Beethoven's music is also supposed to have, qua music, a critical aspect that is lacking in Hegel's philosophy. This is because, unlike the positive conclusion of Hegel's system, which establishes the true essence of all the preceding negatively related elements, the music's synthesis does not judge 'that's how it is' (B, 287/202). However, this advantage on the part of music allows only a temporary respite from Adorno's rigour, and he even seems subsequently to revoke this concession. In Beethoven's employment of the sonata reprise – he is referring to the Ninth Symphony's first movement – which actually seems to say 'that's how it is', the music is 'in the same sense aesthetically questionable as the thesis of identity in Hegel' (B, 39/17).[57] The sonata reprise, in which the formally decisive end of the movement is a conventionally determined repetition of the material of the beginning, mirrors the fact in Hegel that the philosophical system can only claim to be complete by repressing the 'non-identical', the resistance of the real to definitive subsumption under concepts, thus by merely repeating at the end what was already there at the beginning.[58] However, Adorno often seems to think this repression is the same repression as that occasioned by the commodity structure and instrumental reason.

Now this part of what is in many ways a thoroughly illuminating conception of relationships between structures of intelligibility in modernity is basically objective spirit gone mad and is about as 'ontological' as you can get. Art, philosophy, the commodity system, science, all become part of the same process. This conception largely derives from Weber's rationalization thesis and bears many similarities to the later Heidegger's accounts of Western metaphysics' 'subjectification of being'. Once this position is adopted, it necessarily provides the framework for the rest of Adorno's assessment of the meaning of modern music, with the attendant problems we have already considered. More specifically, it makes necessary the idea that 'the idealist "system" in Beethoven is tonality in the specific function it gains in him'. In Beethoven, tonality is therefore 'abstract identity' (B, 40/17), and, after a more complex argument, it is 'identity as expression. The result: That's how it is' (B, 41/18). The result of tonality is, therefore, a kind of apophantic judgement, so that music has effectively become the language of a merely self-confirming reality. This is why Adorno both wishes to separate the truth of music from apophantic truth and has to insist on the need for new music constantly to criticize the 'affirmative' aspects of the music that precedes it.

These ideas actually become more enlightening when Adorno suggests that the 'key to the late Beethoven probably lies in the fact that the idea of the totality as something which is already achieved in this music became unbearable to his critical genius' (B, 36/14), because the totality relied too much on a preestablished convention. This suggestion could be used to bring not just the late Beethoven into interesting contact with the philosophy of Schlegel and Novalis, which, while sharing a similar sense to Beethoven's of a new dynamic in modern forms of articulation, refused to accept the kind of Idealist closure subsequently sought by Hegel. Novalis' assertion in 1796 that the 'Absolute which is given to us can only be known negatively, by our acting and finding that no action can reach what we are seeking' seems apt,[59] even to music, for example, the first movements of the *Eroica* and the Ninth Symphony, which may appear triumphantly to proclaim the Absolute by their reconciliation of beginning and end but are, in one sense, 'only music' and therefore cannot positively know the Absolute.

At the same time as rejecting as ideological the positive idea of totality that he sees in Hegel and Beethoven, Adorno relies on the idea of a negative totality that depends on a sort of inverted history of *Geist* as the increasingly disastrous domination of merely subjective, instrumental reason. Only when music opposes this domination by refusing any kind of reconciliation can it be 'true' as an adequate critical response to history. Rather than realizing – as he sometimes does elsewhere – that there is more than one way to oppose ideological symbolic forms of reconciliation, Adorno tends to equate all kinds of such reconciliation, thus leaving no space to see how these may function differently in different contexts. To the extent to which this conception from *Philosophy of Modern Music* just repeats the ideas of *Dialectic of Enlightenment*, it is best abandoned. Is there, though, another way in which this conception might yet yield some usable results? The fact is that Adorno's position, with all its flaws, does still point to something which is a serious issue in modern music. Why can musicians in modernity rightly be criticized for trying to 'turn the clock back' by merely repeating conventions from the past and failing to engage with contemporary society by new use of musical material? The answer, I believe, lies precisely in the question of music's relationship to language, which is where the issue of the political meaning of music must be confronted.

The 'linguistic character' of music has two sides for Adorno, which in certain respects relate to the dialectic between the literal and the metaphorical. On the one hand, the natural material, like the material of the linguistic signifier, is, as was suggested by the Hegel-Beethoven link, increasingly incorporated into 'a more or less fixed system' – 'convention' – which is both independent of the individual subject and yet at its disposal as a means of trying to express itself. On the other hand, 'the inheritance of the pre-rational, magical, mimetic' survives in music insofar as it is related to language as 'expression'. The mimetic aspect is, though, increasingly 'subjectively mediated and reflected' as an 'imitation of what happens in the inside of people'.[60] This mediation extends the range of convention in modern Western music into the articulation of the most individual aspects of the subject, thereby extending the range of music as language (as 'meaning' in the sense Adorno criticizes) and eventually leading to a crisis of expression based on the feeling that it has all been expressed already. Although it involves a serious problem, this seems to me the dialectic which might form the defensible core of Adorno's conception of musical meaning.

The following passage makes great sense, for example, of why a crisis developed in the European tradition of modern music as a result of a shift away from the productive relationship between convention and expression that was epitomized by Beethoven's use of tonality:

The process of the linguistification of music also entails its transformation into convention and expression. To the extent that the dialectic of the process of enlightenment essentially consists in the incompatibility of these two moments, the whole of Western music is confronted with its contradiction by this dual character. The more it, as language, takes into its power and intensifies expression, as the imitation of something gestural and prerational, the more it at the same time also, as its rational overcoming, works at the dissolution of expression.[61]

Without convention, there can be no way in which music qua expression can be a means of creating symbolic social cohesion. Expression without convention becomes merely radically individual in a way which ceases to have any social significance beyond the manifestation of a refusal to accept anything dictated by convention. As soon as expression ceases to be this, however, it begins to become convention, as it *must* if it is to be significant at all. Expressivity, like uniqueness, is inconceivable without its counterpart, but that counterpart can negate what it helps identify. This dialectic must be interpreted via specific historically located music, otherwise we end up back with Adorno's questionable totalizations and fail to see how the moving relationships between these two notional poles have differing significances at different times in different places. Free jazz can, for example, move from being a vital questioning of the limitations felt at a certain stage of musical development in relation to harmonic and other conventions to being an empty repetition of a conventional refusal to employ tonality and song structure.

The problem in Adorno's version of this idea lies in his tendency simply to identify apophantic language with convention and then to attach the identification to a Hegelian-Weberian story about rationalization as the repression of the 'non-identical'. This identification leads to a tension in his idea of art's link to truth which highlights a series of difficulties inherent in the approach with which we began. These difficulties are not particular to Adorno, and they can only be briefly illustrated, but not analyzed, by a final example. If one interprets the conclusion of Bruckner's Eighth Symphony in terms of its historical constellation, as the apotheosis of 'tonality', it can be understood as a last attempt to restore unity to musical material whose growing divergence and disintegration will soon lead to 'new music'. The resources Bruckner has to employ to achieve this unity are riddled with contradictions, so that past and future jar, even as their confrontation gives rise to something unique. In this way, the dangers of a theologically inspired ideological overcoming of real contradictions in the second half of the nineteenth century can be heard in the power of music which often simply forces together material of divergent kinds. Bruckner's overwhelming coda does not occur at a point of logical musical culmination, and the final major key descending phrase combines affirmative culmination with a desperate sense of relief. This would, for example, be one way of understanding why Furtwängler conducted it so fast.

In terms of musical production, the piece arguably does have a historically specific ideological sense and thus contributes to the problematic nature of subsequent tonal apotheoses. These can become forms of self-deception on the part of a society heading, not for triumph, but actually for disaster – in this respect Adorno's favouring of Mahler's Sixth and Ninth Symphonies, with their non-triumphant conclusions, makes real sense. However, in terms of its reception, which Adorno too often wholly subordinates to the idea of the immanent logic of the work, the meaning of a work like Bruckner's Eighth is dependent on complex interactions between listeners, performers, institutions, and history which, as long as the work is 'alive', demand a more open-ended approach to musical meaning. This approach would allow more space for individual engagement with the work as, for example, an expression of a temporalized, secular transcendence that little else in the modern world can provide and at present may only be accessible via 'judgementless synthesis'. Such an approach, which is sometimes evident in aspects of Adorno's Mahler book and in other writings on specific composers, would, though, require a more consistent engagement with ideas from a hermeneutic tradition which Adorno – for the understandable reason that he found Heidegger morally and politically beyond the pale – was in some ways unable to understand.

NOTES

1. Theodor W. Adorno, *Gesammelte Schriften*, vol. 19, *Musikalische Schriften VI* (Frankfurt: Suhrkamp, 1984), 628.
2. Adorno, *Musikalische Schriften VI*, 628.
3. Adorno, *Musikalische Schriften VI*, 615.
4. Peter Kivy, *The Fine Art of Repetition* (Cambridge: Cambridge University Press, 1993), 19.
5. The same review has been reprinted since, only, as far as I know, by papers on the Left, such as the *Tageszeitung*.
6. Adorno, *Musikalische Schriften VI*, 331.
7. Adorno, *Musikalische Schriften VI*, 638.
8. Adorno, *Musikalische Schriften VI*, 614.
9. Theodor W. Adorno, *Philosophie der neuen Musik* (Frankfurt, Berlin, and Vienna: Ullstein, 1958), 35. Translated by Anne G. Mitchell and Wesley V. Blomster under the title *The Philosophy of Modern Music* (New York: Seabury, 1973), 32. Hereafter PM. Page numbers of the German edition are followed by page numbers of English translation.
10. Carl Dahlhaus, ed., *Einführung in die systematische Musikwissenschaft* (Laaber, Germany: Laaber, 1988), 98.
11. Theodor W. Adorno, *Beethoven: Philosophie der Musik* (Frankfurt: Suhrkamp, 1993), 25. Translated by Edmund Jephcott under the title *Beethoven; The Philosophy of Music* (Cambridge: Polity Press, 1998), 6. Hereafter cited as B. Page numbers of German edition are followed by page numbers of English translation.
12. The point with regard to literary and other non-musical forms is that, without the friction of the aspects of reality which they ultimately wish to oppose, the works would merely contribute to existing deceptions. The novels of Flaubert can suggest what is meant: They are to a large extent constructed of the debased everyday language of Flaubert's time, which they try to transform by the constellations in which it is placed.
13. I shall not attempt to deal here with the undoubted proximity of this idea to the later Heidegger's view of modern technology (on this, see Andrew Bowie, *From Romanticism to Critical Theory: The Philosophy of German Literary Theory* [London and New York: Routledge, 1997]).
14. Hegel makes art a manifestation of 'absolute spirit', because it is not tied to the material world in the way that the sphere of law, property, etc., is.

In this passage, Adorno therefore suggests that what for Hegel belongs to absolute spirit cannot be separated from objective spirit. Habermas, incidentally, argues much the same about Hegel's claim to have access to absolute spirit.

15. The idea of this constellation is, as we shall see, the main source of the connection of Beethoven to the philosophy of German idealism.

16. Nicholas Cook, *Music, Imagination, and Culture* (Oxford: Oxford University Press, 1990), 177–8.

17. 'Apophantic' truth is truth which is expressed in propositions.

18. Theodor W. Adorno, *Ästhetische Theorie* (Frankfurt: Suhrkamp, 1973), 187. Translated by Robert Hullot-Kentor under the title *Aesthetic Theory* (London: Athlone, 1997), 123. Hereafter cited as AT. Pages numbers of German edition are followed by page numbers of English translation.

19. Analogously, we escape the generality inherent in a finite vocabulary by recombining words in new ways in poetry. Such recombination often relies on the 'musical', non-semantic possibilities of language, such as rhythmic repetition or repetition of sounds. I shall return to this idea in relation to metaphor below.

20. Ludwig Wittgenstein, *Philosophische Untersuchungen* (Frankfurt: Suhrkamp, 1971), 227.

21. Martin Heidegger, *Logik: Die Frage nach der Wahrheit* (Frankfurt: Klostermann, 1976), 135. Clearly this conception of truth is not merely semantic, and it involves considerable problems, which Heidegger never really solved: see Bowie, *From Romanticism to Critical Theory*. The essential point here is the claim that meanings are not simply understandable in propositional terms. Exactly how this claim is linked to questions of truth is beyond the scope of this essay.

22. Heinrich Besseler, *Aufsätze zur Musikästhetik und Musikgeschichte* (Leipzig: Reclam, 1978), 45.

23. Roger Scruton, *The Aesthetics of Music* (Oxford: Oxford University Press, 1997), 467.

24. Charles Taylor, *Human Agency and Language* (Cambridge: Cambridge University Press, 1985), chap. 9, 10.

25. Given the worries about the notion of 'expression', I think it is perhaps better to employ the term 'disclosive', for reasons that will become apparent in the rest of the argument.

26. Downing A. Thomas traces the important earlier stages of this shift in the period of the French Enlightenment in *Music and the Origins of Language* (Cambridge: Cambridge University Press, 1995). See also Andrew Bowie, *Aesthetics and Subjectivity: From Kant to Nietzsche* (Manchester: Manchester University Press, 1993; completely rewritten

edition 2002), and my entry on 'Music Aesthetics 1750–2000' in the *New Grove Dictionary of Music and Musicians*.

27. Besseler, *Aufsätze zur Musikästhetik*, 67.
28. Martin Heidegger, *Kant und das Problem der Metaphysik* (Frankfurt: Klostermann, 1973), 93.
29. Immanuel Kant, *Werkausgabe*, vol. 10, *Kritik der Urteilskraft*, ed. Wilhelm Weischedel (Frankfurt: Suhrkamp, 1968), A 190, B 193.
30. See John Neubauer, *The Emancipation of Music from Language. Departure from Mimesis in Eighteenth-Century Aesthetics* (New Haven and London: Yale University Press, 1986); Bowie, *Aesthetics and Subjectivity*.
31. Immanuel Kant, *Werkausgabe*, vols. 3 and 4, *Kritik der reinen Vernunft*, ed. Wilhelm Weischedel (Frankfurt: Suhrkamp, 1968), A 145, B 184.
32. Heidegger, *Logik*, 406.
33. Heidegger, *Logik*, 406.
34. Heidegger, *Logik*, 146.
35. Scruton, *Aesthetics of Music*, 132.
36. Wolfram Hogrebe, *Ahnung und Erkenntnis* (Frankfurt: Suhrkamp, 1996), 10.
37. Whether one can really talk of a 'symbolic order' in any strict sense seems doubtful to me. See Bowie, *From Romanticism to Critical Theory*, chap. 5.
38. On this, see Anke Thyen, *Negative Dialektik und Erfahrung. Zur Rationalität des Nichtidentischen bei Adorno* (Frankfurt: Suhrkamp, 1989); Bowie, *From Romanticism to Critical Theory*, chap. 9.
39. Donald Davidson, *Inquiries into Truth and Interpretation* (Oxford: Oxford University Press, 1984), 263.
40. Davidson, for example, insists that the only *meaning* a metaphor has is its literal meaning. Samuel Wheeler has argued, though, that Davidson merely means by this that most of what matters about language need not be thought of in terms of biconditional statements which define literal meaning, such as '"Snow is white" is true if and only if snow is white'. Instead metaphors, like music, matter because of the world-disclosing capacity that they share with music. Seen in this way metaphors are not parasitic on literal meaning: One does not first have to have grasped an expression's literal sense for it to make you notice something. See Samuel C. Wheeler III, *Deconstruction as Analytic Philosophy* (Stanford: Stanford University Press, 2000).
41. Andrew Bowie, 'The Meaning of the Hermeneutic Tradition in Contemporary Philosophy', in *'Verstehen' and Humane Understanding*, Publications of the Royal Institute of Philosophy, ed. Anthony O'Hear (Cambridge: Cambridge University Press, 1997).

42. Michael Krausz, ed., *The Interpretation of Music* (Oxford: Oxford University Press, 1993), 209.

43. These contentions do not mean that we do not rely on contextual heuristic distinctions between ways in which articulations are intended; they just mean that we do not possess metaphysical certainty about what is literal and what is metaphorical of the kind promised, but hardly delivered, by some versions of formal semantics.

44. See Robert Brandom, *Articulating Reasons* (Cambridge, Mass.: Harvard University Press, 2000).

45. The reasons for this are similar to the reasons Hegel's account of music is inadequate: Brandom sees his project as a version of Hegel's rationalism. See Bowie, *Aesthetics and Subjectivity* (2002 edition).

46. Stanley Cavell, *Must We Mean What We Say?* (Cambridge: Cambridge University Press, 1976), 93.

47. Theodor W. Adorno, *Gesammelte Schriften*, vol. 18, *Musikalische Schriften V* (Frankfurt: Suhrkamp, 1984), 154.

48. Scruton, *Aesthetics of Music*, 341–2.

49. Adorno suggests in the Mahler book that the externality of music, as an objectification of subjectivity, may be an aid in the defense against paranoia generated by pathological narcissism. 'It is rather that an orchestra plays within musical consciousness than that a consciousness is projected onto the orchestra'. (Theodor W. Adorno, *Mahler: Eine musikalische Physiognomik* (Frankfurt: Suhrkamp, 1976), 39. Translated by Edmund Jephcott under the title *Mahler: A Musical Physiognomy*, (Chicago: University of Chicago Press, 1992), 25. Hereafter cited as M.

50. Adorno, *Musikalische Schriften V*, 154.

51. Adorno, *Musikalische Schriften V*, 154.

52. For a critique of the idea of the 'name' in Benjamin, see Bowie, *From Romanticism to Critical Theory*, chap. 8.

53. Adorno, *Musikalische Schriften V*, 157.

54. Given that Beethoven 'is' music, Adorno does not feel the need to specify which 'Seventh'.

55. Adorno, *Musikalische Schriften V*, 158.

56. Friedrich Schlegel, *Kritische Schriften und Fragmente*, vol. 2 (Paderborn, Germany: Ferdinand Schöningh, 1988), 155.

57. The reprise in the Ninth does not sound at all the same as the material from the exposition which is being repeated: It is massively intensified and sonically wholly different. Adorno, though, regards its intensity as a further aspect of its affirmative character.

58. This was already Schelling's objection to Hegel. See Andrew Bowie, *Schelling and Modern European Philosophy: An Introduction* (London:

Routledge, 1993), chap. 6; F. W. J. Schelling, *On the History of Modern Philosophy*, translation and introduction by Andrew Bowie (Cambridge: Cambridge University Press, 1994).

59. Novalis, *Das philosophisch-theoretische Werk*, vol. 2, ed. Hans-Joachim Mähl (Munich and Vienna: Hanser, 1978), 181.
60. Adorno, *Musikalische Schriften V*, 161.
61. Adorno, *Musikalische Schriften V*, 161.

STEFAN MÜLLER-DOOHM

11 The Critical Theory of Society as Reflexive Sociology

In the course of developing his critical theory of society – a project whose philosophical foundations were first explicitly outlined by Max Horkheimer in a programmatic 1937 essay in the *Zeitschrift für Sozialforschung*[1] – Theodor W. Adorno came to formulate his unique concept of sociology. The formulation is the result of a process of learning and reflection whose point of departure is the attempt to make sense of the mutually conditioning relations between music and society. The importance of music theory in Adorno's sociology is also to be explained from the biographical fact that, though Adorno studied philosophy in Frankfurt am Main at the beginning of the 1920s, his heart had been bent on music from childhood.[2] (Adorno studied composition with Alban Berg in Vienna in 1925.)[3] Adorno's abilities as a composer influenced not only his numerous published opera and concert reviews but also his music-aesthetic analyses of individual works. These two areas of interest have in common that both were engaged in discerning the transformation of musical material amid changes in society. The essay "On the Social Situation of Music," which appeared in the first issue of the journal published by the Frankfurt Institute for Social Research, offers a rich preliminary account of his sociological findings in the area of music.[4]

The essay is particularly significant because the analysis of music – in which three aspects of music, its production, reproduction, and reception, are treated – is the first indication of what Adorno intended as the objective of his mature sociological reflection: namely, to uncover social content in the textures of aesthetic manifestation. Adorno's sociological analysis of music[5] takes two things as its point of departure: first, concrete musical material in its aesthetic appearance as well as its compositional forms and techniques, and second,

279

the view that the practice of music in contemporary society arises socially. The young Adorno subscribes to the premise that even the most sublime expression of spirit carries the stamp of existing society and is characterized by its historical development. This insight already contains the category of *social mediation* – to be made explicit only later – which occupies a central position in Adorno's sociological analyses. His early texts permit an understanding of mediation as the specific mutual conditioning between universal and particular, whole and particular appearance, society and individual.[6]

The essay's first sentence already formulates how an analysis which grasps musical phenomena as social phenomena is to be conducted: Despite the claim to autonomy made by musical works and despite the conscious distancing of compositions from the aesthetic conventions of their time, all music of the present draws out "the contradictions and flaws which cut through present-day society" (SSM, 391). Adorno begins the essay by declaring what he takes to be the origin of society's inner antagonism: All products of human action are subjugated to the anonymous rule-mechanisms of exchangeability by the universality of the capitalistic production of goods. Thus a conflict arises between the structurally determined special dynamic of the unshackled movement of capital and the requirements of the individual to realize him- or herself in creative work. If this claim of a structural antagonism is correct, then it must be demonstrable in particular instances how the dynamic of capitalist economy affects social connections all the way down to the sphere of art. What must be uncovered, and with regard to the object, is how the mediation between the economic base and the manifestations of the psychocultural superstructure proceeds. It is this which is the core element of Adorno's wide-ranging sociology. As a social physiognomics of appearance,[7] his sociology wants "to perceive something in the features of the givenness of totality."[8]

I. THE RIDDLE IS THE ANSWER

What radical art shares with sociological theories of society is that both dispense with the idea that a complete foundation for knowledge can be supplied by the totality of what exists. Thus, a theory cannot simply consist in descriptively capturing and classifying categories of given social relations. Just as music breaks with its tradition through atonality, theory becomes critical by negating the injustice, inhumanity, personal selfishness, and alienation which social conditions produce under a capitalist economy. Through critical thinking, social theory has the task of helping to overcome internally contradictory social conditions, just those conditions that could be other than they are. Both composition[9] and theory making rely on an "objective principle of order which is never imposed upon the material from the exterior, but rather extracted from the material itself and brought into relationship with it by means of a historical process of rational transparence" (SSM, 399). Like the autonomous music of the avant-garde, social theory is a relentless critique which distinguishes itself from all previous forms of critique through radical negation. Radical negativity reveals itself as freedom in that it uncovers, through "extreme variation and through-construction," that which is potentially present in material but has not been able to develop under habitual pressures and constraints (SSM, 401).

Adorno's theory of society comes into existence through constructions of unconventional combinations of elements of that same material, and hopes to bring out the subjects embedded in history within social, working, and life nexuses. It depicts something new and gets this newness from nothing less than the concrete givenness of material being. With the help of this theory, it is possible to construct a model depicting how the world could be different – different than it is. These possibilities of otherness are not otherworldly utopian projects. As models of thought, they result rather from the conditions that are historically given in them or at least can be shown to have potentially been given. The given is, according to Adorno, not to be compared to what factually exists in the here and now.

By making evident which devastating consequences social contradictions will bring about, the theory of society might evoke processes of realization, – if necessary, evoke them through conscious exaggeration, just as the autonomous music of the avant-garde might once have accomplished a like realization through the shock of dissonance. The process of theory construction begins by disassembling what is factually visible in order to find out what lies behind the form of appearance.[10] First, theory makes it possible to understand the structural conditions and functionality of society in its existing form. Second, the way in which theory works on the materiality [*Stofflichkeit*] of its object realm makes evident society's particular way of being contingent and shows that it can be modified by dialectical movements in the material. *Only if it proceeds according to the principle of composition and constructs its objects in thought acts* can social theory move beyond the level of a descriptive and orderly reiteration of facticity. The theory of society is thus constructive in two ways for the composer Adorno: It permits insight into the nexus of conditions in social reality through its analytical method, and, by showing society to be historically constructed, it generates consciousness that the nature of social conditions is, in principle, changeable. The social standpoint of conditions consists not merely in the fact that social forms of life have a past *but in the fact that they are open toward the future.*

In an early text, based on his inaugural address as lecturer in philosophy at the University of Frankfurt, Adorno makes clear that this type of social theory, just like the advanced practice of composition of the Second Vienna School, builds on rationally produced constructions. His initial thesis is that one must give up the illusion that one can grasp in thought the whole of a meaningfully imagined reality. This is why all attempts to grasp the empirical through ever more precisely differentiated philosophical systems are condemned to failure. Because reality as such is without intentions and remains principally puzzling, philosophy poses itself the task of solving riddles through thought. According to Adorno, as long as it will allow itself to be challenged by "riddle-figures of that which exists,"[11] philosophy will remain relevant even in a world that has been disenchanted by the rationalism of individual academic disciplines. Attempting to solve such riddles through interpretation does not, however, mean pursuing the traces of some occult truth which might explain everything because it would prove to be the ontological foundation of all things. Rather, it is the "function of the riddle-solving ... to light up the riddle-*Gestalt* like lightning" (AP, 127). Such a momentary coming to consciousness succeeds when the questions posed by the puzzle are encircled by answer variations that attempt to sketch solutions. In this passage, central to the foundation of his mode of knowledge, Adorno says that attempts at philosophical interpretations should be brought into "changing constellations." And these "changing trial combinations" must be conducted experimentally "until they fall into a figure which can be read as an answer, while at the same time the question disappears" (AP, 127). The task of the philosopher is clearly defined here: to interpret reality through "construction." This "construction of figures" itself is made up of the *isolated elements of reality*. For Adorno, the process of understanding becomes compatible with the materialist method because of this relation to being: "interpretation of the unintentional through juxtaposition of the analytically isolated elements and illumination of the real by the power of such interpretation" (AP, 127).

In order to find the solution to the riddle, that is, to bring the contradictions within society to consciousness, philosophy, in its interpretation of the questions which the historical process sketches, must orient itself according to the elements of the riddle and ask about the constitution of the social. Society, like the riddle, contains its own answer. Because the philosopher allows him- or herself to be challenged to come up with a constructive suggestion for a solution, the riddle takes on different forms without ever becoming substanceless. These new forms become an impetus for renewed attempts to interpret the riddle. For Adorno, knowledge here means that models of interpretation set themselves alight at the extreme of what appears other. At this point, he introduces the concept of the dialectic for the first time. The truth content, which can only ever be of a preliminary nature, shows itself to thought. In summary, one could say that even in this early text Adorno already sought to make clear to himself how knowing can be formulated as a dialectical process. The process is one of rational construction made up of a series of varying models of thought. These models of thought pour the historical material of the social – the "lifting off from the world of appearance," as he calls it with reference to Freud – into new forms.

In the inaugural address, Adorno differentiates this philosophical understanding from a *separate logic of research*. Research is the business of the methodologically distinct disciplines, among which Adorno includes sociology. The mutually conditioning relation between philosophical *interpretation* and sociological *research* must be guaranteed by "dialectical communication." Adorno means that the grand plan of a philosophical diagnosis of the contemporary world must aim at "constructing keys, before which reality springs open" (AP, 130). In order to realize this far-reaching epistemological goal of theory construction, the help of "exact fantasy" is needed, which is, however, only safe from pure speculation if it "abides strictly within the material which *the sciences* present to it" (AP, 131; emphasis added). This, according to Adorno, is the function of sociology as well as of the other social sciences: With the help of its research methods, elements of empirical material are made accessible, and these same elements become the igniting fuel for the exact fantasy from which models of thought gain their power to exceed those very elements.

Sociology, however, should not limit itself to confronting those interpretations – inspired by exact fantasy – with the mirror of what really is the case. The science of society must do more than merely survey data and collect facts. Rather, as the most modern discipline of the social sciences, sociology must accomplish the trick of climbing up walls from the outside.[12] This image of the façade climber permits Adorno to claim that sociology must do two things. First, it must enter the rotting edifice of the human sciences, which is in danger of collapsing, and assure itself that the insights of conceptual thinking are valid and can revitalize themselves by relating to contemporary life. Second, Adorno hopes that from the other side of the illusory façade of human coexistence, sociology's disillusioned gaze will be able to bring to daylight something about the nexus of conditions of social practice. But this requires theoretical work. This work is the antidote to the danger that sociology distills its concepts out of the available reality and amounts to an "inconsistent connection of simple this-here determinations which scoffs at every cognitive ordering and in no way provides a critical criterion" (AP, 130–1).

2. SOCIOLOGICAL THOUGHT IN MODELS

At the very start of his academic career, Adorno neither admitted the possibility of a *prima philosophia* nor relinquished his interest in music. Rather, he sought to connect both philosophy and music to sociology. But what is this sociology's relation to philosophy? By connecting to philosophy's heritage, sociology actualizes the philosophical mode of understanding, which proceeds by constitutively appropriating reality. Moreover, the excerpts of reality which sociology makes accessible through the methods of social research are an effective corrective to the speculative spirit of those received philosophies that attempt to sustain claims of absoluteness. Sociology, however, is only adequate to this double demand – reflection of the concept of society and confrontation with facticity – if it is able to take up a self-critical position vis-à-vis its own categorical and methodological instruments, that is, if it remains conscious of its own limits as a particular discipline. On an abstract and general level, these are the tasks that Adorno assigns to sociology. During the last three decades of his career, in which he collected experiences in the realm of theory construction and social research, his concept of sociology took on the defined contours of a specific reflective science.[13]

In the decade spent as an émigré, mainly in New York and Los Angeles, Adorno became familiar with the praxis of social research. In this field, his contributions to media research (The Radio Research Project, The Film-Music Project)[14] as well as the large-scale empirical study of the authoritarian personality are of central importance.[15] A psychoanalytically inspired hypothesis forms the point of departure for the latter investigation (now a sociological classic) into social prejudice, anti-Semitism, and fascistic thought patterns. The study investigates the mutual relation between manifest and latent dimensions of personality. According to the study, it is not only the attitudes and behaviors of the relative minority of self-declared fascists which are dangerous for democratic ways of life but also the syndrome of a potential fascism as the hidden element of authority-bound structures of personality in a multitude of individuals. Research based on this supposition requires complicated connections between research techniques. According to Adorno's methodological claim, the techniques must be capable of seeing past the superficial opinions reflected in quantitative research methods. These techniques, which function independently of each other, include standardized instruments, such as an extensive questionnaire with three scales for the indirect measurement of anti-Semitism, ethnocentrism, and conservatism, as well as projective processes and qualitative interviews. The three scales, which contain chiefly projective-question formulations, are the basis for the "fascism scale" developed in the course of the research; the scale is composed of specific items that can count as valid and reliable indicators of extensive and latent character disposition. With the help of the forty-five–increment meter of the F-scale, it was possible to measure the fundamental character variables that represent the dominant traits of authority-bound personalities. Adorno describes the potentially fascistic character disposition as a structural unity: "Traits like conventionality, willingness to bow to authority and aggressivity, tendencies to project, manipulate and such were usually found to be determining."[16] *The Authoritarian Personality* is an excellent example of the type of empirically interpretative social research which Adorno preferred because of the validity of its findings and which he practiced in the course of the research program of the Institute for Social Research as well as during his time as director of the Institute in Frankfurt. When Adorno decided to reemigrate to Germany with Max Horkheimer in order to rebuild the Institute, which had been destroyed[17] during the war, he made use of the practical experience that he had gained as a social researcher in the United States. It was precisely the international success of the studies on the authoritarian character that encouraged him to contribute to the empirical type of qualitatively oriented sociology – "to interpret phenomena, not ascertain fact, organize and classify facts"[18] (a maxim of interpretative sociology that can be taken as the guiding idea for Adorno's analysis of society).

For Adorno, sociology is an object-specific way of reflection, a work of interpretation, which dives down into particular objects in order to decipher them as expressions of generality. This process of interpretation becomes a critique of society when the analyzed reality of the social is confronted with what could be: when it is shown that society, because of its condition of domination, remains far behind its possibility of being free. The difference between the real and the possible makes necessary both a critique of historically superfluous unfreedom and a critique of social relations in which domination of humans over other humans perpetuates itself. Adorno's sociological reflections locate themselves at the point of tension between being, what ought to be, and being capable. On the basis of an analysis of all circumstances, Adorno investigates the question of whether that which is corresponds to that which human beings set as a goal for themselves. Are things the way they ought to be? This ought is not an arbitrary normative positing but the historical inheritance of an ideal human coexistence that one generation passes down to the next symbolically. The critique of society results from the "field of tension between the possible and the real" (PD, 69, translation altered), that is, from the sociotheoretical evidence that facticity has not lived up to the level of its possibility. Critique does not simply condemn what, in the name of reason, it can show to be unreasonable.

In the uncovering of contradictions, it rather develops a picture of that which should take the place of what has been recognized as untrue. For "the false, once determinately known and precisely expressed, is already the index of the right and the better."[19] The fact that sociological criticism of the condition of the world is capable of changing the world for the better "is founded in the objectivity of the mind itself,"[20] which, by means of negation, is capable of clearly revealing what is false as false. The critique of society as determinate negation must go beyond a pure description of what is given. It requires an immanent analysis, which discovers the object from the inside. Immersing oneself like this in the object requires openness to experience. These unregulated experiences mean, however, that for Adorno any support from the canon of socioempirical methods and concepts is secondary.[21] He demands that sociological reflection consist of "binding statements without a system."[22] Constructing "models of thought" which seek to grasp the specificity of the object is a response to this demand.

Such small format models of sociological thinking can be found in a book that is rarely considered to be part of the canon of sociological literature. I refer to the *dialogue intérieur* of *Minima Moralia*, a collection of over a hundred and fifty aphorisms subtitled *Reflections from Damaged Life*.[23] These reflections have in common that they originate from a thinking back to a significant event or historically important experience. These differing experiences of reality are subjected to a thought process that carefully examines phenomena from the front and back, their surface and depth, in order to determine their position in history and society.[24] The aphorisms are didactic pieces through which one can learn what Adorno means by sociological reflection. They concretely demonstrate how he observed human relations and social conflicts from an inner perspective in order to relate the failure of the individual, enlarged as if under a magnifying glass, to the contradictions that damage life in a reified world. By taking trivial intersubjective relations seriously and examining them analytically, Adorno calls forth that *Aha-Erlebnis* which many readers experience in reading these miniatures. Adorno writes, for example, in one of the many passages replete with experience, "Instead of solving the question of women's oppression, male society has so extended its own principles that the victims are no longer able even to pose the question" (MM, 92).

Through the artistry of formulation, Adorno demonstrates how critical understanding should be realized in the form of counterpunctual thinking or in thoughts that threaten to impale the thinker. It is a mark of these aphorisms that they allow a paradoxical field of tension to develop: "Only by the recognition of distance in our neighbor is strangeness alleviated: accepted into consciousness" (MM, 182). Or: "There is tenderness only in the coarsest demand: that no one shall go hungry any more" (MM, 156). Understanding results from the contradictory form of argumentation. The extreme sides of each contradiction show themselves to be guilty of one-sidedness. Because Adorno illuminates both sides of not just one but all tokens in play, a provocative excess of meaning develops, forcing the reader toward thought. He questions that which has just arisen in him. Thus, Adorno writes, "True thoughts are those alone which do not understand themselves" (MM, 192).

3. SOCIOLOGY AGAINST THE PROHIBITION OF REDUPLICATION

Adorno's mature concept of sociology as a reflective science appears most clearly in his contributions to the so-called positivist dispute in German sociology. The debate, which originated in the early 1960s, concerned the specific logic of the social sciences. It began with a lecture by Karl Popper,[25] then teaching at the London School of Economics, presented at the conference of the German Society of Sociology in Tübingen. Popper outlined a scientific program of critical rationalism in twenty-seven theses. Adorno, in debate with Popper, was charged with explaining in epistemological terms his own dialectical theory of society. In his lecture, Adorno contended that sociology, in contrast to the natural sciences, does not have unqualified data but can include only data which have arisen from the social nexus of life. Those situations available to sociology are thus social down even to their linguistic relations.

Adorno also took this opportunity to clarify the central concept of society, which, according to him, is an objective edifice. Society manifests itself as the totality of a nexus of mediation. And though the totality of society expresses itself in particular phenomena, society remains greater than the sum of its particulars: "System and individual entity are reciprocal and can only be apprehended in their reciprocity" (PD, 107). Since society is internally contradictory, sociological understanding must represent this contradiction and thus cannot be without contradictions itself, that is, it cannot be without contradiction in a formal logical sense. Adorno also introduced a new concept of critique in his debate with Popper. Critique becomes the object-specific negation of a particular fact, which must be overcome and changed: "The critical path is not merely formal but also material.... Critical sociology is, according to its own idea, necessarily also a critique of society" (PD, 114).[26] According to Adorno, this far-reaching claim regarding the critique of society cannot be reconciled with a value-free science. Though critique does not itself depend on a point of view, it is based on the insight that social relations must be altered because they produce suffering, injustice, and coercion. Adorno's concept of critique aims at juxtaposing the question of value-free science with the edifices of society, its relations and institutions. For him, critique is the confrontation between concept and thing and pursues the question "whether the objects of knowledge are what they claim to be according to their own concept" (PD, 23). Positivistic reason, by contrast, limits itself to means-ends rationality, in which the one-sidedness of instrumental reason comes to the fore. Adorno criticizes positivism for ignoring the failure of subjective reason and thus hypostatizing the knowledge form of the subject and its forms of thought. This limitation corresponds to the questionable dependence on available methods and deductive, formal logic. Both lead to a "loss of the spontaneity of knowledge" (PD, 21). Moreover, according to Adorno, critical rationalism's understanding of critique is too narrow, since it limits itself to non-contradictory statements. Pure non-contradiction, however, becomes tautologous: "the empty compulsion to repeat" (PD, 58). For him, thinking as a non-contradictory imitation is a symptom of the totally integrated society.

In his contribution to the positivist dispute, Adorno opposes the primacy of those scientists operating with a posited standard of objectivity and with the "illusion of a somehow natural-transcendental dignity of the individual subject" (PD, 14–5). He contrasts this with the "primacy of the subject": It states that all operations of the subject in the realm of thought and action are determined through an ordering of temporal and spatial objectivity. He summarizes the central points of his criticism in a few sentences:

The core of the critique of positivism is that it shuts itself off from both the experience of the blindly dominating totality and the driving desire that it should ultimately become something else. It contents itself with the senseless ruins which remain after the liquidation of idealism, without interpreting, for their part, both liquidation and what is liquidated, and rendering them true. Instead, positivism is concerned with the disparate, with the subjectively interpreted datum and the associated pure thought forms of the human subject. (PD, 14)

The central object of Adorno's critical theory is the mutually conditioning relation between the multitude of contradictions in society as a totality and the concrete modes of life of its subjects. "Despite all the experience of reification, and in the very expression of this experience, critical theory is oriented toward the idea of society as a subject" (PD, 14). The individual, whose value and character in contemporary society Adorno tries to determine, occupies the central position of this sociological enlightenment. In this sense, his critique of society has a normative aspect: the harmony of the autonomous subject with the necessary conditions of social and systemic integration.

Sociology is the reflection of society on itself. It extends itself over the differentiated objects of a science, which has itself been made separate by the division of labor. Sociology is thus "a piece of intellectual compensation for the division of labor, and should not, in turn, be unconditionally fixed in accordance with the division of labor" (PD, 55). Sociology is thus more than an academic discipline in the usual sense. Adorno describes it via its mode of reflection. Sociology, as becomes clear from his contribution to the positivist dispute, is a heterogeneous edifice and consists of both the method of empirical social research and the construction of categories of critical social analysis. So too does it have a double focus: Its object of interest is subjective and objective, it comprises at once both the intentionality of social actions and the social order as a system.

4. FROM SELF-REFLECTIVE INTEREST TO DISCOURSE: THE LINGUISTIC TURN OF CRITICAL THEORY

No real controversy between differing paradigms emerged from the first round of the positivist dispute. The contributors to the debate limited themselves to taking up positions and describing them. A

sharper debate began only once representatives of the younger generation, especially Hans Albert[27] and Jürgen Habermas,[28] entered the
fray.

Habermas took the controversy as the right occasion to expound
his own understanding of the social sciences in relation to Adorno's
thesis.[29] This clarification of his position led him to distinguish between different types of knowledge interests. Knowledge interests,
as Habermas understands them, are the specific points of view under
which reality can be grasped. These types of interested knowledge
define, especially in scientific claims, the purpose and precognitive
understanding that come with every theoretical unit of knowledge.
Interested knowledge is the "transcendental condition of possible
experience."[30] On the basis of the distinction between empirical-
analytic, historical-hermeneutic, and critically oriented sciences,
Habermas distinguishes between the technical, practical, and emancipatory interests of knowledge. In this phase of the development
of the theory, he is concerned with an anthropologically founded
epistemology that has a socially critical perspective. From this perspective, he shows that the methodological premises of positivistic,
hermeneutic, and critical sciences can be connected back up to socially necessary conditions of reproduction. In this sense, interested
knowledge and the methods of the sciences have a close connection
to the socially necessary practices of instrumental and communicative action.

Scientifically deduced critique has a special status. It goes beyond
the instrumental influence of things (for example, the empirical, analytic sciences) or the understanding (for example, the comprehension of symbolic forms of expression by the historical hermeneutical
sciences); in the framework of the sciences, critique is the first to be
charged with explaining interested knowledge. That interest exists
more or less, for Habermas, as the transcendental condition of the sciences. Second, this critique is based on an empirical insight. Through
the medium of self-reflection, critique brings things to consciousness
and thus aids in the dissolution of dogmatic forms of life. The category of emancipatory interest reveals its purpose: to create freedom
by sublating the social constraints that stem from the particularity
of the dominating interests. Habermas overcomes the category of
pure thought with the category of social totality – which formed the
basis of Adorno's concept of the integrated society as the systematic
functional nexus – by differentiating between types of interested

knowledge and distinguishing between the types of work and interaction (that is, the later dualism between system and life-world). Though Habermas conceptualizes society as a systemically stabilized nexus of socially integrated groups,[31] he notes that society constitutes itself through language, work, and domination. Social domination denotes the object of his critique of society. This critique orients itself by a standard that Habermas calls "the model of the suppression of generalizable interests."[32] It is, however, never clear in advance whether an interest is generalizable and could become evident only through just such a process of justification, that is, through discourse. Such discourses lead to particular hypothetical judgments about whether these claims, after careful examination, are in the general interests of all involved individuals. The concrete content of social criticism develops out of these processes. By clarifying and making more precise the presuppositions and processes of critique, Habermas lays a new foundation for the project of critical social theory. The project claims to have created the framework for a theory of modernity developed in terms of the theory of communicative action.

Habermasian critique, as an open discursive practice of mutual criticism, is fundamentally different from the concept of social criticism in Adorno's theory. For Adorno, the basic impulse for critique is the experience of suffering and the idea of its opposite, the right life, which itself surfaces in the experience of suffering. In Adorno's theory of society, critique is developed as the analysis of false consciousness and as the diagnosis that measures the reality of society in the light of its potential for emancipation. Habermas, by contrast, defines the social-scientific function of social criticism far more carefully. For Habermas, critique is carried by an emancipatory interested knowledge but cannot fall back on any certainty, even less onto a binding conception of the right life. Exactly what such a conception of the good and at the same time the rational might be is a favorite topic of the critical debate. Social criticism can only be effective as sociological enlightenment if it is capable of giving good reasons which could convince those who are affected by society's questionable direction of development of this very questionableness. Social criticism proves itself by showing that its claims to validity can withstand a critical challenge. For this version of critique, there can thus be neither finitude nor a point of completion. Critique is only possible if the critical project is open to error; that is, critique can only be practiced through what Habermas calls discourse. Habermas's great discovery in his linguistic theoretical analysis is, however, that critique becomes possible when the conditions for the possibility of communicatively oriented actions exist. It is this that makes the reconstruction of the conditions of critique possible.

   This linguistic-pragmatic justification of social criticism is again too abstract for a third, younger generation of social theorists, who were initially influenced by Habermas's paradigm of communicative action but then sought to overcome it. First among these is the social philosopher Axel Honneth. Honneth, who now has Habermas's teaching chair in Frankfurt, represents what has recently been called the recognition turn in Critical Theory. The chief question posed here concerns the way individuals and groups achieve their social meaning within the life nexus. Through which prelinguistic experiences does one come to understand who and what one wants to be in society? Can one realize one's own claims? Are they respected or disregarded? Starting from these questions, Honneth tries to develop a theoretical concept whose categories must lead to a practical change in what is open to critique in society. Social theory must relate to those nexuses of experiences in which the injury of those claims that are disregarded in and through society is expressed. According to Honneth, Critical Theory should intervene where claims to identity have not been respected. Honneth has in mind deep-seated anthropological claims about justice, which, as he says, "are connected with respect for one's own dignity, honor and integrity."[33]

   He distinguishes between three types of mutual recognition: (1) emotional care in the intimate space of love relations and friendship, (2) the legal recognition of a person who represents his or her own legitimate interests, and (3) the social valuation of personal achievements through which members of society demonstrate their particular abilities. These concepts of social criticism claim to thematize the moral experiences which stake their claim to emotional, juridical, and evaluative elements in subjective mistreatment. But it is still not clear whether this critical theory will prove fertile by uncovering situations in social reality which are found wanting.

5. OUTLOOK

Despite the attempts by Habermas and Honneth at overcoming the older Critical Theory, striking continuities remain. The critical element of social theory, for Adorno, Habermas, and Honneth, is a sensitivity to the social pathologies of modernity, that is, a sensitivity to injustice. Just as Adorno wanted to bring out the suffering in history with his critique, Habermas takes his cue from the negative idea of gradations of discrimination and suffering. Honneth's understanding of Critical Theory as morally motivated thinking which must essentially be aimed at excluding all conceivable forms of mistreatment and humiliation is hardly different.

Although these similarities concerning the moral point of view are striking, it is now really only possible to speak of critical theory in the plural, for Critical Theory has produced several distinct types of criticism in its development over the past half century. While the older social criticism aims at a historical situation in which one, as Adorno says, "could be different without fear" (MM, 103), the critique of the conditions of communication and the critique of the conditions of recognition are central to the social-theoretical-reflective projects of Habermas and Honneth, respectively.

Compared to the older Critical Theory, the younger ones are significantly more careful where the political-practical dimension of sociological enlightenment is concerned. It is Habermas especially who insists on modesty. He refuses to cede a privileged role to the sciences. Social criticism under its own steam cannot change the world, even if it has a thoroughly conceptually differentiated theory of society. According to Habermas,

What we need is to practice a little more solidarity: without that, intelligent action will remain permanently foundationless and inconsequential. Such practice, certainly, requires rational institutions; it needs rules and communicative forms that don't morally overtax the citizens but rather exact the virtue of an orientation toward the common good in small change.[34]

This statement shows that for Habermas society is not considered merely the raw material with which the theorist believes him- or herself able to work according to his or her insights. Indeed, there is no world spirit to which enlightenment science has privileged access and upon which it might call. The key to professional critical insight must include a willingness to relinquish Critical Theory but so too, conversely, must not be compelled to hold thinking as in principle harmless.

A plural Critical Theory does not at all mean the exclusion of one version or the exclusive validity of the other. The various versions of Critical Theory stand instead to each other in a relationship of mutual complementarity. As a self-reflective discipline Critical Theory is all encompassing: it includes the concrete conditions of life, which devalue human beings and make them unhappy, and it focuses on those unfortunate developmental tendencies that often lead to alienation and the loss of freedom. But as a self-reflective practice Critical Theory must also enlighten itself as to what social criticism is and how it is to be practiced as a discipline. In the practice of self-reflection social criticism must prove itself a better example of that which it seeks to be, namely, the praxis of critical argumentation. The path of such a critique is already part of the praxis of enlightenment, which is precisely what is at stake.

Translated by Stefan Bird-Pollan

NOTES

1. Max Horkheimer, "Traditional and Critical Theory," in *Critical Theory: Selected Essays*, trans. Matthew J. O'Connell (New York: Continuum, 1986), 188–243. Max Horkheimer (1895–1973) was born the son of a Jewish industrialist in Stuttgart. He came to philosophy only after having studied business for some time. His philosophy studies finally brought him to Frankfurt, where he received his doctorate under Hans Cornelius for a dissertation on Kant's *Critique of Judgment*. Horkheimer, then a lecturer, published his work *Anfänge der bürgerlichen Geschichtsphilosophie* (Stuttgart: Kohlhammer) in 1930. A collection of aphorisms, entitled *Dämmerung: Notizen in Deutschland* (Zurich: Oprecht and Helbling), influenced by both humanistic socialism and skepticism, followed in 1934; it was published under the pseudonym Heinrich Regius. Adorno, on whom this book made a great impression, followed this literary example in his 1951 *Minima Moralia: Reflexionen aus dem beschädigten Leben* (Berlin: Suhrkamp). In 1931 Horkheimer took over the leadership of the six-year-old Institute for Social Research; the Institute was associated with the University of Frankfurt, though, because of its endowment, it operated as a relatively independent research institution. The Institute undertook research into issues relating to economics and the social sciences on the basis of a scientific Marxism. Horkheimer's 1937 essay is of particular interest because in it he tries to provide an epistemological basis to clarify the concept of critique.

This concept was at the center of the theory of society that the members of the Institute (by then already institutionally connected to New York's Columbia University) sought to develop. Horkheimer wanted to connect critique with an objective concept of truth, which would coincide with a universal interest of humanity that "consciously constitutes itself into a subject for the first time" (Max Horkheimer, *Kritische Theorie: Eine Dokumentation*, vol. 2, ed. Alfred Schmidt [Frankfurt: Fischer, 1968], 180). The fact that the concept of critical reason also made demands for absoluteness led to a growing skepticism about its historical-practical efficaciousness. And because the dialectic of the historical process was, in principle, incomplete, this efficaciousness further required the correct moment in history. The idea of right life, which was the normative center of power of a critique of society, thus necessarily became dislocated and abstract. Likewise, critique itself retreated into the snail house of an exclusive attitude of general negation.

2. Theodore Wiesengrund-Adorno (1903–69) grew up in Frankfurt in the first decade of the turn of the century in a family that combined the bourgeois pursuits of both business and intellect. His father, Oscar Alexander Wiesengrund, was of Jewish descent. As the owner of an economically flourishing wine distribution company, he represented the characteristic individualism of a businessman in a city of commerce. Adorno was a single child. His talents were not least attributable to the influence of his 'two mothers'. The one, his natural mother Maria, born Calvelli-Adorno della Piana, was active as a singer up until her marriage. Her sister Agathe was a concert pianist. After studying philosophy, sociology, and psychology for four years at the then still new University of Frankfurt and completing his dissertation in philosophy with a dissertation on Edmund Husserl, Adorno moved to Vienna in the spring of 1925 in order to continue his study of composition with Alban Berg. Adorno habilitated in 1931 with his work *Kierkegaard: Construction of the Aesthetic*, translated into English by Robert Hullot-Kentor (Minneapolis: University of Minnesota Press, 1989). After 1934 Adorno left fascist Germany and went to Merton College, Oxford, as an advanced student in order to receive an academic degree. During his stay in the United States (1938–49), Adorno was an official contributor to the New York Institute for Social Research in the field of sociology (where he contributed to the *Authoritarian Personality* [1950] and other research projects). After returning to Frankfurt at age forty-six, Adorno lived for another twenty years. During this period, his most important writings in philosophy, sociology, and literary and music criticism appeared, and he established a name for himself as one of the most important intellectuals of the postwar period and a leading representative of Critical Theory.

3. Berg, composer of *Wozzeck* and *Lulu*, was part of the so-called Second Vienna School, which adhered to the then revolutionary composition model of twelve-tone technique and atonality. The group also included Arnold Schoenberg and Anton Webern.

4. Theodor W. Adorno, "Zur Gesellschaftlichen Lage der Musik," *Zeitschrift für Sozialforschung* 1 (1932). Reprinted in *Gesammelte Schriften*, vol. 18, ed. Rolf Tiedemann et al. (Frankfurt: Suhrkamp, 1984). Translated by Wes Blomster under the title "On the Social Situation of Music," reprinted in *Essays on Music*, ed. Richard Leppert (Berkeley: University of California Press, 2002), 391–436. Hereafter cited as SSM.

5. Music sociology as a distinct path of sociology was uncharted territory in the 1930s, and Adorno trod it as one of the pioneers. Of course, he made express mention of the previous achievement in the sociology of music by Max Weber, who "conceived the history of music in conjunction with an encompassing Occidental process of rationalization, and furnished evidence that only on the basis of this rationalization, thus the continually growing domination over nature, human control over the phonic materials, did the development of great music become possible." In addition, Weber had scientifically pulled the ground out from under the "conception which is still widespread today, and which ultimately amounts to the notion that music fell, so to speak, from the skies and therefore is above any rational or critical examination" (*Aspects of Sociology*, trans. John Viertel [Boston: Beacon Press, 1972], 110). The best introduction to Adorno's sociology of music is his *Einleitung in die Musiksoziologie*, in *Gesammelte Schriften*, vol. 14, 168–433. Translated by E. B. Ashton under the title, *Introduction to the Sociology of Music* (New York: Seabury Press, 1976).

6. The concept of mediation is not, in Adorno, the permeation of, for example, music through society. Rather, mediation is to be found in the phenomenon itself. Mediation can be seen in the way "society objectifies itself in works of art" ("Thesen zur Kunstsoziologie," in *Gesammelte Schriften*, vol. 10, 374). The abstraction society only manifests itself at all as a "mediated nexus" [*Vermittlungszusammenhang*]; that is, it appears as a universal in the particular. From the sociological perspective, mediation appears in the historically determined mutual conditioning between individual and society. For Adorno, this category, taken from the epistemological perspective, embodies his premise of the universal mediation of all things.

7. Rolf Tiedemann has explicated the concept of social physiognomics in his introduction to Walter Benjamin's *Passagen-Werk*: "Physiognomics infers the interior from the exterior; it decodes the whole from the detail; it represents the general in the particular. Nominalistically speaking, it proceeds from the tangible object; inductively it commences

in the realm of the intuitive" ("Dialectics at a Standstill: Approaches to the *Passagen-Werk*," trans. Gary Smith and Andre Lefevere, in Walter Benjamin, *The Arcades Project* [Cambridge, Mass.: Harvard University Press, 1999], 940).

8. Theodor W. Adorno, "Einleitung zum 'Positivismusstreit in der deutschen Soziologie'," in *Gesammelte Schriften*, vol. 8, 315. English translation in Theodor W. Adorno et al., *The Positivist Dispute in German Sociology*, trans. Glyn Adey and David Frisby (London: Heinemann, 1976), 32 (translation altered). Hereafter cited as PD.

9. During his lifetime Adorno produced over thirty musical compositions, including piano songs, string quartets, and orchestra pieces. A great part of his oeuvre is made up of writings primarily concerned with music, compositions, and composers. Of the twenty some volumes in his complete writings, only three contain works on sociology in the strictest sense, but two volumes in the sociology of literature, culture, and art supplement these. His philosophical publications comprise seven volumes. While it is possible to speak of a major work in the area of philosophy, namely, *Negative Dialectics* (1966), this is hardly possible in the area of sociology. Adorno accepted neither the term "pure sociology" nor that of "pure philosophy." Adorno often argued against the "division of labor among disciplines like philosophy, sociology and history," for this division of labor lies not in the subject matter of these fields "but is thrust upon them from the outside. Science, which really is one, is not naively directed straight ahead, but rather is reflected in itself and cannot respect this arbitrary division of labor" ("Thesen zur Kunstsoziologie," in *Gesammelte Schriften*, vol. 10, 373).

10. The basis for this claim lies in the distinction between essence and appearance which has become commonplace since Kant and Hegel (if not since Plato). Still, Adorno criticizes both philosophers by saying that essence should "no longer be hypostasized as a pure intellectual being-in-itself" (*Negative Dialektik*, in *Gesammelte Schriften*, vol. 6, 169; translated by E. B. Ashton under the title *Negative Dialectics* [New York: Seabury Press, 1973], 167).

11. Theodor W. Adorno, "The Actuality of Philosophy," *Telos*, no. 31 (1977): 126. Hereafter cited as AP.

12. The depiction of sociology as a climbing of façades, which becomes a common trope in Adorno, stems from a remark of Martin Heidegger's (cf. AP, 130).

13. Cf. Stefan Müller-Doohm, "Theodor W. Adorno," in *Klassiker der Soziologie*, ed. Dirk Kaesle (Munich: C. H. Beck, 1999).

14. Cf. the Princeton Radio Research Project and Hanns Eisler [and Theodor W. Adorno], *Composing for the Films* (New York: Oxford University Press, 1947).

15. Theodor W. Adorno et al., *The Authoritarian Personality* (New York: Harper, 1950). Reprinted in *Gesammelte Schriften*, vol. 9, pt. 1.

16. Adorno, *Authoritarian Personality* (*Gesammelte Schriften*, vol. 9, pt. 1), 312.

17. One central issue determined Adorno's future philosophical and socio-logical activities as researcher and professor: Sociology and philosophy understood as enlightenment sciences are duty-bound to help ensure – through research on the social origins of the fall back into barbarism – that this horror never be accepted by a people, that they never again sup-port a politics of conquering and systematic destruction. At one point in the second part of *Minima Moralia*, Adorno notes of the crimes com-mitted by the Germans, "Nevertheless, a consciousness that wishes to withstand the unspeakable finds itself again and again thrown back on the attempt to understand it, if it is not to succumb subjectively to the madness that prevails objectively" (*Gesammelte Schriften*, vol. 4, 115; translated by E. F. N. Jephcott under the title *Minima Moralia: Reflec-tions from Damaged Life* [London: New Left Books, 1974], 103; hereafter cited as MM). In the face of the real terror, the attempt to understand seems particularly helpless. Still, Adorno argues, this path of under-standing must be trodden. Adorno's postulate that writing poetry after Auschwitz is barbaric (*Kulturkritik und Gesellschaft*, in *Gesammelte Schriften*, vol. 10, 30; translated by Samuel Weber and Shierry Weber under the title "Cultural Criticism and Society," in *Prisms* [London: Neville Spearman, 1967], 34) insists on this process of relentless intel-lectual understanding of what is in itself unintelligible in order to give an account of that which came to pass and how and why it occurred.

18. Theodor W. Adorno, "Scientific Experiences of a European Scholar in America," *Gesammelte Schriften*, vol. 10, 703; also in *The Intellectual Migration: Europe and America, 1930–1960*, ed. Donald Fleming and Bernard Bailyn (Cambridge, Mass.: Harvard University Press, 1968), and in *Critical Models: Interventions and Catchwords*, trans. Henry Pick-ford (New York: Columbia University Press, 1998), 216.

19. Theodor W. Adorno, "Kritik," in *Gesammelte Schriften*, vol. 10, 793. Translated by Henry Pickford under the title "Critique," in *Critical Models: Interventions and Catchwords* (New York: Columbia Univer-sity Press, 1998), 288.

20. Adorno, *Kulturkritik und Gesellschaft*, 22 ("Cultural Criticism and So-ciety," 28).

21. Given the common misconception on this point, it is necessary to note that Adorno was a critic but never an opponent of empirical social re-search. He insists, "My own position in the controversy between em-pirical and theoretical sociology – which is often...thoroughly mis-interpreted – may be summarized roughly by saying that empirical

investigations, even in the domain of cultural phenomena, are not only legitimate but essential. But they should not be hypostasized and treated as a universal key. Above all, they themselves must terminate in theoretical knowledge. Theory is not merely a vehicle that becomes superfluous as soon as the data are available" ("Scientific Experiences of a European Scholar in America," in *Gesammelte Schriften*, vol. 10, 718; also in *The Intellectual Migration: Europe and America, 1930–1960*, ed. Donald Fleming and Bernard Bailyn [Cambridge, Mass.: Harvard University Press, 1968], 228).

22. Adorno, *Negative Dialektik*, 39 (*Negative Dialectics*, 29).

23. Adorno, *Minima Moralia*.

24. "All thinking is exaggeration, insofar as every thought that is one at all goes well beyond its confirmation by given facts" (Theodor W. Adorno, "Meinung Wahn Gesellschaft," in *Gesammelte Schriften*, vol. 10, 577; translated by Henry Pickford under the title "Opinion Delusion Society," in *Critical Models: Interventions and Catchwords* [New York: Columbia University Press, 1998], 108).

25. Karl R. Popper (1902–1994) is one of the most important philosophers of the twentieth century. He developed his theory of scientific knowledge in dialogue with logical positivism; his theory of science is related to his antidogmatism and his support of democracy and of an open, pluralistic society. Popper opposes the positivistic foundational concept of scientific knowledge according to which a series of hypotheses are gathered from the observation of particular cases, which then permits the deduction of laws. Popper begins from the premise that there can be neither an absolutely certain point of departure for knowledge nor one single possible method. Scientific theories distinguish themselves by being refutable through facts (potential falsifications). The scientist is duty-bound to search out falsifying cases. Scientific progress results from the elimination of what is wrong by the method of trial and error.

26. Popper too incorporates critique into his model of science. In his lecture "The Logic of the Social Sciences," he argues that "the method of science is one of tentative attempts to solve our problems; by conjectures which are controlled by severe criticism. It is a consciously critical development of the method of 'trial and error'. The so-called objectivity of science lies in the objectivity of the critical method. This means, above all, that no theory is beyond attack by criticism" ("The Logic of the Social Sciences," in Theodor W. Adorno et al., *The Positivist Dispute in German Sociology*, trans. Glyn Adey and David Frisby [London: Heinemann, 1976], 89–90).

27. Hans Albert (born 1921) has been a prominent proponent of critical rationalism since the 1960s. He proceeds from the premise that reason is

in principle fallible and that final justifications are impossible. Theories must be formulated in such a way that they can be criticized or falsified. In the course of the positivism dispute, he defended the formalization of arguments because this leads to clarification of the proof structure and thus contributes to critique. For him, logic is an instrument of critique.

28. Jürgen Habermas (born 1929) is the most important and most productive representative the second (i.e., younger) generation of proponents of Critical Theory. In the mid-1950s he was Adorno's assistant at the Frankfurt Institute for Social Research and later the successor to Max Horkheimer's teaching chair. One of the chief concerns of his socio-theoretical project is to clarify the standards of Critical Theory. In his contributions to the positivism dispute, he tried to take up a position between analytic theory of science and dialectics. He attempted to fore-ground the emancipatory meaning of self-reflection against the privi-leged nomological understanding, which depends on the production of technically useful knowledge. According to Habermas, all sociology de-pends on value and thus contains moral judgment, which must be made transparent in the interests of knowledge (i.e., must be justified in the-oretical discourse).

29. Jürgen Habermas, *On the Logic of the Social Sciences*, trans. Shierry Weber Nicholsen and Jeremy Stark (Cambridge, Mass.: MIT Press, 1990).

30. Jürgen Habermas, *Knowledge and Human Interests*, trans. Jeremy Shapiro (New York: Beacon Press, 1972), 126.

31. Jürgen Habermas, *The Theory of Communicative Action*, 2 vols., trans. Thomas McCarthy (Cambridge, Mass.: MIT Press, 1984–9).

32. Jürgen Habermas, *Legitimation Crisis*, trans. Thomas McCarthy (New York: Beacon Press, 1976), 111.

33. Axel Honneth, "Die soziale Dynamik der Missachtung: Zur Ortsbestim-mung einer Kritischen Gesellschaftstheorie" *Leviathan* 1 (1994): 86.

34. Jürgen Habermas, *The Past as Future*, trans. Max Pensky (Lincoln: Uni-versity of Nebraska Press, 1994), 96–7.

12 Genealogy and Critique
Two Forms of Ethical Questioning of Morality

I

Any adequate understanding of morality includes its critical questioning.[1] Critical questioning of this sort looks on morality from the outside, for it views morality as a necessarily limited perspective on our life as a whole. One can therefore characterize this questioning as an "external" reflection on morality. At the same time, however, it would be a misconception of the critical questioning of morality to view it as solely external, for it might then too readily result in a rejection, or even a dissolving, of morality. What leads to this misconception is the overlooking of the fact that the external stance is at the same time linked to a *self*-questioning of morality: The questioning of morality from the outside has its foundations in morality itself. For viewed correctly, morality is constituted such that it contains that which at the same time it is in conflict with from the outside. Objects thus composed may well be called "dialectical." Part of any adequate self-understanding of morality is therefore the examination of the dialectic, or, more precisely, what Adorno would call the *negative* dialectic, of morality.

The thesis of the negative-dialectical constitution of morality is central to the moral philosophy formulated by so-called older Critical Theory, primarily the work of Max Horkheimer but also that of Adorno. At the same time, this thesis illustrates where the older Critical Theory remains most clearly at odds with the "younger" one, namely, the work of Jürgen Habermas. In the new discursive ethical reasoning of morality developed by Habermas, morality was to receive a form which might release it from the negative dialectic of self-questioning and self-limitation. This opposition in the very conception of morality between the two generations of Critical Theory is mirrored in their relationship to Nietzsche's undertaking of a genealogical examination of morality – to that author who devoted himself like no other to the task of molelike digging to "undermine our *faith in morality*."[2] In Habermas's eyes, Nietzsche has nothing to tell us at all, but above all nothing about moral philosophy. For Horkheimer and Adorno on the other hand, Nietzsche's "intransigent critique of practical reason"[3] is part and parcel of a traditional line of modern reflection on morality, one they also intend to continue, albeit in a fundamentally different manner. Genealogy and critique are two forms of the questioning of morality which start with the same problem but end up with conflicting solutions.

The common interest that connects Nietzsche's genealogy with Adorno's critique and separates them from Habermas's discourse ethics can be shown, first of all, by casting a glance into the history of modern moral philosophy. There are two crucial characteristics here. First, modern moral philosophy employs a narrow definition of the concept of morality. In particular, it uses the expression "moral" to depict a mode of behavior or an attitude whose fundamental property is orientation toward the idea of equality, for "moral" means "egalitarian" in modern moral philosophy. The moral attitude considers others as equals; it is an orientation of equal treatment. Second, modern moral philosophy is "a reflective theory of morality."[4] This is to say that moral theory not only expresses moral perception and judgment but makes moral perception and judgment the objects of a reflexive, distanced inquiry. The first intention of such inquiry is foundational: Reflection in modern moral philosophy means first, in both a historic and systematic sense, the foundation of morality – or, to be more precise, the founding of morality on non-moral interests, capacities, or practices. In modern moral philosophy, "founding" is therefore understood in a strong sense as a derivation. Reflection as the foundation of morality means then that something nonmoral is found present in all people (is part of "human nature"), and from this the moral attitude is to be derived.

This idea of the foundation of morality stands in opposition to a second form of reflection in modern moral philosophy referred to by Schiller in his *Letters on Aesthetic Education* as an "anthropological assessment" (in the sense of evaluation) of morality. By this Schiller understood an assessment of morality under the aspect of its consequences for human life as a whole, "where content no less than form, and living feeling too has a voice."[5] In this perspective, the moral attitude appears as but one among many practical directives that determine our life. As the history of modern revolution compellingly demonstrated to Schiller's eyes, the moral attitude of equality can have detrimental consequences for those other, nonmoral directives; it must therefore be questioned reflectively by those. In both forms of reflection, morality is seen from an outside in relation to something else, something not itself moral but nonetheless relevant to morality. In its first form, such reflective relating of morality refers it to its grounds; in its second form, to its consequences. Reflecting on morality in its first form is therefore understood as a justifying of morality, while reflecting on it in its second form is understood as a questioning and limiting of morality.

The comparison of two traditional courses of modern moral reflection allows for a more precise indication of the common ground between Nietzsche's genealogy and the older Critical Theory. Habermas's discourse ethics falls within the first tradition of reflecting on morality. Habermas shares with Kant, but not with Nietzsche or Adorno, the idea of a reflective foundation of morality – a foundation which at the same time is to point out the absolute or categorical validity of moral principles. Adorno, on the other hand, like Nietzsche, belongs to the second tradition, which, along Schiller's line, undertakes a questioning of morality focusing on its consequences. Nietzsche and likewise Adorno want to show what moral norms and practices mean for individuals and, even more, how they might damage their lives. This is the common starting point between Adorno and Nietzsche. At the same time, they differ, even contradict one another, in their results. The opposition between Adorno and Nietzsche is not – like that between Habermas and Nietzsche – an opposition between the founding and questioning of morality but is instead an opposition *in* the questioning of morality, between two of its forms. The opposition between Adorno and Nietzsche, though, is no less far-reaching because of this: It has to do with the *conclusions* drawn from this questioning. For these conclusions, Nietzsche and Adorno use the same figure to begin with: that of a "self-overcoming of morality [*die Selbstaufhebung der Moral*]."[6] Each understands this figure in a completely different way, however. For Nietzsche, self-overcoming of morality is the liberation of the theoretical and practical potentialities of morality – for example, the capabilities of truthful self-scrutiny and sovereign self-control[7] – from their moral purposes for the sake of individual *self*-perfection. Adorno on the other hand regards the self-overcoming of morality as necessary precisely for moral purposes involving *others*. The self-overcoming of morality is to Adorno the liberation of social virtues – Adorno names such virtues as compassion, giving, and solidarity – from the false models of reason and freedom with which they have grown entangled in modern morality. Nietzsche's questioning aims to unmask "our old morality [as] part *of the comedy*,"[8] while Adorno's, on the other hand, aims to convert it into a "liberated practice" [*befreite Praxis*]. The common ground between Adorno and Nietzsche is in the question as to what meaning morality has for the *individual*. Their contrasting stance reveals itself in what this question means for *morality*.

II

Nietzsche often describes the overcoming of morality using aesthetic metaphors: as its turning into comedy, as the achievement of an aesthetic "*freedom above things*" that makes us "*able* also to stand *above* morality."[9] The overcoming of morality however can only be attained – this is the reason that Nietzsche speaks of its *self*-overcoming – through honest, truthful cognition. The overcoming, indeed the dissolution, of morality takes place when we venture into the "immense and almost new domain of dangerous insights" that Nietzsche sees as opened up by a psychology which is viewed "once again as queen of the sciences":

If one has once drifted there with one's bark, well! all right! let us clench our teeth! let us open our eyes and keep our hand firm on the helm! We sail right *over* morality, we crush, we destroy perhaps the remains of our own morality by daring to make our voyage there.[10]

The overcoming of morality is to Nietzsche the prize promised to "the cognizers," those "bold travelers and adventurers," as compensation for the dangers they choose to face; they are able to stand above morality, they can travel beyond morality, because a "*profounder* world of insight" is opened to them.

Again and again this Nietzschean project of dissolving morality through a gaining of cognition has been understood in terms of an objective, even scientistic reduction: as a project that tries to show that moral concepts and moral distinctions are illusory when confronted with the "true" reality of "immoral" facts. In the world of objectively ascertainable facts, so goes this argument, everything that our moral world consists of – such as the distinction between good and evil or the freedom of the subject to act responsibly – does not exist at all. This is not, however, what Nietzsche is concerned with in his questioning of morality. For Nietzsche, that morality is illusion cannot be reason enough for an objection to it – his objection is that morality is an illusion which fails to recognize itself as such. The "moral problem" that Nietzsche seeks to expose concerns not the issue of truth but the *"the value of these* [moral] *values."*[11] Nietzsche's dissolving of morality is a result of his "valuation of the value" of morality:[12] that is to say, his evaluation that the value of morality is base or weak, or, more precisely, that the value of morality is only a value *for* the base or weak. Nietzsche criticizes morality not because the world of morality is not truly real but rather because it is not truly valuable.[13]

Every question of value is for Nietzsche a question of purpose: "The question: what is the *value* of this or that table of values and 'morals'? should be viewed from the most diverse perspectives; for the problem 'value *for what?'* cannot be examined too subtly."[14] What purpose a thing serves, or what it is good for, cannot, however, be generally expounded. That it has value because it is of use for something means that it has value because it is of use to *somebody.* The question of value has a threefold structure: It refers to the value a thing has for someone for some purpose: Every question of value is at the same time for Nietzsche a question of "what for?" and "for whom?" Therefore, according to Nietzsche, "one can still always ask: what does such a claim [that of the value of a thing] tell us about the man who makes it?"[15] To ask about the value of a morality means to ask what significance it has for a person to orient himself using the norms of this morality, and this means regarding the value of morality from the point of view of the person.

In this questioning of the value of morality from the perspective of the person, Nietzsche differentiates between a first step, which is to look at the *"history* of morality,"[16] *"the history of the origins* of these [moral] feelings and valuations," and a second step, the actual "*critique* of moral valuations."[17] And indeed the critique results from the history of morals, if it is consequently followed; this is what takes place in the genealogy of morals. The history of morality leads the various forms of morality back to the "conditions and circumstances in which they grew, under which they evolved and changed."[18] For whom, goes the question here, is a certain kind of moral rule and regulation of value or use, and if it is of use to someone, in what way and with what aim? But the genealogical question does not stop there. It asks not only about the value of a morality but "*why have morality at all*?"[19] In order to answer this question, the genealogist has to give up the objective view of the historian. He cannot answer the question "why have morality at all?" in an "impersonal" way but must take "morality as a problem, and this problem as *his* own personal distress, torment, voluptuousness, and passion."[20] The questioning of morality, which Nietzsche seeks to take as far as its dissolution, is in a double sense personal. It is directed toward the person for whom a certain set of morals has a certain value, and it is a questioning by a person – a questioning in which the genealogist turns morality into one of those problems to which he "has a personal relationship . . . and finds in them his destiny, his distress, and his greatest happiness."[21]

When the genealogist questions in such a personal way the person for whom the moral has significance and value, he goes from being an observer to being a participant in a "struggle" over morality.[22] Genealogy thereby shows the struggle over morality and is itself a strategy in the struggle that it has proved lay in the very origins of morality.[23] That means that genealogy is and acts as a party to the struggle, it distinguishes and decides, it evaluates. Genealogy not only determines for whom, for what sort of person, which morality has which value; genealogy also judges the "value" of each morality, and indeed its value for the kind of person that the genealogist himself is or would like to be. Nietzsche's questioning of morality is not merely nonobjective but rather personal, nor is it relativistic but rather normative. Genealogy asks what value a morality has when one seeks to "make a whole *person* of oneself and keep in mind that person's *greatest good* in everything one does."[24] To state clearly what this means and how it is possible – namely, "to make a whole person of oneself" – is the central task of the "individual ethics"

(*Individual-Ethik*) which Nietzsche already mentioned in his notes in the early 1870s.[25] This individual ethics is indeed of a new kind, but no less normative than that of Epictetes, Seneca, Plutarch, Montaigne, and Stendhal, which he refers to.[26] It describes and promotes a personal, an *own*, in Nietzsche's words, a "nobler" life of "superior" freedom. It is this conception of individual ethics that binds Nietzsche's criticism to the following role for philosophers: their "task, their hard, unwanted, inescapable task," is to be "the bad conscience of their time,"[27] because they are to confront contemporary cultural phenomena with the question of what significance they have for the "personal life" of individuals. That and not the objective cognition of the true composition of reality is the "deeper insight" which allows us, according to Nietzsche's aforementioned formulation, to travel "beyond morality" toward a "noble," a truthfully accomplished (*gelungenes*) life – beyond morality because morality (that is, the then reigning morality of equality) has its basis in an attitude of enmity toward such a life.

Adorno's critical theory shares with Nietzsche's genealogy the project of an individual ethics–guided critique of morality and culture. The "region," as is written at the very beginning of *Minima Moralia*, "that from time immemorial was regarded as the true field of philosophy, but which, since the latter's conversion into method, has lapsed into intellectual neglect, sententious whimsy and finally oblivion" is "the teaching of the good life."[28] Its central ideas are those of "autonomy" and the "happiness" of individual existence. Like Nietzsche's genealogy, Adorno's cultural criticism from the outset refers to a normative standard, one not exhausted by the moral principle of equality but rather one from which the principle of equality can be judged. What Adorno calls "humanity" consists of the achievement of forms of behavior toward others, as well as toward oneself, which cannot be judged by the measure of equality, including solidarity and tact toward others and freedom and fulfillment in relation to oneself, to one's own nature.

At the same time, the achievement of these relationships is not merely "private," that is to say, not merely a question of individually appropriate, even attributable circumstances (which are not a subject of Critical Theory). Far more decisive for the individual's "good life" is the condition of a culture and society, or, more precisely, the cultural condition of a society. However, this must not be taken to mean

that the condition of a culture decides or even *determines* whether
there exists a right life for an individual. (Adorno, too, points out the
contingency upon which individual accomplishment and happiness
depend.) Rather, the condition of a culture determines if and how
we can acquire an appropriate understanding of the right life. Every
single person must decide for himself in which direction he should
seek an accomplished life. But not one person can embark on this
search without drawing on the patterns of achievement proffered by
the culture and practiced on him by the culture. Such patterns dictate what the achievement such a life consists of – indeed not its
content so much as what form this accomplished life should take.
These patterns shape the perception that a culture has of the good
life and imprint themselves on the individual; without this point of
reference no person can reach an understanding of the accomplished
life. Therefore, it is culturally determined, not whether our life succeeds, but how we conceive what such success might be.

Upon this – one could say "hermeneutic" – connection between
the individual accomplished life and the cultural patterns of accomplishment, the undertaking of individual ethics-based cultural criticism has its foundation. For through this connection the condition of
a culture is relevant for accomplishment – not directly for the accomplishment of individual existence but indirectly for the achievement
of the conception or the projection of its accomplishment. That there
is no right life in a false one – "Wrong life cannot be lived rightly" [*Es
gibt kein richtiges Leben im falschen*] – so must this most famous
line of *Minima Moralia* (MM, 42) be understood. In other words,
the false life only knows false representations of the right one, or,
more precisely, "false" culture develops only pictures or models of
life which make it impossible for individuals to lead a right life any
longer. "We shudder at the brutalization of life, but lacking any objectively binding morality we are forced at every step into actions and
words, into calculations that are by humane standards barbaric, and
even by the dubious values of good society, tactless"(MM, 27).[29] It is
one thing to criticize a society for not providing some or even many of
its members with the same opportunity for a good life as others have;
this is criticism of the injustice of that society. It is another thing to
criticize a culture for not providing the models nor expounding the
capabilities which allow individuals simply to achieve an appropriate *idea* of the accomplishment of their individual existence; this is

the inhumanity of the prevailing culture at which Adorno aims his criticism.

This points to common ground between Nietzsche and Adorno: They undertake a critical observation of culture that has as both its starting point and its focus the individual person, the succeeding and failing of individual existence (to the extent that this success and failure is determined by culture). Adorno's "melancholy science" (MM, 15) indeed differs from the "gay science" of Nietzsche in how it deals with this individual ethics–based critique of the prevailing culture. While Nietzsche confronts it with an ideal of the accomplished life, Adorno empathizes with the damage and suffering that it occasions.[30] What both have in common, however, is that their critique of the prevailing culture takes that culture and its effects "personally," as Nietzsche said. And indeed personally in a double sense: Both Adorno and Nietzsche are concerned with the consequences the prevailing culture has for the individuals in their attempt to lead a right life. This only reveals itself to the critic in relation to his *own* attempt to lead a right life. The critical recognition of the prevailing culture is therefore for Adorno and Nietzsche at the same time an experiment of the critic with his own life; he only attains such insight by seeking to make "his own life in the frail image of a true existence" (MM, 26).

For Adorno, morality is one of the cultural practices at which the individual ethics-based critique is aimed, precisely because it damages the right life of individuals. Such is the meaning of the "critics of morality,"[31] developed in the first of the three "models" in his *Negative Dialectics* by way of a debate with Kant. In it Adorno wants to show that, and to what extent, "abstract morality," as he says following Hegel, has "repressive features" (ND, 256) – to what extent it possesses coercive traits. Adorno thereby takes up Nietzsche's diagnosis of the "self-violation" that the moral order signifies for the individual. At its center, for Nietzsche, is the "delight in imposing a form upon oneself as a hard, recalcitrant, suffering material and in burning a will, a critique, a contradiction, a contempt" – the "joy in making [oneself] suffer."[32] In this way, Nietzsche (and Adorno follows his lead) puts the moral subject into the center of his critical examination of morality – the question, therefore, of how an individual, subject to the moral rules of equality, relates to himself, *must* relate to himself. Nietzsche and Adorno share Kant's deduction of morality from autonomy: Moral laws are not "repressive" because they are forced on the individual from the outside. But they are not any less repressive because the individual has imposed these laws on himself. It is far more the free self-imposing of moral laws that Nietzsche refers to as "self-violation" and Adorno refers to as the "repressive features" of morality. Moral freedom, as autonomy, means compulsion for both Nietzsche and Adorno.

Neither Nietzsche nor Adorno understand this claim as asserting that *all* freedom is compulsion *to an equal degree*. Indeed, Nietzsche's genealogy (and Adorno's conception of critique backs him in this) demonstrates that there is no freedom without breaking the compulsion of nature and that this breaking is in its turn itself a compulsion.[33] The compulsion of natural compulsion [*Naturzwang*] is for Nietzsche and Adorno a compulsion opening the door to freedom. More precisely, it is, or rather was, the *moral* compulsion of nature that proved itself in human history to be the freedom-opening compulsion:

If we place ourselves at the end of this tremendous process, where the tree at last brings forth fruit, where society and the morality of custom at last reveal *what* they have simply been the means to: then we discover that the ripest fruit is the *sovereign individual*, like only to himself, liberated again from morality of custom, autonomous and supramoral.[34]

This is the individual capable of leading a "strong" or "distinguished" accomplished life, and for this self-mastering "sovereign" to have "consciousness of his own power and freedom," moral compulsion was necessary and even justified: "The labor performed by man upon himself during the greater part of the existence of the human race, his entire *prehistoric* labor, finds in this its meaning, its great justification, notwithstanding the severity, tyranny, stupidity, and idiocy involved in it."[35] Once, however, this transmoral or individual autonomy has been attained, moral compulsion loses any justification; then it becomes superfluous and therefore unjustified. In Nietzsche's and Adorno's critique of morality, therefore, compulsion and freedom are neither simply opposed nor simply identified. No freedom comes into being and is sustained without compulsion, but not all freedom possesses the same degree of compulsion. Nietzsche and Adorno distinguish between two different forms of freedom both of which are based on compulsion, and yet they can be differentiated, when compared, as freedom and compulsion. That moral freedom is compulsion – this aforementioned central thesis of Nietzsche's and Adorno's critique of morality – therefore means that *moral freedom* is compulsion as opposed and compared to the *individual freedom* of determining and realizing an accomplished life. For Nietzsche and Adorno, morality is a cultural pattern that prevents the accomplished or right life because (1) it initiates an understanding of freedom as (moral) autonomy and (2) this understanding makes it impossible to practice that form of "individual" freedom necessary for the accomplished or right life.

Certainly Nietzsche's and Adorno's analyses differ when it comes to describing more closely the inhibitory consequences of morality – and above all *what* they inhibit. If for Nietzsche the consequences of morality included the "diminution and leveling of European man,"[36] which put an end to the "abundance of creative power and masterfulness" of "the higher man,"[37] Adorno sees therein the "wishful image of an uninhibited, vital, creative man" (MM, 156) and describes such "absolute rule of one's inner nature" (ND, 256) as, quite to the contrary, a consequence of morality. That which is inhibited by morality is characterized by Nietzsche using pictures of heroism and genius and by Adorno, on the other hand, with mimetic reconciliation.[38] And yet here too is a common motif articulated by Nietzsche and Adorno. For in an important respect they envisage in the same way the course of individual freedom weakened by moral freedom. This is the expressive dimension of individual freedom.

Moral freedom, that is to say, the notion of a free relationship with one's self, upon which both the idea and practice of morality are based, is the freedom of a subject behind, or above, its deeds – of a subject responsible for its deeds, as it can act in one way or another. The idea of a free self-subjugation under the moral law is based on the belief "in a neutral independent 'subject.'"[39] For without this belief, according to Nietzsche's argument, there can be no grounds for the moral law's demand regarding "strength": "that it should *not* express itself *as* strength, that it should *not* be a desire to overcome, a desire to throw down, a desire to become master, a thirst for enemies and resistance and triumphs." "Popular morality" speaks of moral responsibility and freedom "as if there were a neutral substratum behind the strong man, which was *free* to express strength or not to do so."[40] That, however, in Adorno's words, is the fiction of an "absolute volitional autonomy" (ND, 256), which cuts off what constitutes free action. "True practice, the essence of acts that live up to the idea of freedom, necessitates full theoretical consciousness. . . . However, such practice also necessitates something else, which is not encompassed by consciousness, but which is bodily [*leibhaft*] mediated by reason and yet distinct from it" (ND, 229, translation amended). This other, which is both "intramental and somatic" (ND, 228), Nietzsche calls "force" and Adorno "impulse." Free action is not as the idea of moral freedom would have it appear, an autonomous acting from a detached decision about the realizing of one's own forces or impulses. Free action is, rather, inaccessibly and uncontrollably expressive, the "expressing" of forces[41] – the release of force to self-expression. True freedom, without which there can be no accomplished life, requires the withdrawal of the doubling up of act and actor and thereby the self-surrender of the subject as an instance of autonomous disposition. This explains why the cultural pattern of moral freedom distorts the practice of individual freedom, even threatens it: The rule of morality develops or imprints a self-relation which so decisively weakens the free capability to allow one's own forces and impulses to assert themselves that the achievement of individual existence is damaged.

III

The opposition between moral and individual freedom is the foundation of Nietzsche's demand for an overcoming of the moral idea of equality. "Today, conversely," Nietzsche writes in a piece on an idea of greatness which the philosopher holds up against his time,

when only the herd animal receives and dispenses honor in Europe, when 'equality of rights' could all too easily be changed into equality in violating rights – I mean, into a common war on all that is rare, strange, privileged, the higher human, the higher soul, the higher duty, the higher responsibility, and the abundance of creative power and masterfulness – today the concept of 'greatness' entails being noble, wanting to be by oneself, being able to be different, standing alone and having to live independently.[42]

Above all else, however, the living of such greatness necessitates a break with the ideas of equality by virtue of which the "*autonomous* herd" disputes "every special claim, every special right and privilege" of the individual; individual life can only succeed as immoral life.[43]

What is wrong with this inference? According to a widely shared reading of it, let us call it the liberal reading, its very premises. Nietzsche reached, as we have seen, his immoral consequence from the starting point of an individual ethics–based questioning of morality: by measuring the worth of morality through the significance it has for those individuals striving for nobility and greatness. In the liberal view, the argument begins with an assessment of morality from the outside, relating it to where an individual (as Nietzsche says in the earlier passage from *The Gay Science*) "finds his destiny, his distress, and his greatest happiness." This starting point must eventually result in the negation of morality, for the standpoint of morality *is* that of equality, the taking into account of everyone. To observe morality from the perspective of the single person means nothing other than observing it immorally: It means avoiding the step into the moral perspective, for this is the very step from the individual to everyone.

Both Nietzsche and his liberal critics accept that to question morality from outside (as the individual ethics view does) is to dissolve morality. Contrary to this, I want to show in what follows that this inference from the individual ethics-based questioning of morality, though not its premise (the individual ethics-based questioning itself), is wrong. This judgment becomes apparent in Adorno. Adorno did not, obviously, draw the same conclusions as Nietzsche from his individual ethics–based critique of morality, which nonetheless in perspective and content agrees with Nietzsche's. If this critique forms the basis for Nietzsche's negation of morality from without, from a "beyond good and evil," for Adorno it is rather a project of unfolding the inner dialectic of morality. Its outline can be taken from what Adorno formulates at one point in *Negative Dialectics* with reference to the idea of fair or equal exchange (ND, 146 ff.). In general, the idea of equality belongs to the reign of the "principle of identification." However, if equality were therefore to be "denied . . . abstractly – if we proclaimed, to the greater glory of the irreducibly qualitative, that parity should no longer be the ideal rule – we would be creating excuses for recidivism into ancient injustice." This is the difference between an "abstract" and the "critical" negation of equality: "When we criticize the barter principle [or the principle of morality] as the identifying principle of thought, we want to realize the ideal of free and just barter. To date, this ideal is only a pre-text. Its realization alone would transcend barter [or morality]" (ND, 147). Such is the conclusion to be drawn from Adorno's critique of morality: the transcendence of the moral law as its true realization. "Skepticism towards *ressentiment* in the bourgeois ideal of equality that does not tolerate any qualitative differences" – that is to say, the skepticism that Adorno shares with Nietzsche – does not lead Adorno, as it does Nietzsche, to an abstract rejection of the moral idea of equality in favor of an order of rank and privilege. Rather, it leads him to a demand for its realization through its transcendence.

With this confrontation, the crux of my comparison of Nietzsche and Adorno is reached. I began this comparison with the question whether – as Nietzsche and his liberal critics believe – the individual ethics-based questioning of morality has to end with its dissolution. Adorno's critique of morality demonstrates that this is not the case: It undertakes an individual ethics-based questioning of morality which understands itself as the realization of morality through its transcendence. But what does "the realization of morality through its transcendence" mean? It sounds, as Adorno concedes in a related context, "paradoxical enough."[44] In order to actually justify the thesis which I have formulated by the comparison of Nietzsche and Adorno – the thesis, once again, that the individual ethics–based questioning of morality does not equal its dissolution – Adorno's project of realizing morality through its transcendence requires an explanation capable of convincingly dispelling its apparent paradoxical nature.

This becomes possible when we extend the comparison of Nietzsche and Adorno, of genealogy and critique, to their essential aspects. We have seen that Nietzsche and Adorno are in agreement in both method and content regarding the importance of critically questioning the *consequences of morality* for the life of the individual. We have also seen that Nietzsche and Adorno differ in their *attitudes toward morality*. For both, however, their *conception* of morality is crucial; it is here that the lines of their agreement and differences intersect. And, indeed, Nietzsche and Adorno are at one as regards the *form* of morality; therefore, they also concur in the description of the consequences of morality for the individual. At the same time, however, Nietzsche and Adorno contradict one another as regards the *ground* of morality; therefore (and not because of capricious preferences or political prejudices), they assume opposing attitudes toward morality.

The form of morality defined by Adorno and Nietzsche in parallel ways is that of a general, universally valid, and internal, self-imposed law which demands an equal taking into account of everyone. This definition of the form of morality cannot, however, make its existence comprehensible. For that purpose, an examination of its origins, its source, is essential. Both Nietzsche and Adorno view the moral law of equal treatment as a systematically secondary phenomenon which stems from an urge *other* than its manifest moral "intention." "We believe that the intention is merely a sign and a symptom that still requires interpretation"[45] – an interpretation which should reveal what the moral idea "*means*; what it indicates; what lies hidden behind it, beneath it, in it; of what it is the provisional, indistinct expression, overlaid with question marks and misunderstandings."[46] In expressed opposition to the rationalistic "attempt... to derive the duty of mutual respect from a law of reason" (DA, 85), thereby destroying its very basis,[47] both Nietzsche and Adorno follow the moral law of equal treatment back to something different which finds in it only limited expression; the moral law conceals where it comes from.

The source of the law of equal treatment, however, is defined by Nietzsche and Adorno in strictly opposing ways; herein lies the crucial difference in their attitude to morality. In Nietzsche's view, the morality of equality is based on *ressentiment*: "The slave revolt in morality [in which this kind of morality came to power] begins when *ressentiment* itself becomes creative and gives birth to values."[48] That is the central thesis in Nietzsche's explanation of morality in which two different steps can be distinguished. The first step follows the proclaimed intention of loving or at least respecting others back to the compulsions of revenge and hatred. According to Nietzsche, there would be even "more justification for placing above the gateway to the Christian Paradise and its 'eternal bliss' the inscription 'I too was created by eternal *hate*.'"[49] Nietzsche defended this implausible thesis (implausible, if one sticks only to the manifest intentions) through a structural analysis of the "mode of valuation" which underlies the morality of equality. The "slave revolt" which created this morality signifies, according to Nietzsche, an "inversion of the value-positing eye" driven by the "need to direct one's

view outward instead of back to oneself": "While every noble morality develops from a triumphant affirmation of itself, slave morality
from the outset says No to what is 'outside,' what is 'different,' what
is 'not itself'; and *this* No is its creative deed."[50] The demand that
everyone be considered equally is based on a hateful nay-saying to
those who in the completion of their life and in all "innocence" (admittedly, the "innocent conscience of the beast of prey")[51] threaten,
constrict, and obstruct the others. These are, according to Nietzsche,
the "strong men" – "replete with energy and therefore *necessarily*
active."[52] They are first of all feared, then hated, and finally declared
"evil": "The man of *ressentiment* ... has conceived 'the evil enemy,'
'*the Evil one*,' and this in fact is his basic concept, from which he then
evolves, as an afterthought and pendant, a 'good one' – himself!"[53]
That the morality of equality is a morality of *ressentiment* is shown
by the fact that, in its basis and center, it is a move against the threatening other.

That is, however, only the first step in Nietzsche's demonstration
that the morality of equality derives from *ressentiment*. A second
step is required as well. If the morality of equality is related to the individual freedom of the other as its negation, this is not only because
it fears such freedom as "dangerous to the community," hates it, and
declares it evil. Even more, the hatred of individual freedom stems
from a self-relation which cuts off one's *own* individual freedom.
In *ressentiment*, the basis of morality, fear, and hatred, in relation
to the other and in relation to the person himself, belong together;
the nay-saying directed to the other as the evil one corresponds to
the "denial of himself, of his nature, naturalness, and actuality."[54]
The man of *ressentiment* believes himself to be forced "to make
necessary and regularly recurring sensations into a source of inner
misery, and in this way to want to make inner misery a necessary
and regularly recurring phenomenon *in every human being*."[55] The
moral person does not want – or, more precisely, the moral person
cannot want – his own accomplished life and therefore fights that of
others.

Thus it becomes clear why, according to Nietzsche, individual
ethics–based questioning of morality has to end with morality's
dissolution. In that questioning Nietzsche sees the restricting effects which the morality of equality has on the accomplished life
of individuals, for it enforces a false understanding of freedom – an

understanding of freedom that makes an accomplished life impossible. In his definition of morality, Nietzsche wants to show moreover
that these effects are morality's true basis. The morality of equality
not only *leads* to a weakening of individual freedom in the pursuit
of the accomplished life but even has its foundation in a will, an
"ill" will, to weaken individual freedom and to demonize the accomplished life as culpable and poisonous. The morality of equality
is for Nietzsche on the whole nothing but a self-forgotten institution
of, and a self-disguising institution for, the weakening and obstruc-
tion of the accomplished life.

It is this homogenizing picture of morality, in which consequences
and foundation run seamlessly together, that Adorno's conception
of morality contradicts most decisively. Adorno can, however, at the
same time connect to a consideration that Nietzsche has brought
up several times but never thought through to its final conclusion.
And with good reason, for its consequences are destructive for his
conception of morality. It has to do with Nietzsche's understanding
of love toward a neighbor or an enemy. As we have seen, Nietzsche
understands the morality of equality, contrary to appearances, as a
morality of hatred. He expands upon this through his claim that, also
contrary to appearances, the virtue of loving your neighbor or enemy
cannot be considered to be based on this morality. Only to the noble ones and, therefore, only by shaking off the norm of equality is
"'*love* of one's enemies' possible – supposing it to be possible at all on
earth. How much reverence has a noble man for his enemies! – and
such reverence is a bridge to love."[56] Nietzsche's argument for the
impossibility of loving your enemy within the morality of equality
is that this morality hates the enemy as an evil one and that the man
of this morality hates himself (and that the evil enemy personifies
outwardly what the man of this morality hates of himself). Contrary
to this, the noble man is in the situation to love his enemy: He does
not have to hate his enemy for he does not hate himself. An accomplished relationship with oneself, as is only possible with a strong
or superior life, is – so claims Nietzsche in his reasoning on loving
your enemy and your neighbor – the prerequisite for being able to
enter into an affirmative relationship with the strong or superior life
of another and not having to hate the other as an evil enemy. This
connection between an (accomplished) self-relationship and (affirmative) relationship with the enemy is expressed most clearly by a

piece from *Daybreak* entitled "Do Not Let Your Devil Enter into Your Neighbor!":

Let us for the time being agree that benevolence and beneficence are constituents of the good man; only let us add: 'presupposing that he is first benevolently and beneficently inclined *toward himself*!' For *without this* – if he flees from himself, hates himself, does harm to himself – he is certainly not a good man. For in this case all he is doing is rescuing himself from himself *in others*: let these others look to it that they suffer no ill effects from him, however well disposed he may want to appear! – But it is precisely this: to flee from the ego, and to hate it, and to live in others and for others – that has hitherto, with as much thoughtlessness as self-confidence, been called 'unegoistic' and consequently 'good'.[57]

In his consideration of goodwill and love, Nietzsche brings modes of behavior into play which are not foreseen in his discussion of the confrontation of modes of valuation in slave and noble morality – which indeed represent in the light of this confrontation a genealogical paradox;[58] they are modes of behavior which arise from directing "one's view outward instead of back to oneself"[59] but in which this "directing outward" is not a reaction of hate but an affirmation of the other made possible through an "affirmation of itself."[60]

Responding to this formulation of loving one's neighbor from an affirmative self-relationship, Adorno describes moral attitudes as not to be affected by the negative verdict on the moral law of equality because it weakens and damages just such self-relationships. The pivotal position in Adorno's reconstruction of Kant in his *Negative Dialectics* is in fact occupied by what he refers to as "the impulse of solidarity with what Brecht called 'tormentable bodies'" (ND, 286). There Adorno treats the feeling of solidarity as standing in contrast to the "rationalizing" of morality in the formulation, justification, and application of a moral law of equality. Solidarity is no "abstract principle" but rather a somatic "impulse" or "spontaneously stirring impatience" (ND, 286). This means, however, at the same time that the impulse of solidarity and the observance of the law of morality imply two different, even opposed, ways of self-relation and freedom. This is also what is meant by the final sentence in Adorno's chapter on Kant, that the remainder of morality, which the individual must eventually settle with, consists of that for which "Kantian ethics – which accords affection, not respect, to animals – can muster only disdain: to try to live so that one may believe himself to have been a good animal" (ND, 299). The action stemming from a feeling of solidarity is the action of a "good animal" – of a subject that does not separate itself from its "forces" or "impulses" for the sake of following the law and in order to make itself feel freed from them but rather whose freedom, indeed, whose very strength, consists of allowing its forces or impulses to express themselves. Only in this way, in "harmony," even in "reconciliation," with himself (that is, with his powers and impulses), can man be good to others.[61] "Men are human only where they do not act, let alone posit themselves, as persons" (ND, 277).

With these reflections on the impulse of solidarity, Adorno adopts Nietzsche's reasoning on love but also decisively changes it. And not only because love and benevolence are bound for Nietzsche to awe and admiration for success[62] whereas for Adorno the feeling of solidarity is essentially determined by the reaction to the suffering of others: "The physical moment tells our knowledge that suffering ought not to be, that things should be different. Woe speaks: 'Go'" (ND, 203). Above all, however, Adorno's solidarity concept and Nietzsche's love concept have completely different, even opposing, relations to morality; for our context, this is the crucial aspect. Because Nietzsche views the morality of equality as arising from nothing but *ressentiment*, he has to place love and benevolence in opposition to it outwardly (one belongs to slave morality, the other to the noble morality); there is supposedly no connection between them. That is, however, neither historically nor psychologically plausible and is entirely the result of Nietzsche's implausible founding of morality in *ressentiment*. Adorno's theory of solidarity is able to avoid this conclusion, for in Adorno's analysis the feeling of solidarity and the law of morality do not stand in external opposition to one another. Indeed, the feeling of solidarity, according to Adorno, is the basis of the law of morality, although nonetheless it is distorted by the very law of morality which it founds.

This means that Adorno, in contrast to Nietzsche, who has a homogenous conception, formulates a (literally) "critical" conception of morality, a conception that distinguishes between two fundamentally different dimensions of morality. Unlike in Nietzsche's genealogy, "critique of morality" means for Adorno the discovery of an opposition, even a contradiction, in morality – the unfolding of a dialectic between, on the one side, the "somatic impulse" (the feeling of solidarity with the other individual) and, on the other side, the "abstract principle" of morality (the principle of equal consideration for everyone). Adorno understands this opposition at the same time as the difference between the foundation and the form of morality. In other words, the impulse of solidarity gives rise to morality, but that impulse, when articulated through the moral law of equality, loses its meaning. Adorno therefore understands the critically disclosed opposition within morality, the opposition between moral impulse and moral principle or law, between foundation and form of morality, also as the opposition between what is true and what is false in morality:

> The lines. ["No man should be tortured; there should be no concentration camps"] are true as an impulse, as a reaction to the news that torture is going on somewhere. They must not be rationalized; as an abstract principle they would fall promptly into the bad infinities of derivation and validity. We criticize morality by criticizing the extension of the logic of consistency to the conduct of man; this is where the stringent logic of consistency becomes an organ of unfreedom. (ND, 285–6)[63]

Also, the moral law of equality stems from the impulse of solidarity and not from the triad of fear, hatred, and self-torture, where Nietzsche saw its origins. At the same time, the moral law of equality "rationalizes" the impulse of solidarity, making it an "abstract principle" – and thus destroys it.

It is this critical conception of morality, as intrinsically conflicting or dialectical, that allows Adorno to assume an attitude toward morality that contradicts that of Nietzsche: the attitude that he described as the "realization" of morality "through its transcendence." This attitude toward morality follows from the individual ethics–based critique of the restrictive consequences which morality has for the "right life" of individuals. That explains why morality must be transcended. Contrary to the homogeneous conception of morality in Nietzsche's genealogy, however, morality does not just consist of a form which can cause harm, as the moral law of equality, to life and freedom of the individuals. Rather this form of morality cannot be comprehended if not viewed as the distorted expression of an impulse at the basis of morality, which aims, as the impulse of solidarity, at individuals and the accomplishment of their lives. Therefore, the transcending of morality is at the same time the realization of morality: The transcending of the moral law of equality is the realization of the moral impulse of solidarity with suffering individuals. Or, more precisely, the transcending of the moral law of equality is *only in so far justified* and not an "excuse for recidivism into ancient injustice" to the extent to which it is the realization of morality, the realization of the moral impulse of solidarity with suffering individuals. That is the double thesis articulated by Adorno's seemingly paradoxical identification of realization and transcendence: To realize morality means to transcend it, for to realize morality means to follow the moral impulse of solidarity with suffering individuals even in opposition to the moral law of equality. On the other hand, to transcend morality means to realize it, for to transcend morality means to oppose the moral law of equality only for the sake of solidarity with suffering individuals.

Through this connection between realization and transcendence of morality, Adorno gives the individual ethics–based questioning of morality a completely different normative status than Nietzsche – as much as their questioning may be in agreement as far as process and findings. Adorno unfolds the individual ethics–based critique of morality in which the demand for its transcendence is founded as a critique of morality, yet still carried out on the basis of morality. Because it questions the moral law in the name of individuals and the accomplishment of their lives, the individual ethics–based critique is in itself an act of solidarity with the individuals who suffer from the damage of their lives. Thus Adorno shows that the claim on which Nietzsche and his liberal critics are at one – the claim that the individual ethics-based questioning of morality results in its dissolution – is false. And Adorno also shows what the false premise of this claim is, namely, the premise that the dimension of morality that is the subject of the individual ethics-based critique – the moral law of equality – is the whole of morality. If one misinterprets morality as being homogeneous, as Nietzsche *and* his liberal critics do, then every criticism of the moral law of equality is a dissolution of morality. If, on the other hand, one recognizes, like Adorno, the contradiction within morality, then the individual ethics–based critique of morality comes into its own as the self-critique of morality.

Translated by Rebecca Morrison

NOTES

1. This essay is an interpretative response to the rather sketchy systematic exposition of the project of a critical reflection of morality in my recent essay "Critique and Self-Reflection: The Problematization of Morality," *Constellations* 7, no. 1 (2000): 100–115. For further elaboration see my *Spiegelungen der Gleichheit* (Berlin: Akademie, 2000), esp. pt. 1.

2. Friedrich Nietzsche, *Daybreak: Thoughts on the Prejudices of Morality*, trans. R. J. Hollingdale (Cambridge: Cambridge University Press, 1982), 2.

3. Max Horkheimer and Theodor W. Adorno, *Dialectic of Enlightenment* (New York: Continuum, 1994), 94. Hereafter cited as DA.

4. Niklas Luhmann, *Paradigm Lost: Über die ethische Reflexion der Moral* (Frankfurt: Suhrkamp, 1990).

5. Friedrich Schiller, *Werke*, vol. 5, *Über die ästhetische Erziehung in einer Reihe von Briefen*, ed. H. Fricke and H. G. Göpfert (Munich and Vienna: Hanser, 1980), 577. Translated by Elizabeth M. Wilkinson and L. A. Willoughby under the title *On the Aesthetic Education of Man, in a Series of Letters* (Oxford: Clarendon Press, 1967), 19.

6. Nietzsche, *Daybreak*, 4. For Adorno's use of this figure, see section III.

7. Nietzsche speaks of the self-overcoming of morality because it is undermined by its own orientation toward uprightness and honesty: "After Christian truthfulness has drawn one inference after another, it must end by drawing its *most striking inference*, its inference against itself" (*On the Genealogy of Morals*, trans. Walter Kaufmann [New York: Vintage, 1989], pt. 3, par. 27. In the same way, individual freedom or "sovereignty" only arises from the moral freedom that it suppresses.

8. Nietzsche, *On the Genealogy of Morals*, preface, par. 7.

9. Friedrich Nietzsche, *The Gay Science*, trans. Walter Kaufmann (New York: Vintage, 1974), par. 107.

10. Friedrich Nietzsche, *Beyond Good and Evil; Prelude to a Philosophy of the Future*, trans. Walter Kaufmann (New York: Vintage, 1966), par. 23.

11. Nietzsche, *On the Genealogy of Morals*, preface, par. 6.

12. Nietzsche, *On the Genealogy of Morals*, pt. 3, par. 25.

13. That should not call into dispute what Bernard Williams pointed out, namely, that Nietzsche's moral psychology claims to be "more realistic" than that of its competitors ("Nietzsche's Minimalist Moral Psychology," in *Making Sense of Humanity* [Cambridge and New York: Cambridge University Press, 1995], 65 ff). However, that cannot be the reason for Nietzsche's dissolution of morality. And that is because the question whether "realistic" or "unrealistic" is in its turn itself for Nietzsche a question of the will and of value. See Jean-Luc Nancy, "'Unsere Redlichkeit!' (über Wahrheit im moralischen Sinn bei Nietzsche),"

in *Nietzsche aus Frankreich*, ed. Werner Hamacher (Frankfurt, Berlin, and Vienna: Ullstein, 1986), 169 ff.

14. Nietzsche, *On the Genealogy of Morals*, part 1, par. 17.
15. Nietzsche, *Beyond Good and Evil*, 99.
16. Nietzsche, *On the Genealogy of Morals*, preface, par. 7.
17. Nietzsche, *The Gay Science*, par. 345.
18. Nietzsche, *On the Genealogy of Morals*, preface, par. 6.
19. Nietzsche, *The Gay Science*, par. 344.
20. Nietzsche, *The Gay Science*, par. 345.
21. Nietzsche, *The Gay Science*, par. 345.
22. Nietzsche, *On the Genealogy of Morals*, part 1, par. 16.
23. See Michel Foucault, "Nietzsche, Genealogy, History," in *Language, Counter-Memory, Practice: Selected Essays and Interviews*, ed. Donald Bouchard, trans. Donald Bouchard and Sherry Simon (Ithaca: Cornell University Press, 1977), 139–64. However, here Foucault still understands the nonobjectivity of the genealogical investigation solely as (epistemic) perspectivism, not yet as (ethical) normativity.
24. Friedrich Nietzsche, *Human, All Too Human : A Book for Free Spirits*, trans. Marion Faber (Lincoln and London: University of Nebraska Press, 1984), pt. 2, par. 95.
25. Friedrich Nietzsche, *Nachlaß*, Winter 1870–1 – Autumn 1872, 8 [115], in *Sämtliche Werke*, vol. 7 (Berlin and Munich: de Gruyter/dtv, 1988), 266.
26. See Hinrich Fink-Eitel, "Nietzsches Moralistik," in *Deutsche Zeitschrift für Philosophie* 41 (1993): 865 ff. On the following discussion, see the perfectionist reading of Nietzsche by Daniel W. Conway, *Nietzsche and the Political* (London and New York: Routledge, 1997). This line of thought can be traced back to Stanley Cavell's "Aversive Thinking: Emersonian Representations in Heidegger and Nietzsche," in *Conditions Handsome and Unhandsome* (Chicago: Chicago University Press, 1990), 33 ff.
27. Nietzsche, *Beyond Good and Evil*, 137.
28. Theodor W. Adorno, *Minima Moralia: Reflections from Damaged Life*, trans. E. F. N. Jephcott (London: Verso, 1974), 15. Hereafter cited as MM.
29. Adorno sees therein the signature of the present day: that the patterns of the right life of bourgeois culture have disintegrated, that, however, from this disintegration no better new ones have emerged, for this disintegration gave birth to the rule of a purely functional instrumental rationality.
30. On the relationship between "negativistic" method (which starts from suffering) and positive normative ideal (which leads to a conception of the good life) in Critical Theory, see Axel Honneth, "Anerkennung und

moralische Verpflichtung," in *Zeitschrift für philosophische Forschung* 51 (1997): 25 ff.

31. Theodor W. Adorno, *Negative Dialectics*, trans. E. B. Ashton (New York: Continuum, 1992), 285. Hereafter cited as ND.

32. Nietzsche, *On the Genealogy of Morals*, part 2, par. 18.

33. On Nietzsche's theory of freedom, see Judith Butler, *The Psychic Life of Power: Theories in Subjection* (Stanford: Stanford University Press, 1997), 63 ff.; on Adorno's theory of freedom, see K. Günther, "Dialektik der Aufklärung in der Idee der Freiheit. Zur Kritik des Freiheitsbegriffs bei Adorno," in *Zeitschrift für philosophische Forschung* 39 (1985): 229 ff.

34. Nietzsche, *On the Genealogy of Morals*, part 2, par. 2.

35. Nietzsche, *On the Genealogy of Morals*, part 2, par. 2.

36. Nietzsche, *On the Genealogy of Morals*, part 1, par. 12.

37. Nietzsche, *Beyond Good and Evil*, 139.

38. Thus is Adorno's view of his contrast with Nietzsche; cf. *Minima Moralia*, par. 60 ("A Word for Morality") and par. 100 ("Sur l'Eau"). See Gerhard Schweppenhäuser, *Ethik nach Auschwitz: Adornos negative Moralphilosophie* (Hamburg: Argument Verlag, 1993), 166 ff.

39. Nietzsche, *On the Genealogy of Morals*, part 1, par. 13.

40. Nietzsche, *On the Genealogy of Morals*, part 1, par. 13.

41. This demonstrates where Nietzsche's and Adorno's understanding of the expressive character of free action differs from that of Charles Taylor: For Taylor, it has to do with the expression of meaning, for Nietzsche and Adorno, with that of forces. See Charles Taylor, *Human Agency and Language*, Philosophical Papers 1 (Cambridge: Cambridge University Press, 1985), 90 ff.

42. Nietzsche, *Beyond Good and Evil*, 138–9.

43. Nietzsche, *Beyond Good and Evil*, 116.

44. In its original context, Adorno's concession refers to the impossibility of a purely "immanent" critique of identity: "Therefore, paradoxically enough, to criticize it [i.e., identity] immanently means to criticize it from outside as well" (ND, 145).

45. Nietzsche, *Beyond Good and Evil*, 44.

46. Nietzsche, *On the Genealogy of Morals*, part 3, par. 23.

47. This is Horkheimer's thesis in the morality chapter of *Dialectic of Enlightenment*: The attempt of enlightenment to found morality solely on reason destroys morality, for, as the "black writers of the bourgeoisie" have shown, "formalistic reason" is not "more closely allied to morality than to immorality" (DA, 117 ff.). Moreover, while the rationalistic enlightenment attempts to seek the sole basis for morality in reason alone, it reproduces the hostility toward all affects and feelings,

including moral affects and feelings, thus destroying the only foundation morality can possibly have. The same thesis is put forth by Nietzsche in pointing out that Kant's attempt to find a foundation for morality "has certainly not led us modern philosophers on more firm and less treacherous grounds." Within Kant's rationale to found the "realm of morality" within pure reason, Nietzsche sees nothing but the involuntary acknowledgement of "the thorough *immorality* of nature and history" (*Daybreak*, par. 3).

48. Nietzsche, *On the Genealogy of Morals*, part 1, par. 10.
49. Nietzsche, *On the Genealogy of Morals*, part 1, par. 15.
50. Nietzsche, *On the Genealogy of Morals*, part 1, par. 10.
51. Nietzsche, *On the Genealogy of Morals*, part 1, par. 11.
52. Nietzsche, *On the Genealogy of Morals*, part 1, par. 10.
53. Nietzsche, *On the Genealogy of Morals*, part 1, par. 10.
54. Nietzsche, *On the Genealogy of Morals*, part 2, par. 22.
55. Nietzsche, *Daybreak*, par. 76.
56. Nietzsche, *On the Genealogy of Morals*, part 1, par. 10.
57. Nietzsche, *Daybreak*, par. 516.
58. Following Yovel's formulation of the "genealogical scandal" that Spinoza represents for Nietzsche by connecting traits which, for Nietzsche, are in opposition. See Yirmiyahu Yovel, *Spinoza and Other Heretics: The Adventures of Immanence*, vol. 2 (Princeton, N.J.: Princeton University Press, 1989), 132 ff.
59. Nietzsche, *On the Genealogy of Morals*, part 1, par. 10.
60. Nietzsche, *On the Genealogy of Morals*, part 1, par. 10.
61. Even if the expressive constitution of freedom, as explained above, does not realize the reconciliation "of nature and the mind," it promotes such reconciliation as a "phantasm" (ND, 229). This reconciliation is accompanied, for Adorno, by a reconciliation of, traditionally speaking, morality and good life. For if morality is an expression of a somatic impulse (the impulse of solidarity), and if succeeding life consists of an unfolding of somatic impulses, then acts in accordance with morality are a completion of succeeding life – or so Adorno seems to conclude (ND, 231 ff.). As to the problematic of this conclusion, see below.
62. One can understand this as the Greek strain in Nietzsche's concept of love; see Hans Joas, *Die Entstehung der Werte* (Frankfurt: Suhrkamp, 1997), 45 ff. Joas refers to Max Scheler, "Das Ressentiment im Aufbau der Moralen," in *Gesammelte Werke*, vol. 3, *Vom Umsturz der Werte* (Bern: Francke, 1955), 70 ff. Fundamental for Scheler is the confrontation between "Greek" and "Christian" (hostile to Jews and women; cf. pp. 43 and 53). Adorno's sense of solidarity, on the other hand, is at odds with this differentiation. For solidarity relates to the suffering other

but does not, unlike Christian love, "bow down to it" (Scheler, "Das Ressentiment").

63. In this version, Adorno forgets the argument against compassion formulated by Horkheimer in the *Dialectic of Enlightenment*, which, *mutatis mutandis*, is also true of the feeling of solidarity: the argument that compassion is limited, that it is "always inadequate" (DA, 103). For like compassion, the feeling of solidarity only refers to individuals. Therein lies its deficiency as compared to the idea of justice as articulated by the moral law of equality; this renders the moral law essential in spite of its deficiency.

13 Adorno's Negative Moral Philosophy

Universalism in moral philosophy has been the source of controversy among theorists in the field for years. One can still acquire a solid view of the ethics debate by sorting out the players according to their acceptance or rejection of universalism. For example, you will find Richard M. Hare, John Rawls, and Jürgen Habermas lined up on one side of the universalism divide, and Charles Taylor, Richard Rorty, and Zygmunt Bauman on the other side, with Martha Nussbaum, Seyla Benhabib, and Alex Honneth poised somewhere in between. What does Theodor W. Adorno have to do with all of this? His reflections about the aporias of the good life *(des richtigen Lebens)*[1] and rational praxis date from the 1940s to 1960s. They arose in the context of the decidedly nonethical discussions of the old critical social theory. Their crucial theorems do not, at first glance, exactly invite the interest of today's moral theorists. In *Minima Moralia*, for example, Adorno points out the inner connection between morality and repression. He maintains the thesis that norms and moral principles have, from antiquity to the present, replicated social domination on a theoretical level and that in the false totality of advanced capitalist society the good life is not possible.[2] The problem of universalism in moral philosophy was never explicitly taken up by Adorno. I do believe, nonetheless, that Adorno has a great deal to contribute to our understanding of this problem. He can help us come to terms with the ambivalence specific to and characteristic of universalism in moral philosophy. To do so is necessary, as the controversy between the universalists and the particularists in the current ethics debate has overlooked this ambiguity.

Deontological moral theories – such as that of Rawls, whom, on this point, Habermas's discourse-ethics follows – treat practical discourse as public discussion and limit the sphere of its possible objects to questions of justice. Only thus is it possible – runs the thesis – to find principles that lend themselves to universalization and can legitimately claim universal validity. The sphere which premodern ethics represented by the concepts of happiness and the good life *(guten Lebens)*[3] is relegated to a private matter and excluded from public discourse. The critics of universalistic moral philosophy prefer, conversely, to formulate ethical systems that are based squarely in this sphere and are valid only within limited communities. These theorists thus overlook the objective of critical normativity without which ethical reflection tends to lose its binding power, even within individual societies but all the more so in the "clash of civilizations."[4] A division of labor, however, limits those who assume universalistic perspectives, whether from a monological or a communicative viewpoint, to questions of justice, and they fail no less to mediate universal questions of justice with particular questions of the good life, questions which no modern moral philosophy ought to overlook.[5]

Discourse ethics focuses on the "moral point of view,"[6] characterized by an impartial interest in justice for and the well-being of all subjects who have the capacity to act and by the willingness and competence to build intersubjective consensus regarding controversial normative issues. Ontogenetically, this level constitutes the highest stage in the measurable development of moral judgment. Phylogenetically, the moral point of view is discussed as a regulative idea, as a figure of rationality become actual we must always strive for but will, perhaps, never attain. Universalistic moral principles are the result of development. Moral actors are convinced that the validity claims of such principles can be decided only through discourse. Modernity's project of moral philosophical enlightenment consists, then, in safeguarding moral principles and establishing binding rules for normative discourse. From the perspective of Adorno's negative moral philosophy, however, the question arises whether we can afford, in taking up this position, to dispense with a dialectical critique of the principles themselves. One fundamental assumption of the *Dialectic of Enlightenment* is that the universal realization of enlightened thought is thwarted when the latter fails to reflect upon its own dark side. If we uncritically accept such concepts as freedom, impartiality, justice, and respect, we would overlook something crucially important. The historical index of these concepts, which binds them to their own reverse sides, is by no means a surface matter. As concepts, they are firmly linked to bourgeois society's history of domination. They thus carry within themselves, as modern *coincidentiae oppositorum*, the opposite of what they explicitly stand for. Freedom is fused with unfreedom as long as it only becomes concrete, for individuals, in the free sale of their labor power as a commodity. Impartiality can mean, in a biased society, partisanship: partisanship for the existing state of things. Respect for the other and recognition of the other are never quite separable from the guidelines of behaving through which we learn them: through obedience and fear. If justice is to be understood as "each according to his or her own," this always means: to each only what, under the existing social conditions, he or she is entitled to.[7]

In his genealogy of morals, Michel Foucault arrived at insights similar to Adorno's, but he drew different conclusions from them. When it comes to normative issues, Foucault's archaeological and genealogical critique of power and rationality is ambiguous, since, as Habermas showed, it reduces, "functionalistically," "validity claims...to the effects of power" and, "naturalistically," "the 'ought' to the 'is'."[8] I want to state the thesis that in Adorno we can, in contrast, study how to integrate the ambivalence of fundamental normative ideas into a critical theory of morality without having to forfeit the normative, critical edge of the validity claims of moral philosophy. Kant and Hegel, as much as, of course, Marx, Nietzsche, and Freud, inspire Adorno's critique of moral philosophy, an immanent critique and an ideology critique at the same time. To Adorno, critique of ideology does not mean consigning morality to the dustbin because of the costs of repression, nor does it mean declaring it irrelevant. Adorno was not concerned with a denunciation of bourgeois moral philosophy that, skeptical of rationality, reduces it to mere ideology of domination.

Adorno's contribution to the current discussion within moral philosophy can, in my view, be reconstructed as follows: We all have an interest in gaining rational and moral control over our own social interactions so as to become and remain aware of the constitutive ambivalence underlying ethical intuitions, for we can change only what we know. In particular, only when we reflect on the ambivalence of moral categories can we utilize their liberating power to shape our lives in an autonomous way and thus prevent being dominated by their oppressive side. We can learn from Adorno much about the reasons why the emancipatory potential of a normativity governed by principles is also jeopardized by its own inner dialectic. To make this potential actual, we need such insight.

I. ETHICS AND MORAL PHILOSOPHY

In the writings published during Adorno's lifetime, the normative foundations of his critical theory are not always obvious. More recently, it has become possible to study these foundations in the light of a series of lectures he gave at the University of Frankfurt entitled "Problems of Moral Philosophy".[9] He gave these lectures for the first time in the 1950s and then again at the beginning of the 1960s. One feature of these lectures is striking: Although Adorno was engaged in reflections about *moral philosophy*, he explicitly denied that work on a new *ethics* was needed. His understanding of the relation between ethics and moral philosophy diverges, in this respect, from that which is prevalent today.

As a rule, when we speak about "ethics," we in fact mean a "theory of morality arising from reflection."[10] The term "ethics" is thus synonymous with "moral philosophy." On the other hand, the two terms are as often used in distinctly separate ways, to mark a difference in content. When used thus, "ethics" and "morality" refer to actions in the life-world, whereas "ethics and moral philosophy" refers to systematic philosophical reflection whose subject matter consists of such actions.

Adorno's thoughts about the identity and difference of the concepts of ethics and morality take another direction. In his view, when we use the concept of morality, we assume that public and individual morality[11] already coincide. For Adorno, to speak of "morals" has restrictive, even repressive, implications in the realm of sexuality (PMP, 170). When one speaks of "ethics," one suggests, in contrast, a recourse to the person – one suggests that what counts in ethics are not actions performed according to public conceptions of what is moral but rather that which follows from the actor's own character, his or her specific way of being. So understood, however, "ethics" does turn out to be only the "bad conscience of conscience" [*Schlechtes Gewissen des Gewissens*]: The just demand that

332 GERHARD SCHWEPPENHÄUSER

individual and public morality coincide is retracted in resignation
(PMP, 15). In the intellectual climate of the 1950s, the general tendency to ontologize – to make human nature as we find it, the way
it happens to be, the normative standard – prevailed in Adorno's
eyes in the concept of ethics. As he said in one of his lectures from
1956–7, "The concept of ethics is much more popular than moral
philosophy. It sounds less rigid, seems to have loftier, more humane
connotations. . . . Ethics is flexible, non-binding. . . . It seems to say,
we should derive from simply the way we are, the way we should
behave."[12] What was important to Adorno was to accentuate, in the
Enlightenment tradition, the opposition between nature and moral
rationality. "The moral order. . . is linked to reason, linked to that,
which allows us to rise above nature. Ethos stands in stark contrast
to Kantian moral philosophy." The latter was a central point of reference for Adorno's own reflections.[13] He thus preferred the concept
of morality, whose fundamental problem he thought was crystalized
in "the relation between freedom and law" (PMP, 16).

As long as we live in an "individualistic society," according to
Adorno, "all the problems of moral philosophy come under the general rubric of private ethics" (PMP, 175–6). Consistently within the
philosophical tradition of the Enlightenment, he characterized the
fundamental problem of moral philosophy as the relationship between the individual and the universal. "The central problem of all
moral philosophy is the relationship between the particular, the particular interests, the behavior of the individual, particular human
being and the universal which stands opposed to it." But it would
be a "mistake, if in this conflict. . . we were" simply "to place all
the blame on the side of the universal." For, in fact, the universal
"always contains an implicit claim to represent a moral society in
which force and coercion have ceased to exist" (PMP, 18).[14] This
is the normative horizon of Adorno's reflections on moral philosophy. For him, moral philosophy's fundamental problem was "how to
bring individual interests and claims to happiness into harmony with
some sort of objective norms, binding on mankind as a whole." Yet,
Adorno believed, we will then always find ourselves in the "realm
[of]. . . tensions and contradictions" (PMP, 14). The "social problem
of the divergence between the universal interest and the particular
interest" (PMP, 19) is simultaneously the problem of moral philosophy.

Even today we can follow Adorno's insight. Social realities continue to be characterized by the fact that every particular interest must be set up as a universal interest. We must represent our particular interests as if particular and universal interests already coincide, and as long as this is so, we find ourselves in an aporetic situation of contradiction. According to Adorno, this means that the question of a good life can only be answered by way of determinate negation. In practical terms, we can attempt to conduct our lives in a decent way, even as society as a whole works against us (PMP, 9–10, 175–6). Adorno understood Kierkegaard's and Nietzsche's ethics of existence (with their implicit aesthetic dimensions), more recently revived by Foucault, in terms of determinate negation. In the resistance to heteronomous socialization – in the resistance, also, to the forms of repressive morality sanctioned by society – he discerned the chance for a life *representative* of a good life, the only chance at all possible when life is lived in the wrong (PMP, 168).

On the level of critical theory, however, such a representative ethics of existence as resistance (PMP, 68) can no longer be defined as "ethics." It can be reconstructed as a moment within a critical or, I would say, a "negative" moral philosophy. In the remainder of this essay, I discuss in some detail just such a moral philosophy by focusing on the following six issues: Adorno's theory of moral impulse; the "aporia" and "determinate negation" of morality (in conjunction with Adorno's Nietzsche interpretation); Adorno's theorem of the "modern"; his relation to Kant and Hegel; the "new categorical imperative" after Auschwitz; and, finally, the implications of a critical theory of moral philosophical universalism.

2. THE MORAL IMPULSE

Adorno's theory of the moral impulse must be viewed in connection with two other theories in the tradition of noncognitive moral philosophy, namely, Jean-Jacques Rousseau's and Arthur Schopenhauer's considerations of compassion. Rousseau defines two principles at work in the human soul which serve as the basis for cultural and moral socialization of the *homme naturel*. On the one hand, there is the principle of selfishness at the root of "self-preservation," on the other hand, the principle which "inspires in us a natural repugnance to seeing any sentient being, especially our fellow man [any like ourselves], perish or suffer."[15] Of course, Rousseau does not go so far as to define "commiseration" as a moral principle; he understands it as a basic human drive, in moral terms neutral. In Schopenhauer's thought, the repugnance at the sight of someone else's suffering reemerges with a positive accent, as "that wonderful disposition... by virtue of [which] one man shares the sufferings of another." Though compassion is itself not rational, it is the only rationally recognizable moral principle, "the sole source of disinterested actions."[16] Compassion is the "true basis of morality" – note that Schopenhauer plays compassion off against Kant's universalizable maxims of reason – because compassion alone gives rise to justice and love of mankind.

Adorno, however, did not resume this tradition and try to establish compassion as an affirmative moral principle. He was not looking for a foundation for morality: rather, he sought an element that would foster mimetic solidarity. The latter, however, was not to be played off against the rationality inherent in norms: It was intended to make the subtle yet undeniable interplay between the two transparent. Adorno's theory of moral impulse attempted to determine, in the individual, the reflexive and somatic-mimetic motives for acting in the face of concrete moral challenges. As Adorno wrote in *Negative Dialectics*,

[M]oral questions are... succinctly posed... in sentences such as: There should be no torture; there should be no concentration camps – while all this continues in Asia and Africa and is repressed merely because, as ever, the civilizing humanity is inhumane toward those it shamelessly brands as uncivilized. But if a moral philosopher were to seize upon these sentences and to exult at having caught the critics of morality, caught them quoting the very same values that are happily proclaimed by philosophers of morals, his cogent conclusion would be false. The sentences are true as an impulse, responding to the news that somewhere some are tortured. They must not be rationalized; as abstract principles they would fall promptly into the bad infinities of derivation and validity.[17]

Mimetic motives stand at the center of Adorno's theory. "Naked physical fear and the sense of solidarity with what Brecht called 'tormentable bodies'" are the core of the moral impulse (ND, 286).[18] According to Adorno, "It is in the unvarnished materialistic motive only that morality survives" (ND, 365). This is why we do not find in Adorno's philosophy, as we do in Wittgenstein's, the fundamental skeptical reflection, characteristic of analytic theories of language, that asks whether it is possible to envision someone else's suffering. Wittgenstein says compassion is "a form of conviction that someone else is in pain." For the philosopher of language games, this gives rise to the problem of the "criterion of identity" of the person above all. "If one has to imagine someone else's pain on the model of one's own, this is none too easy a thing to do: for I have to imagine pain which I do not feel on the model of the pain which I do feel."[19] Thinking of pain and the possibility of communicating it to someone else, Niklas Luhmann similarly starts from the assumption that individuals are basically incompatible monads who nevertheless are able to communicate. If we are concerned, not with the communicability of a type of experience that is essentially not of language, but with the moment Adorno marked with the concept (originating in the context of Max Scheler's material ethics of value) of the "moral addendum,"[20] of what cannot be reduced to mind or spirit but is natural and physical – if we are concerned, that is, with an impulse that must be added to reflection – then something quite different is at stake: the problem of whether moral praxis is possible. And this is what Adorno thinks is so tenuous.

3. THE APORIA AND DETERMINATE NEGATION OF MORALITY

From the perspective of critical theory, the aporia of morality can be described in this way: Morality has a repressive and an emancipatory moment. Both are always present at the same time, and one can only come to the fore against the backdrop of the other. For example, if there as no such thing as freedom, we would have no idea what moral commandments were and therefore would not be able to obey them. A life befitting human beings would be inconceivable. But moral commandments come, necessarily, as imperatives which claim unconditional validity. In their validity, their genesis is eclipsed. Their only source of power is the authority vested in them by convention. This means that moral reflection simultaneously grounds the individual's freedom of action and curtails it. The realm of impulses and the mimetic must be suppressed. However, as we can only articulate and realize particular interests and universally valid ones as long as we are persons with the capacity to act, morality, as an instrument of repression, yet paves the way to freedom.

Against this background, Adorno wanted to defend the promise of morality in the face of its inevitable self-destruction. He discerned an antagonism at work in morality, one that reproduces the social antagonism between particular and general interests. The attitude of the moral philosophers toward their own theoretical conduct must express it as well. Already in his lectures of 1956–7, Adorno had spoken of the "double position toward morality" which, as a critical theorist, he must adopt:

We have to accept the moral universal insofar as it is transparent in its relation to humanity become actual, on the one hand, and, on the other hand, in relation to freedom and self-determination of the individual: while conversely, as far as it is oppressive and repressive, all morality stands open to critique.[21]

The immanent contradiction of morality is as follows: On the one hand, morality holds us responsible, imputes to us a freedom to act we do not have; on the other hand and at the same time, morality as critique of our present actions is the "representative of a freedom to come." As philosophers, therefore, we must "be just as much for as against morality." The critique of morality can set its sights neither on an affirmative countermorality, nor on an abstract negation of morality *tout court* – as Nietzsche, for whom this difference was lost, did – but solely on the "determinate negation" of morality. In other words, it must "see that we confront [morality] with its own concept, that we pose the question: is morality moral, does it satisfy the principles which it contains within itself?"[22]

The determinate negation with which Adorno is concerned is meant, not to do away with morality, but rather to point out when and to what extent morality itself becomes immoral. Adorno uses determinate negation as a method of critique and not, as Hegel had done, as an idealist foundation for a new form of positivity. It is not a transition from morality to a concrete ethical life (*Sittlichkeit*) but a negation of negation in Marx's sense. Traditional moral philosophy in its abstract idealist form negated the historical and social foundations with which it was linked. Adorno went on to negate this negation so that the productive core of moral philosophy is further sublated (in the Hegelian sense) in a critical theory of morality.

It is not surprising that Adorno reproached Nietzsche for having negated morality in an *abstract* manner. In his wholesale rejection of the substance of Western moral philosophy, Nietzsche failed, according to Adorno, to distinguish between its ideological and its true aspects. The values he himself set in place then reproduced the moral commandments he wanted abolished. He merely turned them upside down. In his lectures of 1963, Adorno complains that Nietzsche stopped at

the abstract negation of bourgeois morality, or, to put it differently, of a morality that had degenerated into ideology, into a mask which concealed a dirty business. . . . [H]is analysis of the individual moral problems he faced did not lead him to construct a statement of the good life. Instead . . . he came up with a positive morality that is, in fact, none other than the negative mirror-image of the morality he had repudiated. (PMP, 172)

To Adorno's argument, we could raise the objection that Nietzsche rightly understood his critique to be "self-sublimation of morality,"[23] a critique motivated by a concept of morality which would not allow itself to be corrupted and which would shield moral impulses from being instrumentalized and made ideological. Whoever seeks the "self-overcoming of morality"[24] will not want to condemn moral philosophy wholesale: Nietzsche's "immoralism" was a consequence of his morality. Of course, Adorno understood this. His critique of Nietzsche aimed less at the program than the way in which it was carried out. And here the critique is on the mark, since Nietzsche had categorized all contributions to moral philosophy from Plato to Kant and Schopenhauer as symptoms of "decadence." He also did not want to admit that moral philosophy does not always continue to function as ideological veil but often enough is transformed into the impulse to change reality.[25] In other words, it becomes the demand to order social reality in a rational way and to create the basis for human happiness by means of rational praxis. For Nietzsche, moral rationality was merely the regressive suppression of vitalist instincts, the categorical imperative a "Tartuffery," and the concept of intelligible freedom "nonsense."[26] We also must agree with Adorno when he reproaches Nietzsche for wanting to see the restoration of feudal values (PMP, 173). For in Nietzsche's cult of nobility and his advocacy of a new aristocratic morality, his critique of prevailing ideas about morality is transformed into an affirmative vision of domination and social injustice. But in contrast to Georg Lukács, for example, Adorno did not view this as reason enough to

condemn Nietzsche. He tried instead to find a rational core in Nietzsche's errors. Adorno thought that this much truth sticks in the
"brutalities of Nietzsche's moral philosophy": "[In] a society that is
based on force and exploitation, a violence that is unrationalized,
frank and open and, if you like, an 'expiatory violence,' is more innocent than one that rationalizes itself as good" (PMP, 174).[27] In
a radio discussion with Max Horkheimer and Hans-Georg Gadamer
shortly after Adorno's return to liberated Germany,[28] Adorno already
alluded to the ironic, equivocal nature of Nietzsche's writing. Nietzsche's conception of a "liberated person," Adorno stresses, appears
as the mirror image of someone who is not yet free, of someone under the sway of "lies" and "conventional morality." Nietzsche, when
he postulates the shattering of conventions, wanted to bring the latter into sharp relief. Adorno continues to say that, in Nietzsche,
"the model of freedom appears behind the superficial celebration of
oppression."[29]

The central argument of Adorno's metacritique of Nietzsche's critique of morality is that Nietzsche fell prey to his own definition of
slave morality and was taken in by the false appearance of the social conditions of power which he, perhaps better than anyone, had
tracked down and exposed right through to the microcosm of human
psychology. What Nietzsche portrayed in vitalist terms as the manifestation of the will to power, what he conceived of as substance,
what he hypostatized, should have instead been demystified once
more and shown to be a necessary illusion. This time, it must happen from the perspective of possible freedom from domination.

Nietzsche failed to recognize that the so-called slave morality that he exco-
riates is in truth always a master morality, namely the morality imposed on
the oppressed by the rulers. If his critique had been as consistent as it ought
to have been, but isn't – because he too was in thrall to existing social conditions, because he was able to get to the bottom of what people had become,
but was not able to get to the bottom of the society that made them what
they were – it should have turned its gaze to the conditions that determine
human beings and make them and each of us into what we are. (PMP, 174)

Ultimately, Adorno's immanent critique of morality and moral
philosophy ensues in a Marxist critique of the form of morality, one
that understands morality as a "form of voluntary subordination"[30]
which nevertheless holds the potential for autonomy. All the same,

Adorno was careful to stress that Nietzsche had penetrated deeper into the mechanisms of ideology than Marxism had ever done.

4. THEORY OF MODERNITY

One position in the present discourse on ethics resembles Adorno's negative moral philosophy, above all when it assesses the normative as coercive in character and modern rationality as effecting repressive exclusions. I am referring to the "postmodern ethics" of the Polish-born British sociologist Zygmunt Bauman, the 1998 recipient of the Adorno Prize awarded by the city of Frankfurt. Like Adorno, Bauman reflects on the connection between morality and domination. For both writers, philosophy and the sociology of morals blend together: What academic custodians of philosophy consider materialistic deformation and status consciousness, sociologists suspect of being pure metaphysics. On several important points, however, Bauman's ethics also differ considerably from Adorno's negative morality, above all in that the former abandons the *immanent* critique of modernity.[31]

This can be understood from Bauman's theory of modernity, according to which the "substance" of modernity, the "typically modern practice [as] the substance of modern politics, of modern intellect, of modern life, is the effort to exterminate ambivalence."[32] Modern rational thought and action strive for exact definition and logical classification and suppress and destroy what cannot be defined and classified. Modernity's nightmare is chaos, its objective is order: To complete its project of dominating nature, driven by fear, it attempts to annihilate the alien and the different by means of methodical mass murder. Modernity suppresses and drives out ambivalence and creates order by force. In Bauman's eyes, the Holocaust was the sad pinnacle of modernity, "really existing socialism" was its last bastion. Postmodernity, in contrast, is held up as a chance for modernity[33] because it tolerates ambivalence. Postmodernity also represents a new chance because it has abandoned the attitude of "emotionless, calculating reason," the defensive attitude of modernity toward the spontaneity of human beings and the certainty they achieve through instinct and impulse. Finally, postmodernity has come to realize that the reenchantment of the world is the right response to the lost illusions of modernity. One of the main illusions was the belief that a binding universalistic code of ethics could be established. Today's moral philosophers have learned "to accept contingency," "to acknowledge ambiguities," and to see that the ultimate moral authority lies in the individual's moral intuition. This conception is founded in a "picture of postmodernity as modernized modernity."[34] As the values of modernity are promoted by the market, modernity faces, according to Bauman, one problem: the danger of lapsing into indifference.

Bauman is an advocate of ambivalence; he defends its concerns against modernity and believes that postmodernity takes them up (tendentially) well. Yet to Adorno, modernity was *itself* ambivalent. Since reality is processual, since real social conflicts develop a destructive dynamic in which terms of the antagonism merge into each other, only the dialectical method can decode this ambivalence. Adorno's goal was not to preserve ambivalence but rather to use it as an index for decoding social heteronomy, which had not yet been overcome. Adorno would have hardly welcomed postmodernity as a springboard to individual self-determination.

Adorno was a critic of modernity, both in the subjective and the objective sense of the genitive. His dialectical critique of modernity is the critique of a philosopher who belongs to modernity and does not want to abandon its objectives but rather wants to show how these objectives lead, inevitably, to their own undoing. What was important for Adorno was to understand how the normativity characteristic of modernity, the liberal ideology arising from the formal freedom of exchange relations in a commodity-based society, single-handedly destroys itself or resignedly assists in its own downfall long before it is able to test itself against social reality in any extensive or sustained way.[35] In the *Dialectic of Enlightenment*, Adorno and Horkheimer reconstruct the disenchantment of the world in modern Western rationalism as the "retreat of the individual from the mythic powers."[36] But in the fully enlightened final stage – and this is the point of the book – the repressed powers will, transformed, return. As domination of nature through technological, instrumental rationality proceeds, manmade social relations – based on the logic of domination, rationalized through commodity exchange – shall appear immutable, as a second nature. But with a difference: The destructive forces that the triumph over nature unleashes are more destructive than nature itself. This is, according to Adorno and Horkheimer, itself a form of reenchantment. The latter becomes the object of their critique, beholden to rationality's own self-examination. For them, reenchantment was no magic charm, as it is for Bauman: It announced imminent destruction, not deliverance.

What Bauman understands as emancipation from domination, Adorno would have described as merely a change in the way domination perpetuates itself. Bauman thinks that the rational control of human drives in accordance with moral norms has always been the naked rationalization of social domination. The disappearance of this form of domination would consequently appear to postmodern consciousness as an expansion of freedom. Adorno's is not a reductionist approach. According to Bauman, the "postulate of universality" was "a reflection on the modern practice of universalization." His concept of universalism markedly equivocates between the sociopolitical and the moral-philosophical meanings. Political universalization, to Bauman, means the "uniformizing practices and ambitions of the modern state." The unconditional moral authority to which the modern state lays claim historically presupposed "recognizing as moral only such rules as pass the test of some universal, extemporal and extraterritorial principles."[37] Bauman does not shy away from claiming a unity of philosophical universalism and imperialism: "Empires of unconfined and unchallenged sovereignty, and the truth of unlimited and uncontested universality were the two arms with which modernity wished to remold the world according to the design of perfect order."[38] The disempowerment of the communal, territorial, and temporally conditioned foundations of moral judgment by the process of standardization inherent in Western rationality represents, for Bauman, an internal colonization. "The feverish search for the 'foundations' of moral rules could be only prompted and kept urgent," Bauman thinks, by the "task of convincing" the dominated. "Indeed, coercion by law stands a chance of being accepted with a minimum of murmur if the law in the name of which coercion had been threatened could be shown to be more than just a whim of the legislators."[39] Moral rules' formal similarity to legal principles and their discursive character have the function of lending them the appearance of legitimacy: For this reason moral philosophy makes use of the analogy with law.

5. KANT AND HEGEL

Adorno did not miss this side of the success story of bourgeois domination replicated within. With the help of Sigmund Freud, Adorno enumerated and presented Kant with the immense costs of rigorist moral theory. Internalization perpetuates domination and gives rise to a cycle of repression and the return of violence (ND, 271). In the end, it contributes to the failure of culture. But Adorno did not see only this side. He did not overlook the other, underlying moment, the critical idea of autonomy and the truth content of moral postulates. This is often misrepresented in the literature that addresses Adorno's relation to Kant. Adorno's – to be sure often unjust – critique, in which he specifically emphasizes the way the categorical imperative repressively sublimates the authority of the superego, is often taken to be Adorno's final word on Kant. As a result, many writers have not seen that Adorno also, conversely, uses Kant to take Freud to task. Adorno thoroughly approved of Kant's refusal to subject human conscience to a genetic-psychological critique: he recognized, here, the legitimate claim of moral validity against all relativistic attempts to reduce morality to psychology. The critical and anticipatory truth content of a rationally grounded moral philosophy cannot be credited to the constantly damaged subjectivity of "empirical character." The latter cannot serve as a moral measure. Adorno thought that the claim to validity raised in Kant's moral law anticipates a free form of socialization among autonomous individuals, who only in this way would become capable of acting morally. Adorno describes the "crux" of Kant's doctrine of freedom as "a conception incompatible with any empiricism – that moral objectivity, and the just social order it implies, cannot be measured by the way . . . men happen at any given time to be."[40]

Placing the individual at the center of his ethics of conscience,[41] Kant conceived him adequately as autonomous; abstracting the real state of heteronomous mediation, he hypostasized him no less. In contrast, the content of Hegel's sublation of morality, according to Adorno, is the experience of the individual all but unable to change heteronomous reality through his or her own efforts. Hegel, however, converted this experience to affirmative terms. He did not criticize how irrational conditions obstruct the rational will but passed off these conditions as the adequate realization of the latter. In Adorno's view, Hegel thus legitimized social repression: Individuals are subject to coercive social mechanisms which they have created, and having no awareness of the internal dialectic at work, at whose mercy they nonetheless find themselves, they are exposed to these mechanisms as to forces of nature. Hegel let his theory of moral philosophy pass over into political theory, but this was an abstract negation. "Because Hegel extended the concept of morality into the political realm, he dissolved it."[42] According to Adorno, this dissolution cannot be true, because it remains a theoretical construct to which no real mediation between the political and moral spheres in the world corresponds. If the moral sphere is theoretically dissolved into the political sphere, the individual's spontaneity is as compromised conceptually as in fact it already is under the historical conditions of social heteronomy. Hegel thus only further limits the spontaneity ever to be realized.

To proclaim that freedom has become reality is tantamount to assuming that we can dispense with the notion of morality because its substance has been successfully and completely sublated in an ethical life in the political realm. For this reason, according to Adorno, in the area of moral philosophy, the antipodes Kant and Hegel remain equal as exponents of truth and untruth – until, that is, the social situation itself moves in the direction of a practical reconciliation of the particular with the universal:

Kant's moral philosophy and Hegel's philosophy of right represent two dialectical stages of the bourgeois self-consciousness of praxis. Split as they are between the particular and the universal, the two poles which tear that consciousness apart, both are also false; each is right in opposition to the other so long as no possible higher figure of praxis is revealed in reality.[43]

Adorno's assessment, however, ultimately was not even-handed: He remained a staunch critic of Hegel. Hegel's apology for power, as it evolves in the philosophy of right and philosophy of history, in which Hegel blithely disregards individuals and their experience of the overwhelming force of the social and historical universal, is, to Adorno, ideological. Adorno sided with the individual and strongly argued, in the end, against Hegel's pretended reconciliation of the individual with the totality, as, for example, in his critique of Hegel's subsumption of subjective conscience under the norm of objective ethical life, which takes the shape of positive legal norm (ND, 402).

6. THE NEW CATEGORICAL IMPERATIVE

Just how much Adorno was indebted to Kant's moral philosophy is evident in the extensive commentary on and interpretation of Kant in his lectures of 1963. This comes to light no less in connection with an ethical theorem, especially important to Adorno: the new categorical imperative after Auschwitz.

A new categorical imperative has been imposed by Hitler upon unfree mankind: to arrange their thoughts and actions so that Auschwitz will not repeat itself, so that nothing similar will happen again. When we want to find reasons for it, this imperative is as refractory as the given one of Kant was once upon a time. Dealing discursively with it would be an outrage, for the new imperative gives us a bodily sensation of the moral addendum: bodily, because it is now the practical abhorrence of the unbearable physical agony to which individuals are exposed, even with individuality about to vanish. (ND, 365)[44]

Adorno's new imperative combines fundamental normative reflection with reflection on the historicity of ethical problems rooted in the specificity of the situation. Adorno thus fashioned a new moral principle which, contrary to Kant's imperative, is bound with a unique historical and social constellation.

A categorical imperative, which Kant conceived of as an expression of freedom and moral autonomy, is now "forced on" mankind. Critics who consider this contradiction to be a mistake on Adorno's part have missed the central point. The confidence, justified in Kant, that it is possible to realize autonomy as a principle of socialization for free individuals has, in Adorno, given way to the awareness that the only thing which matters any more is to struggle against the heteronomy of mankind, determined in its antagonistic social relations, as much as possible. The categorical, unconditional, and self-grounding claim to validity of Kant's categorical imperative is guaranteed by its formal character, even though it is also to be considered a "fact of reason." In Adorno's case, the categorical imperative's claim to validity is brought to bear in conjunction with historical experience and our interest in abolishing suffering. As it is heteronomous in this – and only in this – respect, Adorno's imperative does not result in absurdity. Every positively formulated ethical maxim, regardless of whether it relates in terms of content to the good life or in terms of form to moral action, must reflect back the historical actuality of the catastrophe manifested in Auschwitz. Adorno works from the assumption that we are no longer in a position to speak about what should be but only what must not be. Formulated *ex negativo*: Although an emphatic claim to validity can be ascribed to normative critical principles, this claim is no longer "unconditional." It is, rather, determined both by the state of reality, which in moral terms is in need of change, and by our interest in seeing such a change take place, an interest from which we can no longer turn away. This interest, therefore, can never be derived from anything else.

Adorno is here concerned with a self-evident motive of materialist moral philosophy: the notion of humanity at peace. He hesitates to measure his moral imperative against criteria of discursive justification, criteria grounded in logical arguments, but not because he thinks it impossible to cite rational grounds for his moral imperative. Rather, the very requirement of providing logically incontestable grounds, without which a moral imperative, presumably, cannot lay claim to any validity, would make a mockery of the content of Adorno's imperative, its founding experience. In other words, it would itself be morally untenable. This is why the demand seemed blasphemous to Adorno.[45] Such grounding may indeed be possible, but in the face of the suffering wrought by mankind, unfathomable and manifest, it would be presumptuous to require us to legitimate, by skillful argument, our demand to see suffering abolished. It does follow, from these considerations, that theoretical arguments alone cannot found Adorno's new categorical imperative. It does not follow, however, that this imperative must be essentially incompatible with such arguments or be undermined or disproved by them. On the contrary, it is certainly possible to give good theoretical arguments for this imperative, and Adorno, after all, did himself do so, much as Marx was able plausibly to ground his anthropological and emancipatory "categorical imperative to overthrow all conditions in which man is a debased, enslaved, neglected, and contemptible being."[46]

The only problem is that in this case Adorno did not spell out exactly what he meant by "grounding." In the German text, Adorno writes of the predicament of "finding reasons for" the new categorical imperative: "er ist . . . widerspenstig gegen seine *Begründung.*"⁴⁷ That is, the new categorical imperative is refractory against grounding. What does "grounding" mean in Adorno – providing an ontological foundation, rational arguments, or a combination of both? If we look at the issues involved in Adorno's notion of grounding in the context of the current discussion taking place in contemporary practical philosophy, we can perhaps better see what may have been at stake for Adorno. Analytic philosophy has demonstrated that it is logically inadmissible to ground the binding value of a moral principle in yet another moral ground. But analytic philosophy draws the wrong conclusion from this, namely, that it is absolutely impossible to ground moral principles. In contrast, neo-Aristotelian ethics bases its moral principles on a faculty of practical judgment oriented toward human goods, and Kantian deontological ethics, as well as discursive ethics, derives the binding force of its moral principles from formal-universalistic rules of generalization.⁴⁸

To set out an affirmative moral principle and to ground a moral philosophy on the binding nature of such a principle is precisely what Adorno did not want to do. At the heart of his moral philosophy is a negatively formulated categorical imperative that says what must never happen, what must not be. It does not say, in a positive way, how we are to prevent "what must not be." The imperative draws its evidence from historical experience. From a systematic standpoint, it has recourse to nothing other than the moral impulse. Adorno makes this explicit in terms of a materialist theory of the experience of suffering as it spontaneously reflects upon itself.

In the final analysis, however, Adorno's wholesale rejection of the requirement of grounding morality is not plausible. For the question remains, why is it that all discursive arguments must always result in the "bad infinity" of "derivation and validity" (ND, 285)? Why do they have to a priori end up as rationalizations in the form of an ethical philosophy of principles? The question is whether Adorno wanted to reject universalization along with the demand for rational grounds. If we deprive moral propositions of their own theoretical grounds, we can hardly maintain that they are normatively binding for everyone, everywhere, and at all times. This, however, would conflict with Adorno's intention: to pursue a critique of moral philosophy for the sake of the good and the right life. Even if Adorno provides no actual answer to the question of grounds, it is nevertheless possible to try to construct such an answer that takes into account his normative objectives. First, we must see that because negative moral philosophy is not based on nondiscursive moral intuitions, it can be disassociated from irrationalistic arguments for morality. And second, according to Gunzelin Schmid Noerr, Adorno's categorical imperative is not a principle "which could ground morality altogether"; rather, it grounds only a "*minimal morality* of respect for unafflicted life."[49]

7. CRITICAL THEORY OF UNIVERSALISM IN MORAL PHILOSOPHY

Bauman negates moral-philosophical universalism abstractly. The problem in Adorno's case is, rather, that he gives no theory of universalism but merely indications of its immanent dialectic. The following quote will serve as an example. Its context is the aporias of the Auschwitz trials, begun in Frankfurt in 1965. "The incompatibility of every general moral judgment with psychological determination – an incompatibility which nonetheless does not relieve us of the judgment that something is evil – comes from the objective antagonism, not from inconsistent thought" (ND, 286). Adorno clarified what he meant by this in discussing the aporetic situation in which critical consciousness finds itself when it attempts to critique the amoral actions of those involved in the National Socialist system of concentration camps. We must pass moral judgment on the perpetrators, but confronted with a psychological inability to act freely, universalizable moral judgments remain impotent. It does not follow that the perpetrators are thereby excused. The lawful exercise of justice – morally legitimate and necessary – would nonetheless remain locked in the logic of violence which underlay the actions of the perpetrators. As Adorno wrote at the time of the trials, "The latest stand of the moral dialectic concentrates on this point: acquittal would be a barefaced injustice; but a just atonement would be infected with the principle of brute-force, and nothing but resistance to it is humanity" (ND, 286).

Against the backdrop of this extreme situation, the inadequacy of "every universal moral judgment" becomes apparent. Adorno thinks, however, that this is so *in every case*. A critical theory of moral-philosophical universalism begun in this way does not negate, abstractly, the necessary claim of moral judgments to universality; rather, it will formulate the insight into their inescapable aporia. The aporia is *given* to us. Without the claim to universality, we would have no criterion of judgment, yet from this criterion it *does not follow* that empirical actions of empirical individuals are compatible with moral norms that can be universalized.

Questions regarding the criteria for moral action and a normative concept of justice are of central importance today. In phrasing these questions, Bauman's conception of postmodern ethics helps less than Adorno's method of immanent critique (the determinate negation of morality), together with the (Aristotelian) transition from private ethics to the political, a proposal with which Adorno ends his lectures on the *Problems of Moral Philosophy* (165 ff.). This links the older Critical Theory with current attempts to make critical normativity the standard for social praxis. In discussion with Emmanuel Levinas and Jacques Derrida, Axel Honneth has demonstrated that the asymmetrical relationship of responsibility, which Bauman also relies on, cannot be made a principle of morality, even though it may well be a fundamental experience in the emergence of the individual's moral consciousness. Only the universalistic moral point of view of equal treatment can claim validity as a systematic moral principle.[50] It is not at all the case that in modernity this moral point of view has proven to be only a destructive egalitarian ideology aimed at leveling all differences. Instead, it has provided an idea of justice that stands against facts, that obligates all of us to contribute to its general realization in society. In her theory of "interactive universalism," Seyla Benhabib has attempted to supplement the moral point of view with the added dimension of the ability and willingness to "reverse perspectives," the faculty of "enlarged thinking."[51] The faculty of universalization must not finish as a discursive exercise in coming to an understanding and *thinking* in terms of the *universal* other; rather it must also include the capacity to recognize the other as a *concrete* other. Moral-philosophical reflections about justice are mediated with ethical reflections about life-world conditions, which dictate how we act. This specific attempt to mediate the universal with the particular is inspired by the fundamental question of Adorno's moral philosophy: "how to bring individual interests and claims to happiness into harmony with objective norms binding on mankind as a whole" (PMP, 14). Without the continuing influence of Adorno's reflections, current attempts at a sympathetic but self-critical transformation of moral philosophical universalism can hardly be imagined.

Translated by Cara Gendel Ryan and Michael McGettigan;
translation edited by Simon Krysl

NOTES

1. *Translator's note*: Adorno's distinction between the "good life" [*gutes Leben*] of traditional moral philosophy and the "good life" or right life [*richtiges Leben*], the notion or the not-yet of his own negative moral philosophy, has to be respected. In Adorno's German, the allusion of *richtig* to *Recht* – right (life) and *the* right (or *a* right) – is implicit but less obvious than in English. Dialectically, Adorno's "*richtiges Leben*" can be heard to imply what *richtiges Leben* signifies, the negative mediation of good life and the right. In his *Problems of Moral Philosophy* (trans. Rodney Livingstone [Stanford, Calif.: Stanford University Press, 2000], hereafter cited as PMP), Adorno speaks of the "locus of right action" [*richtigen Handelns*] according to Kant, "namely the moment of freedom in the absence of which good [*richtiges*] life cannot be even imagined" (p. 6, but see also p. 1). For a translator, this constellation of concepts *must* present problems: We have chosen to side with Rodney Livingstone (*Problems in Moral Philosophy*) against E. F. N. Jephcott (*Minima Moralia*) and to use "good life" as the translation, but one can as easily go the other way around. The task of the translator may be to explicate as well as to preserve the ambiguity.

2. Theodor W. Adorno, *Minima Moralia: Reflections from Damaged Life*, trans. by E. F. N. Jephcott (London: New Left Books, 1974), 39, 184.

3. The "good life" here stands for the German "*gutes Leben*" (not "*richtiges Leben*").

4. Samuel P. Huntington, *The Clash of Civilizations and the Remaking of World Order* (New York: Simon and Schuster, 1996).

5. Seyla Benhabib, *Critique, Norm and Utopia: A Study of the Foundations of Critical Theory* (New York: Columbia University Press, 1986), 328–30.

6. Discourse ethics thus follows the studies of Lawrence Kohlberg, *The Psychology of Moral Development: The Nature and Validity of Moral Stages* (San Francisco: Harper and Row, 1984). See also Jürgen Habermas, "Remarks on Discourse Ethics," in *Justification and Application:*

Remarks on Discourse Ethics (Cambridge, Mass.: MIT Press, 1993), 19–112.

7. The principle of *suum cuique* is, in itself, problematic enough: It did not, unfortunately, become problematic only when it was perversely inscribed as a motto on the gate of the Nazi concentration camp Buchenwald on the outskirts of Weimar.

8. Jürgen Habermas, *The Philosophical Discourse of Modernity* (Cambridge, Mass.: MIT Press, 1987), 276.

9. The taped lecture course of May-July 1963 has been published as vol. 10, part 4 of Adorno's *Nachgelassene Schriften: Probleme der Moralphilosophie*, ed. Thomas Schröder (Frankfurt: Suhrkamp, 1996); English edition: *Problems of Moral Philosophy*. See note 1 above. The lectures from the winter of 1956–7 (recorded in shorthand) have not been published yet.

10. See Niklas Luhmann, "Ethik als Reflexionstheorie der Moral," *Gesellschaftsstruktur und Semantik* 3 (1989): 358–447 (in English, Niklas Luhmann, "Paradigm Lost: On the Ethical Reflection of Morality: Speech on the Occasion of the Award of the Hegel Prize 1989," *Thesis Eleven* 29 [1991]: 82–94).

11. *Translator's note:* English "morality" translates both German *Moralität* and *Sittlichkeit*. The Hegelian translation is "ethical life," but outside a Hegelian context this brings the unwelcome connotation of *ethics*. We have translated according to context.

12. Adorno's lecture from November 11, 1956, quoted by Gerhard Schweppenhäuser, *Ethik nach Auschwitz: Adornos negative Moralphilosophie* (Hamburg: Argument Verlag, 1993), 7.

13. Adorno, quoted by Schweppenhäuser, *Ethik nach Auschwitz*, 7.

14. Translation modified.

15. Jean-Jacques Rousseau, preface to the "Discourse of the Origin of Inequality," in *The Basic Political Writings*, ed. and trans. Donald A. Cress (Indianapolis, Ind.: Hackett, 1987), 35.

16. Arthur Schopenhauer, *On the Basis of Morality*, trans. E. F. J. Payne, introduction by David E. Cartwright (Providence, R.I.: Berghahn, 1995), 182–3. On Adorno and Schopenhauer, see Gunzelin Schmid Noerr, "Moralischer Impuls und gesellschaftliche Reflexion: Das Verhältnis der Kritischen Theorie zur Mitleidsethik," in Schmid Noerr, *Gesten aus Begriffen: Konstellationen der Kritischen Theorie* (Frankfurt: Fischer, 1997), 153–97.

17. Theodor W. Adorno, *Negative Dialectics*, trans. E. B. Ashton (New York: Continuum, 1983), 285 (translation modified). Hereafter cited as ND. The bad infinity – it may not be necessary to add – refers to the infinite chain of logical justification: As every ground of the sentences requires

a further ground, they can never, in the abstract, be grounded fully. As moral, these principles must have a claim to absolute validity precisely because they are always embedded in a concrete situation. They do not – ideologically – clothe a particular ("civilization") as an abstract universal; they are true in an immediate sense.

18. In his poem about Walter Benjamin, "Zum Freitod des Flüchtlings W.B.," Brecht spoke of the "tormentable body" [*quälbarer Leib*] ("On the Suicide of the Refugee W.B.," in *Poems 1913–1956*, ed. John Willett and Ralph Mannheim [London: Methuen, 1979], 363). In *Negative Dialektik* (Frankfurt: Suhrkamp, 1984), Adorno writes of "*quälbarer Körper*" (p. 281).

19. Ludwig Wittgenstein, *Philosophical Investigations*, trans. G. E. Anscombe, 2nd ed. (Oxford: Blackwell, 1958), pars. 287, 253, 302.

20. Das "*Moment des Hinzutretenden am Sittlichen*" (ND, 365). See Max Scheler, *Formalism in Ethics and Non-formal Ethics of Value* (Evanston, Ill.: Northwestern University Press, 1973), chap. 3; see also PMP, 2.

21. Adorno's lecture from December 6, 1956, quoted in Schweppenhäuser, *Ethik nach Auschwitz*, 177.

22. Adorno's lecture from February 26, 1957, quoted in Schweppenhäuser, *Ethik nach Auschwitz*, 179.

23. *Selbstaufhebung*: Friedrich Nietzsche, preface to *Daybreak: Thoughts on the Prejudices of Morality*, trans. R. J. Hollingdale (Cambridge: Cambridge University Press, 1997), par. 4.

24. *Selbstüberwindung der Moral*: Friedrich Nietzsche, "*Beyond Good and Evil*, in *Basic Writings of Nietzsche*, ed. and trans. Walter Kaufmann (New York: Modern Library, 1966), par. 32.

25. See Gerhard Schweppenhäuser, *Nietzsches Überwindung der Moral: Zur Dialektik der Moralkritik in Jenseits von Gut und Böse und in der Genealogie der Moral* (Würzburg: Königshausen u. Neumann, 1988).

26. *Tartufferie*: Nietzsche, *Beyond Good and Evil*, par. 5; *Unsinn*: Nietzsche, *Twilight of the Idols Or, How One Philosophizes with a Hammer*," in *The Portable Nietzsche*, ed. and trans. Walter Kaufmann (Harmondsworth, England: Penguin, 1976), par. 8 of "The Four Great Errors," p. 500.

27. Adorno takes the notion of "expiatory violence" *(entsühnende Gewalt)* from Walter Benjamin's "Critique of Violence," in *Reflections: Essays, Aphorisms, Autobiographical Writings*, ed. Peter Demetz (New York: Schocken, 1986), 297.

28. Theodor W. Adorno, Max Horkheimer, and Hans-Georg Gadamer, "Über Nietzsche und uns: zum 50. Todestag des Philosophen," in

Max Horkheimer, *Gesammelte Schriften*, vol. 13, ed. Gunzelin Schmid Noerr (Frankfurt: Fischer, 1989), 111–20, quotations from pp. 114–5.

29. Adorno, Horkheimer, and Gadamer, "Über Nietzsche und uns," 115.
30. Wolfgang Fritz Haug, "Marx, Ethik und ideologische Formbestimmtheit der Moral," in *Ethik und Marx: Moralkritik und normative Grundlagen der Marxschen Theorie*, ed. Emil Angehrn and Georg Lohmann (Königstein, Germany: Hain Verlag bei Athenäum, 1986), 46.
31. See Gerhard Schweppenhäuser, "Das Unbehagen an der Moral: Zur Kritik der Ethik bei Adorno und Bauman," *Das Argument* 231–41, no. 4 (1999): 513–26.
32. Zygmunt Bauman, *Modernity and Ambivalence* (Ithaca: Cornell University Press, 1991), 7.
33. See Bauman, *Modernity and Ambivalence*, 257.
34. Wolfgang Bonss, "Die uneindeutige Moderne: Anmerkungen zu Zygmunt Bauman," *Mittelweg* 36, no. 4 (1993): 28.
35. Hauke Brunkhorst, *Theodor W. Adorno: Dialektik der Moderne* (Munich and Zurich: Piper, 1990); in English under the title *Adorno and Critical Theory* (Cardiff: University of Wales Press, 1999).
36. Max Horkheimer and Theodor W. Adorno, *Dialectic of Enlightenment*, trans. John Cumming (New York: Continuum, 1995), 46.
37. Zygmunt Bauman, *Postmodern Ethics* (Oxford: Blackwell, 1993), 39.
38. Zygmunt Bauman, *Modernity and Ambivalence*, 255.
39. Zygmunt Bauman, *Postmodern Ethics*, 65.
40. Theodor W. Adorno, "Sociology and Psychology," trans. Irving N. Wohlfarth, *New Left Review* 46 (1967): 67–80; 47 (1968): 79–97 (quotation from p. 83). See Gerhard Schweppenhäuser, "Die Selbstdestruktion des Kultur-Überichs: Überlegungen zu den Grundlagen von Kultur- und Moralkritik bei Adorno," in *Impuls und Negativität: Ethik und Ästhetik bei Adorno*, ed. Mirko Wischke and Gerhard Schweppenhäuser (Hamburg: Argument-Verlag, 1995), 198–214.
41. The notion of the ethics of moral tenor, viz. conscience [*Gesinnungsethik*], originates in the work of Max Scheler and Max Weber; it is opposed to the ethics of success [*Erfolgsethik*] in Scheler and to the ethics of responsibility [*Verantwortungethik*] in Weber.
42. Theodor W. Adorno, "Marginalien zu Theorie und Praxis," in *Gesammelte Schriften*, vol. 2, pt. 2, *Kulturkritik und Gesellschaft*, 764 ff. Translated by Henry W. Pickford under the title "Marginalia to Theory and Praxis," in Theodor W. Adorno, *Critical Models: Interventions and Catchwords* (New York: Columbia University Press, 1998), 259–78.
43. Adorno, "Marginalien zu Theorie und Praxis," 765.
44. Adorno's "*Frevel*" – here, "outrage" – can also suggest "blasphemy." The religious connotation is at most a connotation, a result of a very

particular reading of Adorno. The discourse on the new categorical imperative is, as a whole, a discourse on the absolute: yet, both like and unlike Kant's, a *materialist* discourse on a *this-worldly* absolute. But this is also to say that *Frevel*, unlike an outrage, is *objective*, not subjective – contrary, shall we say, to moral law, not manners. To dissolve the imperative in a chain of justifications is to laugh in the face of human dignity.

45. See n. 44.
46. Karl Marx, introduction to *A Contribution to the Critique of Hegel's Philosophy of Right*, trans. Gregor Benton, in *Early Writings*, ed. Quintin Hoare (London: New Left Books, 1974), 251.
47. Adorno, *Negative Dialektik*, 385 (emphasis added).
48. Ulrich Steinvorth, *Klassische und Moderne Ethik: Grundlinien einer materialen Moraltheorie* (Hamburg: Rowohlt, 1990), 46–61.
49. Gunzelin Schmid Noerr, "Kritik der Ethik in moralischer Absicht: anlässlich neuerer Versuche, Adornos Ethik zu rekonstruieren," *Allgemeine Zeitschrift für Philosophie* 24, no. 1 (1999): 79.
50. Axel Honneth, "The Other of Justice: Habermas and the Ethical Challenge to Postmodernism," in *The Cambridge Companion to Habermas*, ed. Stephen K. White, (Cambridge: Cambridge University Press, 1995), 318.
51. Seyla Benhabib, *Situating the Self: Gender, Community, and Postmodernism in Contemporary Ethics* (New York: Routledge, 1992), 9 ff., chaps. 1 and 5, and passim.

14   Adorno's Social Lyric, and Literary Criticism Today

Poetics, Aesthetics, Modernity

Theodor Adorno would shudder – then again, maybe not – to see what's become of his celebrated 1957 essay "On Lyric Poetry and Society."[1] Actually, the question of whether he'd be shaken by recent interpretations of the essay may be less interesting than the related matter of whether those analyses are anticipated by Adorno's own theory. That is, the readings at issue, despite or even because of their manifestly left-wing intentions, may stem from what Adorno would see as a grimly predictable, instrumentalist negation of his negative dialectic: a perverse cancellation-by-programmatic-affirmation of the philosophical aesthetics Adorno had developed precisely to trouble the neat dialectical syntheses and closures of fellow Marxian critics.

The relevant interpretations of "On Lyric Poetry and Society" have arisen in mostly academic Anglo-American treatments of late eighteenth century through twentieth-century poetry (though applications sometimes reach back as far as Renaissance lyric); they have more or less assimilated Adorno's essay to the influential theory or argument known, in recent literary criticism, as the "critique of aesthetic ideology," which has at times seemed to make itself almost synonymous with Marxian or Marxian-inflected criticism in general. The critique of aesthetic ideology holds that high romantic poetics and Kantian aesthetics – building on eighteenth-century advances in bourgeois sociopolitical power – establish an essentialist or transcendental theory of cultural value. This is said to be an *ideological* theory whose function, enacted practically through literary/aesthetic experience and form, is to serve bourgeois hegemony by rerouting attention, interest, and energy from the sociopolitical to the artistic-cultural realm. This bourgeois theory's Other, from romanticism through modernism, will consequently be the material, the sociopolitical, and the historical, all of which the critique of aesthetic ideology understands to be subjugated or erased – ideologically *de*formed – by artistic-philosophical form. The critique's overarching analysis (of high romanticism's and then modernism's character and foundationality vis-à-vis canonical notions of literary, artistic, and cultural value) has of course frequently been articulated in the vocabulary and syntax of Marxian or Marxian-inflected methodology. It is therefore not surprising that the critique's analysis has wished to rely in significant part on Frankfurt School Critical Theory, with particular emphasis initially on the work of Walter Benjamin and then, with increasing frequency, on that of Adorno.[2]

But despite shared concerns about the sociohistorical, Frankfurt School theory – Adorno's especially, and above all his decades-long meditation on Benjamin's oeuvre – diverges sharply from critique-of-aesthetic-ideology views about poetics and aesthetics since Romanticism. The divergence is perhaps clearest in the case of poetry. The "lyric formalism" which to aesthetic-ideology critics looks like an escape from the social, like a balefully hermetic, elitist self-involvement that eschews nuts-and-bolts materialism, appears to Adorno as something different; it appears to him as a crucible for the modern artistic experimentalism indispensable to Marxian dialectics and other progressive methodologies of criticism, not to mention Frankfurt School Critical Theory's own project of investigating and knowing the new, of making it available to perception in the first place. (For the Frankfurt School, "the new" is understood ultimately in relation to not yet grasped features of the mode of production and, in fact, of all that is emergent in the social.) Yet recent ideology-critique rehearsals of "On Lyric Poetry and Society" emphasize – understandably – the essay's comments concerning ideology, false consciousness, and class antagonism. They regularly present Adorno's essay as an injunction to demystify poetic language so that critical knowledge of the poem's hidden social ground may be brought to light, as if Adorno were an antiformalist whose primary agenda was the demonstration of auratic lyric form's "aestheticist" mandate, its allegedly reactionary tendency to obscure sociopolitical content and to propagate false consciousness.[3] The point is then made, in Adorno's name, that attention to formal poetics is, at most, to be treated punctually, because the better, less romanticizing or less

aestheticizing strategy is to concentrate on working up a full sociology of the poem's contexts and thus, the argument goes, of the
poem's participation in the sociopolitical.[4]

Adorno's essay does contain language that might be deemed consonant with ideology-critique and with the latter's frequently twinned
impulse of utopian countergesture. Adorno notes, for instance, that
modern lyric "poetic subjectivity is itself indebted to privilege" (NL,
45/88); its remarkable elevated or sublime irony "was always bourgeois" (NL, 42/82); its "self-absorption, its detachment from the social surface, is socially motivated" (NL, 48/84–5) despite any contrary
belief on the poet-subject's part; meanwhile, in its liberatory aspect,
modern lyric becomes "the voice of human beings between whom
the barriers have fallen" (NL, 54/104), and so forth. But Adorno's
argument finally travels in a different direction than might be pre-
dicted from these important registrations of lyric's inextricable connections to existing society, ruling ideologies, and utopian impulse.
Before textually locating that different movement, it's worth pausing
to notice the light shed by the paratexts and by the most contextu-
ally focused commentaries in the essay's Anglo-American reception
history.

Prior to Shierry Weber Nicholsen's indispensable translation of
Noten zur Literatur (1991–1992), the essay's most cited English version was the one Bruce Mayo had made for a 1974 issue of *Telos*,
and as Mayo's *Telos* introduction carefully explains, Adorno's essay
invites historicization as much as any poem or period to which it is
applied.[5] In fact, some of Adorno's most knowledgeable and sympathetic critics have observed that – alongside concerns about the essay's being anachronistically or uncritically pressed into service for
projects inimical to it – there's also cause to wonder about the essay's
status relative to Adorno's other meditations on lyric and the social.
Deeper exploration of the subject may occur, it has been suggested,
in texts where Adorno engages particular poets (as well as historical
and philosophical aesthetics) in a more sustained manner than the
somewhat programmatic character of "On Lyric Poetry and Society"
seems to allow.[6] Still, the essay has for decades been correctly identified as at least sketching Adorno's major positions on the trajectories
of modern poetry and poetics, aesthetics, and criticism, and its acces-
sibility and brevity probably will continue to ensure it a substantial
readership.

So why does "On Lyric Poetry and Society" appear at certain points to stress the sociological over the formal? The answer involves recognition of the complicated double task Adorno actually sets himself: to challenge a reigning German formalism that (often reacting against recent National Socialist policies of saturating aesthetic matters with the hoariest ideological agendas) seeks virtually to divorce aesthetic from sociopolitical concerns and equally to contest a reductionist, Left ideology-critique that finds its raison d'etre in ritual demystifications of artistic illusion, in triumphalist revelations of artworks' sociohistorical determination. The essay's achievement will be to suggest that this double task hardly belongs to it – to criticism – alone; Adorno more than implies that modern lyric itself originates by critically undertaking an inaugural version of such stereoscopic duty or vocation. Hence Adorno begins "On Lyric Poetry and Society" with an elaborate semi-ironic plea for the right even to *think* of saying something sociological about so evidently ephemeral and delicate, so solitary or solipsistic, a phenomenon as the refined, fragile music made in lyric poetry (NL, 37–8/73–4).

Saying is the operative word; this sociologically titled essay originated in the mid-1950s as a radio talk in the Federal Republic of Germany. Commentators have rightly highlighted Adorno's sly attempt to unsettle his original German audience's effectively "new critical" assumptions by working out to the social *from* the formal (as against the audience's likely presumptions about sociology reflexively casting aspersions on, or even dispensing with, poetry's formal elements).[7] But this is hardly a concession; the immanent analysis that always characterizes Adorno's work (and Frankfurt School theory in general) is dedicated to immersion in form, to full experience of and engagement with its textures, syntaxes, rhythms, and tonalities. New critical (or other methodologically formalist) attentiveness to form is not so much discarded as extended into the social and back again, with the proviso that the poem or artwork is conceived, not as an independent object, but, following Benjamin, as part of a constellation or force field [Kraftfeld] that obtains through a series of complex relationships between the work and the social (it being understood that the social is always also, at least microcosmically, within the work). Thus, while Adorno offers his essay as a contribution toward a sociology of lyric, he is nonetheless explicit about a constitutive paradox – a paradox, that is, unless it is effectively ignored in order to find that once the social is reached, the formal simply falls away. The paradox is that if the aesthetic cannot be known without a materiohistorical sociology, so too a radically intended sociology of art must find *its* ground extraempirically, in materialism's Kantian-romantic correlate: the foundationality and indispensability of aesthetic form.

> Social concepts [*Gesellschaftliche Begriffe*] should not be applied to [art]works from without but rather drawn from exacting examination of the works themselves...[N]othing that is not in works of art or aesthetic theory themselves, not part of their own form, can legitimate a determination [*legitimiert die Entscheidung*] of what their substance, that which has entered into their poetry, represents in social terms. To determine that [*Das zu bestimmen*], of course, requires both knowledge of the interior of the works of art and knowledge of the society outside. But this kowledge is binding only if it is rediscovered through complete submission to the matter at hand. Special vigilance is required when it comes to the concept of ideology, which these days is belabored to the point of intolerability. (NL, 39/76–7)

The passage is significant not just for its wariness about "intolerably belabored" ideology-critique, nor even for the immediately following insistence that artworks almost constitutively resist ideology by giving "voice to what ideology hides" (NL, 39/77). For even before the word "ideology" appears, Adorno – while indicating that the social is not simply to be thrown aside in favor of the poem's formal constituents – signals that the very idea of the social determination of artworks earns its theoretical-methodological keep only if "rediscovered" spontaneously through immanent aesthetic and critical experience. However ultimately determining the social may be, such social meaning is lost when intellectual analysis attempts externally or mechanically to impose it in a predetermined manner. In the middle of the passage quoted above ("To determine that..."), Adorno reinforces the point by *not* making those presumably objective, sociological tools with which the passage had begun – *social concepts* – the subject or agent of the sentence in question; for neither social concepts nor their referent, society, will lead us to what is truly social in lyric. Hence, instead of front-loading the crucial sentence with social concepts and with formulations of how they determine the poem, Adorno almost stealthily begins with the *subject's* determination of the poem's social basis ("To determine that, of course, requires both knowledge of . . . ").

Yet Adorno's notion is not that a blithe, free-floating subjectivity should fancifully usurp the power of social reality, arbitrarily issuing *pronunciamentos* that presume to determine a social content or meaning whose determination really ("objectively," as it were) belongs to society and history. Rather, lyric turns out to be a particularly telling instance of how, in aesthetic experience, the subject – effectively reconstructing what Adorno will represent as the artwork's own process of discovering still obscured areas of the social – finds that his or her apparently free aesthetic play is a special kind of labor, a kind of labor that leads precisely to the "binding knowledge" that the artwork and the aesthetic experience of it are objectively social through and through. (This sense of individual aesthetic play miming social labor is implicit throughout the essay, tuned generally to Adorno's use of the terms "collectivity," "objectivity," and "the universal" as designations for, among other things, the social totality and the potentials of a collective labor power.)[8] The key idea is that significant facets of society remain to be discovered and that such discovery is unlikely to occur through use of society's own extant concepts for understanding itself. The passage's narrative sequencing even models the process its thesis projects: Consciousness of previously obscured aspects of the social is won by appropriating for the subject the vocabulary and function of objective (material, sociopolitical, historical) determination; the subject then takes up the word (and activity of) "determination" – then and only then to grasp the reality of objective social determination itself.[9] Thus when Adorno turns, in the essay's last movement, to analyze works by Eduard Mörike and Stefan George, his attention to the poems' experiments in tone, rhythm, rhyme, diction, and levels of style is socially cast; these formal phenomena, Adorno emphasizes, are what allow readers to begin working up a sense of the materiohistorical tensions, the reality, that the poems register and make available.

Given these indications of the essay's consistent focus on the interpenetration of poem and society, it might appear strange that a case would ever have been made that Adorno methodologically elevates sociology and/or ideology-critique above poetics. Whether in the last few decades Anglo-American criticism has belabored the question of ideology less – or more – than the "intolerably-belabored"

Ideologiekritik that Adorno had already criticized in the two Germanies of the 1950s would be worth an essay in its own right; the fact that so many critics have effectively ignored or reversed the essay's strictures regarding ideology-critique calls at least for a historical evaluation of how Frankfurt Marxism has been translated into today's literary and cultural studies. But in all fairness, no small portion of the confusion may be caused by "On Lyric Poetry and Society" itself, along with adjacent Adorno texts. The barbs against bourgeois society and culture that the essay quite gleefully delivers, together with the essay's compressed but stingingly Benjaminian assessment of the static (indeed, ideological) character of the mainstream modern lyric that sidesteps the radical traditions of Baudelairean experimentalism, coincide for many readers with the Adorno known for enthusiastically ratifying Brecht's assessment that the "palace" of canonical culture is – despite its grand pretensions to the contrary – "built from dogshit."[10]

At any rate, the raising of questions about the essay's real direction has scarcely been limited to interventionist Left critics who champion ideology-critique and who highlight the political or socioeconomic. It is too rarely remembered that when Geoffrey Hartman wrote his seminal essay on Keats and modern poetics, he sketched a fascinating charged relationship between his meditation and Adorno's "On Lyric Poetry and Society." On the one hand, Adorno's ideas about ideology as "untruth, false consciousness," were quickly described as classically Marxian and impoverished. On the other hand, Hartman amiably and openly stole the constellative formulation that many have deemed the most important feature of "On Lyric Poetry and Society," where, as a specific alternative to conceptions of the poem as ideology, Adorno approaches "the lyric poem [as] actually capturing the historical moment within its bounds" and sees "the poem as a philosophical sundial telling the time of history" [hält eigentlich das lyrische Gedicht in seinen Grenzen den geschichtlichen Stundenschlag fest; das Gedicht als geschichtsphilosophische Sonnenuhr]. The rest, Hartman seemed happy to suggest (starting with the phenomenon of tour de force experimentalism in Keats), was just modern poetic history enacting Adornian philosophical aesthetics.[11]

If for critics of various stripes there has been some understandable confusion about the status, in Adorno's essay, of formal poetics vis-à-vis history and the sociopolitical, there nonetheless exists a source of evidence, internal to "On Lyric Poetry and Society," that helps clarify matters. This has to do with a word that Adorno never pronounces in the essay but whose concept and history are everywhere present in it. The word is "experiment," and in the more sustained analyses of artistic endeavor presented in *Aesthetic Theory*, Adorno *will* explicitly pronounce and foreground this term (whose modern history, he indicates, virtually begins with romantic and postromantic lyric poetry).[12] In "On Lyric Poetry and Society" Adorno pursues the idea of experiment via the closely related notion of *spontaneity* [*Spontaneität* or *Unwillkürlichkeit*]; the essay repeatedly observes that in the process of spontaneous exploration (undertaken by the artist, the artwork, and the audience), previously occluded aspects of the social are made available.

Commitment to this process leads Adorno militantly to insist that he is "not trying to deduce lyric poetry from society" and that lyric's "social substance is precisely what is spontaneous in it, [is] what does not simply follow from the existing conditions at the time" (NL, 43/84). It follows that "lyric reveals itself to be most deeply grounded in society when it does not chime in with society" (literally, where it does not speak after, or echo, society's own "mouth" [wo sie nicht der Gesellschaft nach Munde redet]), where lyric "communicates nothing" (that is, where lyric resists the abstracted, utilitarian, exchange-value "reification" characteristic of advanced capitalism's modes of "communicative discourse") (NL, 43–4/85–6). And for Adorno as for Benjamin, it then follows historically that the crucial modern poet – the artist who makes lyric poetry modern – is Baudelaire: Baudelaire, who for his subject chooses "the modern itself," who abjures or scorns an already known socioliterary language, so that his "lyric poetry is a slap in the face not only to the *juste milieu* but also to all bourgeois social sentiment," yet whose "tragic, arrogant mask" of advanced technique is nonetheless – indeed, is in consequence – "truer to the masses" than conventional "poor people's poetry" exactly because its experimentalism brings into aesthetic experience the historical reality unavailable to a poetics determined by reigning conventional concepts of what those social conditions are or have been. And clarifying the stakes and trajectory of its argument that "the social substance in lyric is precisely what is spontaneous in it, what does not simply follow from the existing conditions at the time," Adorno's essay ultimately traces this Baudelairean-experimental strain in modern lyric to the formally and *politically* signifying names of Brecht and García Lorca (NL, 44–6/87–90).

In more theoretical terms, how does lyric *give us* the social? How can it be said to provide an understanding of the social that "does not simply follow from" – that is not simply determined by – "existing conditions" or a preexisting grasp of them? Adorno will treat these questions in a far more sustained manner in *Aesthetic Theory*, but already in "On Lyric Poetry and Society," Adorno (following Benjamin) in effect writes – or points to postromantic lyric as that which allows him to write – a Marxian translation of Kantian aesthetics. Underlying Adorno's Kantian account is the aesthetic's *quasi*conceptual and thus *quasi*social quality. The aesthetic, while looking like conceptual-objective, "useful," content-determined thought or activity, quite precisely only *looks like* them, only mimes them at the level of form. Aesthetic thought-experience in some way precedes conceptual-objective, content-and-use-oriented thought; in that sense, the aesthetic is formal because, rather than being determined by, it *provides the form for* conceptual thought or cognition. Aesthetic thought-experience remains free (relative to more properly conceptual thought) from the preexistent rules assumed to govern conceptual thought. In the Kantian lexicon, this makes the aesthetic a site of *reflective* rather than *determinant* judgment. The aesthetic, then, serves as a mold or frame for the construction of conceptual thought (for "cognition in general," as Kant puts it).

The aesthetic serves also as a formal and imaginative engine for new, experimental (because previously nonexistent) concepts. With its quasiconceptual and quasisocial character, the aesthetic can provide a prerequisite of critical thought by offering formal means spontaneously to develop the materials for new (not even necessarily utopian) concepts. Such bringing forward of the materials for the construction of new concepts can enable us to glimpse previously obscured aspects of substantive social reality (aspects of society not already determined by society's own conceptual view of itself). The operative notion is that thought determined by society – by society's own concepts of itself (status-quo, reigning concepts of society) – can never give a satisfactory picture of society. This finally resolves into a fundamental strain of Adorno's aesthetics that can be expressed as follows: Aesthetic experiment helps construct and make available the intellectual-emotional apparatus for accessing, and to that extent helps make available the social material of, the new. To re-iterate, this constructivist theory and practice sees that experiment in the aesthetic realm – the aesthetic *as* experiment – helps make new areas of the modern fitfully available *to* perception in the first place.[13]

But what would make *lyric* such a special case within this theory or view of art and aesthetic experience? For the traditions of poetics in which Adorno and Benjamin participate, modern lyric stands as a, or even *the*, high-risk enterprise, the "go-for-broke-game" [va-banque-Spiel] of literary art. The lyric poem must work coherently in and with the medium – language – that human beings use to articulate objective concepts, even while the lyric explores the most subjective, nonconceptual, and ephemeral phenomena. This theoretical or philosophical difficulty – how simultaneously to think objectivity and subjectivity – also arises practically as lyric's great problem of form construction: How – with language alone as medium – to build a solid, convincing artistic structure out of something as evanescent as subjective song (NL 44/85) and how, in the bargain, to delineate or objectivate the impressively fluid contents of capitalist modernity? (NL 43/85). How, spontaneously yet rigorously, to make thought sing and to make song think? In short, lyric dramatizes with special intensity modern aesthetic quasiconceptuality's more general attempt to stretch conceptual thought proper; this special intensity arises from lyric's constitutive need musically to stretch "objective" conceptual thought's very medium, language – to stretch it all the way toward affect and song, but without relinquishing any of the rigor of conceptual intellection:

The paradox specific to the lyric work, a subjectivity that turns into an objectivity, is tied to the priority of linguistic form in the lyric; it is that priority from which the primacy of language in literature in general (even in prose forms) is derived. For language is itself something double. Through its configurations it assimilates itself completely into subjective impulses; one would almost think it had produced them. But at the same time language remains the medium of concepts, remains that which establishes an inescapable relationship to the universal and to society. (NL, 43/85)

While lyric has always had this special double character, the modern crisis of aura (and lyric's consequent need radically to differentiate itself from reification and the reified communicative discourse that have led to the seeming loss of aura in modernity) exponentially raises lyric's constitutive wager. As mentioned previously, Adorno's essay treats Baudelaire as the watershed in these developments. And of course standing behind the references to Baudelaire in "On Lyric Poetry and Society" are Benjamin's extraordinarily influential writings on the French poet, most of which imply that lyric aura in Baudelaire is won, if at all, at the historical price of announcing its own endgame.[14] Benjamin therefore at times suggests (and later Benjaminians have generally mandated) that a "critical" poetics in the late modern or postmodern period should be anti-lyric, antiaesthetic, and committed to poetic methods ingeniously associated with technologically oriented reproduction, all in order to effect radical defamiliarization and the renewal of sociopolitical commitment. But in "On Lyric Poetry and Society," *Aesthetic Theory*, and related texts, Adorno plays careful variations on Benjamin's themes, arguing that – at least since Baudelaire – the critical force of poetry depends precisely on the formal ability to make lyric itself critical (which is quite distinct from Benjamin's intermittent interest in abolishing or getting beyond auratic lyric subjectivity and modern aesthetic autonomy). Preserving Benjamin's great insights into how Baudelaire brilliantly makes lyric vocation confront the ostensible destruction of its own historical precondition – the kind of temporal-reflective, auratic *experience* apparently no longer possible, Baudelaire's poems seem to declare, in a radically commodified, high-speed, high-capitalist modernity – Adorno nonetheless effectively defends the continuing practice of a lyric poetry that begins by singing song's impossibility but whose refusal of aura *tout court* would be the refusal of critique. In short, Adorno pushes on with the analysis set forth in Benjamin's "On Some Motifs in Baudelaire," where a vexed discovery of lyric aura's power occurs precisely in the moment of marking aura's further dissipation and now seeming impossibility.[15]

This continuing endeavor – in both poetry and criticism – is what Adorno theorizes as a modern phenomenon and as that which makes each new area of the modern fitfully available to perception. Left poetry and criticism that tends to abandon formal poetics and the question of lyric aura (in favor of a hunt for sociohistorical determination) would, from an Adornian perspective, unintentionally serve to efface and ratify, rather than to recognize, contest, or refunction, the phenomenon of reification. This would obtain because the *intentional* abandonment of aura and its formal constituents leads to a failure to register even negatively – through vexed attempts to create or access aura – the crucial modern phenomenon of aura's loss (or at least its apparent loss). What the *intentional* abandonment of aura then produces is *not* the critical objectivation of the reifying process (aura's Other); what then occurs is *not* the bringing to light of the erasure of labor and the commodification of everyone and everything. What results instead is culture's straightforward, affirmational repetition of a consequently unchallenged reification.[16]

All this indicates why ideology-critique readings of his essay probably wouldn't make Adorno shudder. For the shudder or shaking (*Schauer, frisson*, or, most dramatically, *Erschütterung*) is what *Aesthetic Theory*, following "On Lyric Poetry and Society," treats as Baudelairean-modern lyric's mode for conveying the critical potential of an exponentially raised *via-negativa* aura. The effort negatively to register aura's apparent loss stands as a necessary attempt to gesture toward and reinvent aura in the very modernity that all too frequently appears to have banished it, that appears to have erased the sense of quasiphysical, quasicognitive, quasiexperiential otherness in art, an otherness that – to reiterate – is for Adorno fatefully linked to the social and its reality of, among other things, labor.[17] These last are, moreover, perhaps the original and ultimate objects of *Aesthetic Theory*'s simultaneous theorization of aura, "second-reflection," and *Erschütterung*. *Aesthetic Theory* conceives *Erschütterung* as that which, by dint of aura's dynamic of charged distance, can break down the hardening of subjectivity – can break down through this shaking, in other words, "the subject's petrification in his or her own subjectivity" and hence can allow the subject to catch "the slightest glimpse beyond that prison that it [the 'I'] itself is," thus permitting the "I," once "shaken, to perceive its own "limitedness and finitude" and so to experience the critical possibility of thinking otherness.[18] The process of shaking that leads toward knowledge of otherness – including the otherness that is the social itself – is, in other words, what gives critical value to the "I" whose "voice is heard in the lyric" (NL, 41/80); *shaking* is what animates the "paradox specific to the lyric work, a subjectivity that turns into objectivity" (NL, 43/85).

Yet from an Adornian perspective, critical lyric practice has value beyond the new social materials and protoconcepts it helps make substantively, "objectively," available. One way to begin conveying this would be to remember how aura's crisis comes to be so important for Benjamin's (and, through Benjamin's influence, for Adorno's) crucial theory and practice of the *constellation* and *force field* [*Kraftfeld*]. These latter are often and rightly understood as an intellectual attempt nondeterministically to locate and dynamically connect elements (historical, socioeconomic, cultural) that are not initially given as relational but that, when animated (constellated) into conjunction, create or reveal a signifying force field. That force field for its part illuminates the larger social reality whose elements have been brought together in affinity and tension (rather than in a falsely integrative, positivistic totalization) to make the constructivist force field itself visible.[19] The familiar idea in play, developed out of Kant by Benjamin and Adorno (and by others before them, including Nietzsche and Emerson), is that there exists a noninstrumental yet precise, coherent, nonarbitrary mode of thought – the aesthetic – that contributes formally toward and imaginatively reinvigorates conceptual knowledge while itself forgoing substantive conceptuality and the modes and logic of argumentation and discursivity. In short, the aesthetic bridges objective-conceptual knowledge (or the objective world to which such knowledge corresponds) and the subjective human capacity for a critical agency that would be more than arbitrary in relation *to* objective knowledge of existing reality. (Here I can only assert something that deserves full elaboration elsewhere: Contrary to so much of the "anti-aestheticist" hostility of contemporary Marxian and Marxian-inflected theory to aesthetic experience and aesthetic judgment, Marx himself intentionally marshals the aporetic but by no means paralyzing structure of Kantian reflective aesthetic judgment precisely for the "theory of *praxis*" announced in his *Theses on Feuerbach*.)[20]

All of which helps clue us in to another level of the constellation's and the force field's significance. Benjamin, to be sure, employs the constellation and force field to *grasp* the crisis of the apparent loss of aura (especially or ultimately the crisis of *lyric* aura, hardly surprising

given lyric's canonical place in the history of art, aesthetics, and poetics and its place in Benjamin's own thought). But at some point, the
Benjaminian constellation and force field rightly become understood
as inseparable *from* lyric aura. That's another way of saying that the
Baudelairean-Benjaminian crisis of lyric aura (the crisis of the avail-
ability, in capitalist modernity, of the sort of reflective experience
that in its turn makes possible a noninstrumental yet nonarbitrary,
potentially emancipatory capacity for constructing new conceptual-
objective knowledge) is really the crisis-question of whether, and
how, critical thought and agency are still possible. For Benjamin and
Adorno, critical lyric is a "go-for-broke" articulation, in the language
of art and aesthetics (especially poetry), of the condition of possibility
for a more than subjectively arbitrary thought that is nonetheless not
bound by the rule of existing concepts and the argumentation proper
to them. On Benjamin's and Adorno's view, an engaged criticism
will trace this process and seek to elaborate its concept. This is exactly what's at stake when Benjamin – and, following him, Adorno –
enunciates the constellation and force field. In the celebrated phrasing of the "Theses on the Philosophy of History" (which is, among
other things, Benjamin's updating of Marx's aesthetically theorized
rejection, in the *Theses on Feuerbach*, of Left-materialist determinism), the constellative act blasts the *Jetztzeit* (the now-time, the
present, that emerges beyond the picture offered by society's currently ruling concepts) out of the continuum of history, out of the
seeming continuum presented by reigning concepts.[21]

Lest one still imagine that lyric and the constellation and force
field of Frankfurt School Critical Theory merely parallel one another, Benjamin and Adorno repeatedly indicate that the constellation and force field themselves partake fundamentally of aesthetic
theory and artistic practice. This profoundly aesthetic dimension becomes palpable when one considers Benjamin's and Adorno's often
stated specification of what, within criticism, constellative form requires, of how and why it creates or brings into view a force field:
In writing that seeks to present constellative critical thought, each
sentence should strive to point back – formally and substantively –
to a constantly moving center from which that sentence has all
along radiated. That's no small task, and if the ideal of an in-motion
writing that structurally fuses imagination, precision, and formal-
stylistic torque seems to demand the impossible, that's probably

because Benjamin developed the notion and practice largely through his formidable engagements with the formidable artists of the Baude-lairean lyric countertradition.

(The Benjaminian-Adornian mandate further requires that the critic not aestheticize criticism, that he or she not write criticism as if it were lyric poetry, not write as if the links between these modes could be used to declare them by fiat identical or interchange-able. Criticism's relationship to lyric's constellative form is thus best grasped as aesthetic, not aestheticist. The kinship stems from the overlapping but distinct relationships that both criticism and art maintain to *mimesis*, to a mode of thought-representation that does not in the first instance operate via conceptuality and argumentation but through an experience of affinity and difference, although criti-cism finally must work to enunciate, in the language not of mimesis but of conceptuality, the contributions *toward* conceptuality that art, that mimesis, has nondiscursively offered.)

Such an analysis allows us freshly to see that Benjamin's con-stellation and force field jointly stand as one of the great modernist, constructivist reimaginings of that familiar old lyric-aesthetic friend that it thereby radically reinvents (not least by way of a properly modernist parataxis that restages romantic articulations of parts and wholes): organic form. In Adorno's musical formulation, such constructivist reimagining or genuine carrying forward of organic form appears, in advanced modernity, as the simultaneously disso-ciative and structural principle of dissonant composition. On this view, constellative form simply *is* the theory-practice of the critical-progressive, self-consciously modern artwork. If in an earlier, ro-mantic era, organic form attempts to realize a critical dynamism through explicit involvement with lyric risk, constructivist form's greatest challenge, its go-for-broke game in later modernity, involves the effort to constellate and – however covertly or implicitly, how-ever sideways slanted the renderings, however inclusive of ostensibly nonlyric or anti-lyric materials and methods – the effort to approach lyric aura.[22]

Informing the reflections of "On Lyric Poetry and Society" and more clearly theorized in *Aesthetic Theory* is this notion that crit-ical lyric, along with the criticism dedicated to it, is tuned to the very possibility of historically, reflectively accounting for *anything*. Critical lyric aura signifies, or is keyed to, the possibility of an act of understanding that proceeds in a more than merely instrumental *and* more than merely arbitrary manner: It proceeds in a manner directed toward meeting at least the minimal requirements of critical agency. That's why the apparent loss of lyric aura really is such a crisis for Adorno and Benjamin, who consequently conceive the reimagining or reinventing of lyric aura as an ongoing commitment to the possibility of *constellating*, to the possibility of constructing constellative form.

As Adorno insists in "On Lyric Poetry and Society" and his many other elaborations of Benjamin's "On Some Motifs in Baudelaire," the modern inability to hear lyric music – not only lyric's obvious modernist-constructivst dissonances, but also, inside or alongside the latter, the survivals of lyric melodiousness and mellifluousness – is the inability to hear art stretching toward critique. When the rejection of a warmed-over, too-easy programmatic transcendentalism results in the essential abandonment of lyric aura – when the governing interpretive yardstick adopts, in order to stigmatize lyric aura itself, precisely the least realized creations or readings of lyric's emphatically nonempirical, nonrepresentationalist "I" (the "I" actually best understood as a construction-toward-aura that seeks, via necessary fictions, negatively to allow subjects provisionally to transcend their own empirical experiences and consider other subjects and objects) – then the result all too often is the effective abandonment of art's ability to stimulate critical agency.[23] Modernity without critical agency has almost always been a recipe for special disasters, and in Adorno's eyes, the very least that poetry and criticism can do to help prevent such outcomes is to abandon neither lyric nor society.

NOTES

For their responses to earlier versions of this essay, I am grateful to Charles Altieri, Russell A. Berman, Adam Casdin, James Chandler, Norma Cole, Lydia Goehr, Robert Hass, Tom Huhn, Robert Hullot-Kentor, Martin Jay, Shierry Nicholsen, Michael Palmer, and Arthur Strum.

1. See Theodor Adorno, "On Lyric Poetry and Society," in *Notes to Literature*, vol. 1, trans. Shierry Weber Nicholsen, ed. Rolf Tiedemann (New York: Columbia University Press, 1991), 37–54; originally published as "Rede über Lyrik und Gesellschaft," in *Noten zur Literatur*,

vol. 1 (Frankfurt: Suhrkamp, 1958), 73–104. Hereafter cited as NL. Page numbers in English translation are followed by page numbers of German original.

2. For an extended historicotheoretical discussion of the critique of aesthetic ideology's working premises, see Robert Kaufman, "Red Kant, or the Persistence of the Third *Critique* in Adorno and Jameson," *Critical Inquiry* 26 (summer 2000): 682–724. For specific treatment (over against critique-of-aesthetic-ideology interpretations) of a key nexus in nineteenth- and twentieth-century poetry, aesthetics, and criticism, see Kaufman, "Negatively Capable Dialectics: Keats, Vendler, Adorno, and the Theory of the Avant-Garde," *Critical Inquiry* 27 (winter 2001): 354–84.

3. For elaborations of a crucial Frankfurt and Adornian distinction (generally ignored in ideology-critique criticism) between *the aesthetic* and aesthetic*ization*, see Robert Kaufman, "Aura, Still," *October* 99 (winter 2002), pp. 45–80, as well as Kaufman, "Red Kant."

4. Some of these critical accounts and applications of Adorno have also simultaneously or alternatively highlighted "On Lyric Poetry and Society's" utopian strains, in a manner that dovetails with contemporary Marxian criticism's often intertwined theorization of ideology and utopia (powerfully and influentially adumbrated, for example, in Fredric Jameson's "Conclusion: The Dialectic of Utopia and Ideology," in *The Political Unconscious: Narrative as a Socially Symbolic Act* [Ithaca: Cornell University Press, 1981], 281–99); and in certain cases, "On Lyric Poetry and Society" has itself been deemed aestheticist, has itself been deemed to propagate aesthetic ideology.

For representative examples of Anglo-American approaches to "On Lyric Poetry and Society" during the last few decades (approaches which often provide valuable insights while tending generally to work from within some version of the ideology-utopia matrix), see, for example, E. Warwick Slinn, "Poetry and Culture: Performativity and Critique," *New Literary History* 30, no. 1 (1999): 55–74, esp. 65; Terence Allan Hoagwood, "Keats and the Critical Tradition: The Topic of History," in *The Persistence of Poetry: Bicentennial Essays on Keats*, eds. Robert M. Ryan and Ronald A. Sharp (Amherst: University of Massachusetts Press, 1998), 153–64; Mark Jeffreys, "Ideologies of Lyric: A Problem of Genre in Contemporary Anglophone Poetics," *PMLA* 110, no. 2 (1995): 199–200; Anne Shiferer, "Beleaguered Privacies," *Midwest Quarterly* 33, no. 3 (1992): 325–6; Douglas Bruster, "'Come to the Tent Again': 'The Passionate Shepherd,' Dramatic Rape and Lyric Time," *Criticism* 33, no. 1 (1991): 56–7, 71, n. 22; Joseph Chadwick, "Violence in Yeats's Later Politics and Poetry," *English Literary History* 55, no. 4 (1988): 887,

889–90; Annabel Patterson, "Lyric and Society in Jonson's *Under-wood*," in *Lyric Poetry: Beyond New Criticism*, ed. Chaviva Hosek and Patricia Parker (Ithaca and London: Cornell University Press, 1985), 150–2, 162–3; John Brenkman, *Culture and Domination* (Ithaca and London: Cornell University Press, 1985), 108–21; and Margaret Homans, "'Syllables of Velvet': Dickinson, Rossetti, and the Rhetorics of Sexuality," *Feminist Studies* 11, no. 3 (1985): 570.

For one of contemporary Anglo-American criticism's most sustained, thoughtful, and decidedly *un*-ideology-critique encounters with "On Lyric Poetry and Society," see Paul Fry, *A Defense of Poetry: Reflections on the Occasion of Writing* (Stanford: Stanford University Press, 1995), passim. Fry takes up Adorno mostly in relation to British romanticism and its recent reception histories. See too, in this regard, the very brief discussion, but impressively exfoliated application, of "On Lyric Poetry and Society" in the concluding sections of James Chandler, *England in 1819: The Politics of Literary Culture and the Case of Romantic Historicism* (Chicago: University of Chicago Press, 1998), 529–54; and see Forest Pyle, *The Ideology of Imagination: Subject and Society in the Discourse of Romanticism* (Stanford: Stanford University Press, 1995), passim and esp. 120–25.

Interesting engagements with Adorno's lyric theory have also occurred in a criticism increasingly written (perhaps not coincidentally) by poet-critics and focused largely on modern and contemporary experimental poetry; this criticism has in some cases reproduced, and in others moved subtly toward jettisoning, the ideology-utopia axis. Examples include Rachel Blau DuPlessis, "Manifests," *Diacritics* 26, no. 3–4 (1996): 36–7; R. K. Meiners, "Dialectics at a Standstill: Orwell, Benjamin, and the Difficulties of Poetry," *boundary* 2 20, no. 2 (1993): 116–39, and "Mourning for Our Selves and for Poetry: The Lyric after Auschwitz," *Centennial Review* 35, no. 3 (1991): 545–90; Michael Davidson, "From Margin to Mainstream: Postwar Poetry and the Politics of Containment," *American Literary History* 10, no. 2 (1988): 286–7; and Norman M. Finkelstein, "Jack Spicer's Ghosts and the Gnosis of History," *boundary* 2 9, no. 2 (1981): 88–9.

There are of course many studies of Frankfurt School Critical Theory itself, and/or of modern poetries outside the Anglo-American tradition, that offer helpful suggestions about Adorno's concept of lyric; see, for just a few instances, Russell A. Berman, "Lyrik und Öffentlichkeit: Das amerikanische Gedicht," in *Die andere Stimmme: Das Fremde in der Kultur der Moderne*, eds. Alexander Honold and Manuel Köppen (Cologne: Böhlau Verlag, 1999), 231–42, and "Cultural Studies and the Cannon: Some Thoughts on Stefan George," *Profession* (MLA) (1999):

168–79; Shierry Weber Nicholsen, *Exact Imagination, Late Work: Essays on Adorno's Aesthetics* (Cambridge, Mass.: MIT Press, 1997), passim and esp. 59–102; Peter Uwe Hohendahl, *Prismatic Thought: Theodor W. Adorno* (Lincoln: University of Nebraska Press, 1995), passim and esp. 81–103, 105–17, 151–4, 235–7; Fredric Jameson, *Late Marxism: Adorno, or, The Persistence of the Dialectic* (London and New York: Verso, 1990), 205–7; and Martin Jay, *Adorno* (Cambridge, Mass.: Harvard University Press, 1984), 145, 155.

5. See Bruce Mayo, "Introduction to Adorno's 'Lyric Poetry and Society,'" and Theodor W. Adorno, "Lyric Poetry and Society," *Telos*, no. 20 (spring 1974): 52–5, 56–71.

6. See, for example, Nicholsen, *Exact Imagination, Late Work*, 61, 96. Another of Adorno's preeminent translators and interpreters, Robert Hullot-Kentor, has on numerous occasions voiced similar sentiments.

7. See the discussion of the essay's early audiences and the West German analogues of a new-critical poetics in, for example, Mayo's "Introduction to Adorno's 'Lyric Poetry and Society'" and Hohendahl's *Prismatic Thought*.

8. See NL, 45–6/88–90. In *Aesthetic Theory*'s treatments of how aesthetic experience affords insight into problems of determination, Adorno explicitly and repeatedly brings the discussion around to – and he uses the term – *labor* (*Arbeit*); see Theodor W. Adorno, *Aesthetic Theory*, edited, translated and with a translator's introduction by Robert Hullot-Kentor (Minneapolis: University of Minnesota Press, 1997), e.g., 167–8, 174; German original: *Ästhetische Theorie* in *Gesammelte Schriften*, vol. 7, ed. Rolf Tiedemann (Frankfurt: Suhrkamp, 1970), 249–51, 260. For a full discussion of how *Aesthetic Theory* links aesthetic aura – especially *lyric* aura – to an understanding of labor and reification in modernity, see Kaufman, "Aura, Still."

9. If the sequence seems awfully Hegelian, Adorno will elsewhere indicate that his commitment to the artwork's – and aesthetic experience's – quasiconceptuality or nonconceptuality finally yields a quite Kantian critical theory, whose intentional undoing of Hegelian conceptual identitarianism stems from the theoretical pride of place that Kant grants the aesthetic. See Kaufman, "Red Kant."

As throughout his work (and perhaps most frequently in *Aesthetic Theory*), Adorno in "On Lyric Poetry and Society" alternately uses *bestimmen* and *determinieren* to speak both of social causation or determination and intellectual analysis of it (the German *Determination* is also alternatively used in *Aesthetic Theory*). Adorno will speak too, as in the "On Lyric Poetry and Society" quotation in the text above, about making or legitimating a decision [Entscheidung] or about the need to deduce [deduzieren] the elements and/or orders of determination. At all events, the constellation of German terms for causation (or determination) and for attempts to grasp it intellectually have generally been rendered by Adorno's translators as (or as closely aligned with) the English *determine* and *determination*.

10. See Theodor W. Adorno, "Metaphysics and Culture," in *Negative Dialectics*, trans. E. B. Ashton (New York: Continuum, 1973), 366 (translation amended); German original: "Metaphysik und Kultur" in *Negative Dialektik*, reprinted in *Gesammelte Schriften*, vol. 6, ed. Rolf Tiedemann (Frankfurt: Suhrkamp, 1973), 359 [*ihr Palast…gebaut ist aus Hundsscheisse*]. On Brecht's, Benjamin's, and Adorno's sometimes distinct but always overlapping theories of lyric aura, aesthetic experience, and cultural value in poetry since Baudelaire, see Kaufman "Aura, Still."

11. See Geoffrey Hartman, "Poem and Ideology: A Study of Keats's 'To Autumn,'" in *The Fate of Reading* (Chicago: University of Chicago Press, 1975), esp. 125, 126, 324 n. 3. Grasping Adorno's formulation for the purpose of attempting to understand historical *determination* without falling into mechanistic *determinism*, Hartman observed, "It should be possible to consider a poem's *geschichtlicher Stundenschlag* (Adorno) – how it tells the time of history – without accepting a historical determinism" ("Poem and Ideology," 126, quoting from "Rede über Lyrik und Gesellschaft," p. 91 [the passage in "Rede über Lyrik und Gesellschaft" continues to p. 92, where it concludes with *das Gedicht als geschichtsphilosophische Sonnenuhr*]). For the passage in the English text, see NL, 46. For Hartman's more recent engagements with Adorno, see his *The Fateful Question of Culture* (New York: Columbia University Press, 1997).

12. In fact, *Aesthetic Theory*'s discussions of experiment and related issues will frequently restate (and at times virtually quote) passages from "On Lyric Poetry and Society"; see, for example, *Aesthetic Theory*, 55, 99, 133, 122–4, 167–8 (*Ästhetische Theorie*, 88, 152–3, 201–2, 185–8, 249–52).

13. For further treatment, see Kaufman, "Red Kant."

14. See Kaufman, "Aura, Still"; and see, for example, Walter Benjamin, "The Work of Art in the Age of Mechanical Reproduction" and especially "On Some Motifs in Baudelaire" in *Illuminations: Essays and Reflections*, ed. Hannah Arendt, trans. Harry Zohn (New York: Schocken, 1969), 217–51, 155–200, and "The Paris of the Second Empire in Baudelaire," in *Charles Baudelaire: A Lyric Poet in the Era of High Capitalism*, trans. Harry Zohn (London: New Left Books, 1973), 9–106; German originals: "Das Kunstwerk im Zeitalter seiner technischen Reproduzierbarkeit," "Das Paris des Second Empire bei Baudelaire," and "Über einige

Motive bei Baudelaire" in *Gesammelte Schriften*, vol. 1, ed. Rolf
Tiedemann and Hermann Schweppenhäuser (Frankfurt: Suhrkamp,
1972), 431–654. Most of these texts are likewise found in Benjamin,
Illuminationen: Ausgewählte Schriften (Frankfurt: Suhrkamp, 1961).
See also Benjamin, *Charles Baudelaire: Ein Lyriker im Zeitalter des
Hochkapitalismus: Zwei Fragmente*, edited and with an afterword by
Rolf Tiedemann (Frankfurt: Suhrkamp, 1969).

Also see Theodor W. Adorno and Walter Benjamin, *Briefwechsel
1928–1940*, ed. Henri Lonitz (Frankfurt: Suhrkamp, 1994), 138 ff.,
364 ff., and 388 ff.; translated by Nicholas Walker under the title *The
Complete Correspondence, 1928–1940*, ed. Henri Lonitz (Cambridge,
Mass.: Harvard University Press, 1999), 104 ff., 280 ff., and 298 ff.

15. See the final discussions in Adorno's essay on Mörike and George and
Adorno's focus on their negative approach toward aura via omission,
renunciation, dissonance, and so forth. For an important reconsidera-
tion of the "crisis of experience" theory standing behind Benjamin's and
Adorno's thoughts about the loss of aura in modernity, see essay. 5 of
this volume.

16. Broached in the discussion in "On Lyric Poetry and Society" of the tension between reified communicative discourse and poetic language, this
argument about aura, reification, and labor is given definitive treatment
in *Aesthetic Theory*; in the latter text, see, for example, pp. 33, 79, 167–
8, 173–4, 204, 209, 245, and 269 (*Ästhetische Theorie*, pp. 57, 122–4,
249–52, 258–60, 303–4, 311, 363–4, and 401).

17. It should be emphasized that the linkage between aura and labor-
otherness is meant, in Frankfurt School terms, critically to distinguish
via-negativa aura from official culture's blithe or "affirmative" attempts
(in the Marcusean sense) falsely to reenchant and reconcile a world still
scored by profound exploitation and stark inequality.

18. Adorno, *Aesthetic Theory*, 269, 245 (*Ästhetische Theorie*, 401, 364). On
"second-reflection," see Kaufman, "Red Kant," 718–19.

19. For valuable explications of Benjamin's and Adorno's development of the
force field and constellation, see the introduction in Martin Jay, *Force
Fields: Between Intellectual History and Cultural Critique* (New York
and London: Routledge, 1993), esp. 1–3, 8–9; see also the introduction to
Jay's *Adorno* (Cambridge, Mass.: Harvard University Press, 1984), esp.
14–23.

20. For discussion, see, for example, Anthony J. Cascardi, *Consequences of
Enlightenment* (Cambridge: Cambridge University Press, 1999); Frances
Ferguson, *Solitude and the Sublime: Romanticism and the Aesthet-
ics of Individuation* (New York: Routledge, 1992); Howard Caygill, *Art

of Judgment (Oxford: Blackwell, 1989); and Kaufman, "Red Kant" and "Negatively Capable Dialectics."

21. See the fourteenth of Benjamin's "Theses on the Philosophy of History," *Illuminations*, 261; "Über den Begriff der Geschichte" (*Gesammelte Schriften*, vol. 1, p. 730). Compare, for its applicability to the making of constellations, Benjamin's fascinating distinction between *Jetztzeit* and *Jetztsein* [waking-being] in *Das Passagen-Werk* 1, *Gesammelte Schriften*, vol. 5, 494–5 (*The Arcades Project*, 391–2).

22. For a key treatment of the concept and form of constellative thought and writing within criticism, and for the constellation's relationship to the nonarbitrary yet nonargumentative forms of modern art, see Robert Hullot-Kentor, "Foreword: Critique of the Organic," in Theodor W. Adorno, *Kierkegaard: Construction of the Aesthetic*, trans. Hullot-Kentor (Minneapolis: University of Minnesota Press, 1989), x–xxiii. For related discussions of how mimesis informs Adorno's modes and styles of writing, see Jameson, *Late Marxism*, e.g., p. 68, and Martin Jay, "Mimesis and Mimetology: Adorno and Lacoue-Labarthe," in *The Semblance of Subjectivity: Essays in Adorno's Aesthetic Theory*, ed. Tom Huhn and Lambert Zuidervaart (Cambridge, Mass.: MIT Press, 1997), 29–54, reprinted in Jay, *Cultural Semantics: Keywords of Our Time* (Amherst, Mass.: University of Massachusetts Press, 1998), 120–37.

23. See NL, 38–42, 43–6, 53–4/75–83, 84–91, 103–4; and see *Aesthetic Theory*, 55, 99, 133, 122–4, 167–8 (*Ästhetische Theorie*, 88, 152–3, 201–2, 185–8, 249–52). For a parallel critique of various modernist and post-modernist composers' attempts to create an art of sheer materiality and construction (effectively and uncritically leaving expression and aura behind), see Theodor W. Adorno, "Das Altern der neuen Musik," in *Gesammelte Schriften*, vol. 14, 143–67; translated by Hullot-Kentor and Fredric Will under the title "The Aging of the New Music," *Telos*, no. 77 (Fall 1988): 95–116. For indications about how such musical questions translate back into problems of literary art, see Adorno's treatment of sheerly constructivist play with "protocol sentences" and conventions (*Aesthetic Theory*, 154–7, 203–6; *Ästhetische Theorie*, 231–6, 302–7).

15 Adorno's *Tom Sawyer* Opera Singspiel

We can't run away
from this old house...
and if we run somewhere in fear
we still remain inside
this gives us fear and dread.

Adorno
The Treasure of Indian Joe[1]

I

Ever since the academic world came to agree that philosophy is only possible as science, philosophers, who nevertheless cannot escape artistic production, go through life with both the mark of the conceptual poet and a bad conscience for it. The *Phenomenology of Spirit*, giving voice to an already widespread program – Hegel's own poetry notwithstanding – has it that the writers of the French Enlightenment, who presented their most important insights in the form of stories and novels, are too clever; that is to say, they write too well. Literary inferiority would certainly be a good characterization of a large part of the academic community – a community which has successfully lowered its ideal of science from the lofty heights of Hegel's investigation into things themselves down to the modest quest for knowledge about how we know things. The academic community has never forgiven Nietzsche for writing *Thus Spoke Zarathustra* and *The Dithyrambs of Dionysos* and has taken this as an excuse to declare the *Genealogy of Morals* irrelevant to the field as well. At least in Germany these experiences have been cause for caution in intellectual matters and have even intimidated intellectual inquiry.

Those who prefer to write aphorisms rather than stale but transcendentally grounded puns about the being of being would do well to keep their theses to themselves until after they have passed their habilitation. One must be a Sartre and have established oneself independently of teaching at both the Sorbonne and the Collège de France in order occasionally to write a theater piece for Jouvet and Brasseur without losing prestige. But here – in our land – let no artist underestimate the superior power of the professional thinker if he, viewing himself as a thinker, has no wish to wind up unawares in a Beckettian trashcan.

II

Adorno himself, whose literary production amounts to little more than two hidden verses and a series of short prose pieces published under a hitherto undiscovered pseudonym, was not insensitive to the charge of philosophical meddling in literary matters. But even the German of his theoretical writings is far too good to spare him such a charge. It was surely decisive for his reserve in literary matters that "the departmentalization of mind" does its "task all the more reliably since anyone who repudiates the division of labor," according to the measure of his own work, "makes himself vulnerable by its standards in ways inseparable from elements of his superiority."[2] These exposures aim to show the weakness which society teaches each of its members. By placing on the opening page of his first professional philosophical publication – and thereby owning – Hegel's dictum "Now is the time for philosophy to be raised to the status of a science," Adorno seeks not to guard against a literary faculty which suits the work more than he realizes. But he points out that the coexistence of philosophy and literature leaves neither objectively intact.[3] The individual subject is not capable of bringing together again what history and society have torn apart: conceptual knowledge of what is, philosophy as a necessary interpretation of reality, on the one hand, and, on the other hand, the disintegration of philosophy into images or elements of images out of which a nonbeing, an aesthetic semblance, might be constructed.

The separation of intellectual from physical labor, which initially came from the intellect, has not only disfigured intellectual work, but also moved it closer to ideology. The division of labor, even on the individual level, perpetuates itself in such a way that, although the truth content of theory and art converge, access to it may be gained only via a strict renunciation of the methods and techniques of the other sphere of inquiry. No one knew better than Adorno that aesthetic theory was still theory and not aesthetic and that theory placed into artworks unchanged makes the artworks as encrusted as they are theoretically uncompelling. "The social division of labor recoils on man, however much it may expedite the task exacted from him" (MM, 22). Whoever, like Adorno, refuses to allow his work to be made less pleasurable by society and who feels his thought to be "nourished" by the "finest objectification" of the "drives" will refuse to allow thought and drive, emotion and discursivity, concept and image to be muddied by a mixing of these extremes (MM, 122). He will more likely direct his own psychology and will reappropriate society's decision to seek a compromise between the two in the hope that he might temporarily outwit if not outrun the decision. Even if most people nowadays get by by going against the grain, the fact remains that to rebel against even this requires a splinter (MM, 109).

III

Adorno's splinter was theory; literary works remained in his desk and were reserved for friends. The same did not hold for the compositional works, however. Adorno sought publishers and even performances for them. It was probably that the conceptless language of music produced a different relationship between philosophy and composition than exists between philosophy and literature, which use the same medium, both employing words as carriers of meaning.[4] Adorno's early interests and studies were divided equally between philosophy and music, and he refused to decide between the two for a long time. Even after World War II, Adorno writes that he has "felt his whole life" that he was "pursuing the same thing in two diverging realms."[5]

Adorno initially studied composition and piano with Bernhard Sekles and Eduard Jung in Frankfurt, but he left for Vienna in 1925 to study with Alban Berg and Eduard Steuermann. The few of Adorno's own compositions which up to the end satisfied him were produced in the period 1923 to 1945. Shortly before his death, Adorno often spoke of taking up composing again once he was free of his responsibilities as university professor and director of the Frankfurt Institute for Social Research. It never came to that.

Adorno's compositions were played occasionally before 1933 but have been played more often since the 1950s. It was chiefly Carla Henius who took up the piano song cycles, which make up the largest part of Adorno's oeuvre. Adorno also composed pieces for orchestra and chamber music for violins and a cappella choirs, arranged piano pieces by Schumann for a small orchestra, and set French folk songs to music. Only *Sechs kurze Orchesterstücke* (op. 4) are in print, the score having been published in 1968 by Ricordi in Milan. Musicians such as Ernst Křenek, René Leibowitz, and Dieters Schnebel have attested to Adorno's significance as a composer.

Those who are familiar with Adorno's writings on music and know that he regularly wrote opera reviews in the decade preceding 1933 will not be surprised to know that he was also interested in the production of operas. His Singspiel *Der Schatz des Indianer-Joe* (*The Treasure of Indian Joe*), based on Mark Twain's novel *The Adventures of Tom Sawyer*, developed out of this interest between 1932 and 1933.[6]

IV

Adorno often warned against taking the artist to be the best commentator on his own work. The artist's subjective additions to the interpretation are rather cause for skepticism on the side of the critic. What counts is what the artwork realizes objectively; the artist's intention is only one more moment among many, most of which are more significant.[7] Adorno, of course, did allow the artist's intention to form the starting point for his interpretation: By measuring the real work with the intended work, the interpreter can, under certain circumstances, make out more about the work than by simply following the artist's interpretation. If this essay makes reference to Adorno's comments on *Schatz des Indianer-Joe*, this may be appropriate for several other reasons as well. For one, the intent is not to give a full interpretation of the work but rather to provide some indications of how to read the text, since this work presents the reader with a hitherto unknown aspect of Adorno's oeuvre. This other aspect of Adorno's writing does not simply follow his philosophy, as passages from a letter to Benjamin make clear. The different medium of the libretto is well situated to illuminate aspects of his philosophical writing, just as philosophy can shed light on *Schatz des Indianer-Joe* by showing the libretto's proximity to central theoretical themes in Adorno's work. Furthermore, a libretto is certainly not an autonomous work of art. It is no Mörikean "artwork of a genuine sort" but rather, to use a phrase that finally is appropriate, a piece of utility-art (*Gebrauchskunst*). In order to produce anything at all, the composer of the Singspiel "needs" the literary basis. Only fully composed operas themselves might be called artworks in the strong sense, since only they have realized the unity of text and music. *Schatz des Indianer-Joe* did not come this far. What we have – the text itself – ought to be judged on a different scale than a work of art which claims authenticity for itself. The author of this essay however, is grateful to be able to cite a few cursory remarks by Adorno which allow him to defend Adorno against some misconceptions about the work; he may even be able to anticipate a little of what Adorno's project might have looked like had it not been abandoned.

V

Adorno must have shown his libretto to friends soon after finishing it. He even conducted an epistolary exchange with Benjamin, which follows. Benjamin wrote to Adorno on January 29, 1934, from Paris:

There are certain circumstances which only add weight to the difficulties and dangers attendant upon any long period of separation. This is exactly what has happened with regard to "The Treasure of Indian Joe." In the relationship in which we have stood to one another for some years, it has been a rare thing for a major piece by one of us to reach the other simply and directly in its final form. On reading the piece I have occasionally wished that we could have discussed the project in detail with one another earlier. A rather selfish wish, perhaps; but how it would have relieved me in my present predicament, had it been fulfilled. You would soon have realized that this range of material itself – quite apart from the musical question about which I cannot venture any opinion whatsoever – appears to me to be an unpromising one. I am not even sure whether or not you mentioned it to me, at least by title. But if so, this Mark Twain simply remained a title and nothing more to me. But we have had no real contact during the period in which the plan progressed, and the circumstances which occasioned this fact perhaps led you to withdraw even further into your work. However that may be – my protracted silence will certainly have alerted you to the unusual difficulties which have obstructed the expression of my reaction in this case. If I have nonetheless decided to express it now, you will also recognize here – inasmuch as you weigh *that* rather than *how* I do so – an untarnished image of our relationship. I should have much preferred to have congratulated you in detail upon your sketch of children in "Four-Handed Once Again"[8] – the most recent thing of yours which I have read. This piece is closer to me than the atmosphere in which your opera has surrounded childhood. I believe I can imagine what you were attempting here. And unless my suspicion is quite wrong, it is difficult to see, after Cocteau, how such a thing could properly succeed. For in his "Enfants terribles" everything unfolds *more dangerously*. And it is indeed this danger which constitutes the measure for working out what you seem to me – in the very highest sense – to have been intending. You can be sure that I have not overlooked certain very fine things in the piece. Especially the cave scenes, for example. But it is essentially the reduction to the idyllic, as expressed both by the songs and the course of action itself, which is incompatible, in my opinion, with the substantive issues with which you are here concerned. For in fact, childhood could only be invoked so immediately with the spilling of sacrificial blood. And in Cocteau that flows freely enough. But in your case the straightforward, rustic tone of the dialogue only impedes this.

Without seeing in these lines any other claim than that contained in my *most personal* judgment, I would ask you to recognize in them the same solidarity which for my part I shall soon express in my *public* judgment on your Kierkegaard book.[9]

Adorno, still in Berlin, responded to this ultimately devastating criticism on March 4, 1934:

For weeks now I have been carrying around a detailed letter concerned with the question of Tom Sawyer, since your lines are naturally the only thing of substance on the mater which I have received. But in the meantime I have heard from Felicitas [Gretel Karplus, Adorno's wife] about your own highly critical predicament, and under these circumstances I can well imagine that any extended aesthetic discussion would only seem rather insulting in the context.

I have preferred therefore to do something for you. . . .

About "Tom" I will say only this: I believe that the stars which preside over "Les enfants terribles" are not particularly favorable to this piece. What is at issue here is something very different, and something which, I hope, is not merely personal to me. The hearty language is not the heartiness of real children, so much as that encountered in the literature written for children; nor does the course of the action, the focal point of which is of course the cave scene, strike me as that harmless either; if it doesn't sound too arrogant, I would perhaps suggest that I have smuggled a great deal into the piece, that nothing is quite intended in the sense in which it immediately appears, and that I am using the childlike imagery to present some extremely serious things: in this connection I am far more concerned with presenting this image of childhood than I am with invoking childhood as such. The process in which the piece has evolved also possesses something of those perilous moments which you found lacking in it. It is certainly not to be measured in comparison with Cocteau, nor with anything in "epic theater"; if anything, it is most closely related to my Kierkegaard book. The central issue is the violation of the oath and the whole thing represents a projected flight: the expression of fear. Perhaps it will show a different and more congenial face to you if you take another look at it; for I can hardly believe with regard to this work above all that you, its ideal reader, should have failed to appreciate it. – Incidentally, you were familiar not only with the general plan, but also with two scenes (the cemetery and the haunted house) which I read out at Schoen's place, on the very same evening when you read us the first installment of the Ar (I nearly wrote: the Arcades! What a telling lapse!), no, of the Berlin Childhood. So much simply in defense against the charge of launching something wholly unexpected upon you. As far as the music is concerned, that is well underway.[10]

To close the epistolary debate, here is a passage from a letter by Benjamin from Paris, dated March 9, 1934:

I . . . hope that we shall no longer have to put off a meeting between ourselves in the near future. . . . This seems to me all the more urgent since we really do have to discuss "Tom" in some detail with one another. It was quite obvious to me from the first that, as the old Bedouin proverb has it, death is hiding within the fold of Tom's cloak. And the reservations expressed in my letter concerned the execution rather than your central intentions. But everything does indeed depend upon the concept of the "children's approach" itself, and in order to discuss and develop all that I would need you to be here in person.[11]

Adorno and Benjamin probably never again discussed *Schatz des Indianer-Joe*, as their next meeting took place in 1936, when Adorno had already abandoned the composition for the Singspiel and by which time they had a new set of problems to discuss.

VI

Although the key phrase "invocation of childhood" may well have been on the mind of the author of "A Berlin Childhood around 1900,"[12] it represents a serious misunderstanding of what Adorno had in mind. Only someone whose real childhood lacked happiness would seek to recover the right life, forever beaten out of us by the self-conscious life of adults, in dreams of his childhood; such a person's later unhappiness might, in psychoanalytic terms, be blamed on an unhappy childhood. Adorno's childhood was, by all accounts, an exception. It seems to have been so carefree and fulfilled, so "undangerous," that the adult Adorno did not need the fantasy of a happy childhood. He did not have to "invoke" reserves of happiness off of which he could concretely live. Of course, Adorno must also have known moments in which, though he was not faced with a ditch of sacrificial blood, he did face an abyss into which every fantasy inevitably sinks and from which his childhood must have stared back at him. Here he faced the deathly fear of losing that which one believes to be secure to the very last: the continuing promise that seemed to guarantee a happy childhood. This notion, already present in the creative beginnings of *Schatz des Indianer-Joe*, seems to be what the phrase "moments of danger" alludes to. Adorno composed most of the libretto during the first few months of the Nazi regime, when he, socialist and half-Jew, had lost his university post and was restricted to teaching music only to "non-Aryans" but still could not bring himself to emigrate from the country whose language was his native tongue.[13] Simple autobiographical fear is also depicted in the character of Tom Sawyer, but this fear is rather the concrete fear of a thirty-year-old who needs more than a year to abandon the lap of his old house, which has come to represent only fear and dread, than the amorphous fear of a child. It was not until the spring of 1934, while he was still working on the Singspiel, that Adorno moved first to London and then to Oxford. Adorno claims that it was Benjamin's criticism of the libretto, which disheartened him more than he admits in the quoted letter, which caused him to break off the composition. It is also possible, however, that the composition was no longer psychologically important for him. Leaving the country which could no longer afford the composer a dignified life had done "almost nothing" to "make everything better." Even if departure did improve some things, it certainly did nothing to improve that which would have been important for the conception of *Schatz des Indianer-Joe*. Finally, there were subjective as well as objective reasons which forced the artist Adorno to concentrate more on theoretical work. The subjective reasons included the fact that he had to earn a living in exile; the objective reasons were that he was far more expert in the fields of philosophy and sociology and that these disciplines were better at speaking for those whom he had left behind in the house of dread.

VII

"He took your life, /they let me go, /.../ it was I who destroyed you." A Singspiel which opens with a *Totenlied* – even if it is sung by a boy to a tomcat whom he tried to cure with a "painkiller," harmless medicine of his own fabrication, is hardly *for* children, even if its protagonists *are* children. Nothing is intended just as it is written; the author is not so much concerned with what the child does than with what is made out of the child. After Tom has satisfied the convention of the *Totenlied*, he accuses the cat: "He is now useless." The fact that even children see a living being who has died as a useless thing and that they subsequently recognize the corpse as having a use value – the dead cat might be used to remove warts – shows that the quid pro quo which the libretto constitutes between the world of children and that of adults is present even in the opening tableau. The absence of the kitsch love story in *The Adventures of Tom Sawyer* notwithstanding, *Schatz des Indianer-Joe* follows Mark Twain's fable quite closely. The librettist's "intentions" are in part indicated by those small changes which he did feel were necessary. In Twain's novel, for example, Tom gives his cat the medicine only toward the middle of the novel, and the cat escapes by throwing itself out the window, merely bleeding. Nothing indicates, however, that the poor cat will die. (Twain does not indicate how the other cat dies, the one which Tom and Huckleberry Finn try to use to charm away their warts.) But the cat in *Schatz des Indianer-Joe* remains important throughout: Its corpse is present when Dr. Robinson is murdered and becomes a piece of evidence for the solution of the murder case. The cat is also referred to in the last tableau, during which Tom and Huck Finn arrange to bury the cat, as the conciliatory ending of the Singspiel requires, despite the otherwise gruesome material of the story.

The enumeration of "all those beautiful things," themselves already dead and useless, following the death lament in the first tableau sounds at first like a parody of Lautréamont's famous definition of beauty in modernity as "a chance encounter between a sewing machine and an umbrella on an operating table." But Adorno's intentions are quite different. For him, Tom's collector frenzy is an image of the ubiquitous and already irrational society in which everything is exchangeable, be it the "apple core with a little bit of apple left," the "knife without a handle," or the "piece of window frame" which was received in payment for the privilege of painting Aunt Polly's fence – all junk. In order to show the absurdity of exchanging abstract labor for abstract goods, in which the use value necessary for the reproduction of labor is merely "dragged with it," as Adorno says, the process is reversed: It is not Tom who, as the entrepreneur, buys the labor of his friends, but rather the little painters, convinced by Tom of the value and privilege of painting the fence, who pay *him*. One must be thankful for any work, even if it is without pay or even requires payment. It is this Hebelian lesson which may have persuaded the author, who was writing during the economic crisis in the early 1930s, to keep the scene from Twain's novel. The junk heap "of all the beautiful things, which I have traded," depicted with so much care in the libretto, reads like a caricature of our present society, which could not have been imagined at the time it was written. The scene is a piece of truth content which, according to Adorno's later *Aesthetic Theory*, is only made manifest through the story.

Schatz des Indianer-Joe proceeds by mediated demonstration, by Brechtian showing (even if Adorno would have rejected the term) rather than by immediate invocation. Using material from a mid-nineteenth century American children's story, which seems as exotic now as so-called primitive peoples might have seemed during the Enlightenment, was as much a means for the librettist to distance himself and alienate himself from the content (to use Brecht's phrase) as the dialogue itself. Vis-à-vis Benjamin, Adorno insisted that the Singspiel had nothing to do with the language of children. The patter out of which the dialogue is constructed was pregiven, not by Mark Twain, who only realized that he had written a children's book after the novel's enormous success, but by children's book authors of a certain type, themselves infantile, who, by imagining how children speak, actually lead children to speak in this way once they have read sufficient amounts of this garbage. In order to avoid any doubt about the dialogue's artificiality, Adorno adds bits of Frankfurt dialect to the language of his young protagonists from Hannibal on the Mississippi; clarity is more important than credibility in the sense of some verism. The dialogue in *Schatz des Indianer-Joe* proceeds through and against certain language patterns – by ironizing he turns against it, by exaggeration he moves with it – in order to depict the "very serious things" which Adorno has in mind. The America portrayed in *Schatz des Indianer-Joe* is neither the real America nor Mark Twain's America; it rather resembles the dreamlike America depicted in Franz Kafka's novel of the same name. Adorno tries to depict this mystical world of the petit bourgeoisie which orients itself only according to money and polite behavior and which is experienced as the nightmare it in fact is only by those, like Tom and Huck, who do not completely belong to that society.[14]

VIII

The two boys accidentally witness Indian Joe commit a murder, for which he then successfully frames the blind drunk Muff Potter. Reigning judicial as well as moral practice requires a statement by a witness, possibly under oath, to give a correct account of the events. When the influence of natural right theories of justice waned, moral and judicial legitimacy fell apart; however, that which natural theories of justice aimed at and which was replaced by the formalisms of positivist theories of justice survives in the oath. The oath contains an element of an earlier world, a bending back of history into prehistory, which Adorno, following Benjamin, calls the mythos. "The Song of Watching" (*"Das Lied vom Zusehen"*) shows succinctly what this means for the breakdown of law, for that guarantee of justice which bourgeois society believes will suffice to uphold the law. The song in the second tableau reads thus: "Someone is murdered / no one saw it / no one is guilty / ... / someone is murdered / another person did it / two watched it happen / all are guilty, / as long as they don't speak." A system of justice which depends on observation, on the existence of witnesses and on their willingness to testify, must protect itself by requiring its witnesses to take an oath to prevent per-jury. If they do commit perjury, they are threatened with the same punishment as the criminal. The system of justice thus reverts to a mythical definition of justice which is only seemingly superan-nuated and which Aristotle attributes to a nameless predecessor of Thales. According to Thales, the gods themselves had to swear the oath: "[T]he most honorable is the oldest, the oath is the most hon-orable" – this seems also to have been Aristotle's opinion. The oath of the gods then turned into the ορκos which humans pledged to the gods and which, as Aristotle knew well, was used to legitimate unverifiable statements to which only the gods could attest.[15] This is not very different than the way the oath works in our modern law courts, which, though they have taken to prosecuting perjury, only reluctantly allow people to swear by anything but the Bible. Kant, the incorruptible citizen, recognized that the oath was a means of "blackmail" and saw that the oath depended on mythical determina-tion and was a point at which enlightened self-determination failed; as a bourgeois, however, he recognized that such "blackmail" was indispensable for legal practice.[16]

Tom and Huck, though they have witnessed the murder, are reluc-tant to testify, as their fear of the murderer's revenge outweighs their trust in the courts. The fearful individual thus experiences himself as relying on himself only and as opposed to society in general. In circumstances where this opposition remains sufficiently general, an evildoer – in this case Indian Joe, who threatens to "butcher" the children – functions as an agent of this false society in which no one is safe. Society then refers the threatened party to a second mythi-cal principle, but it can do no better than a second oath, this time not a legal one, since the object is to evade exactly that, but an oath which will bring the deviants and outsiders together in a commu-nity which opposes the anonymous society at large: "Tom Sawyer and Huck Finn / swear at the open Grave, that they / will breathe nothing of this / now and for all times." This oath, the invocation, is similar and yet different than the ορκos. The two children seem to be living what can be read about one hundred years later in Sartre's *Critique of Dialectical Reason*. By swearing to be silent "now and for ever," they come together to protect themselves from a murderer and from a society which is not able to protect them. This deed is "the origin of humanity" ("*le commencement de l'humanité*"),[17] in the sense that both are equals as they seek to extricate themselves from the amorphous myth – Sartre speaks of *limon* (mud) – which determines society. The conjuration of *"la Terreur,"* however, remains the same as *"la peur"* (fear) from which it springs. That which comes from fear and requires terror to be implemented ("We hope to die if we ever break the oath and breathe a word to anyone" is merely self-directed terror), even if it is humanity itself, is hardly more humane than that which it seeks to resist. It is ultimately the oath the two boys swear which imprisons them in the same society, one that has revealed its mythical nature by requiring the legal oath, which they try to escape from by their second oath.

IX

It is more humane to break the oath than to keep it since the oath is meant to save Tom and Huck's skins by hiding the truth. Not only does it save the life of an innocent man and reinstate the truth, it also demythologizes the world a bit more. Tom's decision to break the false oath is not motivated by pity for Muff Potter, who is to hang for a crime he has not committed. None of the great idealist philosophers who justified the oath or at least believed the oath to be necessary felt completely comfortable doing so. Kant held the oath to be "fundamentally wrong... since even in the civil condition coercion to take oaths is contrary to human freedom, which must not be lost."[18] Hegel considered the oath to be a last recourse but really only subjective in nature,[19] while Schopenhauer even granted "people the right to lie in certain circumstances."[20] Schopenhauer's pity is ultimately a better principle by which to live a good life than according to even a logically deduced or a posited set of rigorous ideas which leave the world merely as it is. Thus Tom effects more by breaking the oath than only saving Potter: "And here, I think it is also an adventure when someone breaks an oath." The least significant element in the decision is probably the recognition that the oath is immoral; the two boys realized this from the very beginning. Pity is accompanied by the ever present but unconscious opposition to a society which must reach back to the legal institution of the oath as a "final recourse," to the purely subjective and empty oath in the midst of objective resistance. Tom's protest against such a society manifests itself in the search for adventure, in bandit and pirate games and in the hunt for buried treasure. Nor does his fantasy lack the image of the beautiful woman who, once she has been brought to land by the pirates and has fallen in love with her captor, is difficult to rid oneself of. Adorno even remodels the boys' superstition, their belief in ghosts and goblins as well as their attempts to rid themselves of warts, all taken directly from the Twain novel; they present the mirror image of the desire for an alternative to the ordinary. Adorno once cautioned, "Reason, as governor of stupidity, concerned or mockingly worries that one should not over-interpret texts."[21] Even if it is overinterpretation, one must say that *Schatz des Indianer-Joe* is also *objectively* a work of art which itself deals with art: The boys' longing for freedom and openness which they seek to satisfy, at least at times, is nothing less than the longing of *all* art, only on a higher level.

Tom and Huck's adventurous escape into the unknown, their flight to Jackson's Island, and the treasure hunt in the caves are all purchased at the price of new anxieties: "The central issue is the violation of the oath and the whole thing represents a projected flight: the expression of fear," these three terms belong together in the Singspiel and in real life. The story makes clear that the desire for adventure and freedom, the source of all hope, is tied to the fear of Indian Joe's revenge and hence to the impossibility of living a truly free life. Tom and Huck are *also* children, not just adult types; this can be seen in a pattern of fear which is ineluctable in a world permitting no one to break free of it and which accompanies the two in their hesitant attempts to break out of the world of grown-ups. But fear is dialectical, an "overreaching generality," as Hegel's *Logic* calls this figure of thought: It is not *merely* fear but fear *and* its opposite, the final freedom from fear. Here is Adorno's theoretical formulation: "The capacity for fear and for happiness are the same, the unrestricted openness to experience amounting to self-abandonment in which the vanquished rediscovers himself" (MM, 200). This insight, demonstrated through a childish image and presented in the form of a Singspiel, seems at first harmless but suggests a far-reaching power. Whatever small happiness Tom and Huck experience, their openness to new experiences – which are no longer possible for adults and which they anyway seek to beat out of children – comes finally from their willingness to suffer fear or to stop playing along when the game becomes too dangerous.

X

Less than a year after Hitler came to power and half a year before Adorno started work on *Schatz des Indianer-Joe*, Adorno wrote the following about a new production of *The Magic Flute* in Frankfurt:

In a time in which the word "Enlightenment" has become a term of abuse and in which the divinely mystical powers of blood have begun to call on the spirit, the idea that the age of music which is still called classical in Germany, and which was started with a work not merely enlightened in its text, but in the very being of its reconciling sounds is thoroughly enlightened, without thereby betraying its nature, gives us hope that the power of nature itself turns toward enlightenment and reconciliation.[22]

The Singspiel, which initially came from the French comic opera but subsequently became a specifically German form, has always been critical of society: Adorno's libretto admits this freely. It is almost as if Adorno the librettist has anticipated the theoretician by having already developed the dialectic of enlightenment in 1933. Here enlightenment is no longer celebrated in Mozart's sense as the "liberation of the human from the spell of the mother and the reconciliation with the ground of nature."[23] In *Schatz des Indianer-Joe*, freedom can no longer be found in nature, either on the island in the Mississippi or in the cave in the forest. The boys are as unsuccessful at escaping the mythical spell of society as humans have been in reuniting with nature since the time of *The Magic Flute*. The hated world of the citizens of Hannibal, the core of capitalist production, has become second nature and has poisoned and disfigured the first. For Adorno, the adventures, the pirate games, and the treasure hunt represent something rendered impossible by society: They are attempts to overleap society and create a reconciled world. This impossibility is registered by the piece – in art humans still remain captives of the spell. Fear soon catches up with the boys, who are fishing and living an outdoor life in disfigured nature. Even here they are unlucky and cannot find the adventures they are looking for. Benjamin's criticism of the idyllic quality of the play, most merited by the island tableau, is shown to be unjust by the tableau itself: "We cannot escape / from this old house, / the house is much too large, / there we rest as in our mother's lap, / and if we run somewhere for fear, / we are still in it [mother's lap], / this makes us afraid and disgusts us / we cannot escape." In the sixth tableau, the house – a symbol associated with the mother by psychoanalysis – turns into a cave. The mythos catches up to what once sheltered humans from mythical nature: mother, cave, and house. The nineteenth-century interior, which Adorno interprets, in his book on Kierkegaard, just like Benjamin, appears to have been moved into nature in *Schatz des Indianer-Joe*; the scenes in the sixth tableau are literally a series of interiors representing the inescapable cave. "The forest outside" seems "completely different" to Tom once he finds his way out: "As if it were only painted. Not a real forest at all." For *Schatz des Indianer-Joe*, the motto that there is no right life in falsehood means that there is no true nature where society is false.

XI

Hope, without which a Singspiel cannot progress, is present, if at all, only in hopelessness. Redemption does not come from fleeing the world but, following Marx, from *changing* it: "We cannot find adventure, / we are freer in Hannibal, / ... / there we will always argue, /we have our own thoughts, / there we will make everything new." Adorno never thought of reconciled nature as the abstract antithesis of domination and social disfiguration but rather as the transformation of the nature-dominating principle through its own self-reflection. But Tom and Huck are not social revolutionaries, they are characters in a Singspiel and cannot be expected to make *everything* new. The very serious things in *Schatz des Indianer-Joe* which Adorno wrote to Benjamin about befit the Singspiel: The treasure which the two find at the end allows them at least to live a decent life in an inhospitable society. The right society would be not completely different but, as Adorno says in the words of a Jewish mystic, a world in which everything is like it is here and now, only a little different. "Almost nothing has made everything all right" goes a line toward the end of the "Song of Thanking." By remaining so close in tone to the poetry of German romanticism, especially to the *Wunderhorn* songs, the poems of the Singspiel sound not like parody but rather like disillusioned poetry. The elements of the folk song which seem to provide comfort and safety are revealed to be lying about their proximity to home. This becomes especially clear when Muff Potter, accused of murder and waiting to be hanged, sings unseen from his prison cell, "In the forest, in the beautiful green forest" and "Sleep in peace." Occasionally, however, Adorno entrusts the serious things which he "means" to individual verses or strophes. These can be found in "The Song of Thanking," in the children's choir at the beginning of the cave scenes, and in "The Song of Fear." Here all false sense of the romantic is left out, and one believes oneself to have refound in the fictional quotation what one has merely forgotten, just as children listen to fairy tales which anticipate what they have not yet lived. "Almost nothing has made everything all right": This is *also* a theory of the fairy tale, ahead of all science. "We step into the cave / and play one afternoon / in the hope that no one will be lost / at the last tolling of the bell." Here Benjamin's "invocation" of childhood and Adorno's insistence on enlightenment finally sound in unison. If invocation is still a mythical act, then "only what gives myth its due can provide liberation from myth" (NL, 145). *Schatz des Indianer-Joe* hoped to represent fear in the same way music does, namely, by articulating the fears "of helpless human beings" to "signal help for the helpless, however feebly and distortedly. In doing so it would renew the promise contained in the age-old protest of music: the promise of a life without fear."[24] If one undertook the difficult task of articulating the content of Adorno's libretto in the language which is common to both Adorno and Benjamin, one might say that the aim was to show that what corresponds to mythos is fear and the world which has still forgotten hunger but must concretely abolish it (as is stated in a decisive materialist phrase at the end of the second finale); music, on the other hand, corresponds to that gentle and healing power which humans have only succeeded in representing through symbols in fairy tales. Representing fear through music thus aims at nothing less than the reconciliation between mythos and fairy tale. It would be difficult to imagine a more serious or ambitious task for a Singspiel. Even the Mozart of *The Abduction from the Seraglio* and of *The Magic Flute* could not accomplish this task.

XII

If one were to offer *Schatz des Indianer-Joe* as pre-Christmas entertainment, perhaps completed by someone else in a spectacular rubato and performed in high comic style, the piece would hardly fail to impress. But one must not, as this would almost certainly be the exact opposite of what Adorno himself had intended to bring to the stage. Only the composition is capable of fully bringing out what the author has let seep into the text. Unfortunately, too little of the composition is extant for the work to be completed. Adorno did not plan to publish the libretto independently of the music; he know too much about literature to consider the libretto by itself to be poetry.

Translated by Stefan Bird-Pollan

NOTES

1. Theodor W. Adorno, *Der Schatz des Indianer-Joe; Singspiel nach Mark Twain*, ed. Rolf Tiedemann (Frankfurt: Suhrkamp, 1979), 57.
2. Theodor W. Adorno. *Minima Moralia: Reflections from Damaged Life*, trans. E. F. N. Jephcott (London: New Left Books, 1974), 21. Hereafter cited as MM.
3. Theodor W. Adorno, *Kierkegaard: Construction of the Aesthetic*, trans. Robert Hullot-Kentor (Minneapolis: University of Minnesota Press, 1989), 3. Hereafter cited as KKA.
4. Theodor W. Adorno. *Quasi una fantasia: Essays on Modern Music*, trans. Rodney Livingstone (New York: Verso, 1992), 6.
5. Letter of July 5, 1948, to Thomas Mann, unpublished manuscript.
6. The libretto, which had previously only been published in excerpt in the *Frankfurter Opernheften* (vol. 6, no. 3, December 15, 1976), was not based on the original English text, since at that time Adorno's command of English was not yet very good. Instead it was based on several German translations of *Tom Sawyer*. The text is contained in his papers and is typewritten with many corrections by the author both in ink and pencil. Sometimes there are several versions without indication as to which the author preferred. In these instances, the decision about which to include was the editor's.
7. Cf. Theodor W. Adorno, *Notes to Literature*, vol. 1, trans. Shierry Weber Nicholson (New York: Columbia University Press, 1991), 110. Hereafter cited as NL.
8. Cf. Theodor W. Adorno, *Impromptus: Zweite Folge neu gedruckter musikalischer Aufsätze* (Frankfurt: Suhrkamp, 1968), 142.
9. Theodor W. Adorno and Walter Benjamin, *The Complete Correspondence, 1928–1940*, ed. Henri Lonitz, trans. Nicholas Walker (Cambridge, Mass.: Harvard University Press, 1999), 23–4. For his judgement on Adorno's book on Kierkegaard, see Walter Benjamin, *Selected*

Writings, vol. 2 (1927–1934), ed. Michael W. Jennings et al., trans. Rodney Livingstone et al. (Cambridge, Mass.: Harvard University Press, 1999), 703–5.

10. Adorno and Benjamin, *Complete Correspondence*, 25–6.

11. Adorno and Benjamin, *Complete Correspondence*, 28.

12. In Benjamin, *Selected Writings*, vol. 2, 595–637; translated as "A Berlin Chronicle."

13. Theodor W. Adorno and Ernst Křenek, *Briefwechsel*, ed. Wolfgang Rogge (Frankfurt: Suhrkamp, 1974), 43.

14. Adorno's "*Schatz des Indianer-Joe*," set in the nineteenth century in the United States, deals with the same issues that Benjamin had already approached in his study of Paris in the nineteenth century; both diagnosed the rapidly aging figures of fathers and grandfathers as primordial figures. This, however, is the topic of Benjamin's *Arcades Project*, which we witnessed Adorno write as a parapraxis – in his March 4, 1934, letter to Benjamin – when he meant to write "A Berlin Childhood around 1900." It was ultimately the close resemblance between what had been intended in the *Arcades Project* and in "*Schatz des Indianer-Joe*" which hindered Benjamin from seeing Adorno's text as an effort to follow Benjamin's lead.

15. Cf. Aristotle *Metaphysics* 983b; *Rhetoric to Alexander* 1432a.

16. Cf. *Kant on History and Religion*, trans. Michael Despland (Montreal and London: McGill–Queen's University Press, 1973), 295.

17. Jean-Paul Sartre, *Critique de la raison dialectique*, vol. 1, *Théorie des ensembles pratiques* (Paris: Gallimard, 1960), 453; translated by Alan Sheridan-Smith under the title *Critique of Dialectical Reason*, vol. 1 (London: New Left Books, 1976).

18. Immanuel Kant, *The Metaphysics of Morals*, trans. Mary Gregor, ed. Roger J. Sullivan (Cambridge: Cambridge University Press, 1996), 119.

19. G. W. F. Hegel, *The Philosophy of Right*, trans. T. M. Knox (Oxford: Oxford University Press, 1952), 143–4.

20. Arthur Schopenhauer, *Parerga and Paralipomena; Short Philosophical Essays*, vol. 2, trans. E. F. J. Payne (Oxford: Clarendon Press, 1974), 264–6.

21. Theodor W. Adorno, "Geklärt" (unpublished manuscript).

22. Theodor W. Adorno [*Opernkritik*] in *Die Musik* 24 (1931–2), 368.

23. Adorno [Opernkritik], 368.

24. Theodor W. Adorno, *In Search of Wagner*, trans. Rodney Livingstone (London: New Left Books, 1981), 156.

SELECT BIBLIOGRAPHY

ADORNO'S GERMAN PUBLICATIONS

Gesammelte Schriften. 20 vols. in 23 books. Edited by Rolf Tiedemann. Vol. 5, 7, and 13 are coedited by Gretel Adorno. Vol. 9 is coedited by Susan Buck-Morss. Frankfurt: Suhrkamp, 1970–1986. Date of original publication or composition appears in brackets.

1 *Philosophische Frühschriften.*
"Die Transzendenz des Dinglichen und Noematischen in Husserls Phänomenologie" [1924].
"Der Begriff des Unbewussten in der transzendentalen Seelenlehre" [1927].
"Die Aktualität der Philosophie" [1931].
"Die Idee der Naturgeschichte" [1932].
"Thesen über die Sprache des Philosophen" [early 1930s].
2 *Kierkegaard: Konstruktion des Ästhetischen* [1933].
3 *Dialektik der Aufklärung: Philosophische Fragmente* (with Max Horkheimer) [1944].
4 *Minima Moralia: Reflexionen aus dem beschädigten Leben* [1951].
5 *Zur Metakritik der Erkenntnistheorie: Studien über Husserl und die phänomenologischen Antinomien* [1956].
Drei Studien zu Hegel [1953].
6 *Negative Dialektik* [1966].
Jargon der Eigentlichkeit: Zur deutschen Ideologie [1964].
7 *Ästhetische Theorie* [1970].
8 *Soziologische Schriften I* [various].
9.1 *Soziologische Schriften II: Erste Hälfte.*
"The Psychological Technique of Martin Luther Thomas' Radio Addresses" [1943].
Studies in the Authoritarian Personality [1950].
9.2 *Soziologische Schriften II: Zweite Hälfte*
The Stars Down to Earth [1957].

Schuld und Abwehr [1955].

10.1 *Kulturkritik und Gesellschaft I.*

Prismen [1955].

Ohne Leitbild: Parva Aesthetica [1967].

10.2 *Kulturkritik und Gesellschaft II.*

Eingriffe: Neun kritische Modelle [1963].

Stichworte [1969].

11 *Noten zur Literatur* [1958, 1961, 1965, 1974].

12 *Philosophie der neuen Musik* [1949].

13 *Die musikalischen Monographien.*

Versuch über Wagner [1952].

Berg: Der Meister des kleinsten Übergangs [1968].

Mahler: Eine musikalische Physiognomik [1960].

14 *Dissonanzen: Musik in der verwalteten Welt* [1956].

Einleitung in die Musiksoziologie: Zwölf theoretische Vorlesungen [1962].

15 *Komposition für den Film* [1944, 1969].

Der getreue Korrepetitor [1963].

16 *Musikalische Schriften I–III.*

Klangfiguren [1959].

Quasi una fantasia [1963].

17 *Musikalische Schriften IV.*

Moments Musicaux [1964].

Impromptus: Zweite Folge neu gedruckter musikalischer Aufsätze [1968].

18 *Musikalische Schriften V* [various].

19 *Musikalische Schriften VI* [various].

20.1 *Vermischte Schriften I* [various].

20.2 *Vermischte Schriften II* [various].

Nachgelassene Schriften [NS]. Approximately thirty volumes of posthumous writings are planned as "Editions of the Theodor W. Adorno Archive." Frankfurt: Suhrkamp, 1993– . The following have thus far been published.

Beethoven: Philosophie der Musik. Fragments and texts. Edited by Rolf Tiedemann. Frankfurt: Suhrkamp, 1993. [NS I.1].

Zu einer Theorie der musikalischen Reproduktion. Edited by Henri Lonitz. Frankfurt: Suhrkamp, 2001. [NS I.2].

Kants "Kritik der reinen Vernunft." Edited by Rolf Tiedemann. Frankfurt: Suhrkamp, 1995. [NS IV.4].

Ontologie und Dialektik. Edited by Rolf Tiedemann. Frankfurt: Suhrkamp, 2002. [NS IV.7].

Probleme der Moralphilosophie. Edited by Thomas Schröder. Frankfurt: Suhrkamp, 1996. [NS IV.10].

Zur Lehre von der Geschichte und von der Freiheit. Edited by Rolf Tiedemann. Frankfurt: Suhrkamp, 2001. [NS IV.13].
Metaphysik: Begriff und Probleme. Edited by Rolf Tiedemann. Frankfurt: Suhrkamp, 1998. [NS IV.14].
Einleitung in die Soziologie. Edited by Christoph Gödde. Frankfurt: Suhrkamp, 1993. [NS IV.15].
Vorlesung über Negative Dialektik. Edited by Rolf Tiedemann. Frankfurt: Suhrkamp, 2003. [NS IV.16].

ADDITIONAL GERMAN PUBLICATIONS

Erziehung zur Mündigkeit: Vorträge und Gespräche mit Hellmut Becker, 1959–1969. Edited by Gerd Kadelbach. Frankfurt: Suhrkamp, 1970.
Philosophische Terminologie: Zur Einleitung. Edited by Rudolf zur Lippe from lectures given in 1962–3. 2 vols. Frankfurt: Suhrkamp, 1973–4.
Der Positivismusstreit in der deutschen Soziologie. Theodor W. Adorno et al. Neuwied and Berlin: Luchterhand, 1969. (Adorno's contributions are reprinted in *Gesammelte Schriften*, vol. 8).
Theodor W. Adorno und Alban Berg: Briefwechsel 1925–1935. Edited by Henri Lonitz. Frankfurt: Suhrkamp, 1997.
Theodor W. Adorno und Ernst Křenek: Briefwechsel. Edited by Wolfgang Rogge. Frankfurt: Suhrkamp, 1974.
Theodor W. Adorno und Max Horkheimer: Briefwechsel 1927–1937. Edited by Henri Lonitz. Frankfurt: Suhrkamp, 2003.
Theodor W. Adorno und Thomas Mann: Briefwechsel 1943–1955. Edited by Henri Lonitz. Frankfurt: Suhrkamp, 2002.
Theodor W. Adorno und Walter Benjamin: Briefwechsel 1928–1940. Edited by Henri Lonitz. Frankfurt: Suhrkamp, 1994.
Über Walter Benjamin. Edited by Rolf Tiedemann. Frankfurt: Suhrkamp, 1970.
Vorlesungen zur Ästhetik 1967–68. Zurich: H. Mayer Nachfolger, 1973.
Walter Benjamin: Briefe. 2 vols. Edited by Gershom Scholem and Theodor W. Adorno. Frankfurt: Suhrkamp, 1978.

ADORNO'S BOOKS IN ENGLISH

The abbreviation GS, followed by volume number and, where applicable, page numbers, indicates the location in the *Gesammelte Schriften* corresponding to the English translation. NS refers to the location in the posthumous writings.
The Adorno Reader. Edited by Brian O'Connor. Oxford: Blackwell, 2000.

Aesthetic Theory. Translated by C. Lenhardt and edited by Gretel Adorno and Rolf Tiedemann. London: Routledge and Kegan Paul, 1984. [GS 7].

Aesthetic Theory. Translated by Robert Hullot-Kentor and edited by Gretel Adorno and Rolf Tiedemann. Minneapolis: University of Minnesota Press, 1997. [GS 7].

Against Epistemology: A Metacritique: Studies in Husserl and the Phenomenological Antinomies. Translated by Willis Domingo. Oxford: Basil Blackwell, 1982; Cambridge, Mass.: MIT Press, 1983. [GS 5: 7–245].

Alban Berg: Master of the Smallest Link. Translated by Juliane Brand and Christopher Hailey. New York: Cambridge University Press, 1991. [GS 13: 320–490].

Aspects of Sociology. Frankfurt Institute for Social Research. Translated by John Viertel. Boston: Beacon Press, 1972.

The Authoritarian Personality. T. W. Adorno, Else Frenkel-Brunswik, Daniel J. Levinson, and R. Nevitt Sanford, in collaboration with Betty Aron, Maria Hertz Levinson, and William Morrow. *Studies in Prejudice.* Edited by Max Horkheimer and Samuel H. Flowerman. Vol. 1. New York: Harper and Brothers, 1950. Chapters 1, 7, 16, 17, 19, and 19 appear in GS 9.1: 143–509 under the title *Studies in the Authoritarian Personality.*

Beethoven: The Philosophy of Music: Fragments and Texts. Translated by Edmund Jephcott and edited by Rolf Tiedemann. Cambridge: Polity Press, 1998. [NS I.1].

Can One Live after Auschwitz: A Philosophical Reader. Theodor W. Adorno et al. Stanford: Stanford University Press, 2003.

The Complete Correspondence, 1928–1940. Theodor W. Adorno and Walter Benjamin. Translated by Nicholas Walker and edited by Henri Lonitz. Cambridge, Mass.: Harvard University Press, 1999.

Composing for the Films. With Hanns Eisler. New York: Oxford University Press, 1947. The book appeared under only Eisler's name until Adorno published a German version in 1969 titled *Komposition für den Film.* This version and an account of the manuscript's history appear in GS 15: 7–155. *Composing for the Films.* With Hanns Eisler. Introduction by Graham McCann. London: Athlone Press, 1994.

The Correspondence of Walter Benjamin, 1910–1940. Translated by Manfred R. Jacobson and Evelyn M. Jacobson and edited and annotated by Gershom Scholem and Theodor W. Adorno. Chicago: University of Chicago Press, 1994.

Critical Models: Interventions and Catchwords. Translated by Henry W. Pickford. New York: Columbia University Press, 1998. [GS 10.2: 455–799.]

The Culture Industry: Selected Essays on Mass Culture. Edited by J. M. Bernstein. London: Routledge, 1991.

Dialectic of Enlightenment. With Max Horkheimer. Translated by John Cumming. New York: Continuum, 1972. [GS 3].

Dialectic of Enlightenment: Philosophical Fragments. With Max Horkheimer. Translated by Edmund Jephcott and edited by Gunzelin Schmid Noerr. Stanford, Calif.: Stanford University Press, 2002. This edition is translated from vol. 5 of Max Horkheimer, *Gesammelte Schriften: Dialektik der Aufklärung und Schriften 1940–1950*, edited by Gunzelin Schmid Noerr. Frankfurt: Fischer, 1987.

Essays on Music. Translated by Susan H. Gillespie and selected, with introduction, commentary, and notes, by Richard Leppert. Berkeley and Los Angeles: University of California Press, 2002.

Hegel: Three Studies. Translated by Shierry Weber Nicholsen. Cambridge, Mass.: MIT Press, 1993. [GS 5: 247–381].

In Search of Wagner. Translated by Rodney Livingstone. London: Verso, 1984. [GS 13: 7–148].

Introduction to Sociology. Edited by Christoph Gödde. Translated by Edmund Jephcott. Stanford: Stanford University Press, 2000. [NS IV.15].

Introduction to the Sociology of Music. Translated by E. B. Ashton. New York: Continuum, 1988. [GS 14: 168–433].

The Jargon of Authenticity. Translated by Knut Tarnowski and Frederic Will. Evanston: Northwestern University Press, 1973. [GS 6: 413–526].

Kant's "Critique of Pure Reason." Translated by Rodney Livingstone and edited by Rolf Tiedemann. Stanford: Stanford University Press, 2001. [NS IV.4].

Kierkegaard: Construction of the Aesthetic. Translated by Robert Hullot-Kentor. Minneapolis: University of Minnesota Press, 1989. [GS 2].

Mahler: A Musical Physiognomy. Translated by Edmund Jephcott. Chicago: University of Chicago Press, 1992. [GS 13: 149–319].

Metaphysics: Concepts and Problems. Translated by Edmund Jephcott and edited by Rolf Tiedemann. Stanford: Stanford University Press, 2000. [NS IV.14].

Minima Moralia: Reflections from Damaged Life. Translated by E. F. N. Jephcott. London: New Left Books, 1974. [GS 4].

Negative Dialectics. Translated by E. B. Ashton. New York: Continuum, 1983. [GS 6: 7–412].

Notes to Literature. 2 vols. Translated by Shierry Weber Nicholsen and edited by Rolf Tiedemann. New York: Columbia University Press, 1991–2. [GS 11].

Philosophy of Modern Music. Translated by Anne G. Mitchell and Wesley V. Blomster. New York: Continuum, 1985. [GS 12].

The Positivist Dispute in German Sociology. Theodor W. Adorno et al. Translated by Glyn Adey and David Frisby. London: Heinemann, 1976. [GS 8: 280–353].

Prisms. Translated by Samuel Weber and Shierry Weber. London: Neville Spearman, 1967; Cambridge, Mass.: MIT Press, 1981. [GS 10.1: 9–287].

Problems of Moral Philosophy. Translated by Rodney Livingstone and edited by Thomas Schröder. Stanford: Stanford University Press, 2000. [NS IV.10].

The Psychological Technique of Martin Luther Thomas' Radio Addresses. Stanford: Stanford University Press, 2000. [GS 9.1: 7–141].

Quasi una fantasia: Essays on Modern Music. Translated by Rodney Livingstone. New York: Verso, 1992. [GS 16: 249–540].

Sound Figures. Translated by Rodney Livingstone. Stanford: Stanford University Press, 1999. [GS 16: 7–248].

The Stars Down to Earth and Other Essays on the Irrational in Culture. Edited by Stephen Crook. New York: Routledge, 1994.

ADORNO'S ARTICLES IN ENGLISH

Date of original publication or composition appears in brackets.

"The Actuality of Philosophy" [1931]. *Telos*, no. 31 (Spring 1977): 120–33. Reprinted in *The Adorno Reader*, 23–39.

"The Aging of the New Music" [1955]. *Telos*, no. 77 (Fall 1988): 95–116. Reprinted in *Essays on Music*, 181–202.

"Alienated Masterpiece: The *Missa Solemnis*" [1959]. *Telos* 28 (Summer 1976): 113–24. Reprinted in *The Adorno Reader*, 304–18, and *Essays on Music*, 569–83.

"Analytical Study of the NBC Music Appreciation Hour [1938–1941]." *Musical Quarterly* 78 (Summer 1994): 325–77.

"Anti-Semitism and Fascist Propaganda." With Leo Löwenthal and Paul Massing. In *Anti-Semitism: A Social Disease*, edited by Ernst Simmel, 125–37. New York: International Universities, 1946. Reprinted in GS 8: 397–407, and in *The Stars Down to Earth*, 162–71.

"Bibliographical Musings" [1965]. *Grand Street* 10, no. 3 (1991): 135–48.

"Bloch's Traces: The Philosophy of Kitsch" [1960]. *New Left Review*, no. 121 (May–June 1980): 49–62.

"Bourgeois Opera" [1959]. In *Opera through Other Eyes*, edited by David J. Levin, 25–43. Stanford: Stanford University Press, 1993.

"Commitment" [1962]. *New Left Review*, nos. 87-88 (November–December 1974): 75–90. Reprinted in Ronald Taylor, ed., *Aesthetics and Politics: Debates between Bloch, Lukács, Brecht, Benjamin, Adorno,* afterword by Fredric Jameson (London: New Left Books, 1977; Verso, 1980), 177–95, and in Andrew Arato and Eike Gebhardt, eds., *The Essential Frankfurt School Reader* (New York: Continuum, 1982), 118–37.

"Contemporary German Sociology" [1959]. *Transactions of the Fourth World Congress of Sociology*, vol. 1, pp. 33–56. London: International Sociological Association, 1959.

"Culture and Administration" [1960]. *Telos*, no. 37 (Fall 1978): 93–111. Reprinted in *The Culture Industry*, 93–113.

"Culture Industry Reconsidered" [1963]. *New German Critique*, no. 6 (Fall 1975): 12–19. Reprinted in Stephan Eric Bronner and Douglas MacKay Kellner, eds., *Critical Theory and Society: A Reader* (New York: Routledge, 1989), 128–35; in *The Culture Industry*, 85–92; and in *The Adorno Reader*, 230–38.

"The Curves of the Needle" [1928]. *October*, no. 55 (Winter 1990): 49–55. Reprinted in *Essays on Music*, 271–276.

"Education for Autonomy" [1969/1970]. With Hellmut Becker. *Telos*, no. 56 (Summer 1983): 103–10.

"The Essay as Form" [1958]. *New German Critique*, no. 32 (Spring–Summer 1984): 151–71. Reprinted in *The Adorno Reader*, 91–111.

"The Form of the Phonograph Record" [1934]. *October*, no. 55 (Winter 1990): 56–61. Reprinted in *Essays on Music*, 277–82.

"Freudian Theory and the Pattern of Fascist Propaganda" [1951]. In *Psychoanalysis and the Social Sciences*, vol. 3, edited by G. Róheim, 279–300. New York: International Universities Press, 1951. Reprinted in GS 8: 408–33; in *Critical Theory: The Essential Readings* edited by David Ingram and Julia Simon-Ingram (New York: Paragon House, 1992), 84–102; and in *The Culture Industry*, 114–35.

"Functionalism Today" [1966]. *Oppositions*, no. 17 (Summer 1979): 31–41.

"Goldmann and Adorno: To Describe, Understand, and Explain" [1968]. In Lucien Goldmann, *Cultural Creation in Modern Society*, translated by Bart Grahl, 129–45. Oxford: Basil Blackwell, 1976.

"How to Look at Television." *Quarterly of Film, Radio and Television* 8 (Spring 1954): 213–35. Reprinted as "Television and the Patterns of Mass Culture," in Bernard Rosenberg and David Manning White, eds., *Mass Culture: The Popular Arts in America* (Glencoe, Ill.: The Free Press, 1957), 474–87. Also reprinted in Ingram and Simon–Ingram, *Critical Theory*, 69–83, and in *The Culture Industry*, 136–53.

"Husserl and the Problem of Idealism" [1940]. *Journal of Philosophy* 37 (1940): 5–18.

"The Idea of Natural History" [1932/1973]. *Telos*, no. 60 (Summer 1984): 111–24.

"Is Marx Obsolete?" [1968]. *Diogenes*, no. 64 (Winter 1968): 1–16. The title of the German essay is *"Spätkapitalismus oder Industriegesellschaft,"* in GS 8: 354–70.

"Jazz" [1946]. In *Encyclopedia of the Arts*, edited by Dagobert D. Runes and Harry G. Schrickel, 511–13. New York: Philosophical Library, 1946.

"Late Style in Beethoven" [1937]. *Raritan* 13 (Summer 1993): 102–7. Reprinted in *Essays on Music*, 564–8.

"Letters to Walter Benjamin" [1930s]. *New Left Review*, no. 81 (September-October 1973): 46–80. See also *Aesthetics and Politics*, 110–33.

"Looking Back on Surrealism" [1956]. In *The Idea of the Modern in Literature and the Arts*, edited by Irving Howe, 220–4. New York: Horizon Press, 1967.

"Lyric Poetry and Society" [1951]. *Telos*, no. 20 (Summer 1974): 56–71. Reprinted in Bonner and Kellner, *Critical Theory and Society*, 155–71, and in *The Adorno Reader*, 211–29.

"Messages in a Bottle" [1951]. *New Left Review*, no. 200 (July 1993): 5–14.

"Metacritique of Epistemology" [1956]. *Telos*, no. 38 (Winter 1978–9): 77–103. Reprinted in *The Adorno Reader*, 112–36.

"Modern Music Is Growing Old" [1955]. *The Score*, no. 18 (December 1956): 18–29. (For an alternate translation, see "The Aging of the New Music.")

"Music and Technique" [1958]. *Telos*, no. 32 (Summer 1977): 79–94.

"Music and the New Music: In Memory of Peter Suhrkamp" [1960]. *Telos*, no. 43 (Spring 1980): 124–38. New translation in *Quasi una fantasia*, 249–68.

"Music, Language, and Composition" [1956]. *Musical Quarterly* 77 (Fall 1993): 401–14. Reprinted in *Essays on Music*, 113–26.

"New Music and the Public: Some Problems of Interpretation" [1957]. In *Twentieth-Century Music*, edited by Rollo H. Myers, 63–74. London: Calder and Boyors, 1968.

"Odysseus or Myth and Enlightenment." *New German Critique*, no. 56 (Spring–Summer 1992): 109–41. (Translation of a chapter from *Dialektik der Aufklärung*, GS 3: 61–99.)

"Of Barricades and Ivory Towers: An Interview with T. W. Adorno." *Encounter* 33 (September 1969) 3: 63–69.

"On Jazz" [1937]. *Discourse* 12 (Fall–Winter 1989–90): 36–69. Reprinted in *Essays on Music*, 470–95.

"On Kierkegaard's Doctrine of Love." *Studies in Philosophy and Social Science* 8 (1939–40): 413–29.

"On Popular Music." With the assistance of George Simpson. *Studies in Philosophy and Social Science* 9 (1941): 17–48. Reprinted in *Essays on Music*, 437–69.

"On Some Relationships between Music and Painting" [1965]. *Musical Quarterly* 79 (Spring 1995): 66–79.

"On the Fetish-Character in Music and the Regression of Listening" [1938/1956]. In Arato and Gebhardt, *The Essential Frankfurt School Reader*, 270–99. Reprinted in *The Culture Industry*, 26–52, and in *Essays on Music*, 288–317.

"On the Historical Adequacy of Consciousness" [1965]. With Peter von Haselberg. *Telos*, no. 56 (Summer 1983): 97–103.

"On the Logic of the Social Sciences" [1962]. In *The Positivist Dispute in German Sociology*, 105–22.

"On the Question: 'What is German?'" [1965]. *New German Critique*, no. 36 (Fall 1985): 121–31. Reprinted in *Critical Models*, 205–14.

"On the Score of Parsifal" [1956]. *Music and Letters* 76 (August 1995): 384–97.

"On the Social Situation of Music" [1932]. *Telos*, no. 35 (Spring 1978): 128–64. Reprinted in *Essays on Music*, 391–436.

"On Tradition" [1966]. *Telos*, no. 94 (Winter 1993): 75–81.

"Opera and the Long-Playing Record" [1969]. *October*, no. 55 (Winter 1990): 62–6. Reprinted in *Essays on Music*, 283–7.

"Perennial Fashion – Jazz" [1953]. In *Prisms*, 119–32. Reprinted in *Critical Theory and Society*, 199–209, and in *The Adorno Reader*, 267–79.

"Progress" [1964]. *The Philosophical Forum* 15 (Fall–Winter 1983–84): 55–70. New translation in *Critical Models*, 143–60.

"Punctuation Marks" [1956]. *Antioch Review* 48 (Summer 1990): 300–305.

"The Radio Symphony: An Experiment in Theory." In *Radio Research 1941*, edited by Paul F. Lazarsfeld and Frank N. Stanton, 110–39. New York: Duell, Sloan and Pearce, 1941. Reprinted in *Essays on Music*, 251–70.

"Reconciliation under Duress" [1958]. In *Aesthetics and Politics*, 151–76.

"Resignation" [1969]. *Telos*, no. 35 (Spring 1978): 165–8. Reprinted in *The Culture Industry*, 171–5.

Review of Jean Wahl, *Études Kierkegaardiennes*; Walter Lowrie, *Kierkegaard*; and *The Journals of Soren Kierkegaard*. In *Studies in Philosophy and Social Science* 8 (1939): 232–5.

Review of Wilder Hobson, *American Jazz Music*; and Winthrop Sargeant, *Jazz Hot and Hybrid*. With the assistance of Eunice Cooper. *Studies in Philosophy and Social Science* 9 (1941): 167–78.

"Richard Strauss at Sixty" [1924]. In *Richard Strauss and His World*, edited by Bryan Gilliam, 406–15. Princeton, N.J.: Princeton University Press, 1992.

"Scientific Experiences of a European Scholar in America." In *The Intellectual Migration: Europe and America, 1930–1960*, edited by Donald

Fleming and Bernard Bailyn, 338–70. Cambridge, Mass.: Harvard University Press, 1968–9.

"A Social Critique of Radio Music." *Kenyon Review* 7 (Spring 1945): 208–17.

"Society" [1966]. *Salmagundi*, nos. 10–11 (Fall 1969–Winter 1970): 144–53. Reprinted in Robert Boyers, ed., *The Legacy of the German Refugee Intellectuals* (New York: Schocken Books, 1969), 144–53; Bonner and Kellner, in *Critical Theory and Society*, 267–75; and in Ingram and Simon-Ingram, *Critical Theory*, 61–8.

"Sociology and Empirical Research" [1957]. In *The Positivist Dispute in German Sociology*, 68–86. An excerpt under the same title is contained in Paul Connerton, ed., *Critical Sociology: Selected Readings* (Harmondsworth, England: Penguin, 1976), 237–57. Also reprinted in *The Adorno Reader*, 155–173.

"Sociology and Psychology" [1955]. *New Left Review*, no. 46 (November–December 1967): 63–80; no. 47 (January–February 1968): 79–97.

"The Sociology of Knowledge and Its Consciousness" [1937/1953]. In Arato and Gebhardt, *The Essential Frankfurt School Reader*, 452–65.

"Spengler Today." *Studies in Philosophy and Social Science* 9 (1941): 305–25.

"The Stars Down to Earth." *Jahrbuch für Amerikastudien* 2 (Winter 1957): 19–88. See also "The Stars Down to Earth: The Los Angeles Times Astrology Column," *Telos*, no. 19 (Spring 1974): 13–90. Reprinted in *The Stars Down to Earth*, 34–127.

"'Static' and 'Dynamic' as Sociological Categories" [1956/1961]. *Diogenes*, no. 33 (Spring 1961): 28–49.

"Subject and Object" [1969]. In Arato and Gebhardt, *The Essential Frankfurt School Reader*, 497–511. Reprinted in *The Adorno* Reader, 137–152, and *Critical Models*, 245–58.

"Theory of Pseudo-Culture" [1959]. *Telos*, no. 95 (Spring 1993): 15–38.

"Theses against Occultism" [1951]. *Telos*, no. 19 (Spring 1974): 7–12.

"Theses on the Sociology of Art" [1967]. *Working Papers in Cultural Studies* (Birmingham), no. 2 (Spring 1972): 121–8.

"Theses upon Art and Religion Today." *Kenyon Review* 7 (Autumn 1945): 677–82.

"Transparencies on Film" [1966]. *New German Critique*, nos. 24–25 (Fall–Winter 1981–2): 199–205. Reprinted in *The Culture Industry*, 154–61.

"Trying to Understand *Endgame*" [1961]. *New German Critique*, no. 26 (Spring–Summer 1982): 119–50. Previously published as "Toward an Understanding of Endgame," in Gale Chevigny, ed., *Twentieth Century Interpretations of Endgame* (Englewood Cliffs, N.J.: Prentice-Hall, 1969), 82–114.

"Veblen's Attack on Culture: Remarks Occasioned by the Theory of the Leisure Class." *Studies in Philosophy and Social Science* 9 (1941): 389–413.

"Wagner, Nietzsche and Hitler" (review). *Kenyon Review* 9 (Winter 1947): 165–72.

"Wagner's Relevance for Today" [1964/1965]. *Grand Street* 11, no. 4 (1993): 32–59. Reprinted in *Essays on Music*, 584–602.

"What Does Coming to Terms with the Past Mean?" [1960]. In *Bitburg in Moral and Political Perspective*, edited by G. Hartman, 114–29. Indianapolis: Indiana University Press, 1986.

"What National Socialism Has Done to the Arts" [March 1945]. In GS 20.2: 413–29. Reprinted in *Essays on Music*, 373–90.

"Why Philosophy?" [1962/1963]. In *Man and Philosophy*, 11–24. Munich: Hueber, 1964. Reprinted in Ingram and Simon-Ingram, *Critical Theory*, 20–30, and in *The Adorno Reader*, 40–53.

SELECTED WORKS ON ADORNO AND CRITICAL THEORY

"Adorno: Love and Cognition." *Times Literary Supplement*, March 9, 1973, 253–5.

Alway, Joan. *Critical Theory and Political Possibilities: Conceptions of Emanicipatory Politics in the Works of Horkheimer, Adorno, Marcuse, and Habermas.* Westport, Conn.: Greenwood Press, 1995.

Antonio, Robert. "The Origin, Development, and Contemporary Status of Critical Theory." *Sociological Quarterly* 24 (Summer 1983): 325–51.

Arato, Andrew. "Introduction: The Antinomies of the Neo-Marxian Theory of Culture." *International Journal of Sociology* 7 (Spring 1977): 3–24.

——— "Critical Theory in the United States: Reflections on Four Decades of Reception." In *America and the Germans: An Assessment of a Three-Hundred-Year History.* Vol. 2, *The Relationship in the Twentieth Century*, edited by Frank Trommler and Joseph McVeigh, 279–86. Philadelphia: University of Pennsylvania Press, 1985.

Arnold, Heinz Ludwig, ed. *Theodor W. Adorno.* Munich: Edition Text + Kritik, 1983.

Bahr, Ehrhard. "Art Desires Non-Art: The Dialectics of Art in Thomas Mann's *Doctor Faustus* in the Light of Theodor W. Adorno's *Aesthetic Theory.*" In *Thomas Mann's Doctor Faustus: A Novel at the Margin of Modernism*, edited by Herbert Lehrnert and Peter C. Pfeiffer, 145–66. Columbia, S.C.: Camden House, 1991.

Bauer, Karin. *Adorno's Nietzschean Narratives: Critiques of Ideology, Readings of Wagner.* Albany: State University of New York Press, 1999.

Baugh, Bruce. "Left-Wing Elitism: Adorno on Popular Culture." *Philosophy and Literature* 14 (April 1990): 65–78.

Behrens, Roger. *Adorno-ABC*. Leipzig: Reclam, 2003.

Benhabib, Seyla. *Critique, Norm, and Utopia: A Study of the Foundations of Critical Theory*. New York: Columbia University Press, 1986.

Benjamin, Jessica. "The End of Internalization: Adorno's Social Psychology." *Telos*, no. 32 (1977): 42–64.

Berman, Russell A. "Adorno, Marxism and Art." *Telos*, no. 34 (Winter 1977–8): 157–66.

"Adorno's Radicalism: Two Interviews from the Sixties." *Telos*, no. 56 (Summer 1983): 94–97.

Modern Culture and Critical Theory: Art, Politics, and the Legacy of the Frankfurt School. Madison: University of Wisconsin Press, 1989.

Bernard, Andreas and Ulrich Raulff, eds. *Minima Moralia neu gelesen*. Frankfurt: Suhrkamp, 2002.

Bernstein, J. M. *Adorno: Disenchantment and Ethics*. Cambridge: Cambridge University Press, 2001.

"Aesthetic Alienation: Heidegger, Adorno, and Truth at the End of Art." In *Life after Postmodernism: Essays on Value and Culture*, edited by John Fekete, 86–119. New York: St. Martins Press, 1987.

"The Death of Sensuous Particulars: Adorno and Abstract Expressionism." *Radical Philosophy* 76 (1996): 7–18.

The Fate of Art: Aesthetic Alienation from Kant to Derrida and Adorno. Cambridge: Polity Press, 1991.

"Philosophy's Refuge: Adorno in Beckett." In *Philosophers' Poets*, edited by David Wood, 177–81. London: Routledge, 1990.

Bernstein, Susan. "Journalism and German Identity: Communiques from Heine, Wagner, and Adorno." *New German Critique*, no. 66 (Fall 1995): 65–93.

Blomster, W. V. "Sociology of Music: Adorno and Beyond." *Telos*, no. 28 (Summer 1976): 81–112.

Blumenfeld, Harold. "Ad Vocem Adorno." *Musical Quarterly* 75 (Winter 1991): 263–84.

Boehmer, Konrad. "Adorno, Musik, Gesellschaft." In Tibor Kneif, ed., *Texte zur Musiksoziologie* (Cologne: Arno Volk, 1975), 227–38.

Born, Georgina. "Against Negation, for a Politics of Cultural Production: Adorno, Aesthetics, the Social." *Screen* 34 (Autumn 1993): 223–42.

Boulez, Pierre. "T. W. Adorno." In *Orientations: Collected Writings by Pierre Boulez*, translated by Martin Cooper and edited by Jean-Jacques Nattiez, 517–18. Cambridge, Mass.: Harvard University Press, 1986.

Bowie, Andrew. "Adorno." In *Profiles in Contemporary Social Theory*, edited by A. Elliott and B. S. Turner, 59–69. London: Sage Publications, 2000.

Aesthetics and Subjectivity: from Kant to Nietzsche. Manchester: Manchester University Press, 1993. New, completely revised edition, 2003.
From Romanticism to Critical Theory: The Philosophy of German Literary Theory. London and New York: Routledge, 1997.
"German Philosophy Today: Between Idealism, Romanticism and Pragmatism." In *German Philosophy After Kant*, Royal Institute of Philosophy Lectures, edited by A. O'Hear, 357–98. Cambridge: Cambridge University Press, 1999.
"Music, Language, and Modernity." In *The Problems of Modernity: Adorno, Benjamin*, edited by Andrew Benjamin, 67–85. London and New York: Routledge, 1989.
"Non-Identity: The German Romantics, Schelling and Adorno." In *Intersections: Nineteenth Century Philosophy and Contemporary Theory*, edited by T. Rajan and D. Clark, 243–60. Albany: SUNY Press, 1995.
Brunkhorst, Hauke. "Adorno, Heidegger, and Postmodernity." In *Universalism vs. Communitarianism: Contemporary Debates in Ethics*, edited by David Rasmussen, 183–96. Cambridge, Mass.: MIT Press, 1990.
Theodor W. Adorno: Dialektik der Moderne. Munich and Zurich: Piper, 1990. In English under the title *Adorno and Critical Theory*. Cardiff: University of Wales Press, 1999.
Bubner, Rüdiger. "Über einige Bedingungen gegenwärtiger Ästhetik." *Neue Hefte für Philosophie*, no. 5 (1973): 38–73.
Buck-Morss, Susan. *The Origin of Negative Dialectics: Theodor W. Adorno, Walter Benjamin and the Frankfurt Institute*. New York: The Free Press, 1977.
Burgard, Peter J. "Adorno, Goethe, and the Politics of the Essay." *Deutsche Vierteljahresschrift für Literaturwissenschaft und Geistesgeschichte* 66 (March 1992): 160–91.
Bürger, Christa. "Mimesis and Modernity." *Stanford Literature Review* 3 (Spring 1986): 63–73.
Bürger, Peter. "Adorno's Anti-Avant-Gardism." *Telos*, no. 86 (Winter 1990–1): 49–60.
Butterfield, Bradley. "Enlightenment's Other in Patrick Suskind's *Das Parfüm*: Adorno and the Ineffable Utopia of Modern Art." *Comparative Literature Studies* 32 (1995): 401–18.
Cahn, Michael. "Subversive Mimesis: Theodor W. Adorno and the Modern Impasse of Critique." In *Mimesis in Contemporary Theory: An Interdisciplinary Approach*. Vol. 1, *The Literary and Philosophical Debate*, edited by Mihai Spariosu, 27–64. Philadelphia: John Benjamins, 1984.
Caughie, John. "Adorno's Reproach: Repetition, Difference and Television Genre." *Screen* 32 (Summer 1991): 127–53.
Champion, James W. "Tillich and the Frankfurt School: Parallels and Difference in Prophetic Criticism." *Soundings* 69 (1986): 512–30.

Clark, Michael. "Adorno, Derrida, and the Odyssey: A Critique of Center and Periphery." *Boundary 2* 16 (Winter–Spring 1989): 109–28.

Claussen, Detlev. *Theodor W. Adorno: Das letzte Genie*. Frankfurt: Fischer, 2003.

Cochetti, Stefano. *Mythos und Dialektik der Aufklärung*. Meisenheim: Verlag Anton Haim, 1985.

Cook, Deborah. *The Culture Industry Revisited: Theodor W. Adorno on Mass Culture*. Lanham, Md.: Rowman and Littlefield, 1996.

Cooper, Harry. "On *Über Jazz:* Replaying Adorno with the Grain." *October* 75 (1996): 99–133.

Dahlhaus, Carl. "Adornos Begriff des musikalischen Materials." In *Zur Terminologie der Musik des 20. Jahrhunderts*, edited by Hans Heinrich Eggebrecht, 9–21. Stuttgart: Musikwissenschaftliche Verlags-Gesellschaft, 1974.

——— "Soziologische Dechiffrierung von Musik: Zu Theodor W. Adornos Wagner-Kritik." *International Review of the Aesthetics and Sociology of Music* 1 (1979): 137–47.

Dallmayr, Fred R. "Phenomenology and Critical Theory: Adorno." *Cultural Hermeneutics* 3 (1976): 367–405.

Demirovic, Alex. *Der nonkonformistische Intellektuelle: Die Entwicklung der Kritischen Theorie zur Frankfurter Schule*. Frankfurt: Suhrkamp, 1999.

Dews, Peter. *Logics of Disintegration: Post-Structuralist Thought and the Claims of Critical Theory*. London and New York: Verso, 1987.

Dineen, Murray. "Adorno and Schoenberg's Unanswered Question." *Musical Quarterly* 77 (Fall 1993): 415–27.

Donougho, Martin. "The Cunning of Odysseus: A Theme in Hegel, Lukács, and Adorno." *Philosophy and Social Criticism* 8 (Spring 1981): 11–43.

Dunn, Allen. "The Man Who Needs Hardness: Irony and Solidarity in the Aesthetics of Theodor Adorno." In *Germany and German Thought in American Literature and Cultural Criticism*, edited by Peter Freese, 470–84. Essen, Germany: Blaue Eule, 1990.

Eagleton, Terry. *The Ideology of the Aesthetic*. Oxford: Basil Blackwell, 1990.

Edgar, Andrew. "An Introduction to Adorno's Aesthetics." *British Journal of Aesthetics* 30 (January 1990): 46–56.

Engh, Barbara. "Adorno and the Sirens: Tele-phono-graphic Bodies." In *Embodied Voices: Representing Female Vocality in Western Culture*, edited by Leslie C. Dunn and Nancy A. Jones, 120–35. New York: Cambridge University Press, 1994.

Fehér, Ferenc. "Negative Philosophy of Music – Positive Results." *New German Critique*, no. 4 (Winter 1975): 99–111.

"Rationalized Music and Its Vicissitudes (Adorno's Philosophy of Music)." *Philosophy and Social Criticism* 9 (Spring 1982): 41–65.

Fenves, Peter. "Image and Chatter: Adorno's Construction of Kierkegaard." *Diacritics* 22 (Spring 1992): 100–114.

Fetscher, Iring and Alfred Schmidt, eds. *Emanzipation als Versöhnung: Zu Adornos Kritik der "Warentausch"-Gesellschaft und Perspektiven ihrer Transformation*. Frankfurt: Neue Kritik, 2002.

Figal, Günter. *Theodor W. Adorno: Das Naturschöne als spekulative Gedankenfigur: Zur Interpretation der "Ästhetischen Theorie" im Kontext philosophischer Ästhetik*. Bonn: Bouvier Verlag Herbert Grundmann, 1977.

Floyd, Wayne Whitson, Jr. "Transcendence in the Light of Redemption: Adorno and the Legacy of Rosenzweig and Benjamin." *Journal of the American Academy of Religion* 61 (Fall 1993): 539–51.

Fluxman, Tony. "Bob Dylan and the Dialectic of Enlightenment: Critical Lyricist in the Age of High Capitalism." *Theoria* 77 (May 1991): 91–111.

Frow, John. "Mediation and Metaphor: Adorno and the Sociology of Art." *Clio* 12 (Fall 1982): 57–65.

Früchtl, Josef. *Mimesis: Konstellation eines Zentralbegriffs bei Adorno*. Würzburg: Königshausen and Neumann, 1986.

"Zeit und Erfahrung: Adornos Revision der Revision Heideggers." In *Martin Heidegger: Innen- und Aussensichten*, 291–312. Forum für Philosophie, Bad, Homburg. Frankfurt: Suhrkamp, 1989.

Früchtl, Josef and Maria Calloni, eds. *Geist gegen den Zeitgeist: Erinnern an Adorno*. Frankfurt: Suhrkamp, 1991.

Gandesha, Samir. "Enlightenment as Tragedy: Reflections on Adorno's Ethics." *Thesis Eleven* (May 2001): 109–30.

"Schreiben und Urteilen: Adorno, Arendt und der Chiasmus der Naturgeschichte." In *Arendt und Adorno*, edited by Dirk Auer, Lars Rensmann and Julia Schulze Wessel, 199–233. Frankfurt: Suhrkamp, 2003.

Gendron, Bernard. "Theodor Adorno Meets the Cadillacs." In *Studies in Entertainment: Critical Approaches to Mass Culture*, edited by Tania Modleski, 18–36. Bloomington: Indiana University Press, 1986.

Geuss, Raymond. "Berg and Adorno." In *The Cambridge Companion to Berg*, edited by Anthony Pople, 38–50. Cambridge: Cambridge University Press, 1997.

Gillespie, Susan. "Translating Adorno: Language, Music, and Performance." *Musical Quarterly* 79 (Spring 1995): 55–65.

Goehr, Lydia. "Adorno, Schoenberg, and the *Totentanz der Prinzipien*: in 13 Steps." *Journal of the American Musicological Society* 56 (2003): 595–636.

The Quest for Voice: On Music, Politics and the Limits of Philosophy. Oxford: Oxford University Press, 1998.

Gracyk, Theodore A. "Adorno, Jazz and the Aesthetics of Popular Music." *Musical Quarterly* 76 (Winter 1982): 95–105.

Grenz, Friedemann. *Adornos Philosophie in Grundbegriffen: Auflösung einiger Deutungsprobleme.* Frankfurt: Suhrkamp, 1974.

Gross, Harvey. "Adorno in Los Angeles: The Intellectual in Emigration." *Humanities in Society* 2 (Fall 1979): 339–51.

Habermas, Jürgen. "The Entwinement of Myth and Enlightenment: Re-Reading *Dialectic of Enlightenment.*" Translated by Thomas Y. Levin. *New German Critique,* no. 26 (Spring–Summer 1982): 13–30.

"A Generation Apart from Adorno." Interview by J. Früchtl. Translated by James Swindal. *Philosophy and Social Criticism* 18, no. 2 (1992): 119–24.

The Philosophical Discourse of Modernity: Twelve Lectures. Translated by Frederick Lawrence. Cambridge, Mass.: MIT Press, 1987.

Philosophical-Political Profiles. Translated by Frederick G. Lawrence. Cambridge, Mass.: MIT Press, 1983.

Hamilton, Carol V. "All That Jazz Again: Adorno's Sociology of Music." *Popular Music and Society* 15 (Fall 1991): 31–40.

Hansen, Miriam. "Of Mice and Ducks: Benjamin and Adorno on Disney." *South Atlantic Quarterly* 92 (Winter 1993): 27–61.

Harding, James Martin. *Adorno and "A Writing of the Ruins": Essays on Modern Aesthetics and Anglo-American Literature and Culture.* Albany: State University of New York Press, 1997.

Hjort, Ann Mette. "'Quasi una Amicizia': Adorno and Philosophical Post-modernism." *New Orleans Review* 14 (Spring 1987): 74–80.

Hohendahl, Peter U. "Autonomy of Art: Looking Back at Adorno's *Ästhetische Theorie.*" *German Quarterly* 54 (March 1981): 133–48.

"The Dialectic of Enlightenment Revisited: Habermas' Critique of the Frankfurt School." *New German Critique,* no. 35 (Spring–Summer 1985): 3–26.

"The Displaced Intellectual? Adorno's American Years Revisited." In *Die Resonanz des Exils: Gelungene und misslungene Rezeption deutschsprachiger Exilautoren,* edited by Dieter Sevin, 110–20. Amsterdam: Rodopi, 1992.

Prismatic Thought: Theodor W. Adorno. Lincoln: University of Nebraska Press, 1995.

Reappraisals: Shifting Alignments in Postwar Critical Theory. Ithaca, N.Y.: Cornell University Press, 1991.

Honneth, Axel. "Communication and Reconciliation: Habermas' Critique of Adorno." *Telos,* no. 29 (Spring 1979): 45–61. A complete translation is reprinted as "From Adorno to Habermas: On the Transformation of Critical Social Theory," in Honneth, *The Fragmented World of the Social*, 92–120.

The Critique of Power: Reflective Stages in a Critical Social Theory. Translated by Kenneth Baynes. Cambridge, Mass.: MIT Press, 1991.

The Fragmented World of the Social: Essays in Social and Political Philosophy. Edited by Charles W. Wright. Albany: State University of New York Press, 1995.

Huhn, Tom. "Adorno's Aesthetics of Illusion." *Journal of Aesthetics and Art Criticism* 44 (Winter 1985): 181–9.

"The Concept of Sublimation in Adorno's Aesthetics." In Roblin, *The Aesthetics of the Critical Theorists*, 291–307.

"Diligence and Industry, Adorno and the Ugly." *Canadian Journal of Political and Social Theory* 12 (1988): 138–46.

"The Movement of Mimesis: Heidegger's 'Origin of the Work of Art' in Relation to Adorno and Lyotard." *Philosophy and Social Criticism* 22 (1996): 45–69.

Huhn, Tom, and Lambert Zuidervaart, eds. *The Semblance of Subjectivity: Essays in Adorno's Aesthetic Theory.* Cambridge, Mass.: MIT Press, 1997.

Hullot-Kentor, Robert. "Back to Adorno." Telos, no. 81 (Fall 1989): 5–29.

"The Impossibility of Music: Adorno, Popular and Other Music." *Telos*, no. 87 (Spring 1991): 97–117.

"Notes on *Dialectic of Enlightenment:* Translating the Odysseus Essay." *New German Critique*, no. 56 (Spring–Summer 1992): 101–8.

"Popular Music and Adorno's 'The Aging of the New Music.'" *Telos*, no. 77 (Fall 1988): 79–94.

Huyssen, Andreas. "Adorno in Reverse: From Hollywood to Richard Wagner." *New German Critique*, no. 29 (Spring–Summer 1983): 8–38.

After the Great Divide: Modernism, Mass Culture and Postmodernism. Bloomington: Indiana University Press, 1986.

Israel, Nico. "Damage Control: Adorno, Los Angeles, and the Dislocation of Culture." *Yale Journal of Criticism* 10 (Spring 1997): 85–113.

Jacoby, Russell. *Dialectic of Defeat: Contours of Western Marxism.* Cambridge: Cambridge University Press, 1981.

Jameson, Fredric. "Introduction to Adorno." *Salmagundi*, nos. 10–11 (Fall 1969–Winter 1970): 140–43.

Late Marxism: Adorno, or, The Persistence of the Dialectic. London and New York: Verso, 1990.

Marxism and Form: Twentieth-Century Dialectical Theories of Literature. Princeton: Princeton University Press, 1971.

Jarvis, Simon. *Adorno: A Critical Introduction.* New York: Routledge, 1998.

Jauss, Hans Robert. "The Literary Process of Modernism: From Rousseau to Adorno." *Cultural Critique* 11 (Winter 1988–9): 27–61.

Jay, Martin. *Adorno.* Cambridge, Mass.: Harvard University Press, 1984.

"Adorno in America." *New German Critique*, no. 31 (Winter 1984): 157–82.

"Adorno and Kracauer: Notes on a Troubled Friendship." In *Permanent Exiles: Essays on the Intellectual Migration from Germany to America*, 217–36. New York: Columbia University Press, 1985.

The Dialectical Imagination. 2d ed. Berkeley: University of California Press, 1996.

"The Frankfurt School in Exile." In *Permanent Exiles: Essays on the Intellectual Migration from Germany to America*, 28–61. New York: Columbia University Press, 1985.

Marxism and Totality: The Adventures of a Concept from Lukács to Habermas. Berkely: University of California Press, 1984.

"Mass Culture and Aesthetic Redemption: The Debate between Max Horkheimer and Siegfried Kracauer." In *On Max Horkheimer: New Perspectives*, edited by Seyla Benhabib, Wolfgang Bonss, and John McCole, 365–86. Cambridge, Mass.: MIT Press, 1993.

Kaufman, Robert. "Aura, Still." *October* 99 (Winter 2002): 45–80.

"A Future for Modernism: Barbara Guest's Recent Poetry." *American Poetry Review* 29 (July/August 2000): 11–16.

"Legislators of the Post-Everything World: Shelley's Defense of Adorno." *English Literary History* 63 (Fall 1996): 707–33.

"Negatively Capable Dialectics: Keats, Vendler, Adorno, and the Theory of the Avant-Garde." *Critical Inquiry* 27 (Winter 2001): 354–84.

"Red Kant, or The Persistence of the Third *Critique* in Adorno and Jameson." *Critical Inquiry* 26 (Summer 2000): 682–724.

"Sociopolitical (i.e., *Romantic*) Difficulty in Modern Poetry and Aesthetics." *Romantic Circles Praxis Series* (June 2003) <http://www.rc.umd.edu/praxis/poetics.ns/kaufman/kaufman.html>

"The Sublime as Super-Genre of the Modern, or, *Hamlet* in Revolution: Caleb Williams and His Problem." *Studies in Romanticism* 36 (Winter 1997): 541–74.

Kellner, Douglas, and Rick Roderick. "Recent Literature on Critical Theory." *New German Critique*, no. 23 (Spring–Summer 1981): 141–70.

Kemper, Peter. " 'Der Rock ist ein Gebrauchswert': Warum Adorno die Beatles verschmähte." *Merkur* 45 (September–October 1991): 890–902.

Kerkhoff, Manfred. "Die Rettung des Nichtidentischen: Zur Philosophie Th. W. Adornos." *Philosophische Rundschau* 20 (1974): 150–78; 21 (1975): 56–74.

Kistner, Ulrike. "Writing 'after Auschwitz': On the Impossibility of a Postscript." *Acta Germanica: Jahrbuch des Germanistenverbandes im Südlichen Afrika* 21 (1992): 171–83.

Knapp, Gerhard. *Theodor W. Adorno.* Berlin: Colloquium, 1980.

Knoll, Manuel. *Theodor W. Adorno: Ethik als erste Philosophie.* Munich: Fink, 2002.

Koch, Gertrude. "Mimesis and *Bilderverbot*." *Screen* 34 (Autumn 1993): 211–22.

Koch, Traugott, Klaus-Michael Kodalle, and Hermann Schweppenhäuser. *Negative Dialektik und die Idee der Versöhnung: eine Kontroverse über Theodor W. Adorno.* Stuttgart: Kohlhammer, 1973.

König, Hans-Dieter. "Adornos psychoanalytische Kulturkritik und die Tiefenhermeneutik." *Zeitschrift für kritische Theorie*, Heft 10 (2000): 7–26.

Krukowski, Lucian. "Form and Protest in Atonal Music: A Meditation on Adorno." *Bucknell Review* 29, no. 1 (1984): 105–24.

Kuspit, Donald B. "Critical Notes on Adorno's Sociology of Music and Art." *Journal of Aesthetics and Art Criticism* 33 (Spring 1975): 321–7.

Lang, Peter Christian. *Hermeneutik, Ideologiekritik, Ästhetik: Über Gadamer und Adorno sowie Fragen einer aktuellen Ästhetik.* Königstein, Germany: Forum Academicum, 1981.

Lehmann, Hans Thies. "Nach Adorno: Zur Rezeption ästhetischer Theorie." *Merkur* 38 (June 1984): 391–8.

Levin, Thomas Y. "Nationalities of Language: Adorno's *Fremdwörter*, an Introduction to 'On the Question: What Is German?'" *New German Critique*, no. 36 (Fall 1985): 111–19.

"For the Record: Adorno on Music in the Age of Its Technological Reproducibility." *October* 55 (Winter 1990): 23–47.

Levin, Thomas Y., with Michael von der Linn. "Elements of a Radio Theory: Adorno and the Princeton Radio Research Project." *Musical Quarterly* 78 (Summer 1994): 316–24.

Löbig, Michael and Gerhard Schweppenhäuser, eds. *Hamburger Adorno-Symposium.* Lüneburg: Zu Klampen, 1984.

Löwenthal, Leo. "Recollections of Theodor W. Adorno." *Telos*, no. 61 (Fall 1984): 158–65. Reprinted in *An Unmastered Past: The Autobiographical Reflections of Leo Löwenthal*, translated by Sabine Wilke and edited by Martin Jay (Berkeley and Los Angeles: University of California Press, 1987), 201–15, and in Leo Löwenthal, *Critical Theory and Frankfurt Theorists: Lectures–Correspondence–Conversations* (New Brunswick, N.J.: Transaction, 1989), 62–72.

Lunn, Eugene. *Marxism and Modernism: An Historical Study of Lukács, Brecht, Benjamin, and Adorno.* Berkeley: University of California Press, 1982.

Lyotard, Jean-François. "Adorno as the Devil." *Telos*, no. 19 (Spring 1974): 127–37.

Markus, Gyorgy. "Adorno's Wagner." *Thesis Eleven* 56 (February 1999): 25–55.

Mayer, Günter. "Zur Dialektik des musikalischen Materials." In Tibor Kneif, ed., *Texte zur Musiksoziologie* (Cologne: Arno Volk, 1975), 200–226.

McCormack, W. J. "Seeing Darkly: Notes on T. W. Adorno and Samuel Beckett." *Hermathena* 141 (Winter 1986): 22–44.

McHugh, Patrick. "Ecstasy and Exile: Cultural Theory between Heidegger and Adorno." *Cultural Critique* 25 (1993): 121–52.

Menke, Christoph. *The Sovereignty of Art: Aesthetic Negativity in Adorno and Derrida.* Translated by Neil Solomon. Cambridge, Mass.: MIT Press, 1998.

"Critical Theory and Tragic Knowledge." Translated by James Swindal. In *The Handbook of Critical Theory*, edited by David M. Rasmussen, 57–73. Oxford: Blackwell, 1996.

Mörchen, Hermann. *Macht und Herrschaft im Denken von Heidegger und Adorno.* Stuttgart: Klett-Cotta, 1980.

Adorno und Heidegger: Untersuchung einer philosophischen Kommunikationsverweigerung. Stuttgart: Klett-Cotta, 1981.

Morris, Martin. *Rethinking the Communicative Turn: Adorno, Habermas, and the Problem of Communicative Freedom.* Albany: State University of New York Press, 2001.

Müller, Harro. "Gesellschaftliche Funktion und ästhetische Autonomie: Benjamin, Adorno, Habermas." In *Literaturwissenschaft: Grundkurs 2*, edited by Helmut Brackert and Jörn Stückrath, 329–40. Reinbeck bei Hamburg: Rowohlt, 1981.

Müller-Doohm, Stefan. *Im Niemandsland: Theodor W. Adornos intellektuelle Biographie.* Frankfurt: Suhrkamp, 2003. English translation forthcoming: *In No-Man's Land: An Intellectual Biography of Theodor W. Adorno.* Frankfurt: Suhrkamp.

Die Soziologie Theodor W. Adornos: Eine Einführung. Frankfurt: Campus Verlag, 1996.

Naeher, Jürgen, ed. *Die Negative Dialektik Adornos: Einführung–Dialog.* Opladen, Germany: Leske and Budrich, 1984.

Nägele, Rainer. "The Scene of the Other: Theodor W. Adorno's Negative Dialectic in the Context of Poststructuralism." In *Postmodernism and*

Politics, edited by Jonathan Arac, 91–111. Minneapolis: University of Minnesota Press, 1986.

Narskii, I. S. "Adorno's Negative Philosophy." *Soviet Studies in Philosophy* 24 (Summer 1985): 3–45.

Nicholsen, Shierry Weber. *Exact Imagination, Late Work: On Adorno's Aesthetics.* Cambridge, Mass.: MIT Press, 1997.

"Subjective Aesthetic Experience in Adorno and Its Historical Trajectory." *Theory Culture and Society* 10 (May 1993): 89–125.

"Toward a More Adequate Reception of Adorno's *Aesthetic Theory*: Configurational Form in Adorno's Aesthetic Writings." *Cultural Critique*, no. 18 (Spring 1991): 33–64.

Nye, William P. "Theodor Adorno on Jazz: A Critique of Critical Theory." *Popular Music and Society* 12 (Winter 1988) 4: 69–73.

Oppens, Kurt and others: *Über Theodor W. Adorno.* Frankfurt: Suhrkamp, 1968.

Osborne, Peter. "Adorno, Theodor W." In *A Dictionary of Cultural and Critical Theory*, edited by Michael Payne, 13–16. Cambridge, Mass.: Blackwell, 1996.

Paddison, Max. *Adorno, Modernism and Mass Culture: Essays on Critical Theory and Music.* London: Kahn and Averill, 1996.

Adorno's Aesthetics of Music. New York: Cambridge University Press, 1993.

"The Critique Criticised: Adorno and Popular Music." *Popular Music* 2 (1982): 201–18.

"Immanent Critique or Musical Stocktaking? Adorno and the Problem of Musical Analysis." In *Adorno: A Critical Reader*, edited by Nigel Gibson and Andrew Rubin, 209–33. Oxford: Blackwell, 2002.

"Stravinsky as Devil: Adorno's Three Critiques." In *The Cambridge Companion to Stravinsky*, edited by Jonathan Cross, 192–202. Cambridge: Cambridge University Press, 2003.

Paetzold, Heinz. *Neomarxistische Ästhetik.* Pt. 2, *Adorno, Marcuse.* Düsseldorf: Pädagogischer Verlag Schwann, 1974.

Pensky, Max, ed. *The Actuality of Adorno: Critical Essays on Adorno and the Postmodern.* Albany: State University of New York Press, 1997.

Pepper, Thomas. "Guilt by (Un)free Association: Adorno on Romance *et al.*" *MLN* 109 (December 1994): 913–37.

Phelan, Shane. "Interpretation and Domination: Adorno and the Habermas-Lyotard Debate." *Polity* 25 (Summer 1993): 597–616.

Pickford, Henry. "Under the Sign of Adorno." *MLN* 108 (April 1993): 564–83.

Posnock, Ross. "Henry James, Veblen and Adorno: The Crisis of the Modern Self." *Journal of American Studies* 21 (April 1987): 31–54.

Prokop, Dieter. *Mit Adorno gegen Adorno.* Hamburg: VSA, 2003.

Puder, Martin "Adornos Philosophie und die gegenwärtige Erfahrung." *Neue Deutsche Hefte* 23 (1976): 3–21.

"Zur *Ästhetischen Theorie* Adornos." *Neue Rundschau* 82 (1971): 465–77.

Recki, Birgit. *Aura und Autonomie: Zur Subjektivität der Kunst bei Walter Benjamin und Theodor W. Adorno.* Würzburg, Germany: Königshausen and Neumann, 1988.

Rehfus, Wulff. "Theodor W. Adorno. Die Rekonstruktion der Wahrheit aus der Ästhetik." Inaugural dissertation, University of Cologne, 1976.

Ries, Wiebrecht. "'Die Rettung des Hoffnungslosen': Zur 'theologia occulta' in der Spätphilosophie Horkheimers und Adornos." *Zeitschrift für philosophische Forschung* 30 (1976): 69–81.

Riethmüller, Albrecht. "Adorno musicus." *Archiv für Musikwissenschaft* 47 (1990): 1–26.

Ritsert, Jürgen. "Das Nichtidentische bei Adorno – Substanz-oder Problembegriff?" *Zeitschrift fur kritische Theorie* 4 (1997): 29–51.

Roberts, David. *Art and Enlightenment: Aesthetic Theory after Adorno.* Lincoln: University of Nebraska Press, 1991.

"Crowds and Power or the Natural History of Modernity: Horkheimer, Adorno, Canetti, Arendt." *Thesis Eleven* 45 (1996): 39–68.

Robin, Ronald, ed. *The Aesthetics of the Critical Theorists: Studies on Benjamin, Adorno, Marcuse, and Habermas.* Lewiston, N.Y.: Edwin Mellen Press, 1990.

Robinson, J. Bradford. "The Jazz Essays of Adorno: Some Thoughts on Jazz Reception in Weimar Germany." *Popular Music* 13 (January 1994): 1–25.

Rochlitz, Rainer. "Language for One, Language for All: Adorno and Modernism." *Perspectives of New Music* 27 (Summer 1989): 18–36.

Rose, Gillian. *The Melancholy Science: An Introduction to the Thought of Theodor W. Adorno.* London: MacMillan, 1982.

Ryan, Michael. *Marxism and Deconstruction: A Critical Articulation.* Baltimore: Johns Hopkins University Press, 1982.

Sample, Colin. "Adorno on the Musical Language of Beethoven." *Musical Quarterly* 78 (Summer 1994): 378–93.

Sauerland, Karol. *Einführung in die Ästhetik Adornos.* Berlin: Walter de Gruyter, 1979.

Savile, Anthony. "Beauty and Truth: The Apotheosis of an Idea." In *Analytic Aesthetics*, edited by Richard Shusterman, 23–46. Oxford: Basil Blackwell, 1989.

Schmidt, James. "Language, Mythology, and Enlightenment: Historical Notes on Horkheimer and Adorno's *Dialectic of Enlightenment.*" *Social Research* 65 (Winter 1998): 807–38.

Schmid Noerr, Gunzelin. "Bloch und Adorno – bildhafte und bilderlose Utopie." *Zeitschrift fur kritische Theorie* 13 (2001): 25–55.

Schmucker, Joseph F. *Adorno–Logik des ZerFalls.* Stuttgart: Frommann-Holzboog, 1977.

Schoberth, Wolfgang. *Das Jenseits der Kunst: Beiträge zu einer wissenssoziologischen Rekonstruktion der ästhetischen Theorie Theodor W. Adornos.* Frankfurt: Peter Lang, 1988.

Schönherr, Ulrich. "Adorno and Jazz: Reflections on a Failed Encounter." *Telos*, no. 87 (Spring 1991): 85–96.

———. "Adorno, Ritter Gluck, and the Tradition of the Postmodern." *New German Critique*, no. 48 (Fall 1989): 135–54.

Schoolman, Morton. "Toward a Politics of Darkness: Individuality and Its Politics in Adorno's Aesthetics." *Political Theory* 25 (February 1997): 57–92.

Schultz, Karla L. *Mimesis on the Move: Theodor W. Adorno's Concept of Imitation.* New York: Peter Lang, 1990.

Schweppenhäuser, Gerhard. *Adorno zur Einführung.* Hamburg: Junius Verlag, 2003.

———. "Adornos Begriff der Kritik." In *Kritische Erziehungswissenschaft – Moderne – Postmoderne*, edited by Wilfried Marotzki and Heinz Sünker, 75–100. Weinheim: Deutscher Studien Verlag, 1992.

———. "Ästhetische Theorie, Kunst und Massenkultur." In *Modelle kritischer Gesellschaftstheorie. Traditionen und Perspektiven der Kritischen Theorie*, edited by Alex Demirovic, 340–65. Stuttgart and Weimar: Metzler, 2003.

———. "Am Ende der bürgerlichen Geschichtsphilosophie: Max Horkheimer/ Theodor W. Adorno: 'Dialektik der Aufklärung.'" In *Jahrhundertbücher*, edited by W. Erhardt and H. Jaumann, 184–205. Munich: Beck, 2000.

———. *Ethik nach Auschwitz: Adornos negative Moralphilosophie.* Hamburg: Argument Verlag, 1993.

———. "Zur kritischen Theorie der Moral bei Adorno." *Deutsche Zeitschrift für Philosophie* 40 (1992): 1403–17.

———. "Das Unbehagen and der Moral: Zur Kritik der Ethik bei Adorno und Zygmunt Bauman." *Das Argument: Zeitschrift für Philosophie und Sozialwissenschaften* 4 (1999): 513–26.

Schweppenhäuser, Gerhard, and Mirko Wischke, eds. *Impuls und Negativität: Ethik und Ästhetik bei Adorno.* Hamburg: Argument Verlag, 1995.

Schweppenhäuser, Hermann. "Theodor W. Adorno: Denken in Konstellation – konstellatives Denken." In *Philosophen des 20. Jahrhunderts*, edited by Margot Fleischer, 204–15. Darmstadt: Wissenschaftliche Buchgesellschaft, 1990.

"Bilder der Natur in der kritischen Theorie." *Zeitschrift für kritishe Theorie* 13 (2001): 7–24.

"Zur Dialektik der Subjektivität bei Adorno." *Zeitschrift für kritische Theorie* 4 (1997): 5–27.

"Das Individuum im Zeitalter seiner Liquidation: Über Adornos soziale Individuationstheorie." In *Vergegenwärtigungen zur Unzeit*, 42–69. Lüneburg: zu Klampen, 1986.

"Spekulative und negative Dialektik." In *Aktualität und Folgen der Philosophie Hegels*, edited by Oskar Negt., 81–93. Frankfurt: Suhrkamp, 1970.

Schweppenhäuser, Hermann, editor. *Theodor W. Adorno zum Gedächtnis: Eine Sammlung*. Frankfurt: Suhrkamp, 1971.

Siebert, Rudolf. *The Critical Theory of Religion, the Frankfurt School: From Universal Pragmatic to Political Theology*. Berlin and New York: Mouton, 1985.

Simon, Richard Keller. "Between Capra and Adorno: West's *Day of the Locust* and the Movies of the 1930s." *Modern Language Quarterly* 54 (December 1993): 513–34.

Slater, Phil. *Origin and Significance of the Frankfurt School: A Marxist Perspective*. London: Routledge and Kegan Paul, 1977.

Specht, Silva. *Erinnerung als Veränderung: Über den Zusammenhang von Kunst und Politik bei Theodor W. Adorno*. Mittenwald, Germany: Mäander Kunstverlag, 1981.

Steinberg, Michael P. "The Musical Absolute (Adorno's Writings on Music)." *New German Critique*, no. 56 (Spring–Summer 1992): 17–42.

Subotnik, Rose Rosengard. *Developing Variations: Style and Ideology in Western Music*. Minneapolis: University of Minnesota Press, 1991.

Deconstructive Variations: Music and Reason in Western Society. Minneapolis: University of Minnesota Press, 1996.

Sullivan, Michael, and John T. Lysaker. "Between Impotence and Illusion: Adorno's Art of Theory and Practice." *New German Critique*, no. 57 (Fall 1992): 87–122.

Sunner, Rüdiger. "Tanz der Begriffe: Musikalische Elemente im Sprachstil von Nietzsche und Adorno." In *Neuere Studien zur Aphorisitk und Essayistik*, edited by Giulia Cantarutti, 184–202. Frankfurt: Peter Lang, 1986.

Tichy, Matthias. *Theodor W. Adorno: Das Verhältnis von Allgemeinem und Besonderem in seiner Philosophie*. Bonn: Bouvier Verlag Herbert Grundmann, 1977.

Tiedemann, Rolf. *Dialektik im Stillstand*. Frankfurt: Suhrkamp, 1983.

Toole, David. "Of Lingering Eyes and Talking Things: Adorno and Deleuze on Philosophy since Auschwitz." *Philosophy Today* 37 (Fall 1993): 227–46.

Townsend, Peter. "Adorno on Jazz: Vienna versus the Vernacular." *Prose Studies* 11 (May 1988): 69–88.

Ulle, Dieter. "Bürgerliche Kulturkritik und Ästhetik: Bemerkungen zu Theodor Adornos Schrift *Ästhetische Theorie*." *Weimarer Beiträge* 18, no. 6 (1972): 133–54.

van Reijen, Willem, et al. *Adorno: An Introduction.* Translated by Dieter Engelbrecht. Philadelphia: Pennbridge Books, 1992.

Varadharajan, Asha. *Exotic Parodies: Subjectivity in Adorno, Said, and Spivak.* Minneapolis: University of Minnesota Press, 1995.

Waldman, Diane. "Critical Theory and Film: Adorno and 'The Culture Industry' Revisited." *New German Critique*, no. 72 (Fall 1997): 39–60.

Walther, B. K. "One God among the Gods: Traces of Hölderlin in Adorno and de Man." *Orbis litterarum* 51 (1996): 1–10.

Weitzman, R. "An Introduction to Adorno's Music and Social Criticism." *Music and Letters* 52 (1971): 287–98.

Wellmer, Albrecht. "Metaphysics at the Moment of Its Fall." In *Literary Theory Today*, edited by Peter Collier and Helga Geyer-Ryan, 35–49. Ithaca, N.Y.: Cornell University Press, 1990.

The Persistence of Modernity: Essays on Aesthetics, Ethics, and Postmodernism. Translated by David Midgley. Cambridge, Mass.: MIT Press, 1991.

"Reason, Utopia, and the Dialectic of Enlightenment." *Praxis International* 3 (July 1983): 83–107. Reprinted in Richard J. Bernstein, ed., *Habermas and Modernity* (Cambridge, Mass.: MIT Press, 1985), 35–66.

"Truth, Semblance, and Reconciliation: Adorno's Aesthetic Redemption of Modernity." *Telos*, no. 62 (Winter 1984–5): 89–115.

Welsch, Wolfgang. "Adornos Ästhetik: Eine implizite Ästhetik des Erhabenen." In *Das Erhabene. Zwischen Grenzerfahrung und Grössenwahn*, edited by Christine Pries, 185–213. Weinheim, Germany: VCH Acta Humaniora, 1989.

Werkmeister, O. K. "Das Kuntswerk als Negation. Zur geschichtlichen Bestimmung der Kunsttheorie Theodor W. Adornos." In *Ende der Ästhetik*, 7–32. Frankfurt: Fischer, 1971.

Whitebrook, Joel. "Fantasy and Critique: Some Thoughts on Freud and the Frankfurt School." In *The Handbook of Critical Theory*, edited by David M. Rasmussen, 287–304. Oxford: Blackwell, 1996.

Perversion and Utopia: A Study of Psychoanalysis and Critical Theory. Cambridge, Mass.: MIT Press, 1995.

Wiggershaus, Rolf. *The Frankfurt School: Its History, Theories, and Political Significance.* Translated by Michael Robertson. Cambridge, Mass.: MIT Press, 1995.

Theodor W. Adorno. Munich: C. H. Beck, 1987.

Wilke, Sabine. "Adorno and Derrida as Readers of Husserl: Some Reflections on the Historical Context of Modernism and Postmodernism." *Boundary 2* 16 (Winter–Spring 1989): 77–90.

"Kritische und ideologische Momente der Parataxis: eine Lektüre von Adorno, Heidegger und Hölderlin." *MLN* 102 (April 1987): 627–47.

Zur Dialektik von Exposition und Darstellung: Ansätze zu einer Kritik der Arbeiten Martin Heideggers, Theodor W. Adornos und Jacques Derrida. New York: Peter Lang, 1988.

Witkin, Robert W. *Adorno on Music.* New York: Routledge, 1998.

Wohlfart, Günter. "Anmerkungen zur ästhetischen Theorie Adornos." *Philosophisches Jahrbuch* 83 (1976): 370–91. A revised version appears in *Zeitschrift für Ästhetik und allgemeine Kunstwissenschaft* 22 (1977): 110–34.

Wohlfarth, Irving. "Hibernation: On the Tenth Anniversary of Adorno's Death." *Modern Language Notes* 94 (December 1979): 956–87.

Wolin, Richard. "The De-Aestheticization of Art: On Adorno's *Aesthetische Theorie.*" *Telos*, no. 41 (Fall 1979): 105–27.

"Utopia, Mimesis, and Reconciliation: A Redemptive Critique of Adorno's *Aesthetic Theory.*" *Representations* 32 (Fall 1990): 33–49.

Zenck, Martin. *Kunst als begriffslose Erkenntnis: Zum Kunstbegriff der ästhetischen Theorie Theodor W. Adornos.* Munich: Wilhelm Fink, 1977.

Zimmermann, Norbert. *Der ästhetische Augenblick: Theodor W. Adornos Theorie der Zeitstruktur von Kunst und ästhetischer Erfahrung.* Frankfurt: Peter Lang, 1989.

Zuidarvaart, Lambert. *Adorno's Aesthetic Theory: The Redemption of Illusion.* Cambridge, Mass.: MIT Press, 1991.

"The Artefactuality of Autonomous Art: Kant and Adorno." In *The Reasons of Art: Artworks and the Transformations of Philosophy*, edited by Peter McCormick, 256–62. Ottawa: University of Ottawa Press, 1986.

"The Social Significance of Autonomous Art: Adorno and Bürger." *Journal of Aesthetics and Art Criticism* 48 (Winter 1990): 61–77.

INDEX

422   Index

Adorno's writings (cont.)
  fear, 389
  Heimat, 101, 121–122
  melancholy science, 310
  redemption, 141, 187
  as reflective sociology, 287–288
  wrong life, 309
  Negative Dialectics, 2, 5, 19, 20, 30,
    32, 34–38, 48–49, 52, 56–69, 86,
    97–99, 101, 103
    abstract morality, 310
    authenticity, 204
    autonomy of volition, 313
    barter (exchange), 133–134, 141,
      314–315
    collective regression, 143
    differentiation, 223
    experience, 106–107, 140
    good, 122
    identity theory, 205, 314–315
    on Kant, 319
    materialistic motive of morality,
      334
    metaphysical experience, 143
    reification, 143
    reconciliation, 320
    suffering, 168, 320
    unutterable, 102
  "On an Imaginary Feuilleton", 139
  "On Lyric Poetry and Society",
    354–369
    spontaneity, 361
  "On the Present Relationship
    between Philosophy and
    Music", 266–267
  "On Proust", 140
  Philosophische Terminologie, 82,
    86–87, 89, 90, 92
  The Philosophy of New Music, 154
    authenticity, 198–199
    Horkheimer's reading of, 158
    lamentation, 165–166
    material of art, 253
    Schoenberg's relation to
      authenticity, 204–205
    Schoenberg's response to, 164–165
    on Stravinsky, 204
  "The Position of the Narrator in the
    Contemporary Novel", 129
  The Positivist Dispute in German
    Sociology, 289

"Presuppositions: On the Occasion of
  a Reading by Hans G. Helms",
  130
Prisms, 106, 168
"Problem des neuen Menschentypus,"
  (June 23, 1941) Adorno Archive
Problems of Moral Philosophy,
  331–333, 337
Quasi una fantasia, 228
  traditional music, 102
"Reaktion und Fortschritt", 206
"Reflexionen zur Klassentheorie", 94
Der Schatz des Indianer-Joe; Singspiel
  nach Mark Twain, 376–393
"The Schema of Mass Culture", 246
In Search of Wagner, 209–210
"On the Social Situation of Music",
  279
"Sociology and Psychology", 57
"Theory of Pseudo-Culture", 130
"Those Twenties", 199
"Trying to Understand Endgame",
  30–32, 58, 127
"What National Socialism has done to
  the Arts", 190
"Words from Abroad", 125
Zur Metakritik der Erkenntistheorie,
  111
aesthetics, 57, 181–182, 189, 240
  of music, 198–218
Agamben, Giorgio, 141–142
Albert, Hans, 291
anti-semitism, 156, 161–163, 285
Apel, Karl-Otto, 99
Arendt, Hannah, 104
art and artwork, see Hegel, see Adorno,
    Aesthetic Theory, 6–8, 17, 20,
    70, 95, 113, 117, 144, 168, 183
  and aesthetic judgment, 257, 354
  autonomy of, 199, 206–210, 240–241,
    249, 252, 281
  dissatisfaction with, 181–182
  And expression, 214, 272
  failure and success of, 218
  and form, 203
  and longing, 389
  material of, 253
  and National Socialism, 190
  and reconciliation, 194–195
  radical art and social theory, 280
  resigned art, 199

Index

427

nature, 20, 26, 65–70, 77, 91–92, 112
Neumann, Franz, 156
Nietzsche, Friedrich, 10, 12, 20, 54–55,
    104, 137, 140, 154
  aesthetics, 366, 376
  gay science, 310
  and music, 207, 209
  Human, All Too Human, 209,
    245–246
  and morality, 303–322, 333, 336,
    338–339
  self-overcoming of morality, 305
  "Truth and Lies in a Nonmoral
    Sense", 108–110
  appearance in Mann's *Doctor Faustus*,
    155
Novalis (Friedrich von Hardenberg), 102,
    132, 270
Nussbaum, Martha, 328

oaths, *see* Kant, *see* Witnessing
object, objective, objectivity, 3, 5–8,
    10–14, 20, 23–25, 27–29, 32–39,
    41–46, 51–65, 69, 71–72, 83–84,
    86, 98–99
  art's stance toward objectivity, 215,
    379
  in Bach's music, 203
  morality non-objective, 307
  in music, 205
  primacy of, 110, 182
  of society, 288
  in sociology, 286–287

particularity, 101–102
  of the object, 106
phenomenology, 111, 112
Pietism, 203
pleasure, 80, 227, 230
Plutarch, 308
poetics, 354–369
Pöggeler, Otto, 117–118
Pollock, Friedrich, 93, 157
Popper, Karl, 288–289
positivism, 97, 201
  debate in German sociology, 288–294
  Heidegger on, 107
Proust, Marcel, 140, 141
psychoanalysis, 52–54, 66
Putnam, Hilary, 258

Raphael (Raffaello Sanzio), 191
Rawls, John, 328
reason, 27–28
  instrumental, 252
reconciliation, 52, 72, 320
  in art, 194–195
  mimetic, 312
redemption, 141, 187
reflection
  art as critical reflection, 215
  and morality, 303, 304
  sociology as reflection, 290
regression, 193
  collective, 143
  and familiarity, 193
resentment, 229
Romanticism, 188, 255, 260, 262, 268,
    354, 391
Rorty, Richard, 328
Rousseau, Jean-Jacques, 260, 333–334
Russell, Bertrand, 263

Sartre, Jean Paul, 54, 255, 377, 387
sacrifice, 194
scars, 198
Scheler, Max, 335
Schelling, F. W. J., 261
Schiller, Friedrich, 303
Schirach, Baldar von, 249
Schlegel, Friedrich, 132, 268
Schleiermacher, Friedrich, 260, 261
Schmid Noerr, Gunzelin, 347
Schnädelbach, Herbert, 100
Schnebel, Dieters, 379
Schoenberg, Arnold, 102, 148–150,
    164–165, 181, 198, 204–205,
    218, 222–228, 230–233,
    235–236, 244, 248, 255
  appearance in Mann's *Doctor Faustus*,
    155–156
  Erwartung, 167, 223–224
  Die Glückliche Hand, 224
  Gurrelieder, 227
  Moses und Aron, 236
  Survivor from Warsaw, 161–166, 168
Schopenhauer, Arthur, 84, 333, 388
  on music, 226
Schumann, William, 210–211, 257
Scruton, Roger, 259, 263, 265, 267
Second Vienna School, 282

Made in the USA
San Bernardino, CA
18 January 2014